Reading the Modernist Bildungsroman

UNIVERSITY PRESS OF FLORIDA

Florida A&M University, Tallahassee
Florida Atlantic University, Boca Raton
Florida Gulf Coast University, Ft. Myers
Florida International University, Miami
Florida State University, Tallahassee
University of Central Florida, Orlando
University of Florida, Gainesville
University of North Florida, Jacksonville
University of South Florida, Tampa
University of West Florida, Pensacola

Reading the
Modernist Bildungsroman

GREGORY CASTLE

University Press of Florida
Gainesville/Tallahassee/Tampa/Boca Raton
Pensacola/Orlando/Miami/Jacksonville/Ft. Myers

11 10 09 08 07 06   6 5 4 3 2 1

Library of Congress Cataloging-in-Publication Data
Castle, Gregory.
Reading the modernist Bildungsroman / Gregory Castle.
p. cm.
Includes bibliographical references and index.
ISBN 0-8130-2983-X (acid-free paper)
1. English fiction—19th century—History and criticism. 2. English
fiction—20th century—History and criticism. 3. Bildungsroman—
History and criticism. 4. Modernism (Literature)—England. I. Title.

PR868.B52C37 2006
823'.809354—dc22   2005058240

The University Press of Florida is the scholarly publishing agency
for the State University System of Florida, comprising Florida A&M
University, Florida Atlantic University, Florida Gulf Coast University,
Florida International University, Florida State University, University
of Central Florida, University of Florida, University of North Florida,
University of South Florida, and University of West Florida.

University Press of Florida
15 Northwest 15th Street
Gainesville, FL 32611-2079
http://www.upf.com

To my muse, Camille

Contents

Acknowledgments

I have been working on the subject of the Bildungsroman for a long time. My own first effort at understanding the form, published while I was a graduate student, now seems to me a woefully inadequate response to the complexities of a genre that has managed to retain its basic contours while adapting to new environments. This book is an attempt to do justice to those complexities. I have many people to thank for this effort. First, I want to thank the University Press of Florida for giving me the opportunity of putting my work into a finished form. I am especially grateful for the support and encouragement of my editor, Amy Gorelick. I also owe a tremendous debt to my friend and mentor John Paul Riquelme, who advised me on all matters of importance but especially on the Wilde and Joyce chapter. I owe a similar debt to Margot Gayle Backus, who read the manuscript at an early stage and helped make it a better book, in large part because she had the reader always in the forefront of her mind. Other colleagues who have helped to shape my thinking about the Bildungsroman include Joseph Valente, Sean Latham, Patrick Bixby, Katie Conrad, and Marilyn Richtarik. I would like to thank too my colleagues and friends at Arizona State University who provided opportunities to talk about my ideas and who offered their advice and support, especially Mark Lussier, Neal Lester, Trevor Helminski, John Lynch, and Corbett Upton. No substantial intellectual project can be completed without the help of students, so I want to thank those students who attended my courses and seminars on the Bildungsroman over the last ten years and who were crucial in shaping my ideas. I also thank Johanna Wagner, who helped with some of the preliminary research for this project, and William Martin, who provided a willing ear and sharp mind whenever I needed to talk out some knotty problem or other. My parents and brothers patiently put up with my midnight compositions while on vacation. Like most academic writers, I appear to work in isolation, but in reality I am assisted by many wonderful and valuable people, and my work could not be done without them.

I want to thank previous publishers for their permission to reprint parts of the following essays: "Colonial Discourse and the Subject of Empire in Joyce's 'Nausicaa,'" in *Joyce: Feminism, Postcolonialism*, edited by Ellen Carol Jones, European Joyce Studies 8 (Amsterdam: Rodopi, 1998), 115–44; "Confessing Oneself: Colonial *Bildung* and Homoeros in Joyce's *A Portrait of the Artist as a Young Man,*" in *Quare Joyce*, edited by Joseph Valente (Ann Arbor: University of Michigan Press, 1998), 157–82; and "Coming of Age in the Age of Empire: Joyce's Modernist Bildungsroman," in *James Joyce Quarterly* 40.4 (2003): 665–90.

Finally, I would like to express my gratitude to the men and women of Godspeed You! Black Emperor and Silver Mt. Zion, whose music occupied and disturbed my thoughts and can be heard still in the spaces between every line of this book.

And Camille, who slept on the floor as I wrote, and provided love and ice cream.

Introduction

The Pathways to Inner Culture

*"The subject is the lie, because for the sake of its own absolute rule it will deny
its own objective definitions. Only he who would refrain from such lies—
who would have used his own strength, which he owes to identity,
to cast off the façade of identity—would truly be a subject."*

Theodor Adorno, *Negative Dialectics*

This study began as an attempt to understand James Joyce's *A Portrait of the Artist as a Young Man* in terms of its peculiar failure to conform to the strict generic demands of the Bildungsroman form.[1] When I began to write about Joyce, in the late 1980s, little work had been done on the modernist Bildungsroman, a circumstance that may reflect the fact that genre studies had fallen out of vogue after the advent of poststructuralist theories in the United States from about the mid-1970s. While a great deal of work has since been done on the Bildungsroman, the situation with respect to the modernist tradition has not changed materially.[2] I believed then, as I believe now, that Joyce's Bildungsroman is far from an isolated example of such generic failure in the twentieth century. *Reading the Modernist Bildungsroman* sets out to understand this failure or, to put my point another way, to discover how this failure signals a successful resistance to the institutionalization of self-cultivation (Bildung). I am principally concerned with the different approaches of English and Irish modernists to the failure of the Bildungsroman in an era of emergent late modernity, in which we see the beginnings of trends that will define the entire twentieth century. It is my contention that the critique of Bildung is part of a general modernist project of recuperation and revision of the Enlightenment concept of aesthetico-spiritual Bildung, which had been rationalized and bureaucratized in the course of the nineteenth century. This recuperation of an earlier, classical form of Bildung is a profoundly radical gesture, one that seeks to reinstate the values of aesthetic education and individual freedom within processes of self-development. This recourse to tradition in the interests of overcoming the constrictions of overly rationalized and bureaucratized societies (capitalist and colonialist) is a signature concern for both British and Irish modernists. Modernism thus can be regarded as a dynamic critical project in which aesthetic (especially literary) experimentation is directed at one of the most pressing concerns of the time: How do we define what it is to be a human being? How do we acquire our selfhood, our identity? These questions are paramount in modernist literature, the basis for so many representations of alienation, depersonalization, and anomie.[3] As I will demonstrate throughout this study, the failure of the modernist Bildungsroman is a complex and contradictory phenomenon, for where the *Bildungsheld* (hero of the Bildung plot) fails to achieve inner culture or harmonious socialization, the genre itself appears to assert its integrity in powerful new ways, to exploit the formative and transformative power of failure in order to effect a rehabilitation of the Bildungsroman genre and a justification of the raison d'être of the form, Bildung.[4]

Modernist aesthetic practices are often discussed in terms of innovation and experimentation, and in terms of the relation between such practices of modernity and the traditions that they are meant to displace. I want to alter slightly this typical approach by suggesting that the modernist Bildungsroman presents us with a quite different case, especially with respect to Bildung. If modernist novelists embrace the classical tradition of Bildung, they do so in order to enjoy the fruits of modernity. Innovation and experimentation emerge as the novelist employs new artistic means to translate the longing for wholeness and harmony. For it is this longing that dominates the motivations and actions of modernist *Bildungshelden*, young heroes willing to do anything, create in any way, so long as they are thoroughly modern, thoroughly whole, thoroughly *themselves*.

In referring to tradition and modernity in this comparative fashion, I mean something different from Terry Eagleton's formulation in *Heathcliff and the Great Hunger*. In that volume Eagleton argues that Irish modernism emerged out of a situation of uneven economic and industrial development, a situation in which "archaic" social traditions mixed with technological modernity. "An archaic moral superstructure thus served an increasingly modern base."[5] While I agree with Eagleton about the social conditions for Irish modernism, I want to stress a relation between epochs of modernity, a relation in which an earlier Enlightenment moment generated moral, ethical, and aesthetic traditions for a later time, thus creating the effect of a tradition within modernity. My conception of this division within modernity is closer to that of Fredric Jameson, who discerns a "pre-modern moment within modernity as such."[6] In this sense, tradition is native to modernity, not a hostile, archaic remnant. How this division in modernity plays out in an Irish context, where traditions not native to modernity play an active role in self-formation, will be addressed in chapter 3.

In keeping with modernism's radical conservatism, modernist novelists rejected the nineteenth-century tradition of socialization, or socially pragmatic Bildung, and looked to the eighteenth-century German Enlightenment, which had created and nurtured a tradition of aesthetico-spiritual (or classical) Bildung, for innovative models of understanding and representing self-cultivation. However, the modernist Bildungsroman harbors a powerful sense of frustration with the dialectical structure of classical Bildung, so evident in the work of Enlightenment thinkers like Johann Wolfgang von Goethe and Wilhelm von Humboldt. This frustration finds expression in a form of "negative" critique, which I hope to illuminate by drawing on Theodor Adorno's "negative dialectics." Negative dialectics refuses the traditional dialectical structure of relations in which the negative term exists solely to guarantee the self-identity of the positive term; it refuses what Adorno calls the "coincidence of identity and positivity."[7] Instead, it seeks to value the negative moment as a critical intervention in the presumed harmony of dialectical structures and as evidence of the very material (or "negative") stratum that is often occluded by the abstract, idealist harmonies of dialectical synthesis. What we perceive to be the failures of Bildung in modernist Bildungsromane can thus be read as critical triumphs. In each of the novels I analyze, the desire for autonomous self-formation both rescues a classical ideal of Bildung (one that had been transformed into the socially pragmatic form described above) and at the same time subjects that ideal to what Adorno calls an "immanent critique," one that allows for more sensitive negotiations of complex problems concerning identity, nationality, education, the role of the artist, and social as well as personal relationships. According to Adorno, "The dialectical critic of culture must both participate in culture and not participate. Only then does he do justice to his object and to himself." This form of immanent critique "takes seriously the principle that it is not ideology in itself which is untrue but rather its pretension to correspond to reality." Language, rhetoric, discourse: all can mystify as well as enlighten. Because of this, "immanent criticism cannot take comfort in its own idea."[8] It is this kind of critique that I see happening in the modernist Bildungsroman, a critique that emerges in part through deliberate adherence to the conventions of the genre. What changes is a new questioning of the ideological subtexts concerning the nature and function of the subject and a new concern for the structure and goal of self-cultivation. As I will show throughout this study, immanent critique does not entail the repudiation of a traditional value; on the contrary, the reinstatement of classical Bildung, even under critical pressure and transformation, provides the crucial opportunity of devising alternatives to socially pragmatic Bildung. It is this double gesture of recuperation and critique that characterizes the modernist Bildungsroman.

It should be noted at the outset that a critique of Bildung and capitulation to its imperatives (of self-sufficiency, of harmonious development) can easily become confused with one another, especially when a critique of normative modes of development is conducted within the strict formal limits of the Bildungsroman. One immediately sees the difficulty of critiquing conceptions of the self, subjectivity, social or national identity—the array of topoi associated with modernism—within a genre whose conventions are tied in myriad ways to just these conceptions in their most stultifyingly normative forms. Is it possible to remain within the main coordinates of the Bildungsroman tradition and at the same time create a hero who *dissents* from that tradition? Is it possible that dissent can propel the genre toward new modes of expression and new modes of inharmonious but *achieved* development? These are the broad questions that frame this study.

Because I am making a fairly broad historical argument—I regard this study as a chapter in the literary history of a genre—a chronological organization is of obvious utility. However, *Reading the Modernist Bildungsroman* also concerns quite specific social thematics. I believe that this dual approach will help account for the productive continuance of an almost rigidly traditional genre within a process of *generic resistance*. In simple terms, this means that the struggle with genre guarantees its survival and its relevance. For while modernist writers resist certain generic conventions and conventional themes and problematics, they nevertheless enact this resistance within those conventions. Just as the sonnet form has succeeded, despite resistance, in continuing to be relevant for modern poets long after Petrarch and Shakespeare, so the Bildungsroman continues to be relevant for novelists who may generally repudiate the values of the German Enlightenment, but who embrace its core value of Bildung. Like the sonnet, the Bildungsroman is tremendously elastic, its conventions so few and relatively simple that resistance to them beyond a certain point is tantamount to putting them aside altogether. Where this does in fact happen, as in the novels of Samuel Beckett, one can still discern the rudiments of the form—a biographical narrative, problems of socialization, the influence of mentors and "instrumental" women, the problem of vocation—even when such rudiments are pared down to their essence, then to their absence. More often, as with many postcolonial Bildungsromane, these generic rudiments are not only retained but embraced with new vigor—a vigor often ironic and stylized, but vigor nonetheless.

This generic resiliency is not always appreciated by critics of the Bildungsroman. Many critics who work within the German tradition or who are affiliated professionally with German studies, like Jeffrey Sammons and Martin Swales, tend to disregard most non-German and twentieth-century Bildungsromane, canonizing a series of texts beginning with Christoph Martin Wieland and Goethe and running through Thomas Mann and Hermann Hesse. Important studies by Franco Moretti and Marc Redfield concentrate on the nineteenth-century German and French traditions. Moretti's position is especially provocative, for it sees in the English Bildungsroman, at the dawning of the twentieth century, the exhaustion of the form.[9] I take the opposite view, that it is precisely the breakdown of traditional forms of identity and of normative, harmonious socialization that gives the Bildungsroman a new sense of purpose. This can best be illustrated in analyses of those twentieth-century modernist exemplars that critics like Sammons and Moretti scant by tethering the genre too closely to a German origin or nineteenth-century field of relevance.[10] *Reading the Modernist Bildungsroman* begins with a reading of two early English modernist Bildungsromane, Thomas Hardy's *Jude the Obscure* and D. H. Lawrence's *Sons and Lovers.* In some ways these texts exemplify the exhausted English tradition of the late nineteenth century, but in other ways they look forward to the kinds of innovations and departures that we see in the 1920s and 1930s. It is important to provide a firm sense of the work done by early English modernists in order to comprehend fully the innovations of Irish writers like Joyce and Oscar Wilde and feminist modernists like Virginia Woolf. Especially important for my argument are Woolf's *The Voyage Out* and *Mrs. Dalloway*, which challenged the masculinist cultural hegemony that Bildung had come to signify in the early twentieth century. Indeed, the problem of gender has only recently been recognized as a significant factor in the development of the Bildungsroman. As John Smith notes, "*Bildung*, and its narrativization in the *Bildungsroman*, is not an 'organic' but a social phenomenon that leads to the construction of male identity in our sex-gender system by granting men access to self-representation in the patriarchal symbolic order. As such *Bildung* is a central form of the institutional cultivation of gender roles."[11] However, the problematic of gender ought not to be isolated within the limits of a reactive generic formation, the so-called "female Bildungsroman."[12] Woolf's critique of the Bildungsroman, her "version" of the form, is also an embrace of the core value of Bildung, one that retrieves it from a recent history of institutionalization within state educational systems. Much the same motive can be found in Irish colonial writers, who were able to translate their disempowerment into Bildung plots of survival and triumph—even if survival means exile and triumph means death. It is in the Irish colonial experience especially that this breakdown in socialization is most pronounced, and that the effects of development outside an imperial European context are the most catastrophic.

In the Irish modernist Bildungsroman, the problems of gender, sexuality, and politics arise in unique ways, calling into question the narrative conventions by which self-development is represented as well as challenging the prevailing attitudes in imperial European societies about the subject and subjectivity, the role of women, and the nature of social mobility. The Irish modernist Bildungsroman, for complex reasons having to do with a history of colonial domination combined with cultural and geographical isolation from Europe, exhibits a greater capacity for generic resistance and for the revival of certain elements found in the classical Bildungsroman, by which I mean the late-eighteenth- and nineteenth-century canon of German, French, and English exemplars. The word "classical" here signals the persistence of generic, aesthetic, and philosophical elements throughout the nineteenth century and in different national settings.[13] For English modernist writers, the Bildungsroman is an inheritance—perhaps an exhausted, vitiated one—and this relationship to literary and intellectual history places certain demands on these writers. These demands are often ignored or rejected, to be sure, but demands are made nonetheless, seconded by readers who have come to expect from the Bildungsroman a satisfying conclusion to the trials of a "coming of age" story. Irish modernists had no such inheritance. Their relationship with the Bildungsroman tradition is one of indebtedness: the form is borrowed and transformed under Irish colonial conditions in order better to represent the self-development of the colonial subject. One way of describing this debt to literary history, a debt incurred without the intention of repayment, is to use the term "transculturation," which has emerged out of the study of the postcolonial Bildungsroman and refers to the appropriation of literary forms and techniques that originate in the literary traditions of imperial societies. Transculturation thus refers to the transfigurations and resignifications of these forms and techniques in order that they might serve new needs within new postcolonial national literatures.[14]

I have referred above to the "coming of age" story and have placed the phrase in quotation marks. I do this in order to alert the reader to problems of nomenclature, thematics, and literary history. The Bildungsroman emerged

in late-eighteenth-century Germany in a climate of intense aesthetic and philosophical exploration and creative production; it emerged not only as the signature narrative expression of the concept of Bildung but also as the "genre
of aesthetics."[15] Historically, the Bildungsroman has thematized this concept,
which had been from the start associated with German national identity but
later with national identity in France and England—and, to a lesser degree, elsewhere in Europe and the United States. The phrase "coming of age," or the similar though less often used "rites of passage," has, over the course of time, been
used as an English equivalent of *Bildung*. And not without good reason, for the
English tradition was very much concerned with the sociojuridical thematic
that this term tends to imply. As we shall see, there is some justification for the
argument that Goethe's *Wilhelm Meister's Apprenticeship* (1795–96) sets a precedent for such a thematic. Be that as it may, the culture of late-eighteenth- and
early-nineteenth-century Germany—specifically of the Weimar region where
so many intellectuals of the period gravitated to write, teach, or reflect—was
dominated less by this sociojuridical concept of Bildung than by an aesthetico-
spiritual one that emerged out of a confluence of Enlightenment humanism,
Protestant Pietism, and the new idealism of Immanuel Kant, Johann Fichte,
and G.W.F. Hegel. More appropriate usages in English, like "self-development,"
"self-formation," and "self-cultivation,"[16] do not quite capture the emphasis on
aesthetic education and a spiritualized inner culture, on the harmony of one's
intellectual, moral, spiritual, and artistic faculties, or on achieving a dialectical
harmony of self and society, of personal desire and social responsibility. I will
tend to use the English equivalents more or less synonymously to indicate the
"classical" concept of Bildung that is associated with the German tradition. In
referring to the socially pragmatic dynamics implied by the phrase "coming of
age," I will tend to use the terms "socialization" and "social mobility."

These problems of nomenclature are not trivial, for the different usages carry
within them associations with national and ideological thematics and modes of
narrative emplotment that have arisen in the course of literary history in Germany, France, and England. For this reason, perhaps the best introduction to the
problems faced by English and Irish modernist writers who experimented with
the Bildungsroman form is to trace this literary history and provide the reader
with a discussion of the classical Bildungsroman tradition. I shall therefore turn,
in the next section, to Goethe's *Wilhelm Meister's Apprenticeship* and some of
its critics in order to raise some of the most salient issues and problems relating
to the classicism of the form. A brief discussion will follow of some French and
English Bildungsromane, which will illustrate how the classical Bildungsroman

was transformed, under the pressure of new social and artistic conditions, from a genre concerned with spiritual development and the aesthetics of self-cultivation to one concerned with the pragmatics of socialization and social mobility. I will conclude with a brief outline of the chapters of this study.

George Moore, in his *Confessions of a Young Man* (1888), observed that "each century has its special ideal; the ideal of the nineteenth century is the young man."[17] This state of affairs could exist only in a culture in which youth, both as a practical reality and as a philosophical ideal, had achieved a privileged position. Many factors contributed to this complex sociohistorical phenomenon. The "long" nineteenth century in Europe and America, a period of revolution and restoration extending from 1776 to 1914, saw the rise of democracy and liberalism, as well as the persistence of a Romantic sensibility that emphasized the individual's control over destiny and the repudiation of absolute authorities, secular and sacred.[18] Against this tumultuous history the figure of youth stands as both a metaphorical and a literal embodiment of an age. Indeed, for Franco Moretti, youth is the figure of modernity itself: "Virtually without notice, in the dreams and nightmares of the so called 'double revolution' [the simultaneous rise of mobility and interiority], Europe plunges into modernity, but without possessing a *culture* of modernity. If youth, therefore, achieves its symbolic centrality, and the 'great narrative' of the *Bildungsroman* comes into being, this is because Europe has to attach a meaning, not so much to youth, as to *modernity*."[19] Youth becomes the "material sign" of modernity "because of its ability to *accentuate* modernity's dynamism and instability."[20] But it is this dynamism and instability that the young heroes of nineteenth-century Bildungsromane must overcome and master in order to enact the drama of socialization. Thus the hero's conflict with social authority (typically a real or symbolic father) ultimately leads to an affirmation of that authority in the social sphere and in the choice of a vocation. Depending on which tradition one examines, this affirmation may take the form of spiritual apprenticeship (as in the classical German tradition), social conformity (as in the English tradition), or artistic success (as in the French tradition). In any case, the primary function of the classical Bildungsroman up to the turn of the twentieth century had been to narrativize the dialectical harmony of this affirmation. If the process failed, as it often did in the French Bildungsroman, it did not mean that society had somehow failed in its duty nor that dialectics had failed to signify the ideal relations of the individual to the social totality. Rather, such failures remind the hero (and the reader) that social maturity involves knowing one's limits and accepting one's place in the order of things. Failure must therefore be understood as a failure to participate or to accept one's role in a dialectic of personal desire and social responsibility, of "reflection and action."[21]

"A symbolic animal, man yearns for a symbolic form that may heal the gap between the values 'within' and the world 'without.'"[22] The classical Bildungsroman serves precisely the function of symbolic legitimation to which Moretti refers. It simultaneously valorizes existing structures of power and prevailing models of socialization. The *Bildungsheld* of the classical form breaks from familial and social authorities in order to experience the world freely; but youthful rebellion turns out to be a forgivable, even necessary interlude before a symbolic reconciliation with those same authorities. Personal destiny ultimately aligns itself with historical destiny in the dialectical harmonies of Bildung. The *Bildungsheld*'s destiny harmonizes with his sociohistorical world, a world that still believes in the perfection of humanity and of social institutions—a world of self-assured modernity, of the "all-round, self-realizing individual."[23] He is a bourgeois hero, in rebellion from the father and the social values he represents, seeking an apprenticeship to life in symbolic journeys and edifying sojourns. In the end the *Bildungsheld* returns to the fold, still young but a little wiser—a prodigal son, artistic rebel, *and* good bourgeois—returns to close the circle.

As I have suggested, the prototype of the classical Bildungsroman is Goethe's *Wilhelm Meister*.[24] The first part of the novel details Wilhelm's comfortable life in a small German town and the loss of his first love. Shortly after losing Mariane, Wilhelm embarks on a long business trip, making introductions and calling in debts for the family business. En route, he falls in with a traveling dramatic troupe. *Wilhelm Meister* thus narrates the achievement of self-cultivation through a process of aesthetic education linked to the theater and its role in forging personal and national identity. "The theater was very much in people's minds," writes Eric Blackall, "not merely as cultural entertainment, but as an educative force toward raising the level of culture." The tension that Blackall notes between Goethe's "lofty conception of the theater as a moral institution and the desire to present a true picture of the life of actors, which was often immoral"—a tension that Goethe presents ironically, fully aware of the delusory nature of his "lofty conception"[25]—duplicates the more encompassing tension between "personal Bildung" and the requirements of the state. But Wilhelm's sojourn in the marginal world of the theater is only one stage toward the *telos* of his self-development, for he is ultimately inducted into an elite Society of the Tower, a group of sensitive and enlightened men and women who have created an ideal capitalist society. It is remarkable how much of the novel is devoted to business affairs and how these affairs are again and again opposed to the bohemian life of the freethinking, freely mobile artist. Through a series of co-incidences and, as it turns out, not so coincidental manipulations, Wilhelm comes into contact with the members of the Society, who ultimately welcome him into the fold. "We can now justly consider you as one of us, and therefore it would be unreasonable not to introduce you further into our mysteries. . . . when [a man's] development has reached a certain stage, it is advantageous for him to lose himself in a larger whole, learn to live for others, and forget himself in dutiful activity for others."[26] He is presented with a Certificate of Appren-ticeship by the Abbé, spiritual advisor of the Society, and later another of his mentors, Jarno, allows him access to the scroll that indicates the full extent of the Society's influence on his development. What Wilhelm sees in the scroll is "a picture of himself, not like a second self in a mirror, but a different self, one outside of him, as in a painting." Immediately afterwards he writes to Therese, the woman with whom he has fallen in love, without consulting his friends, in large part in rebellion against the determinism he has mistaken for free will. "Perhaps it was the feeling," he reflects, "that, as emerged quite clearly from the scroll, there had been so many occasions in his life when he thought he was act-ing freely and unobserved, only to discover that he had indeed been observed, even directed."[27] The implication, of course, is that Wilhelm's self-formation is made possible and guaranteed by the existence of a larger social institution in which he plays an integral part—down to his marriage to Therese, the capstone of his destiny. Closure in his life history comes when he recognizes the authors of his destiny and readily accepts the fitness of his fate: "I don't know about kingdoms . . . but I do know that I have found a treasure I never deserved. And I would not exchange it for anything in the world."[28]

This emphasis on development and "inner culture" enables Goethe's Bil-dungsroman to accomplish what other biographical forms could (or would) not. Unlike most eighteenth-century novels, the Bildungsroman accentuated dynamic psychological changes and developments as well as the possibility of *managing* such changes and developments. Wilhelm Dilthey believed that this possibility is due to the genre's proximity to "the new developmental psychol-ogy established by Leibniz" and "the idea of a natural education in confor-mity with the inner development of the psyche." The *Bildungsheld*'s life and ambitions are gathered into a coherent story that subsumes and resolves all contradictions in a harmonious and dialectical process that follows an inexo-rable pattern: "A lawlike development is discerned in the individual's life; each of its levels has intrinsic value and is at the same time the basis for a higher level. Life's dissonances and conflicts appear as necessary transitions to be withstood by the individual on his way towards maturity and harmony."[29] Dilthey underscores the emphasis on development in the Bildungsroman, which "begins with naive perfection, deriving from one's nature alone, and . . . aims at the ideal to which we can elevate ourselves through a rigorous education. In between we observe highlights of the eccentric development of [the] heroes." *Wilhelm Meister* became for him the touchstone of a genre that expresses the "optimism of personal development" more "joyously and confidently" than any other work.[30]

As some critics have pointed out, *Wilhelm Meister* reveals the difficulty in attaining the ideal of Bildung, in harmonizing desire with history, reflection with action. W. H. Bruford, for example, notes that Wilhelm's induction into the Society of the Tower functions as a symbolic affirmation of the very bourgeois society from which he tries to escape. Wilhelm's initial refusal to take up his inheritance and to enter into his father's business is symbolically retracted when he acquiesces in the schemes of Jarno and the Abbé and accepts a form of individualism predicated ultimately on conformity with the state. Within the Society, as within the social world at large, the individual finds his or her unique place: "The leading idea of the theorists of the Tower is the inability of the individual to live happily for himself alone. For one thing he, like everyone else, will be gifted in some directions but not in others, so that in any civilized society there must be scope for all kinds of complementary activities. The division of labour on which middle-class society is founded is therefore reaffirmed, but the ideal of harmony is not forgotten, the harmony of mind and body in the individual . . . and the harmony of the diversified activities of a society."[31] As the symbolic expression of social unification, the Society of the Tower triumphs over the ideal of self-determination; but the hero is grateful for that triumph. When Wilhelm's narrative closes, he understands the narrative of his life and acknowledges the mastery of the Society and of the fate of which the Society stands as emblem. In Todd Kontje's reading, Wilhelm "sees an alienated version of attained harmony in the creation of the *Turmgesellschaft* [Society of the Tower] and mistakes it for his own."[32] He is asked to accept and even embrace a fate over which he has had no conscious control and to do so because the higher level to which he thus attains more than compensates for the loss of free will. Wilhelm, of course, obeys willingly: "I consign myself entirely to my friends and their direction," he tells Jarno, "for it is useless trying to act according to one's own will in this world. What I most wanted to keep, I have to let go, and an undeserved benefit imposes itself upon me."[33] For Martin Swales, the Bildungsroman dramatizes the dialectical tensions at the root of this capitulation to authority, the struggle between ethical and aesthetic autonomy and the increasingly intrusive pressures of an emergent capitalist state. The Bildungsroman form "derives its very life from the awareness both of the given experiential framework of practical reality on the one hand and of the creative potential of human imagination and reflectivity on the other."[34] This dialectical structure is preserved despite tensions that often lead to critique and render impossible any easy triumph over free-spirited individualism. Swales allows for the possibility that the prosaic and factitious nature of social institutions could conceivably be transformed by the hero's poetic effort of formation. But he concedes that the practical world will "prevail over the hero's dreams, desires, and fantasies."[35]

Recent critics like Swales and Kontje complicate the picture drawn by Dilthey of Goethe's "archetypal Bildungsroman" by stressing the potential for ironic tension between "the sheer complexity of individual potentiality" (*Nebeneinander*, one alongside another) and "practical reality" (*Nacheinander*, one after another), a tension that exemplifies a "necessary dimension of the hero's self-realization."[36] The ambivalent relationship between the *Bildungsheld* and the social world undermines any coherent or definitive conclusion to the Bildung plot, at least according to Swales: "the meaning of the growth process, of the *Werden* [becoming], is to be found in the process itself, not in any goal whose attainment it may make possible.... The Bildungsroman, then, is written for the sake of the journey, and not for the sake of the happy ending toward which that journey points."[37] What is at issue here is the narrative structure of the Bildungsroman, not the dialectical harmony of Bildung, which underwrites the hero's *Werden*. The two emphases that we see in the criticism of Goethe—on a "lawlike development" and on a processual *Werden*—correspond to tendencies that coexisted in late-eighteenth-century German cultural discourse, in which historicist thinking imbricates with the temporality of becoming. Goethe's text itself illustrates this coexistence, for while *Wilhelm Meister* foregrounds the journey and the hero's *Werden*, it also suggests, in its treatment of Wilhelm's ritualistic induction into the elite Society of the Tower, that the goal of the journey is important in and of itself.

Perhaps because the prototype of the form so fittingly exemplifies the complexities of the German Enlightenment, critics tend to point to a German origin for the Bildungsroman.[38] Those who, like Dilthey, affirm the German origin of the Bildungsroman and the dominant influence of the Goethean prototype are responding to its nationalist character, a reading that regards the genre as increasingly less "authentic" the farther it travels from the Goethean context. A tradition of conservative generic formalism has thus led to some rather hard-line positions. Jeffrey Sammons, for example, believes "that if the category *Bildungsroman* is to have meaning, it needs to exhibit two features: the term itself, with its elaborate and heavily charged connotations, ought to have some relevance to the character of the texts it claims to subsume; and it ought to subsume more than two or three or even a half-dozen texts, especially if large claims are made as to its literary-historical dominance and social representative-ness."[39] Sammons then goes on to claim that after Goethe's *Wilhelm Meister* there are only two and a half legitimate exemplars of the form![40] Surely this position is untenable outside a very narrow literary historical framework. Else-where Sammons argues persuasively that the use of the term outside the Ger-man context is highly problematic. For him, the term Bildungsroman "came to lay claim to a particular German tradition with its philosophical origins in the Classical-Romantic age of *Humanitätsphilosophie.*"[41] Unfortunately, the term designates a "phantom genre," says Sammons: "There is no nineteenth-century Bildungsroman genre because no major writer after Goethe could envision a social context for *Bildung.*"[42] Goethe's preeminence in literary history survives despite the ironic tensions noted above. Marc Redfield argues, "If the failure of *Bildung* can be transformed into the knowledge of failure, *Bildung* can re-discover itself as the production of an ironic consciousness and as the assump-tion of human finitude, while the *Bildungsroman* can become the narrative of its own inability to achieve self-definition."[43] This ironic element is more fully evident in the work of Wilhelm von Humboldt, one of the Weimar intellectu-als who contributed to the formation of the concept of Bildung (though not of the Bildungsroman form). As I will demonstrate in the next chapter, Humboldt was instrumental in forming the social context of Bildung for the nineteenth century, in Germany and in England, a context in which the personal and philo-sophical ideal of Bildung was transformed into an ideology of pragmatic indi-vidualism.

If the Germany of Goethe can be said to have invented the Bildungsroman, it is in France and England that the form began to realize its full potential as a pragmatic ideological discourse. We find, particularly in the French Bildungsro-man, a certain skepticism concerning the aesthetico-spiritual form introduced by Goethe and a shift toward a social pragmatics of Bildung that emphasizes socialization and social mobility. Dialectical harmony is still prized, but its achievement is typically oriented toward the smooth integration of the indi-vidual into the operations of the state and its institutions. The desire for social success governs all levels of plot, for without it there would be no story. Rather than experiencing the world, the hero merely does the bidding of that world in the pursuit of fame and fashion. The hero striving for harmonious inner culture degenerates into the parvenu intent on success at the expense of self-formation.

In Stendhal's *The Red and the Black*, for example, the hero, Julien Sorel, idealizes Napoleon, but his idealizations will get him nowhere in the society that has established itself in the wake of Napoleon's defeat. "All my reputation ruined," Julien says to himself, "destroyed in a single instant! . . . And my reputation is all I have, it's my whole life . . . and yet, good heavens, what a life!"[44] Julien's idealism does not condemn him: he is guilty merely of not sufficiently understanding the social world into which he desires entry. But without this understanding, his success could only be ephemeral, a passing fancy; true success in the new social world would depend on how smoothly the individual manipulated the system for personal gain. Julien's "loving effusions" written on the back of Napoleon's portrait, though primarily the longings of a young man who rails at a social world in which he cannot rise, must be kept hidden because of the change in political fashion: in order for him to rise in the world, he must first adapt to it. His hypocrisy is born of an insatiable desire to succeed. When it becomes clear to him that the Church has superseded the army as the path to social advancement, he drops his interest in Napoleon and embarks on a clerical career. But just below the surface of his priestly vocation is the disruptive fury of a passionate desire; and the objects of that desire—success, glory, the love of women—though dependent on society and its members, become bound up in the desire to destroy society itself, to conquer a world that resists his own ambitions.

We have come a long way from the world of Wilhelm Meister, whose happy future is determined by a social class that welcomes him as an equal. But then, reality—the matrix of social relationships in which the hero inevitably becomes entangled—changes radically in the years after Napoleon. "Reality is no longer the infinitely perfectible material it was thought to be during the Enlightenment and throughout the Revolution," writes Moretti; "as Waterloo has shown, history moves not only forward, in harmony with reason, but it can also resist change and bring back the past. Reality then—such is the plain but disturbing discovery of this age—is characterized by mere existence, independent of any symbolic legitimacy. In fact, the more reality is felt to be illegitimate and unjust, the more 'real' it seems."[45] The hero's experience with the social world yields no meaningful relationship with it; that is to say, the hero gleans no meaning of himself through his normative connections with that world. The social contexts for Bildung—vocation and recreation, personal relationships (marriage, parenthood, friendship), social obligations—persist but with a sense of cynicism and loss. The reality of socialization, which ceases to resemble the Goethean notion of Bildung, begins to approximate the forms of ideological interpellation proper to the emergent capitalist societies in western Europe.[46] The *Bildungsheld* is compelled to submit to a state-sponsored regime of socialization, to which, if we follow the absolute and unforgiving logic posited by Louis Althusser, there can be no material resistance: "ideology has always-already interpellated individuals as subjects, which amounts to making it clear that individuals are always-already interpellated by ideology as subjects, which necessarily leads us to one last proposition: *individuals are always-already subjects*."[47] The grim inevitability of this formulation can be overcome only by the exercise of an immanent critique of the dialectical structure of socially pragmatic Bildung, a critique that surrenders not only the belief in sovereign bourgeois subjectivity but also the naïve belief in a total resistance to that subjectivity. In the nineteenth-century Bildungsroman, in England as well as France, contestation rather than connection, interruption rather than completion, ostracism rather than assimilation characterize the hero's narrative of development.

The French Bildungsroman in the mid-to-late nineteenth century, according to Moretti, represents an emergent capitalist order that values pragmatism and social mobility more highly than the aesthetico-spiritual ideals of the late German Enlightenment. Most heroes after Stendhal's, like Lucien de Rubempré in Balzac's *Lost Illusions*, pursue social success for its own sake and not in the service of a higher power. Old traditions and social values lose relevance. Concerning the value of success, Moretti claims: "With Balzac all uncertainty ceases, and the desire for success appears for the first time as a wholly 'natural' impulse needing no justification whatsoever—while the social system, for its part, appears legitimated precisely because it makes individual mobility possible. . . . the new criterion of legitimacy is not characterized by an agreement *over principles*, but by the 'Thermidorian' possibility of satisfying immediate and 'material' interests."[48] "Thermidorian" is ironic here, for the violence we see in Balzac is neither revolutionary nor anarchic; it is the violence of cutthroat ambition. Lucien is a young man of humble provincial origin with a modicum of talent who allows himself to be seduced by a fading provincial aristocrat, Madame de Bargeton. His cynical manipulation of her is linked genetically with his later careerism: "His love for her was mingled with ambition."[49] An almost pathological desire to succeed leads to the sublimation of other desires (to be an artist, to express himself, to empathize with others, to reflect) into the vast sexual energy involved in social climbing. Failure to succeed leads to isolation or, worse, to irrelevance: "So ardent were his desires that he gave a priori assent to any means of advancement. But not to succeed is to commit the crime of social *lèse-majesté*. Has not a man who comes to defeat done to death all those middle-class virtues on which society is built?"[50] That Lucien soon realizes the folly of his hopes to force his way into the aristocracy and instead finds himself trying to force his way into literary and journalistic circles only indicates a change in venue rather than any reconsideration of what constitutes success. His cavalier inconsistency is heightened by his unawareness of being trapped within an endless series of social identities, each one further implicating him in the very social subjectivity to which he assumes, in his arrogant self-assurance, he is immune. Lucien's entrée into literary society occurs after a long siege, and he must force himself past a multitude of possible rivals and enemies. The endless circularity of ambition, of the drive for social success, is underscored at the conclusion when Lucien, returning to Paris destitute and despondent, receives some very pointed advice from the Spanish diplomat Carlos Herrera, canon of Toledo: "Why did I tell you to measure up to society? Because in these days, young man, society has gradually arrogated to itself so many rights over the individual that the individual finds himself obliged to fight back against society. There are no longer any laws, merely conventions, that is to say humbug: nothing but *form*."[51] The canon bestows upon him the "educational digest" that will enable him to make his way in the world. "The code for ambitious people" is finally the only way: "There's no choice: either one must bury oneself in a monastery—and there too the world is often to be found in miniature—or one must accept this code."[52]

A Machiavellian cynicism pervades this worldview, which signals the great distance between Goethe's Society of the Tower (which retains the qualities of a benign feudalism) and Balzac's world of industrial capitalism. Whether he forces his way or forces his way back, Lucien, like so many other nineteenth-century *Bildungshelden*, enters a circulatory economy in which the repetition of ambitious schemes substitutes for an inner life that has been suppressed by institutional pressures and the desires of others. "Whether they want to conquer a woman or obtain a position," writes Moretti, "their life will be a sequence of battles, a sort of personal campaign. Here [in the French Bildungsroman] youth does not find its meaning in creating countless 'connections' with the existing order, but in breaking them. It is not appeased by the happiness of synthesis, but lives, and dies, in the harshness of conflict."[53] The "happiness of synthesis," which characterizes the harmonious development narrated in the classical German Bildungsroman, no longer obtains in the French form, where the hero's assent to "the way of the world" comes at the expense of this very happiness. The French hero does not aspire to an ideal vocation or a marriage that symbolizes the union of spiritual and temporal desires. There is no symbolic Society of the Tower that can lead him to an authentic and unified self.

The mode of social advancement implied by "forcing one's way" describes also the social techniques of Frédéric Moreau in Flaubert's *Sentimental Education*. Unlike Lucien, whose attempt to force his way into the aristocracy fails because he has no social foundation, Frédéric enters Paris a well-educated son of the solid middle class. His ambitions—"In ten years, [he] had to be a deputy; in fifteen a minister; why not?"[54]—are, therefore, at least not unfounded. Not content to dream of conquering French politics, Frédéric also aspires to conquer French women: "He could see nothing in the future before him but an endless succession of years filled with love."[55] As with Julien and Lucien, Frédéric conflates social ambition with sexual desire; it finally matters very little by which path he attains his success, for if one path fails, he will quickly try another. The world of literary salons and publishing houses continuously places before the hero objects of desire that prove unreachable, unsatisfying, potentially fatal. The climate in which young men like Frédéric pursue success cannot support the complex web of commitments that careers and marriages require. As with Balzac before him, Flaubert departs from the ideal of marriage put forward in *Wilhelm Meister*. In Goethe's text, marriage functions as a microcosm and material sign of the hero's acquisition of Bildung. In Flaubert's, mercenary cunning and an "endless succession" of lovers substitute for marriage and signal a quite different relation to the dialectics of Bildung: "The impossibility of possessing [a woman] served as a justification for [Frédéric's] deceitful behaviour, which sharpened his pleasure by providing constant variety; and the more he deceived one of his mistresses, the more she loved him, as if the two women's passions stimulated one another and each woman, out of a sort of rivalry, were trying to make him forget the other."[56] The socially pragmatic ideal of Bildung symbolized by Frédéric's relationships with women belongs to an era of alienation and the capitalist mode of production and consumption. The question of the hero's formation is posed in relation to a social world whose conflicting authorities and possibilities for knowledge proliferate and efface traditional absolutes. Frédéric moves in the city where antisocial behavior—predatory cunning and calculated manipulation, dissimulations and mystification—determines social survival and where youthful enthusiasm is transformed into the bitter and vain desire for lost opportunities. Moretti believes that "Frédéric can protract his youth: as always, thanks to money."[57] But then youth becomes pathological, the object of a fetish; there is no longer any sense of achieved wisdom, only the endless extension of desire—even once the hero returns, ingloriously, to his humble provincial origins in Nogent-sur-Seine where he and his friend Deslauriers "exhumed their youth" and "asked each other after every sentence: 'Do you remember?'"[58] The fable of the prodigal son, which in Goethe's Bildungsroman is transformed into a narrative of the hero's triumphant ascension to an achieved and harmonious Bildung, in the French form is retold as the narrative of defeat, of frustrated rebellion and co-optation. This difference in the representation of return translates the idealistic and utopian aspirations of aesthetico-spiritual Bildung into the socially pragmatic variant that emerges in the course of nineteenth-century modernization.

In the English tradition, as in the French, the socially pragmatic variant of Bildung legitimizes the rise to power of a certain class of young men, rewarding those whose desires for self-development are identical to the demands of the social system. Theodor Adorno provocatively suggests, "Identity is the primal form of ideology." Identity is the means by which a social formation assimilates that which is antithetical to it, bringing otherness into its sphere and conquering it. "We relish [identity] as adequacy to the thing it suppresses; adequacy has always been subjection to dominant purposes and, in that sense, its own contradiction."[59] Though the drive to find adequate identifications between self and society aligns the English Bildungsroman with other European exemplars, there are some significant differences between them. Swales, for example, argues that the English form avoids the "problematic elusiveness" of the hero's relationship to social life found in the German Bildungsroman, which entails a "greater closeness to the actuality of the hero and of the situations with which he is trying to come to terms."[60] For Moretti, the distinction has to do with the stability and conformity of English political culture, which he describes as "a solid world, sure of itself and at ease in a continuity that fuses together 'tradition' and 'progress.' It is a world that cannot and does not want to identify with the spirit of adventure of modern youth."[61] The predilection in the English tradition for a "happy ending" would seem to indicate that an unproblematic assimilation into social institutions is not only possible but desirable; "in England," Moretti writes, "between the insipid normality of the hero, and a stable and a thoroughly classified world, no spark will ever flash. We have to look for another element. . . . A monster *inside* an unyielding system," a villain who "generates plot merely by existing."[62] The journey undertaken to restore order and overcome the monster is forced upon heroes who must "always leave against their will, and without having in any way deserved such a fate."[63] Moretti's focus on the villain in English fiction is appropriate, certainly, but what he does not point out is that the English Bildungsroman urges us to see the monster in the social system as that person who wishes to become socially mobile, to move fluidly upward into a higher social class. Such movements, which began with an insurrectionary force in the early part of the nineteenth century, soon became integrated into the system itself and played a significant role in determining the specific narrative and thematic valences of the Bildungsroman.[64]

One of the chief characteristics of the nineteenth-century English Bildungsroman is an emphasis on work and vocation, a socially pragmatic sense of Bildung that we see in the work of Charles Dickens, Charlotte Brontë, George Meredith, and George Eliot, where self-development is often coupled with discourses of moral and social improvement. These discourses draw the individual into social relationships that in varying degrees determine the nature and quality of personal Bildung. Social class and the importance of work in making upward mobility possible play a key role. The most significant expression of this English form of socially pragmatic Bildung is the narrative of becoming a gentleman, a narrative that reveals the influence of the aristocratic classes on ideas of self-identity and social mobility even, perhaps especially, at a time when those classes were losing ground to the industrial and commercial middle classes. A paradigmatic example is Dickens's *Great Expectations*, where the emphasis falls on Pip's desire to transcend his humble origins and take his place in polite society. Though his desire is thwarted when it is revealed that his rise in status has been funded by Magwich, a transported felon, Pip nevertheless manages to improve his lot in the colonial civil service. In Dickens's tale, the gentleman is seen as normative but not admirable, and the lesson Pip learns is that any rise in status must be justified by his own talents and abilities. The social pedagogy involved in the process of becoming a gentleman among the upper classes is nowhere more clearly articulated, and brilliantly satirized, than in the work of George Meredith. In *The Ordeal of Richard Feverel* (1859), Sir Austin Feverel offers up a system of instruction that guarantees the orderly succession of the young man to the status of gentleman: "The gist of the System set forth . . . that, by hedging round the Youth from corruptness, and at the same time promoting his animal health, by helping him to grow, as he would, like a Tree of Eden, by advancing him to a certain moral fortitude ere the Apple-Disease was spontaneously developed, there would be seen something approaching to a perfect Man, as the Baronet trusted to make this one Son of his, after a receipt of his own."[65] The paternal model that motivates Sir Austin's System—based on "the science of Life . . . a Scientific Humanist, in short"[66]—serves the same function as the Society of the Tower in *Wilhelm Meister*; in both cases we are confronted with symbolic representations of a social structure of power that is inherently patriarchal (Meredith's subtitle—"A History of Father and Son"—makes this explicit) and that aims, within certain conventionally determined limits, at the perfection of the individual. In *The Egoist* (1879), Meredith offers a satiric reflection on this social pedagogy in his depiction of Sir Willoughby, who "cultivated himself" and who "would not be outdone in popular accomplishments. Had the standard of the public taste been set in philosophy, and the national enthusiasm centred in philosophers, he would at least have worked at books. He did work at science, and had a laboratory." The concerns of classical Bildung, no longer relevant in late-nineteenth-century England, are supplanted by science, "the sole object worth a devoted pursuit."[67] Meredith's Bildungsromane draw on both the classical German Enlightenment notion of *Humanitätsideal* and on a native English tradition of philosophical pragmatism to represent the context of a moral-pedagogical system the intent of which is to guarantee the perfect development of the gentleman.

Linked to this thematic of social pedagogy is the orientation toward vocation that we see in George Eliot. The example of Eliot is an important one, and not only because her novels, especially *Middlemarch* (1871–72), reach back for inspiration to the classical form of Goethe. It is important additionally because it marks a terminus in the history of the form, at least for Moretti, whose admiration for Eliot's work underscores the elegiac quality of his argument in the final pages of *The Way of the World*. According to Moretti, Eliot's work narrates a "dream—the notion that one's identity is to be created, and not 'inherited'—[which] brings us back to the beginning of our investigation: to the ideal of *Bildung* which Eliot, with her excellent knowledge of *Meister* and German culture, reformulates as 'vocation.' A vocation which may be political, religious, social, scientific, artistic; but which embodies in every case the synthesis of individual expression and collective benefit."[68] In *Middlemarch*, Dorothea's projects and her ultimate resolution to toil "for the growing good of the world" in her "hidden life"[69] underscore the gulf between what the world expects of individuals and what they expect from themselves, "the 'tragic' split that the modern world has produced between 'life' and 'profession.'"[70] Eliot stands out from other English novelists in large measure because she resists the temptation to valorize in narrative terms the alternatives to vocation—inheritance, careerism, indolence—but also because she places a high value on inner culture. It is for this reason that Dorothea becomes disenchanted with Casaubon, whose admirable intellectual ambitions are transformed in the end into a compulsive drive to control an increasingly chaotic and irrelevant world of knowledge. Nothing could be farther from the goal of an aesthetic education. As for Dorothea, she emerges quietly as the hero of her own Bildung plot, not the instrumental helpmate of Casaubon—or of Will Ladislaw, for that matter.

In England the social conditions that made the Bildungsroman such a powerful and compelling mode of "symbolic legitimation"—the dynamic and unstable developments of capitalism in the nineteenth century through the 1870s—had undergone decisive transformations. One conclusion we can draw, that Moretti does in fact draw, is that social conditions rendered the Bildungsroman inadequate as a model for identity formation or for harmonious socialization—even, it would seem, for the same bourgeois class symbolically configured in Goethe's *Wilhelm Meister*. Moretti argues that the "unhistoric acts" to which Dorothea refers in the final paragraph of the novel "indicate that the standpoint of vocation has been abandoned."[71] For him, this signals the end of the Bildungsroman tradition in English literature, but he could just as easily have taken this abandonment of an essentially masculinist notion of vocation as a starting point for a critique of vocation as a gendered, class-specific expression of the dialectical structure of classical Bildung. Such a critique, which we can discern in many Bildungsromane written by women, focuses on the female *Bildungsheld*, who is doubly constrained in her pursuit of Bildung, since the limitations placed on the young male hero in pursuit of social mobility are compounded for young women by interdicts based on gender difference. For this reason, the Bildungsroman featuring female protagonists may be a better index of the subversive potential of the genre in the nineteenth century, for the "culture of everyday life" (as Moretti puts it) is given a new meaning and emphasis, one that is missing in the "fascinating" stories of Balzac and other male writers. Indeed, we are more likely to find other extremes: the finely drawn machinations in Jane Austen's novels, the Gothic horror of the Brontës, or the provincial obscurity of George Eliot's *Middlemarch*. In such texts, the questions of "inner life" are keyed far more often to themes not typically found in the classical Bildungsroman featuring young male heroes—themes involving romantic love, domestic relationships, emotional well-being, and the potential of "awakening" from the oppressive conditions so often found as the pervasive context for such themes.

In the most important female Bildungsromane of the era—for example, Emily Brontë's *Wuthering Heights* (1847) and Charlotte Brontë's *Jane Eyre* (1847) and *Villette* (1853)—we find some fairly dramatic deviations from the conventions. The motif of "repristination," of a prodigal return to the innocence of origins, is critically redeployed by Emily Brontë in *Wuthering Heights*. According to Sandra Gilbert and Susan Gubar, this redeployment effectively grants to Emily Brontë's female protagonists a level of effective agency by situating their life stories within the context of a Bildung plot that takes them from innocence to experience, but not back to some retrievable innocence. To some extent, the pedagogical aspect of the novel is Gothicized, contrasting dramatically with what we find in Dickens or Meredith.[72] In *Jane Eyre*, too, we see a trajectory from innocence to experience; but it is not a simple transition, for Jane's innocence is from the start colored by her experience with unjust masculine authority, while her later experience negotiating a relationship with Rochester to some degree returns her to the relative purity of her childhood motives. Karen Rowe argues that female Bildungsromane like *Jane Eyre* are strongly influenced by "folktale patterns" that suggest conventional and idealistic patterns of development. Yet the "limited pattern for female maturation" offered up by romantic fairy tales is one that Charlotte Brontë only "initially finds appealing, but later renounces because it subverts the heroine's independence and human equality."[73] In fact, it is just these qualities that seem, early in the narrative, to work against both folktale patterns and Jane's own tendency toward passive obedience to masculine authority. After her servitude at Lowood School and on the eve of her relocation to Rochester's Thornfield, Jane speaks the language of liberty that is in some significant ways a direct inheritance from the era of classical Weimar: "I tired of the routine of eight years in one afternoon. I desired liberty; for liberty I gasped; for liberty I uttered a prayer; it seemed scattered on the wind then faintly blowing. I abandoned it, and framed a humbler supplication; for change, stimulus: that petition, too, seemed swept off into vague space; 'Then,' I cried, half desperate, 'Grant me at least a new servitude!'"[74] We recognize, of course, the ideas of both John Stuart Mill and Thomas Carlyle in this emphasis on liberty and a voluntarist, spiritualized form of servitude. But because a woman desires these values, we are confronted with the "monster" in the system to which Moretti refers. On this view, Rochester's monstrousness is really misleading, since it is always in the service of claiming Jane and containing her within a patriarchal social structure. His insistence on marrying her, despite his being already married, underscores the extent to which the symbolic function of marriage in Goethe's Bildungsroman has been corrupted in the service of a socially pragmatic Bildung. We see the same kinds of Gothicized marriages in George Eliot and Emily Brontë, where a coercive dialectics is the sign of the suppression of female Bildung.

Far from signaling the end of the form, as Moretti suggests, the nineteenth-century English Bildungsroman, particularly when featuring a female protagonist, marks out the space for a provocative if limited immanent critique of the dialectics of Bildung.[75] The primary effect was to highlight the gap between aesthetico-spiritual forms of Bildung and the socially pragmatic variants that follow from it, between the hero's desire to work out a personal destiny and society's demand that personal Bildung function as the symbolic legitimation of existing social conditions. The Bildungsroman, in its turn, reduplicates in literary form a cohesive set of cultural codes whose primary function is to govern social integration in such a way that young men and women *fit into society*. The formation of the hero becomes both the locus and model of history: "in the classical *Bildungsroman*," Moretti argues, "the significance of history does not lie in the 'future of the species,' but must be revealed within the more narrow confines of a circumscribed and relatively common individual life. . . . It thereby follows that the novel exists not as a critique, but as a *culture of everyday life*. Far from devaluing it, the novel organizes and 'refines' this form of existence, making it ever more alive and interesting—or, with Balzac, even fascinating."[76] If the socialization process failed, as it often did in the French Bildungsroman, it did not mean that society had somehow failed; it was the young hero's "unrealistic" aspirations that prevented his desired integration into the social world. The retreat to the provinces really amounts to finding one's way back to where one began, which appears, to the chagrin of the chastised hero, to be one's *proper* place. In the systematic logic of co-optation, all roads lead back home. Thus, for the nineteenth century generally, the heroes of the Bildungsroman are always returning to the authorities they have spurned, not because they have seen "the error of their ways," but because they have, for all their efforts, found no other home.

Starting in the 1890s, the modernist Bildungsroman begins to critique the very society it was meant to validate and legitimize; it carries on the project put forward in the Bildungsromane of women writers who attempted to resignify Bildung in order to represent more faithfully the self-formation of young women. Had this critical tendency not emerged, the Bildungsroman might well have followed the Edwardian family romance into obscurity. It should come as no surprise that the artist, who by the late nineteenth century had become the most potent symbol of nonconformity and rebellion, became the normative *Bildungsheld* of the modernist Bildungsroman, and that identity was increasingly defined in terms of aesthetic education and aesthetic sensibilities. Like other disenfranchised or marginalized members of society, artists had few opportunities for Bildung—few, at least, that they could readily and with a good conscience enter into. On the other hand, their marginalization left them relatively unaffected by the appeal of the various pragmatic discourses of social recruitment. The modern hero, marginalized by race, class, education, nationality, or gender, refuses socialization and assimilation into social institutions that do not advance his or her artistic designs. If Stephen Dedalus must flee his native land in order to try to achieve his goals, if Jude Fawley fails to achieve his goals of self-cultivation and slips into fatal illness, if Rachel Vinrace dies before she can even find out what her goal is, the failure is not that of Bildung, which remains an ideal for all of these young people, but that of the specific social conditions of their development. In the modernist Bildungsroman, Bildung so often turns out to be a dissent from social order, from the bourgeois appropriation of self-cultivation, a dissent as well from the ideas of pedagogy and parenting that sanction restrictive and punitive models of development. Precisely those elements that demanded stability and predictable development in the classical Bildungsroman—harmonious identity-formation, aesthetic education, meaningful and rewarding social relations, a vocation—become problematic in the twentieth century. The modernist Bildungsroman carries on the struggle between desire and "great expectations," but the struggle no longer resembles the dialectical processes so elegantly narrativized in *Wilhelm Meister*.

It is my contention that the English and Irish forms respond in quite different ways to these prior traditions and that, for this reason, they best demonstrate the points of conflict and contrast between modernist traditions and the classical Bildungsroman of the nineteenth century. The English modernist Bildungsroman follows out some of the implications of the realist phase of the classical form, which is concerned primarily with socialization and social mobility, while the Irish tradition, in part because of its long-standing antagonistic relation to English colonial rule and the English literary tradition, resists this tendency toward socially pragmatic forms of Bildung. More resolutely than the English form, the Irish Bildungsroman, like the later modernist novels of Woolf, goes back to the bedrock of the form, Bildung, the ideal of self-sufficiency achieved through aesthetic education. That Irish writers achieved this more successfully than English writers was due, I think, to specific differences in social conditions. Over against the imperial culture of England, Ireland exhibited a combination of unstable social conditions, isolation from major European centers of political and cultural power and influence, and a sense of urgency about the status of the individual and his or her relation to the dominant authorities in Irish society. In Ireland, these conditions were connected to the history of colonial rule, which lent to them specific political, social, and cultural valences. That these sociocultural and political features should have resulted in the resurgence of classical conventions in a transculturated colonial and post-colonial Bildungsroman tradition is not as surprising as it might at first appear. Modernism, especially in Ireland, flourished in uneven social conditions, precisely the kind of conditions that historians have described in late-eighteenth- and early-nineteenth-century Germany, the era in which classical Bildung first emerged. If the humanist values of Bildung enjoyed a resurgence in the early twentieth century, it is because modernist artists recognized in the humanism they resisted the only weapon against a far worse threat: the dehumanization of technological modernity, neatly symbolized by the socially pragmatic variant of Bildung that had come to dominate the educational system and the professionalization of labor.

Paul Sheehan, in his study of the relationship between humanism and modernism, notes the critical role that the Bildungsroman plays in the modernist period. The Bildungsroman, he argues, "is essential to an emplotment of the transactions between the human (humanism, *humanitas*) and the novel. Its antagonist is the experimental, formally diverse modernist novel, with its fraught negotiations between *anthropos* and narrative. This literary form offers a powerful commentary on the various struggles to break free of narrative—or at least to find a different order for its particular conventions. In doing so it illuminates the persistent fixation on the 'human,' and the ways in which it is implicated within narrative understanding and orientation, through the hundred-year anthropometric era, from the 1850s to the 1950s."[77] If I understand Sheehan's point correctly, he is arguing that there is a productive tension between the conventionality of the Bildungsroman form (both its narrative structure and its humanist thematics) and the procedures of experimental modernism. What I offer in the chapters that follow is a meditation on this productive tension, which I see in terms of a critique of the dialectical structure of the Bildungsroman form as well as of the concept of socially pragmatic Bildung that so often provided its ideological core. In the modernist Bildungsroman, a critical perspective reconfigures the conventional structures of narrative, while retaining most of its main elements (plot trajectory, characterization, thematic emphases), and reinstates a revalued classical Bildung as the goal of the modernist *Bildungsheld*. Many critics of the Bildungsroman in modernist literature (which is not to say the modernist Bildungsroman) speak of inversion of or opposition to the conventions of the form. My intention in this study is to speak of quite the opposite, to speak of a resurgence and rehabilitation of Bildung grounded in an immanent critique of the Bildungsroman and its totalizing dialectical processes.

That modernist Bildungsromane so frequently deal with failure suggests a critique of the cultural conditions in which Bildung takes place and which deprive individuals of the freedom to think critically about their identities and how they relate to structures of power. In what follows, I connect this cultural problematic to the problem in philosophy that Theodor Adorno diagnoses in *Negative Dialectics*—that is, I connect the failure of culture to the failure of Enlightenment thinking about the subject, subjectivity, identity, and dialectics, to the failure of a way of thinking that produced the Bildungsroman as the quintessential narrative of the sovereign and autonomous, harmoniously self-identical subject of Bildung. The modernist Bildungsroman, then, in its critique of the classical tradition and in its radical recapture of the concept of Bildung, anticipates Adorno's critique of modernity. "The culture of its environment has broken thought of the habit to ask what all this may be, and to what end; it has enfeebled the question what it all means—a question growing in urgency as fewer people find some such sense self-evident, as it yields more and more to cultural bustle. Enthroned instead is the being-thus-and-not-otherwise of whatever may, as culture, claim to make sense."[78] The alternative to the cultural enfeeblement of modernity is a form of immanent critique that refuses any arrogant stance outside the domain of a contested culture, that in fact strategically inhabits, as a starting point and base of operations, the very culture it criticizes. In modernist hands, the Bildungsroman is critiqued from the standpoint of its tendency toward dialectical harmony, toward reconcilement of the self and the external social world that is preserved as utopian vision in Goethe and that is mourned as a lost paradisaical dispensation in the French and English Bildungsromane throughout most of the nineteenth century. The modernists I treat in this study orient themselves to this tradition from within it, much as Adorno's "negative dialectics" begins precisely through dialectics itself. "Totality is to be opposed by convicting it of nonidentity with itself—of the nonidentity it denies, according to its own concept. Negative dialectics is thus tied to the supreme categories of identitarian philosophy as its point of departure."[79]

In my discussion of the modernist Bildungsroman, I identify a turn toward nonidentity, an attempt to emphasize or draw out the nonidentical as such, rather than simply to assume its "pivotal" role in constituting identity within a classical dialectics. Negative dialectics, which is a form of immanent critique, is not to be confused with the conventional function of dialectical negation, in which the "other" in a binary opposition to the "same" is crucial to the self-identity of the "same" by standing in for or negating all that is not the "same." Nor is it simply a reversal of standard dialectical operations. To confront "the customary formula of 'identity in nonidentity'" with "a purely formal reversal," Adorno warns, "would leave room for the subreption that dialectics is *prima philosophia* after all, as '*prima dialectica.*'"[80] The turn toward nonidentity, then, is a turn toward justice, an attempt to achieve the promise of a more just harmony of self and society by transcending the "pretext" of justice inscribed in the socially pragmatic forms of Bildung and in the classical Bildungsroman.[81] In the modernist Bildungsroman, the goal is not to celebrate the unity and totality of the dialectical terms that constitute the characteristic narrative logic of the form, but to discover the principles of their disharmony and the "logic of disintegration" that alone can make "sense" of the suspicion of identity.[82] It is finally not the structure of the Bildungsroman but what it excludes that is the issue; only a logic of disintegration can attempt to include what has not yet been integrated into a structure that exists by virtue of its absence. The point is not to privilege or celebrate this absence (and thus to reify it in its negative glory) but to indicate its elusive presence, to acknowledge nonidentity ("something," matter, entity, nonconceptuality) *as such*. "It is the matter," insists Adorno, "not the organizing drive of thought, that brings us to dialectics."[83]

In chapter 1, I argue that the key to understanding the survival of the Bildungsroman is the persistence of the concept of Bildung, which in the twentieth century is inextricably tied to the history of modernity, a history in which the intelligentsia of Weimar played a decisive role. Equally important was the work of Wilhelm von Humboldt, whose conception of Bildung, though not expressed in literary or narrative terms, proved extremely influential in the development of socially pragmatic forms of socialization, specifically in educational systems, that became normative in the nineteenth century. I conclude by suggesting that the modernist Bildungsroman, while failing to measure up to the generic conventions it inherits from the classical tradition, nevertheless succeeds to varying degrees in recuperating a classical notion of Bildung that incorporates the crucial elements of individual freedom and aesthetic education. That Bildung is so often frustrated or detoured does not detract from the general project of self-cultivation narrated in modernist Bildungsromane. For this recuperative project seeks not to circumvent or "opt out" of socialization processes, but rather to develop new conceptions of self-cultivation, which often take the form of a liberatory *depersonalization* and which respond more effectively and productively to the demands of modern social conditions. The modernist Bildungsroman may fail in terms of genre, but that failure only serves to articulate more effectively its singular triumph, the abstract affirmation of Bildung as a cherished ideal. The constitutive irony of the modernist Bildungsroman lies in this affirmation made from the perspective of the subject who, in the final analysis, can feel only its absence.

In chapters 2 through 4, I analyze key Bildungsromane in the modernist tradition, focusing on the problems and issues unique to each text as well as to the critical tradition that has accumulated around them. One of my chief assumptions is that the thematics of the modernist Bildungsroman represent a continuance of the concerns of the classical form. A related assumption, one to which I have already alluded, is that the destiny of Bildung and the transformation of the Bildungsroman proceed quite differently in England and Ireland (to say nothing of America and the rest of Europe). For this reason, I treat the English and Irish traditions separately, beginning in chapter 2 with a discussion of two major exemplars of the modernist Bildungsroman by Thomas Hardy and D. H. Lawrence. The dialectics of self-development in their work is strongly determined by issues of class, especially with respect to social mobility and the pursuit of appropriate vocations, and by an antagonistic stance toward humanist ideals of education and identity. In both writers, the instrumental function of women and the role of sexuality and marriage are of fundamental importance to a general critique of genre and to a general rehabilitation of classical Bildung.

Similar problems and themes are discovered in the Bildungsromane of Oscar Wilde and James Joyce, which I discuss in chapter 3, but they are complicated by the colonial conditions in which their very different Bildung plots take shape. Of critical importance is the work of Wilde, whose problematic status as an Anglo-Irishman lies behind his displaced narratives of self-development. In *The Picture of Dorian Gray*, Wilde links the Bildungsroman to an Anglo-Irish Gothic tradition, thereby performing a crucial critical function of destabilizing the dialectical foundation of aesthetics and ethics that subtend not only the classical Bildungsroman but also Wilde's modernist variant of the form. It is through this critical destabilization that aesthetics reemerges as the foundation of a complex mode of self-formation. Both Wilde and Joyce employ the modernist strategy of depersonalization as a commentary on identity formation under colonial conditions. *Dorian Gray* and the essays on aesthetics that make up its essential context constitute a complex attempt to underscore the profound transformations that await those who submit to an aesthetic education outside the institutional framework of the dominant colonial culture. Joyce's *Portrait of the Artist as a Young Man* accomplishes much the same goal, but without making the same kind of generic departures that we see in Wilde. In some ways, Joyce's Bildungsroman more assiduously rehabilitates the conventions of the classical form in order more compellingly to suggest the difficulties of such a form for the colonial subject. With respect to Joyce, the situation is complicated still further by the influence of an institution with strong interests in pedagogy and in creating good subjects—the Roman Catholic Church. Among other things, this complicates the representation of confession in the narration of Bildung, specifically as a model for new modes of communication and social interaction.

Chapter 4 focuses on the representation of Bildung for women, especially as it is transformed in high modernist innovations in narrative, characterization, and thematics. I approach the "Nausicaa" episode of *Ulysses* as an example of a foreshortened Bildung plot that focuses on the kind of aesthetic self-fashioning possible for a young Irish Catholic woman. I contrast this high modernist achievement with a similar one in Woolf's *Mrs. Dalloway*, which complicates the foreshortened Bildung plot of Elizabeth Dalloway by presenting it as part of a retrospective Bildung plot featuring her mother, Clarissa Dalloway. Woolf, who gives an ambivalent assent to Bildung as an ideal of self-sufficiency achieved through aesthetic education, refashions humanism around a new sense of the self. My discussion of Woolf's novel is prefaced by a consideration of her earliest engagement with the Bildungsroman tradition, *A Voyage Out*, a novel about a young woman confronted with a humanistic tradition that seeks to define her even as it excludes her and her attempt to find an alternative to it. In both Joyce and Woolf we see high modernist narrative innovations brought to bear on the vexed problem of self-development, refusing in a decisive way the narrative emplotment typically associated with the Bildungsroman, but nevertheless narrating the aspiration toward Bildung in new and startling formats. They both underscore emphatically the aesthetic dimension of Bildung—even to the point of calling into question the very notion of the subject, the self, and of self-development.

1

Modernity, Modernism, and the Idea of Bildung

The history of the Bildungsroman is the history of a genre in crisis. As it traversed the nineteenth century, the Bildungsroman underwent dramatic transformations, especially concerning Bildung and its role in education. The concept of Bildung had, during this period, become increasingly tied to pragmatic discourses of social recruitment and social mobility. This is especially true in the English tradition, in which social responsibility tended to triumph over personal Bildung, thus creating an ambivalent, at times contradictory, relationship between socialization and individualism, between social mobility and self-sufficiency, between personal desire and social demand. Many modernists resisted this pragmatic model of intersubjectivity and attempted to devise ways by which the presumed failure of the subject to satisfy the demands of society (especially in contexts of education and work) could be revalued and transformed into new forms of identity. One way of doing this was, paradoxically, to retrieve the classical conception of Bildung and redeploy it in a progressive fight against "rationalized" forms of socialization and in the search for satisfying modes of self-cultivation.

In this chapter, I consider closely the concept of Bildung and how, in the course of its development in the nineteenth century, it dominated thinking about the subject, subjectivity, and subject formation.[1] Of special interest are the social and cultural contexts for Bildung, the "harmony of aesthetic, moral, rational, and scientific education" that Fritz Martini believes to be the hallmark of self-cultivation.[2] Though Martini's formulation emphasizes rational and scientific education, and though the lives of Goethe and Humboldt so dramatically demonstrated its importance, the overriding concern of the theorists of Bildung was aesthetic education. Moral reflection and action were an important part of what is understood by the concept of the aesthetic, especially in the harmonious and spontaneous cultivation of the self. Crucially important to such an education was freedom. As Humboldt notes, "if there is one aspect of development more than any other which owes its highest beauty to freedom, it is precisely the cultivation of character and morals."[3] The emphasis on beauty here and elsewhere in the work of Humboldt and his contemporaries reinforces the aesthetic dimension of self-cultivation, a dimension in which "the individual, drawing on the best from the world around him and from history, should seek to 'form' his unique personality as an artist would seek to create a masterpiece."[4]

The development of the concept of Bildung, from the Weimar theorists to the English and Irish modernists, is best understood in the context of modernity and modernization, categories of historical explanation that enable certain linkages, specifically between the subject and the social and cultural institutions that shape and direct subjectivity. My focus on developments in nineteenth-century England is essential to an understanding of how the modernist Bildungsroman responds to a specifically English tradition of humanism, individualism, and liberalism. In the English context, too, we see the displacement of aesthetico-spiritual Bildung and the ascendancy of new pragmatic modes of socialization. Given the pedagogical thematics of so many modernist Bildungsromane, the idea of education—both formal, state-sponsored forms and those initiated and developed by individuals for their own aesthetic needs—will be a focus of discussion throughout this study. It is the key to understanding how Bildung becomes institutionalized and how social mobility contributes to the "production" of subjects. Also important will be the specific modalities of resistance to these mechanisms that we see in nearly all modernist Bildungsromane.

If we read it as a mode of generic resistance, the Bildungsroman might be said to harbor a "political unconscious," which, according to Fredric Jameson, constitutes the ideological basis of literary texts. Literary criticism would then seek to detect "traces" of the "uninterrupted narrative" of social history—specifically, the buried history of "the collective struggle to wrest a realm of Freedom from a realm of Necessity." Criticism brings "to the surface of the text the repressed and buried reality of this fundamental history."[5] This historical narrative is tangled up with the history of the Bildung concept, which I will discuss in the first section of this chapter. I will be concerned with Humboldt's theory of Bildung and the centrality of aesthetics in education and with the transformation of Humboldtian Bildung into the rationalized pragmatic form that first emerges in John Stuart Mill's theories of individualism. In the next section, I shift my focus to England in the second half of the nineteenth century and look closely at social mobility and the increasingly rationalized educational system. The term "rationalization," which I borrow from Max Weber and Theodor Adorno, refers to the process by which bureaucracies and other institutions refine their operations, making them more efficient, standardized, and easily managed. I draw on the work of Ernest Gellner and Michel Foucault to talk about the rationalization and institutionalization of Bildung in both metropolitan and colonial contexts. The final section pursues the problematic development of the modernist Bildungsroman. Of particular interest is the relationship between modernism and the humanist tradition of Bildung. Theorists of modernity like Anthony Giddens, Adorno, Foucault, and Jameson provide a perspective from which to view critically the pedagogical and humanist dimensions of the modernist Bildungsroman, its embrace, as it were, of a classical project of aesthetic education and self-cultivation. The return to Bildung in the modernist Bildungsroman is not, however, an "innocent" return, a Humboldtian dream of self-sufficiency. In the pedagogical and vocational dynamics of the modernist Bildungsroman, we see the trials and tribulations of this return. But more than this, we see the critical potential of a recuperated classical Bildung, a radical conservatism that is at one and the same time an immanent critique.

MODERNITY AND THE RISE OF BILDUNG

The term "modernity," according to Anthony Giddens, can be used, "in a very general sense, to refer to the institutions and modes of behaviour established first of all in post-feudal Europe, but which in the twentieth century increasingly have become world-historical in their impact."[6] The early phase of modernity embraces the humanist project of the Renaissance as well as the scientific developments of seventeenth- and eighteenth-century Enlightenment movements across Europe.[7] Some of the most important trends in modernity, especially after the midpoint of the eighteenth century, include the dominance of industrial capitalism, the development of nation-states, the rise of bureaucracies, the instrumentalization of reason, and the requirement of universal literacy, the last a key element in state-sponsored educational systems. The acceleration and consolidation of these trends correspond to a late phase of modernity, *modernization*. One of the most important developments of modernity, which is of central importance to all of these trends, was the emergence of the subject as sovereign and self-identical, epitomized in the Lockean conception of personal identity. According to Locke, a person "is a thinking intelligent being, that has reason and reflection, and can consider itself as itself, the same thinking thing, in different times and places; which it does only by that consciousness which is inseparable from thinking, and, as it seems to me, essential to it: it being impossible for any one to perceive without *perceiving* that he does perceive." We are aware of ourselves in our present perceptions by virtue of our consciousness: we are present to ourselves as ourselves. "[I]n this alone consists personal identity, i.e., the sameness of a rational being: and as far as this consciousness can be extended backwards to any past action or thought, so far reaches the identity of that person; it is the same self now it was then; and it is by the same self with this present one that now reflects on it, that that action was done."[8] Locke thus links self-awareness to historical thinking, as well as rationality, guaranteeing that the self will remain sovereign and self-identical in the face of irrational or "nonidentical" forces and the kinds of distance and disparity that impinge on one's present sense of self and all past versions of that self.

Some commentators in the mid-eighteenth century, like Thomas Reid, challenged Locke on the grounds that personal identity was bound up with the capacity to *remember* the self; however, recent critics have attempted to clarify the issue by pointing to Reid's category mistake in emphasizing *memory* over *consciousness*.[9] Peter Loptson identifies the complexity of the Lockean self as an "explicit contra-Cartesian view" in which "we are not conscious at all times at which we exist." It lies precisely in the capacity of the self to sustain the condition of self-identity across time, even in the temporary absence of consciousness. Consciousness "*can* be numerically identical in temporally separated events," writes Loptson. And it can be interrupted. "When it returns, following interruption, Locke's view is that, not a new qualitatively resembling consciousness has appeared, but the same old consciousness, revived and restored."[10]

By the late eighteenth century, this notion of the continuous, self-identical consciousness, one that can undergo changes without undergoing a commensurate break into a separate "qualitatively resembling consciousness," had become complicated by new theories of education and self-cultivation. These new theories, which drew on the confessional tradition, both Christian and secular, situated the self as part of an ongoing Enlightenment project that involved the conscious cultivation of the self (Bildung) through the combination of innate capacities and the advantages of birth and social circumstance. A new model of the sovereign subject emerged from this tradition of classical Bildung, a harmonious and unified inner culture formed through social freedom and a secular aesthetic education. This model is at the heart of the Bildungsroman, the literary form that, in the 1790s, began to diverge from the more typical forms of biographical narrative, which M. M. Bakhtin describes as realistic accounts of "the total life process" that are "limited, unrepeatable, and irreversible." The hero's "positive and negative features . . . are fixed and ready-made, they are given from the very beginning." The hero of biographical discourse, then, "lacks any true process of becoming or development."[11] Wilhelm Dilthey draws a similar conclusion, arguing that biographical forms lead "necessarily to an account focusing on significant moments of this life in their typical forms" and that the Bildungsroman differs from them because it "intentionally and artistically depicts that which is universally human in such a life-course."[12] As we have seen in Dilthey's analysis of Goethe, this universal aspect of human life is represented in the term "Bildung" and in the mode of emplotment of the Bildungsroman.

Few concepts in literary and cultural studies are as tied to a specific time and place as the concept of Bildung. Though part of a broad development in eighteenth-century England, France, and Germany that saw the rise of culture in the modern sense of literary, aesthetic, and social achievement, Bildung is often regarded as the singular product of a few German intellectuals in Weimar, Jena, and Berlin in the last two decades of the century. These intellectuals—principally Johann Gottfried von Herder, Christoph Martin Wieland, Friedrich von Schiller, Goethe, and Humboldt—collaborated on a vision of humanism (*Humanitätsideal*) that produced a unifying language for a region of Europe that had no national existence, "a language that could explore inward and elusive experience with an assuredness and differentiation rare in other European languages. Such a language, usually associated with religious or mystical experience, became a potent contribution to the autobiographical and biographical narrative form with the advent of the complex phenomenon of secularization in the second half of the eighteenth century."[13] This "phenomenon of secularization" was nowhere more pronounced than in the work of Herder, whose historicist approach to human history was extremely influential among Weimar intellectuals. He began, as one might expect of a young clergyman, by arguing that the ideal of cultivation was the image of God in the individual: "To the beasts Thou gavest instinct, in the soul of man Thou didst implant Thine image, religion, and humanity." This comes from the second part of Herder's *Ideen*, published in 1785. Only two years later, in the third part, his views had become much more secular, the emphasis falling on the values of human thought and "inwardness." As W. H. Bruford puts it, "The culture of the individual (Bildung) has become a substitute for salvation, a salvation itself conceived in terms reminiscent as much of Greek ideas as of Christian."[14]

Herder's *Ideen* was perhaps the most important early work to promote the idea of Bildung, and Goethe was only one of the more famous writers to elaborate on the concept. Goethe's own treatment of this concept, as I indicated in the introduction, involved the goal of social integration represented in *Wilhelm Meister* by the idealized and benign authoritarianism of the Society of the Tower. At the foundation of this goal and this ideal society was the ideal of self-cultivation, expressed most clearly by the uncle and guardian of the "beautiful soul" whose narrative of pious development inspires Wilhelm and serves as a kind of object lesson for female self-development:

> The whole world is spread out before us like a stone quarry before a builder, and no one deserves to be called a builder unless he can transform these raw materials into something corresponding to the image in his mind, with the utmost economy, purposefulness and sureness. Everything outside us is just material, and I can well say the same about everything about us: but within us there lies the formative power which creates what is to be, and never lets us rest until we have accomplished this in one way or another in or outside ourselves. . . . we strive to know the full extent of our sensual being and actively promote its unification.[15]

The metaphor of building (*Bildung*, in one definition, refers to a complex construction or entity; it derives from *Bild*, "picture" or "image") and the references to "transformation" and "formative power" are oriented toward an inner culture "imaged" in the mind whose unification is actively pursued as a project of conscious construction. It is significant that this quintessential expression of the goal of Bildung is found in book 6 of *Wilhelm Meister*, "Confessions of a Beautiful Soul," for the "Confessions" emphasizes the spiritual aspect of Bildung, which was, as I have suggested, a key feature of Enlightenment thought, especially in the work of Herder and Wieland. Indeed, the German Enlightenment was so strongly tied to Protestant Pietism that it could "almost be described as a branch of progressive Protestant theology."[16] The "Confessions" also underscores the gender dynamics of aesthetic education and classical Bildung. According to Michael Minden, it enables the "sophisticated introjection of otherness . . . which actually *displaces* the male hero," an "authentic female voice" that articulates "a woman's religious self-development . . . bracketed off from the vicissitudes of interaction with the world of activity."[17] Marianne Hirsch emphasizes the ambivalence of this self-development, for while the "Confessions" represents "a creative response to impoverishing and diminishing social circumstances," the Bildung plot devoted to the "beautiful soul" is structurally subordinated to Wilhelm's. This structural subordination signals her otherness and nonidentity: "her voice is confined and contained, balanced in such a way as to make her experience no more than the example of one extreme of human development."[18]

The gender dynamics of the Goethean Bildung plot reproduce a more general narrative structure in which self-identity is achieved in an engagement with the "world of activity." Giddens regards narrative as the preeminent mode of conceptualizing self-identity and subjectivity in modernity: "A person's identity is not to be found in behavior, nor—important though this is—in reactions of others, but in the capacity *to keep a particular narrative going.*"[19] It seems to me that this notion of self-identity bears a family resemblance to the Lockean notion of the self as a consciousness capable of remaining consistent with itself even after "interruption." The significant difference lies in what Giddens refers to as "reflexivity," the practice, unique to modernity, of constant revision and negotiation of self-identity in the face of new information and situations. Another way of putting this difference is to say that the *self* (a "generic phenomenon") is distinct from *self-identity*, which "is not something that is just given, as a result of the continuities of the individual's action-system, but something that has to be routinely created and sustained in the reflexive activities of the individual."[20] A specifically *narrative* continuity evolves out of the self-conscious creation of a biography of the self. It is, in short, "continuity as interpreted reflexively by the agent."[21]

From Locke to Giddens, then, self-identity tends increasingly toward narrative expression, a development entirely commensurate with the strong orientation toward narrative knowledge in modernity generally.[22] In the late eighteenth century, the transformation of an uninflected and static biographical narrative into a highly nuanced record of the self-cultivation of inner life (a "pre-modern" manifestation of Giddens's concept of reflexivity) marks a turning point in modernity.[23] Goethe, working within a novel tradition that had already become conventional enough to warrant Laurence Sterne's parody of it in *Tristram Shandy* (1765–69), understood the importance of finding narrative forms of representing self-development, specifically that masculine form of development that he evidently felt could not exclude the "vicissitudes of interaction with the world of activity." The elements and values of Bildung were formulated in a region of Europe that was constantly undergoing population shifts, invasions, religious pressures, intellectual discoveries. It was a time of intense political and social turmoil during which geographical and cultural boundaries were traversed and redrawn with impunity. The French Revolution and the Napoleonic conquest and reorganization of much of the German territories significantly influenced the way intellectuals like Goethe, Schiller, and Humboldt, among so many others, conceived the role of the individual in a complex, changing world and how self-development is conducted under rapidly changing social conditions. Goethe's novel was written in the relatively halcyon early 1790s, when events in France could still be regarded favorably by liberal-minded Enlightenment thinkers elsewhere. The thematics of socialization that we see in *Wilhelm Meister*, therefore, reflect confidence in the possibilities of a rapprochement between the individual who seeks the aesthetic unity of his faculties and a benign, authoritarian, protocapitalist agrarian utopia unscathed by potentially hostile neighbors.[24]

This is a tall order, to be sure, but in the 1790s, in the intellectually stimulating enclaves of Weimar and Jena, it was a reasonable expectation and *Wilhelm Meister* a less than fanciful narrative expression of it. Goethe's own varied life experiences in Weimar from the 1770s on are remarkable: in addition to producing major literary writings, he was Geheimer Rat (something like a privy councilman) and member of the central ruling Conseil of Weimar, which included the affairs of the University of Jena; he played a leading role in Weimar's amateur theater, practiced various branches of the natural sciences, and contributed widely to literary and scholarly journals as well as to literary and philosophical societies—all of this in addition to corresponding with the leading savants of the day. Goethe's life experience would seem to indicate that an aesthetic education predicated on the freedom to express oneself fully and without restraint not only was possible but could be accomplished as part of a more general harmony of social practices.[25] It also testifies to the positive effects of Weimar's qualities of smallness, isolation, and provinciality. As early as 1783, Bruford notes, Weimar had become a "definite concept," a center of culture not despite but precisely because of these qualities. And it was these qualities that kept Goethe in Weimar far longer than he expected. His "Auf Miedings Tod" contains a paean to this "little capital": "O Weimar! dir fiel ein besonder Los! / Wie Bethlehem in Juda, klein und gross / Bald wegen Geist und Witz beruft dich weit / Europens Mund, bald wegen Albernheit."[26] The development of the nearby University of Jena into a powerhouse of philosophical and scientific research and scholarship suggests that the production of an ideological foundation for Bildung was possible without excessive or negative statist inference. Sympathetic rulers, like Karl August, Duke of Sachsen-Weimar, guaranteed some financial support for the university, but it was really the general excitement of intellectual freedom that attracted Goethe, Schiller, and Johann Fichte (and later G. W. F. Hegel) to the region. It is important to bear in mind that this kind of integration was really possible only to men of the privileged middle and aristocratic classes, who had the economic freedom and social status to pursue Bildung and the ideal of harmonious socialization narrativized in *Wilhelm Meister* and exemplified by Goethe's career.[27] Goethe, like other prominent individuals of his acquaintance, was aware of his own privilege, and some of his projects in Weimar contributed to the aim of making what Franco Moretti calls "the 'aesthetic' dimension of everyday life" available to a wider circle of people.[28] Clearly, such efforts do not detract significantly from the elitist orientation of the project of self-cultivation; in view of the generally conservative orientation of intellectual life in Germany at the time, however, Weimar represented, for a short while at least, a promising potential for the dialectical integration of self and society that is the essence of classical Bildung.

A very short while indeed, for events elsewhere in Europe effectively curtailed the social experiments in Weimar. The first of these events, the French Revolution, was not, in and of itself, a strong deterrent to the work of most German intellectuals. David Blackbourn, echoing contemporaries of Goethe and modern historians, sees the conservative nature of the German Enlightenment as a sufficient protection against French radicalism: "even the pungent German critics of the 1790s were more closely tied to the existing order than their French counterparts, through patronage or employment. Progressive public opinion had always looked to reforms from above for solutions, and in that sense Enlightenment Absolutism acted as a form of 'immunization' against revolution."[29] Far more devastating for the intellectual and cultural life of Weimar was the war France waged in German territories, beginning in 1792 and lasting through the Napoleonic years. "A whole generation grew up in its shadow," Blackbourn writes; "it affected everything from levels of consumption to religious observance. The war also had an ideological component absent from earlier dynastic struggles, and this left its mark on the reshaped German state-system."[30] Up until the early nineteenth century, Germany was a congeries of small states and principalities, free towns and papal cities, some divided into far-flung, geographically separate territories, some so small as to consist largely of a single extended family's property. This fragmented geopolitical terrain suffered serious setbacks during the period of French domination, including loss of life and territory, conscription, food shortages, and reparation costs.[31] The catastrophic defeat of the Prussian army at Jena in 1806 brought the war right into the precincts of Weimar and effectively put paid to its "classical" period.[32] Conflict in the region accelerated during the long period of French occupation and the geopolitical repositioning that led up to the German Confederation of 1815. During this time, the states that had survived occupation embarked on ambitious reforms that "established the state as the motor of modernization."[33] This was especially true in Prussia, where men like Wilhelm von Humboldt were involved in attempting to build into such reforms an awareness of the value of individual Bildung.

For Humboldt even more insistently than for Goethe, Bildung involved a bracketing off of external forces in order to guarantee the sovereignty, autonomy, and harmony of inner culture, which Goethe associated with noble sentiments, sincere intentions and a "natural way of thinking and acting."[34] It was not meant to signify the achievement of self-cultivation in harmony with the state, however much the state was idealized in narrative representations of Bildung. Rather, it involved a distanced and dispassionate position with respect to society, an autonomy of selfhood that could best be characterized as self-sufficiency. Humboldt was not concerned, as Bruford notes, about "what we learn or how we improve the world outside" but only, as Humboldt puts it, about "the improvement of our inner selves, or at least about satisfying the inner restlessness which consumes us."[35] Indeed, in private correspondence Humboldt expresses a view that anticipates the modernist emphasis on the subject as spectator. Though he was a skilled administrator and diplomat, he nevertheless felt the need of detachment and distance, "of looking at the world as a spectacle, rather than as a serious concern in which one must actively intervene," and "of learning to see one's actions as a negligible factor in the world process and only important for one's private view of things and private evaluation of them."[36] This aspect of Humboldt's thinking about Bildung also anticipates the deconstructive or "depersonalizing" strategies of modernism. Like Friedrich Nietzsche, he understood the subject not as a universal category but as a creative project. "*One thing is needful*," writes Nietzsche in *The Gay Science*. "To 'give style' to one's character—a great and rare art! It is practiced by those who survey all the strengths and weaknesses of their nature and then fit them into an artistic plan until every one of them appears as art and reason and even weaknesses delight the eye. . . . It will be the strong and domineering natures that enjoy their finest gaiety in such constraint and perfection under a law of their own; the passion of their tremendous will relents in the face of all stylized nature, of all conquered and serving nature."[37] Humboldt describes himself in Nietzschean terms as a man who has "complete control of [his] self-directive will" and is "thoroughly inward-oriented," one "whose entire effort goes to transform the world in its most manifold shapes into his own solitude."[38] However, as Marianne Cowan notes, he was "a thoroughgoing activist, even a manipulator, a man who lived with singular vivacity for the moment and the moment's enjoyment." The combination of traits noted here prompts Cowan to claim, with reference to the passage from Nietzsche just cited, that the words "might have been written of Humboldt or even by Humboldt."[39] It is this Nietzschean aspect—one that undermines any simplistic notion that personal Bildung must entail harmonious dialectical integration with society—that differentiates Humboldt's thinking from others of his time and that makes his work so suggestive when theorizing the modernist Bildungsroman and its critical recuperation of classical Bildung.

Unlike Goethe, Humboldt was not a literary artist; his writings were largely scholarly investigations of Greek language and culture or reflections on political science. Bildung was for him intimately bound up with classical humanism and the social, ethical, and aesthetic values of the ancient world. He was very much influenced by the cult of Greece, which followed upon Johann Joachim Winckelmann's groundbreaking work. An early essay, "Concerning the Study of Antiquity, and of Greek Antiquity in Particular" (1792), articulates a view of the importance of Greek ideas concerning culture, the individual, and the relation between the two that was to determine so much of his later thinking about Bildung and education. Humboldt's biographer Paul R. Sweet summarizes the main point of the argument: "From the Greeks it was uniquely possible to obtain 'some sort of idea' of a human perfection wherein maximum manysidedness was marvelously integrated into a harmonious whole."[40] The Greek ideal of Bildung supplied Humboldt with a model of sociality that stressed influence over integration. "The truly great person," he wrote to his friend Georg Forster, a celebrated traveler, "the man who is truly cultivated in the intellectual and moral sense, exerts by these qualities alone more influence than all others, simply because such a man exists among men, or has existed."[41] The process of Bildung, then, is not divorced from social institutions and relations; but neither is it one of dialectical give-and-take. The individual comes first, and the cultivated individual is to be regarded as possessing social capital that the uncultivated do not have. The crucial point for understanding Humboldt's humanistic pedagogy is that the cultivated have a responsibility to educate those who lack the means and opportunity to cultivate themselves. The cultivated become, in a sense, role models. "The first law of morality is: cultivate thyself; and the second is: influence others by what thou art."[42] His understanding of Bildung as analogous to Greek ideals of human perfection and as something that can be modeled and taught to everyone uncannily anticipates the modernist Bildungsroman, in which Bildung is represented as a social and cultural value sought by individuals typically marginalized by an elite intelligentsia.

Humboldt arrived in Jena in the early 1790s, while on an extended hiatus from his duties to the Prussian government, and quickly became friends with Goethe and Schiller. He was especially close to Schiller, whose *Letters on the Aesthetic Education of Man* emphasized the crucial link between an aesthetic comprehension of the world and the development of a many-sided, harmonious personality. The theological strains that Bruford hears in Schiller's work—"pure doctrine of inwardness, of 'Bildung,' unconsciously relying on a benevolent Providence"[43]—may not have appealed to the more staunchly secular Humboldt, but they would not have prevented him from recognizing the significance of Schiller's conception. In such cases, it is important not to overemphasize a tendency on the part of Weimar humanists to carry over into their secular work the hallmarks of the Pietism that was everywhere evident in the general intellectual culture. And while Humboldt may not have followed Schiller's abstract method of articulating his point,[44] he was sympathetic with the aim of promoting aesthetics not as a specialized branch of knowledge but as something more general and fundamental. Writing to Christian Körner, he sums up his thinking about aesthetics: "the feeling of beauty derives neither from the theoretical nor practical reason, but rather from *all* rational faculties combined, and is actually what binds all human capacities together in a single whole." It is from this holistic viewpoint that thinkers like Kant and Schiller acquire for Humboldt "the greatest interest, for I would very much like to see at last the knowledge of man and the principles of his *Bildung* in the largest context."[45] Though Humboldt does not devise a systematic theory of aesthetics, the importance of an aesthetic sensibility as the foundation of Bildung is evident in much of his work, including *The Limits of State Action*. In this work, which was to prove profoundly influential in the development of English intellectual trends in the nineteenth century, he was able to formulate a theory of the state that would accommodate the ideal of Bildung and, in fact, protect the very processes by which the individual achieves it.

The Limits of State Action was written in 1791–92 but was not published until 1854, nearly twenty years after Humboldt's death. Sweet summarizes the main argument well: "The true aim of man is to achieve the highest *Bildung* of which his creative energies are capable; and creative energies prosper best in a climate of freedom."[46] Though Humboldt does not pursue Goethe's project of narrativizing Bildung in fictional terms, he does follow him in insisting on the importance of "creative energies" in the project of self-cultivation. For both thinkers, self-cultivation involved the intertwined processes of intense self-awareness and an equally intense communication of this awareness to intimate friends who were engaged in similar projects of self-cultivation. Many of Humboldt's ideas about self-cultivation were expressed in letters sent to his wife and friends in the late 1790s. These letters reveal his interest "in the analysis of his own psychological states and the . . . urge to reveal them to a sympathetic woman."[47] As was the

case with Goethe's relationship with Charlotte von Stein, Humboldt's relationships with women, many of whom were Jewish intellectuals like Henriette
Herz and Dorothea Veit (daughter of Moses Mendelssohn), opened up a whole
new world of ideas. He formed a group, a *Tugendbund* (virtuous circle), which
included Herz and Veit and, later, the woman who was to become his wife,
Karoline von Dacheröden, all of whom were devoted to the free expression
of their thoughts and feelings, with a view to "mutual self-improvement."[48]
Bruford regards these letters as central to our understanding of the concept
of Bildung as it developed in the late eighteenth century: "The emotional currents revealed in the correspondence between these young people, a year before
the French Revolution, are a fascinating psychological study, and the climate
of feeling behind these letters is perhaps just as important as any intellectual
factors for a sympathetic understanding of the German passion for 'Bildung'
in that age."[49]

These letters, together with those written to men like Schiller, express in a
personal register what *The Limits of State Action* sets out as a basic principle
of politics and social organization. The emotional and intellectual candor revealed in the letters could not have existed without a firm belief in reason as
the foundation of personal Bildung, the same reason that provides "the basis
of every political system": "reason cannot desire for man any other condition
than that in which each individual not only enjoys the most absolute freedom
of developing himself by his own energies, in his perfect individuality, but in
which external nature itself is left unfashioned by any human agency, but only
receives the impress given to it by each individual by himself and of his own
free will, according to the measure of his wants and instincts, and restricted
only by the limits of his powers and his rights."[50] In Humboldt's view, nature
is not subdued or conquered by reason. Rather than being "fashioned"—or
exploited—by an abstract "human agency," nature bears merely the "impress"
of individuals who freely and moderately give to it only what is in their power
to give. Nature is part of the complex process of self-cultivation, indeed it is
its germinating moment, for "whatever man receives externally, is only like
the seed. It is his own active energy alone that can turn the most promising
seed into a full and precious blessing for himself."[51] Goethe's Wilhelm Meister
makes a similar point once he has discovered that he is a father and has been
inducted into the Society of the Tower:

> His apprenticeship was therefore completed in one sense, for along with
> the feeling of a father he had acquired the virtues of a solid citizen. His
> joy knew no bounds. "All moralizing is unnecessarily strict," he exclaimed.

"Nature turns us, in her own pleasant way, into what we should be. Strange indeed are those demands of middle-class society that confuse and mislead us, finally demanding more from us than Nature herself. I deplore all attempts at developing us which obliterate the most effective means of education by forcing us towards the endpoint instead of giving us a sense of satisfaction along the way."[52]

The individual is part of the natural world, but his education, his full "flowering" (Humboldt uses such botanical metaphors) is a fundamentally personal and self-sufficient process in which the natural world becomes part and parcel of the individual's "inner moral and intellectual being." Humboldt believed that nothing should intervene to disturb the process by which "human pursuits" created inner culture.[53]

The proper practice of Bildung, then, required absolute freedom, a requirement that is echoed in John Stuart Mill and other champions of liberty and democracy who followed him in the nineteenth century. "The true end of Man," Humboldt writes, in a passage that Mill himself uses in *On Liberty*, "or that which is prescribed by the eternal or immutable dictates of reason, and not suggested by vague and transient desires, is the highest and most harmonious development of his powers to a complete and consistent whole. Freedom is the first and indispensable condition which the possibility of such development presupposes."[54] Freedom, as Humboldt conceives it and develops it in *The Limits of State Action*, is specifically the freedom from "positive" forms of state interference in moral, spiritual, or cultural development. (Some forms of "negative" action, those having to do with security "against the attacks of foreign enemies and internal dissentions," are regarded as necessary.[55]) The law prescribes a limit to the cultivation of Bildung but, more important, it guarantees—or *should* guarantee—the absolute freedom for such cultivation. "Every citizen must be in a position to act without hindrance and just as he pleases, so long as he does not transgress the law; everyone must have the right to maintain, in reply to others, and even against all probability, so far [as] others can tell, 'However closely I approach the danger of transgressing the law, yet will I not succumb.'"[56] Freedom requires a certain proximity, which must be respected, to the danger of transgression, for it is in this outer limit that the individual comes into contact with the law that guarantees freedom.

For Humboldt, "the diverse and changing wishes of individual men are to be preferred to the uniform and unchangeable will of the State."[57] These diverse wishes are the wellspring of the "humanist ideal of the fully rounded, harmonious personality," and of an "aesthetics of personality."[58] Such an aesthetics is fostered by the two principal elements of human experience, inquiry and creativity: "Before inquiry can get to the root of things, or to the limits of reason, it presupposes, in addition to profundity, a rich diversity and an inner warmth of soul—the harmonious exertion of all the human faculties combined." This rich diversity and warmth includes, for Humboldt, the poet's realm of sensations—"the pleasures of sense and fancy"—as well as the philosopher's realm of perceptions. Indeed, the context in which these remarks are made—a discussion of Kant's treatment of morals and aesthetics—constitutes a critique of a tendency in philosophy to ignore the important element of sensation and what Schiller calls "play." Intellectual projects ("inquiry") require a predisposition to Bildung, but so too do the more mundane realms of life, for "the man whose sensibility is thus cultivated and developed, displays the full beauty of his character when he enters into practical life." For the "individuality of energy and self-development" is not only the basis of one's own originality and "individual vigor," it is absolutely necessary for anyone who wishes to have any influence on others. This necessity springs from Humboldt's belief that the ideal "co-existence of human beings" does not consist in social organizations in which the state determines the mode of individual life, either by oppressive or reformist measures, but in "a union in which each strives to develop himself from his own inmost nature, and for his own sake."[59] The impulse toward a form of aesthetic education is an important part of this sociality in which harmonious Bildung is derived from a union with others under conditions of freedom.

Humboldt's general aim, as he states it at the conclusion of *The Limits of State Action*, is to discover "the most favourable position which man can occupy as member of a political community."[60] Unlike Goethe, who regarded such a "favourable position" in terms of the individual's passive induction into a paternalistic social order, Humboldt imagined the ideal position to be one that allowed the individual actively to incorporate external influences in the formation of inner culture. Bildung "was an individual thing," writes Sweet, "limited by what each person had to start with 'in the recesses of his soul.'" But at the same time, "Self-cultivation and self-fulfillment ... involved a very active process. The individual, drawing on the best from the world around him and from history, should seek to 'form' his unique personality as an artist would seek to create a masterpiece."[61] Humboldt looks forward to Mill's quite similar attempt to accommodate the requirements of individualism to those of a rapidly developing industrial society. Where Mill differs is in his championing of a Coleridgean "clerical" class of artists and thinkers who would serve as cultural guides for a society whose primary function was to guarantee the freedom of such guides to do their work. "There are but few persons," Mill writes in *On Liberty*, "in comparison with the whole of mankind, whose experiments, if adopted by others, would be likely to be any improvement on established practice. But these few are the salt of the earth; without them, human life would become a stagnant pool." The role of the mass of people is to "preserve the soil" in which they grow. "Genius can only breathe freely in an *atmosphere* of freedom."[62] Humboldt tended to advocate a more democratic access to Bildung, at least in theory: "the most diverse individuality and the most original independence coexisted equally with the most diverse and profound associations of human beings with each other—a problem which nothing but the most absolute liberty can ever hope to solve."[63] As he found out for himself while laying the groundwork for the University of Berlin, "absolute freedom" was an unattainable ideal.

The events of the period leading up to the establishment of the University of Berlin in 1810 were hardly propitious for the founding of an entirely new educational system in which Bildung would become available to a broad segment of the population. However, Humboldt's background in the humanities, especially the study of ancient Greek culture and language, and his experience in the Prussian civil service prepared him well for the difficulties he faced in his determination to provide an institution for *Allgemeinbildung*, or general humanist education, an institution that would emphasize pure *Wissenschaft* (knowledge, scholarship) and personal Bildung and that would avoid the French style of specialized education.[64] By extending educational reforms beyond the university level to the *Gymnasium*, Humboldt believed it was possible to spread the culture of Bildung beyond the elite classes, making it a social and cultural entitlement. As he put it in a memorandum on the school plans for Königsberg and Prussian Lithuania: "Every person, even the most impoverished, would receive a complete humane *Bildung*."[65] Education as Humboldt conceived it was designed to give access to Bildung to the "entire mass of the nation,"[66] with no special treatment given to children of the nobility. Moreover, his concern for the individual meant that there should be no rigid curriculum. Thus "every type of mind would find its appropriate place, and no decision on a vocation would have to be taken until, in his general development, the individual was ready for it."[67] As for the university, it ultimately evolved into an institutional compromise between the needs of an increasingly bureaucratic society and the ideal of Bildung at its ideological center.

Throughout the nineteenth century, the general effect of this compromise was to "rationalize" the Bildung process and transform self-development into

the production of viable subjects fully socialized to function within increasingly differentiated and technologically complex social systems. Humboldt's
educational reforms were designed to some extent to close the gap between
the idealism of Bildung as it existed in the discourse (novelistic and otherwise) of the Weimar writers like Goethe and Schiller and the prevailing social
conditions in Prussia, which tended to move in the direction of greater state
control of social institutions and rationalization of bureaucratic functions
within them. The institutionalization of Bildung was part of this process, but
Humboldt sought to retain the high ideals he had formulated in his unpublished papers and letters (including *The Limits of State Action*). Ideally, Bildung
would result in what Jean-François Lyotard, in his reading of Humboldt, calls
the "fully legitimated subject of knowledge and society."[68] To a very considerable extent Humboldt succeeded in his plan to create an educational system
that was democratic and that focused on pure *Wissenschaft* and personal Bildung—and this despite the gap that opened up, in the decades following the
establishment of the University of Berlin, between Humboldt's educational
ideals and the actual structure and operation of the university.[69] Institutional
compromises reflected the changes going on in society at large. As Bruford
points out, Humboldt's idea of the university was a "splendid ideal for those
who had the ability and the means to follow it," but the simple fact was that
most people were "eager to learn how to develop the forces of nature and to
make their mark among their fellowmen."[70] We hear in this summation the
priorities of a society that will offer either vocationalism or well-nigh scholastic
specialism, leaving the Humboldtian ideal of Bildung to occupy an excluded
middle ground.

Humboldt's idealism set the stage for this ever-widening gap, an idealism
that reflects the Hegelian tendency, in this phase of modernity, to regard the
state as an abstraction whose "essence" subsumed, and thus defined the exis-
tential limits of, the individual. In "The State as Realization of Spirit," part 3
of *Introduction to "The Philosophy of History,"* Hegel posits the state as "the divine idea, as it exists on earth." Within such a state, the individual's "subjective
will" (that is, "passion") is dependent and thus limited: "This essential being
is itself the union of two wills: the subjective will and the rational will. This is
an ethical totality, the *state*."[71] The "positive freedom" that emerges from this
union defines the limits of Bildung once it is released from the fantasy of its
autonomy and confronted with real social conditions.[72] Humboldt foresaw
both the union and the "positive freedom" that could be made possible by virtue of it. He acknowledged that "the state as he conceived it was, above all, the

custodian of culture, of *Bildung*."[73] However, because he conceived of the state as something less than a "divine idea," his custodial vision of the state implies a laissez-faire attitude toward the individual that Hegel's conception does not permit. This is perhaps one of the reasons Mill and other English writers found him so attractive. If we assume an equivalency between the "positive freedom" of the individual and the institutional autonomy of the university, then it is possible to conclude that Humboldt's emphasis falls less on the dependent position of the university with respect to the state than on the state's recognition that the university is acting in the state's best interest. "In general . . . the state must not demand anything from the universities simply for its own needs, but should adhere to the profound conviction that if the universities achieve their highest purpose, they will also fulfill the purposes of the state."[74]

Humboldt's desire for an autonomous university, then, was the desire for *limited* autonomy within the larger totality of a state that he himself regarded as a necessary social institution, but one that must be organized to allow for the development of genuine personal freedoms. What he did not foresee—or, rather, what he chose not to foresee, since after 1810 he had little to do with education in the state-sponsored form that he inaugurated—was the instrumental role that education came to play in a state that required an ever-expanding and ever-diversifying workforce. I am, of course, referring to the modern nation-state as it developed during the monopoly or imperial stage of capitalism, a state whose institutions had become increasingly intertwined with private industries and, as a result, increasingly concerned with efficiency and productivity. The state came to require not the development of individuals whose faculties would be united in what Moretti calls the "happiness of synthesis" that comes about through the creation of "countless 'connections' with the existing order."[75] What it came to require was a complaisant but productive individual who could perform specific functions and could be replaced by another individual from the trainable masses that constituted modern industrial societies.

THE PRODUCTION OF THE SUBJECT

Nineteenth-century England provides a particularly fruitful context for an exploration of the institutional compromises that transformed the Goethean and Humboldtian ideals of aesthetico-spiritual Bildung into more socially pragmatic regimes of socialization and social mobility. This development was strongly determined by the potential for mobility within a highly stratified class structure, and the English Bildungsroman both reflected and legitimized this social determination. What concerns me here is the underlying discourse of Bildung and how it was transformed in an English context, one that includes developments in colonial Ireland. As I have shown, there are important differences between Goethe's and Humboldt's conceptions of Bildung. Both men desired the harmonious development of inner culture, but while Goethe advocated a mystical apprenticeship and induction into an elite, paternalistic society, Humboldt favored a more pragmatic strategy of humanistic education and participation in a free and democratic nation. This difference in thinking about Bildung is duplicated in the English context.[76] On the one hand we have Thomas Carlyle (at least in his early work) and Matthew Arnold, who follow the Goethean path and advocate a notion of Bildung strongly associated with the arts and with the idea that art, especially literature, could do the work of religion in a secular age. On the other hand we have John Stuart Mill, who follows the Humboldtian path and argues for a form of individualism firmly grounded in political realities but devoted nonetheless to the pursuit of self-cultivation by means of an aesthetic education.

Carlyle is an important, if idiosyncratic, figure in the early history of the English Bildungsroman. His translation of Goethe's *Wilhelm Meister* did much to popularize the Weimar notion of Bildung, while his *Sartor Resartus* expresses a peculiarly English form of it. According to G. B. Tennyson, Carlyle's *Sartor Resartus* establishes a unique English pattern: "That Carlyle's concept of affirmation, his so-called Calvinizing of Goethe's *Entsagen* [to renounce], is not the same thing as the Weimar circle's concept of *Bildung* is to be expected, and it is a measure of the way in which a somewhat aristocratic and characteristically metaphysical German notion was domesticated."[77] As so much of Carlyle's writing indicates, it is work, disciplined action governed by spiritual belief in the efficacy of the task at hand, that guarantees the "sincerity" of one's inner life. "All true Work is sacred," he states in *Past and Present*; "in all true Work, were it but true hand-labour, there is something of divineness."[78] Carlyle reworks the aesthetic and speculative aspects of Bildung in practical and at the same time religious terms: "he expresses them in the earnest quasi-Biblical language of evangelical piety ('Work thou in Well-doing,' for example). The effect, however, is not a denial of Bildung but a transmutation into a more British frame of reference."[79] This frame of reference is often defined in terms of the conjunction of work and morality (as Tennyson's parenthetical quotation so succinctly captures), a tendency that we see also in novels by Dickens, Charlotte Brontë, Elizabeth Gaskell, George Eliot, and so many others.

Arnold's importance in developing this Goethean strand of English Bildung lies not in his contributions to the Bildungsroman but in his development, in an English context, of an essentially Goethean ideal of culture. Arnold's interest in classical culture, especially as it was expressed in his poetry of the late 1840s and 1850s, placed him in a line of development at odds with the practical Christianity of writers like Charles Kingsley as well as with pragmatic thinkers like Mill. As David DeLaura points out, Arnold's work in this period was greeted with dismay by reviewers who found it too closely tied to the tradition of abstract German Romanticism. "Arnold was the poet of culture, not merely because he was classical and scholarly and (as we might say) elitist, but because he had almost single-handedly created in mid-Victorian England a new and challenging view of life—*his* culture and *his* self-culture were too Greek, too 'pagan,' too German and Goethean, too quietistic, to be endorsed readily in an England absorbed by prosperity, activism, and the splendors of the Crystal Palace."[80] While the negative reactions continued well into the 1880s, Arnold himself modified his early Goethean cultural ideal, though he never developed the kind of socially pragmatic notions of culture that we find in Mill or in the pedagogical work of John Henry Cardinal Newman. His critical work in the 1860s shows less evidence of a Goethean strain of pagan classicism or of elitist self-culture, and a text like *Culture and Anarchy*, in its radical, nondialectical polarization of the spheres of culture and practical life, deviates from the cultural ideal of works like *Wilhelm Meister*. We can account for this drift away from Goethe's ideal by recalling that Arnold's conception of culture is a specifically English and nineteenth-century one. DeLaura argues that it was Arnold's recognition of "the unblinkable *facts* of the unsolved nineteenth-century social problem" that was forcing him to "put aside, however reluctantly, his early dreams of a detached and elevated mode of consciousness and creativity—the Goethean paradigm of the self-culture of the artist."[81] I think this reluctance to distance himself from the "Goethean paradigm" is evident in Arnold's unwillingness to surrender the idea that culture is a privileged sphere presided over and protected by a coterie of intellectual elites. In "The Function of Criticism at the Present Time" (1864–65), Arnold decries "the mania for giving an immediate political and practical application" to the "fine ideas of the reason" and condemns English intellectuals for being too engrossed in politics, "catchwords and party habits," and other "practical" matters. His advocacy of the critic as a guardian of culture, and of criticism as a disinterested endeavor free of the contamination of politics, is problematic because it presupposes a cultural ideal that privileges personal perfection over social responsibility. Criticism's "best spiritual work ... is to keep man from a self-satisfaction which is retarding and vulgarizing, to lead him towards perfection, by making his mind dwell upon what is excellent in itself, and the absolute beauty and fitness of things."[82] The emphasis on "the absolute beauty and fitness of things" situates the critic within a project of aesthetic education that anticipates Oscar Wilde's modernist Bildungsroman and his belief in the self-development of the "critic as artist."[83] Though skeptical of the dogmatism of Arnold's aesthetic criteria, early modernists like Wilde and Joyce owe much to his vision of criticism as a serious cultural practice.[84]

More central to the nineteenth-century tradition of Bildung is Mill's theory of individualism, which develops the Humboldtian concept of Bildung and connects it more securely to English institutions and an English tradition of liberalism, to the whole historical process of "Victorian Britain's idiosyncratic modernization."[85] Mill's theory follows Humboldt's in defining self-cultivation in terms of personal freedom and social pragmatism and in emphasizing the aesthetic education that is so important to all the Weimar theorists. The socially pragmatic form of Bildung that we find in the work of Humboldt and Mill is much the same as that which subtends the mainstream English Bildungsroman, as I have described it in the introduction. In what follows I will set out the main aspects of this form of Bildung—individualism, social mobility, and education—and discuss the implications of it for the modernist Bildungsroman in England and Ireland.

Mill's reflections on individualism and the role of social power with respect to individual development are of crucial importance for understanding the broad framework of English liberalism and social reform within which Bildung developed new socially pragmatic criteria of viability that ultimately would displace almost entirely the aesthetico-spiritual criteria of harmonious inner culture and dialectical integration of self and society. Mill's *On Liberty*, as I have noted, is indebted to Humboldt's *Limits of State Action*, especially with respect to the concept of individualism, which is a reasonable English translation of the German concept of Bildung, and the importance of culture as a way of fostering self-development. In this, Mill follows Samuel Taylor Coleridge, who, according to Raymond Williams, was the first to use the term "cultivation" to refer to "a general condition, a 'state or habit' of mind." Williams cites a key passage in *On the Constitution of the Church and State* in which Coleridge insists that civilization be grounded in "cultivation, in the harmonious development of those qualities and faculties that characterize our humanity."[86] This notion of civilization presupposes, according to Mill, a condition of liberty in which the individual, who has "arrived at the maturity of his faculties," can "use and interpret experience in his own way": "A person whose desires and impulses are his own—are the expression of his own nature, as it has been developed and modified by his own culture—is said to have a character."[87] Mill emphasizes the importance of individuality in an explicitly Humboldtian vein, but he is also concerned with a more socially pragmatic style of Bildung in which the autonomy and integrity of the individual are preserved. Mill believes that the level of energy in a given society at a given stage of development is always balanced by a "social principle" that keeps excessive energy from overpowering and destroying the social system. This is the aspect of sociality that Humboldt neglected, perhaps because of an overly sanguine view of the individual's intentions with respect to freedom and the development of personal Bildung. Humboldt also had a tendency toward transcendentalist idealism: "the greater the diversity and individuality of man's development, and the more sublime his feelings become, the more easily his gaze turns from the limited, temporary things around him to the notion of an infinity and totality which includes all limits and all changes—whether he hopes to find a being corresponding to this conception or not." Paradoxically, it is just this gaze toward infinity that prepares people, under conditions of optimum freedom, for social interactions. "The greater a man's freedom," Humboldt continues, "the more self-reliant and well-disposed towards others he becomes."[88]

Writing a half century after Humboldt, Mill is able to assess the impact of self-development in ways that Humboldt could not have foreseen and in a context quite different from the princely states that made up the Germany of Humboldt's time. Mill equates the virtues and values of Bildung with the general social condition of liberty—"the spirit of liberty, or that of progress or improvement"—and sees as the greatest enemy to both the "despotism of custom." "Customs are made for customary circumstances, and customary characters"; and "though the customs be both good as customs, and suitable to [an individual], yet to conform to custom, merely *as* custom, does not educate or develop in him any of the qualities which are the distinctive endowment of a human being." Instead of custom, which calls only for the "apelike [faculty] of imitation," Mill advocates the exercise of choice, "discerning or . . . desiring what is best."[89] It is through such choices that one acquires the kind of education that is fundamental to being human, and I would argue that the education to which Mill refers is a distinctly aesthetic one: "Among the works of man, which human life is rightly employed in perfecting and beautifying, the first in importance is surely man himself." Like Humboldt, Mill insists on self-sufficiency as the primary motive force of aesthetic education, one of "the inward forces which make [the individual] a living being."[90] Against "Christian self-denial" he prefers "Pagan self-assertion," a Greek "ideal of self-development" that dovetails with the Humboldtian variety.[91] Mill also insists that individuals' freedom to educate and develop themselves be in no way impeded by social responsibilities. Human life, he argues, is made richer and more diversified when individuals develop their faculties to the utmost. "In proportion to the development of his individuality, each person becomes more valuable to himself, and is therefore capable of being more valuable to others." In short, the more life in the individual the more life in the social totality. A corollary of this principle is that no one should be allowed to expend excessive energy in such a way as to injure another or prevent another from expressing his or her individuality. "To be held to rigid rules of justice for the sake of others developes [*sic*] the feelings and capacities which have the good of others for the object."[92] Mill here refashions, within the framework of English liberal humanism, the foundational "laws" of Humboldt's theory of Bildung: "The first law of morality is: cultivate thyself; and the second is: influence others by what thou art."[93]

Like many English novelists in the nineteenth century, Mill offers a model of individualism that differs from the classical model of Bildung primarily in its pragmatic, ameliorist approach to the vexed relationship between the individual and the state. His vision stresses a compromise between the requirements of the state and the desire of the individual to pursue self-development, a compromise that modifies, under specific English conditions, what Humboldt advocates in *The Limits of State Action*. Mill's vision, more than Arnold's, reflects the mainstream liberalism of the mid-nineteenth century, with its emphasis on social reform and indirect governance, and is certainly more compatible with the thematics of the Bildungsroman of the period. And it is this aspect of English liberalism that constitutes a significant departure from Humboldt's political sociology, for social reform, which for Humboldt would have constituted undesirable positive interference in the moral or cultural well-being of the individual, had become integrated into the way English social and cultural institutions managed power and resources. As Lauren Goodlad points out, the "specific rationalities" of these institutions were able to overcome whatever pernicious effects followed from the fact of outside "positive" influence, and this is evidenced by its pervasiveness in Victorian culture and society: "the positive impulse to develop individuals and encourage social betterment by collective means of some kind permeated a variety of reformist discourses, including Victorian literature."[94] The English Bildungsroman is a good example of the mode of socialization typical of nineteenth-century liberal society, for it had, as Moretti puts it, "absorbed and propagated one of the most basic expectations of liberal-democratic civilization: the desire that the realm of the law be certain, universalistic, and provided with mechanisms for correction and control."[95] The nineteenth-century English Bildungsroman narrates these "basic expectations." However, over time the processes that Max Weber so well describes—bureaucratization, rationalization, instrumentalization—transformed the desire to cultivate oneself, to nurture one's inner culture, into the desire for social success and for a social pedagogy that teaches young men and women the "the way of the world."

Broadly speaking, in the nineteenth century the social framework for successful subject formation in England was fairly stable, especially for the middle classes. Moretti's characterization of England as "a solid world, sure of itself and at ease in a continuity that fuses together 'tradition' and 'progress,'"[96] is echoed by many social historians. This "solid world" emerged as a result of patterns of social mobility that reinforced the dynamics of class formation that had begun early in the century; the educational system directly affected (and was in turn affected by) this new mobility and, more globally, transformed the very nature of what it meant to be a "social subject." As a result of these linked trends, the identitarian structures of Bildung, traditionally dedicated to the formation of a unified and harmonious inner culture, were now dedicated to the formation of a subject regarded increasingly in terms of viability and productivity in the workplace and in consumer markets.

Social mobility in the modern sense began to take shape as industrial economies moved through their adjustment phase (roughly 1815–65) and then settled into a phase of consolidation that has been characterized as monopolistic or imperialistic capitalism. Of special importance for this study are two interlinked processes—social mobility and education—that accelerated at various points during these phases. Social mobility was a slippery phenomenon, tending to create a more "open" society while simultaneously restricting mobility to certain movements within classes and, less frequently, between the working and lower-middle classes. Andrew Miles argues that social mobility in nineteenth-century England, and elsewhere throughout Europe, was by and large "forced" by the "changing shape of the social division of labor." These developments, stretching from the 1830s to the First World War, resulted in a society in which mobility was "heavily structured" and in which social classes were "profoundly unequal."[97]

Education in this period also had a stratified, unequal nature. It was a crucial mechanism of social advancement (this is especially true of literacy) but it also had the effect of creating new social conditions in which existing class distinctions were reinforced by new educational opportunities. These new opportunities, which created new valences of inequality, did in fact lead to upward mobility among the working and lower-middle classes, but there were limits as to how far up one could go and the nature of the change in social status. The rise of the clerk in the nineteenth century testifies to the creation of new occupational categories that required literacy but that did not come with a commensurate rise in social prestige.

For women, the division of labor remained unequal throughout most of the century, providing few opportunities for social mobility. The "marriage market" was often seen as the most reliable option. Although Miles offers a qualification—"This is not to argue that women were merely passive recipients of male generated social identities, or that their impact on mobility and class formation was confined to their role as daughters and wives"[98]—marriage was unquestionably a primary source of social status and prestige for women throughout most of the nineteenth century. By the 1890s, however, other factors had begun to come into play, especially the introduction of new occupational categories in new commercial and government institutions, which meant an increase in bureaucratic and "service sector" positions, and the elimination of others, in part as a result of a general migration from the countryside to towns and cities. An influx of women in the labor markets to fill these new positions restructured the routes of mobility within the various classes and labor sectors; "in the developing bureaucracies of the early twentieth century the closing down of career routes involving class mobility coincided with the construction of other ladders within classes based around employment status and economic improvement."[99]

The creation of new routes for social mobility necessitated a change in the function and nature of education, insofar as new job opportunities required new modes of training or formal credentials. "Crucially," Miles writes, "informal mechanisms of training and recruitment were gradually being challenged by more structured, meritocratic, and bureaucratically mediated routes into the labour market."[100] In this new environment, education extended beyond the limits of formal instruction in a schoolroom to encompass the various modes of modern apprenticeship, certification, and on-the-job training that accompanied many occupations, especially those involving skilled office work and general literacy.

State-sponsored education in this period took on new meaning and value once it became apparent to industrialists and legislators that the labor market required not only skilled workers but also docile social subjects.[101] As an important element of state ideology, school systems (including primary and secondary schools, universities and colleges) took on a dual responsibility: to consolidate class formations and to rationalize the processes of socialization. This aspect of English modernization highlights the distance traveled from the heyday of classical Weimar, where Bildung promised both self-sufficiency and the potential for a social union "in which each strives to develop himself from his own inmost nature, and for his own sake."[102] What we see in the nineteenth century is the sundering of this union, the emergence of a contradiction between the community and the individual which, as Marx has noted, takes on the form of the modern state.[103]

Throughout nineteenth-century Europe the practices of Bildung that inspired thinkers like Humboldt and Goethe became rationalized and normalized; educational institutions, complete with a new pedagogy of standardization, competence, and efficiency, became producers of viable citizens of the state, a situation that created a class-driven diversification of educational opportunities. England, like much of Europe, developed steeply stratified educational systems that tended to exacerbate existing class divisions. In the last third of the nineteenth century, education in England was undergoing profound changes at all levels, a development put into play, in part, by the Taunton Commission of 1867, which gave official sanction and impetus to the organization of primary and secondary education along class lines. The Education Act of 1870 refined this trend toward rationalization and class division and also drove home the point that national supremacy depended upon systematic national education.[104]

It is in this cultural environment that Mill, Arnold, and Newman found themselves torn between humanism and pragmatism, between two modes of pedagogy and self-cultivation: one an idealist and progressive program associated with Humboldt, the other a far more pragmatic, technical, and specialized program designed to meet the need for highly trained, literate workers in state and corporate bureaucracies. Despite the general tendency toward pragmatism in schools, intellectual discourse remained committed to the goals of humanistic education. This was true especially in the ancient universities of Oxford and Cambridge, which continued to offer a curriculum grounded in the humanist ideal of Bildung to a middle- and upper-class clientele. Newman, for example, argued that the university should be charged not with the propagation of useful knowledge but with the "enlargement or expansion of mind" and with instilling in students "a wise and comprehensive view of things."[105] Though there were conflicts in Newman's work between his belief in the necessity of religious training and his stated desire for a liberal education, his desire that a liberal education be made generally available, even to the Catholic subjects of Ireland, pushed his ideas beyond the arena of sectarian factionalism and into the realm of general public debate over education that began in earnest in the 1860s.[106] The more secular Arnold linked the English concern for liberal education directly to the Humboldtian project of *Allgemeinbildung*: "The truth is that when a nation has got the belief in culture which the Prussian nation has got, and when its schools are worthy of this belief, it will not suffer them to be sacrificed to any other interest; and however greatly political considerations may be paramount in other departments of administration, in this they are not."[107] As in the Prussian reforms, "other interests" did come into play, even in the ancient universities, and the result was that liberal education tended to promote a socially pragmatic form of Bildung that was more suitable to the civil service, the military, and business than to the "complete humane Bildung" that Humboldt had in mind. The orientation toward pragmatism was even more dramatic in the new provincial universities, vocational schools, and extension programs beginning to emerge in the 1870s, which offered more practical training and nonclassical humanities curricula to working- and lower-class students and women. These colleges sacrificed the ideal of Bildung in order to satisfy the vocational goals of their students and future employers. However, a combination of factors—principally cost and the reinforcement of class divisions in the various levels of primary and secondary education—led to a situation in which decreasing numbers of the working and lower classes had access to a university education, and this despite the many provincial universities and university extension programs in major cities. According to some critics, this situation resulted from the ambivalence of liberal reformers, who wanted to open up the universities to disenfranchised men and women but were at the same time afraid that these same men and women would be lured away from "more appropriate occupations."[108] As Patricia Ingham sums up the situation in the 1890s, the liberals' response was "to deny any attempt to open the jealously guarded professions to 'overcrowding' and to claim that they offered only self-cultivation in the form of 'true knowledge and intellectual progress.'"[109] This claim would be less troubling if the institutions in question were genuinely engaged in the cultivation of classical Bildung; however, since they typically defined Bildung more and more in terms of vocational and professional training, it is difficult to find any justification for not opening up the professions to people who were seeking professional training. Indeed, the ambivalence of liberal reformers concerning education reflects their uneasiness about a changing social landscape, one in which even the working and lower classes would require basic literacy and some level of professional training.

Ernest Gellner believes that the process of rationalizing education in a "high (literate, training-sustained) culture" is an inevitable one in the modern industrial nation-state. "The ideal of universal literacy and the right to education is a well-known part of the pantheon of modern values," he writes, noting that education is so important that it is rarely ignored. "What is so very curious, and highly significant, about the principle of universal and centrally guaranteed education, is that it is an ideal more honoured in the observance than in the breach. In this it is virtually unique among modern ideals."[110] State-sponsored educational systems guarantee the "social achievement" of constant communication among people. They are "indispensable," though the individuals who teach in them are more or less replaceable by others in the population. For the individual who goes through the system, an education is a distillation of specialized training. It "is by far his most precious investment, and in effect confers his identity upon him."[111] Only "an educational machine" is "capable of providing the wide range of training required for the generic cultural base." This machine alone guarantees the "quality control" in the "most important of industries, the manufacture of viable and usable human beings."[112] In this analysis, the "instrumentalization" of Bildung amounts to the emergence of an entirely new sense of what it means to "create" a self. The Lockean and Humboldtian notions of the self become obsolete in the face of a rationalized educational system and a bureaucratized market economy. Self-cultivation becomes subject formation, inner culture becomes socialization, and the paths toward Bildung become the "mediated routes" of social mobility.

It is my contention, which I develop more fully in chapter 3, that these processes took on an entirely different complexion and produced very different effects in "semi-colonial" Ireland, where modernization had been at best an uneven process, in large part because colonial rule tended to retard development in some sectors of society and to encourage it in others. An impoverished "metrocolony" of the British Empire, dominated spiritually by the Catholic Church and politically by the British and, to some degree, the Protestant Ascendancy, Catholic Ireland entered the twentieth century with few bourgeois liberal political institutions and no secular, humanist educational tradition; its legacy was largely one of political resistance to oppressive authority and painful self-questioning about the methods and aims of this resistance. The death of Charles Stewart Parnell, and the consequent sense among many Irish nationalists of betrayal at the hands of the Church, culminated a long century of frustration and defeat.[113] Terry Eagleton, in *Heathcliff and the Great Hunger*, describes colonial Ireland as caught "on the hop" between uneven colonial modernization and pockets of "archaic" tradition. In such colonial situations, identity formation and the "viability" of the educated colonial subject are themselves unstable processes in which sectarian and nationalist tensions complicate the formation of class groupings, which thus develop along paths quite different from those in England. For example, two distinct middle classes had emerged by the early twentieth century: the Anglo-Irish and the Catholic, the former a client ruling class of the British Empire, the latter an indigenous formation which gained strength and prestige with the passage, in the late-nineteenth and early twentieth centuries, of the Land Acts.[114] Those people who could not afford to buy land were driven into the cities, where some were able to advance into the middle classes, either in the service sector or in industry; others, the "strong farmers," bought up parcels of land and established a rural petite bourgeoisie. This process accelerated as the century drew to a close. There was, of course, a similar acceleration in England of the bureaucratization of the labor market and an increase, after Forster's Education Act in 1870, of opportunities in the civil service and service sectors for men and, after the turn of the century, for women. But unlike Britain, which witnessed the rise of a powerful industrial middle class alongside a "traditionalist landowning order" that was "the oldest *capitalist* formation in Europe," Ireland was at home to "a peculiarly archaic, unreconstructed style of landlordism," which was, as Eagleton puts it, "every bit as much as its British counterpart, a capitalist formation. . . . But it was a woefully inert brand of rural capitalism, an old-fashioned form of modernity which lacked the challenge of an industrial middle class to spur it into life" — except, that is, in northeast Ulster.[115] Eagleton refers to the Anglo-Irish here, but the Catholic middle class was making its own strides toward modernizing Ireland, particularly in agriculture and, to a lesser degree, in urban industries. And while there were still archaic elements combating Ireland's modernizing projects, they were not strong enough to sustain a traditional Gaelic society. Nor were they truly archaic, in the sense that they were unaffected by modern English or European values. Indeed, one reading of the Celtic Revival would emphasize the way that archaic or traditional elements were cordoned off and sanitized, transformed into the artifacts of a bygone culture. Revivalists like W. B. Yeats and J. M. Synge can well be accused of a form of cultural preservation that relied on modern aesthetic and ethnographic techniques.[116] In any case, Eagleton's claim that an emergent Catholic middle class effectively buried this traditional Gaelic society is confirmed by many revisionist historians who argue that Ireland was no exception to the processes of modernity. Kerby Miller, referring to the persistence of certain myths about Ireland's traditional character, notes that "what are now scored as the cultural residues of 'traditional' Ireland (family, faith, and fatherland) were elaborated in relatively recent times, both to repair the damage caused by nineteenth-century shocks and to ensure the hegemony of the Catholic-Nationalist (or in the North, Protestant-Unionist) middle classes that emerged triumphant from the wreckage of the old order."[117]

Another important dynamic that comes into play in Ireland's uneven modernity is the influence of the Roman Catholic Church, which had a traditionalizing effect on social life, providing continuity and support during times of social instability. Though by and large the Catholic Church in Ireland supported nationalism, its support was always contingent upon nationalist groups abiding by Church orthodoxies, especially in respect to morality and education. Joyce's *Portrait of the Artist as a Young Man* and Kate O'Brien's *The Land of Spices* offer illuminating representations of these often interlocking concerns, the former in its depiction of the effect of Parnell's fall and the latter in its treatment of the role nationalism played in religious schools. It is in this intersection of nationalism, religion, and education that Ireland differs most dramatically from England. Donald Akenson points out that "the national system of education in Ireland ... provide[s] a shattering exception to the generalization that advanced educational systems can develop only in economically and socially advanced societies."[118] By 1831, when Lord Stanley formalized a system of state-run national schools that had been developing during the previous decade, Ireland boasted a school system far superior to that in England. Another way of putting this, of course, is to say that the Irish national schools proved to be an important laboratory for developing the kinds of institutional relations of power required for the production of "viable" subjects. It is important to note, especially in view of the educational experiences we see in Joyce, that the hegemony of *national* education was challenged on the one hand by national*ist* movements of political education sponsored by the Gaelic League and other institutions of cultural revivalism, which had a long history extending back to the era of the penal laws and the "hedge-schools," and on the other hand by denominational schools that were subject to the pressures of nationalist groups. The hedge schools were particularly effective in providing Catholic children in the rural areas with a modicum of education in the period before Catholic emancipation (1829). In addition to teaching the rudiments of a humanist curriculum, including English and classical languages, the hedge schools promoted Gaelic language instruction and Irish history. Of course, this kind of curriculum often resulted in a hodgepodge of subjects inconsistently taught, as Brian Friel illustrates in his play *Translations*.[119] However, despite curricular inconsistencies, the hedge schools were crucial to the formation of early resistance to British regimes of socialization. In the denominational schools, there were two strong alternative paths for resistance: inward toward religious vocation and outward toward nationalist commitment. The latter is especially important in the period beginning with the 1890s, when cultural nationalism began to advocate radical pedagogies within highly politicized forums of popular education. It is to explain the paradox of the educated colonial subject that Irish Bildungsromane pay so much attention to scenes of instruction—and I mean formal classroom experiences in both national and sectarian schools as well as alternative forms of popular education sponsored by municipalities, political parties, cultural societies, and "native intellectuals" like Yeats, Douglas Hyde, and other revivalists.

The Irish colonial experience, especially the formation of the colonial subject in the Irish Bildungsroman, thus shares with the English experience a confrontation with social pragmatism and the near extinction of classical Bildung. Gellner's view that education was consolidated within the institutional structure of the state is a fair enough generality for the Irish context, provided one bears in mind the colonial context of the Irish state and its subordinate relation to history and the international global economy. I would also modify slightly Gellner's approach by turning to Foucault, whose theory of the subject in relations of power makes room for an *agonism*, "a relationship which is at the same time reciprocal incitation and struggle; less of a face-to-face confrontation which paralyzes both sides than a permanent provocation." This agonism is "a permanent political task inherent in all social existence." In an educational institution, these power relations are part of a complex "block of capacity-communication-power," in which relations of power overlap and interact with systems of communication and "finalized activities" in complex, multivalent, sometimes unpredictable ways.[120] Power relations acquire a singularity in educational institutions, in part because of their relative autonomy, a feature of such institutions on which I have already commented in my discussion of Humboldt. An educational institution is defined by very specific relationships of space and subjects; of special interest are "the meticulous regulations which govern its internal life," which Foucault describes in terms of apprenticeship and the subject of knowledge: "The activity which ensures apprenticeship and the acquisition of aptitudes or types of behavior is developed [in educational institutions] by means of a whole ensemble of regulated communications (lessons, questions and answers, orders, exhortations, coded signs of obedience, differentiation marks of the 'value' of each person and the of levels of knowledge) and by the means of a whole series of power processes (enclosure, surveillance, reward and punishment, the pyramidal hierarchy)."[121] Foucault claims that social "discipline" is not a matter of absolute obedience or "assembling in barracks" but rather a case of society seeking a "better invigilated process of adjustment . . . —more and more rational, more economic—between productive activities, resources of communication, and the play of power relations."[122] This is certainly in line with Gellner's emphasis on specialized training and "constant communication." Foucault, however, draws our attention in a way that Gellner does not to a fundamental aspect of all relations of power, especially those involving the institutional production of the subject: precisely the freedom that Humboldt claimed was a crucial presupposition for Bildung. "Power is exercised only over free subjects, and only insofar as they are free. By this we mean individual or collective subjects who are faced with a field of possibilities in which several ways of behaving, several reactions and diverse comportments may be realized."[123] The converse of this claim is that without freedom, and the "insubordination" that it engenders, there would be no relations of power.

Humboldt's formulations haunt the discourse of modernity. Like him, Gellner, Giddens, and Foucault all stress the complex mechanisms by which the subject is "produced" by institutions. Humboldt was well aware, as we have seen, that Bildung could never be entirely free of some dimension of institutionalization; what distinguished the form of Bildung he advocated from that which followed later in the nineteenth century was a belief in the possibility that the state would put no roadblocks in the path of self-cultivation and, indeed, that it would nurture and protect it by funding state university systems. Bildung, for Humboldt, amounted to a semiautonomous form of reflexive self-formation under the control of an individual who, ideally, enjoys a maximum of social freedom in which to manage the cultural capital necessary for the Bildung process. It should come as no surprise, then, that the modernist critique of socially pragmatic Bildung should entail the recapture of an essentially Humboldtian form of aesthetico-spiritual Bildung. The "reflexive project" of the self, as Giddens puts it,[124] conforms to the dialectical harmonies of classical Bildung, but only as a starting point for an immanent critique of Bildung itself. I turn throughout this study to Adorno's "negative dialectics" to describe this form of critique as I see it unfolding in modernist Bildungsromane. Negative dialectics is based on a refusal to become caught up in a traditional dialectical structure of relationships, an identitarian structure in which what is negated is sacrificed in order to shore up the essence or being of what is being positively constructed. The modernist Bildungsroman, in its critique of such dialectical relations, illustrates the ambivalence of modernity at large. As Giddens remarks, "In respect both of social and natural scientific knowledge, the reflexivity of modernity turns out to confound the expectations of Enlightenment thought—although it is the very product of that thought."[125] This betrayal is precisely what we see in the destiny of Bildung in late modernity, for the utopian self-assurance of classical Weimar is in short order undermined by the social mechanisms that come into play in the nineteenth and twentieth centuries, specifically as a result of Humboldt's far-reaching but ultimately impractical plan to bring Bildung to the "entire mass of the nation."[126]

THE DIALECTICS OF MODERNISM

At stake in late modernity, the era of modernism and of the modernist Bildungsroman, are the subjects of Bildung, who are transformed, under new social conditions and forces, into the viable subjects of variously differentiated modes of socialization. These new social conditions exploit a tension that has subtended Enlightenment thinking from the start, a tension between self-assurance, what Giddens calls the "certainty of knowledge," and the doubt that motivates the processes of self-reflexivity, even in the "core domains of natural science."[127] In other words, even as the Enlightenment sought certainty in knowledge, it was creating the very conditions in which that knowledge would fail the test of certainty. As Giddens puts it, "the Enlightenment project of replacing arbitrary tradition and speculative claims to knowledge with the certainty of reason proved to be essentially flawed. The reflexivity of modernity operates, not in a situation of greater and greater certainty, but in one of methodological doubt."[128] In some respects, Giddens reduplicates in a sociological framework the "dialectic of Enlightenment"—a continuous process of demythologization that extends from the dawning of the Enlightenment to a thoroughly disenchanted modern age—put forward by Max Horkheimer and Theodor Adorno. "Just as the myths already realize enlightenment, so enlightenment with every step becomes more deeply engulfed in mythology. It receives all its matter from the myths, in order to destroy them; and even as a judge it comes under the mythic curse."[129] Fredric Jameson's more recent meditation on modernity posits a similar relationship between temporal rupture and periodization, a "dialectic of the transformation of the break into a period in its own right."[130] The same dialectic can be found in "aesthetic modernism," especially in its drive for innovation, which begins as early as the Romantic era. What is the destiny of Bildung in the twentieth century, when the "backward glance" or sense of the past inscribed in its narrative dynamics is so pervasive as to produce both an obsession with past epochs and the fetishization of innovation?[131] "Each subsequent generation, beginning, if you like, with the Romantics," Jameson writes, "feels the unsatisfactory inherited linguistic schema of subjectivity to be an artificial convention, which it is challenged to replace with some newer representational substitute. What looked like the progressive uncovering of new realms of subjectivity . . . is now seen to be a perpetual process of unnaming and refiguration which has no foreseeable stopping point (until, with the end of the modern itself, it reaches exhaustion)."[132] Another way of putting this, following Jürgen Habermas, is to speak of modernity as an incomplete or unfinished project.[133]

It is my contention that the modernist Bildungsroman, in its representation of an unbridgeable chasm, highlights this specific aspect of late modernity: that the project of the self that began in the late eighteenth century, which should, theoretically, extend itself into the future forever, exhausts itself in the failure of cultural representations to offer satisfying narratives of self-development. The return to Bildung, specifically to the aesthetico-spiritual variety developed by the Weimar theorists, is one of the chief motivating forces in the modernist Bildungsroman—indeed, a strong force in modernism at large—which thereby intensifies the critique of prevailing modes of socialization and social mobility. The recapture of classical Bildung and a new emphasis on self-formation paradoxically depends on the techniques and technologies of "depersonalization." By adducing the progressive potential of depersonalizing effects, Jameson corrects the tendency in Giddens to regard self-reflexivity as the production of *personality*. For Jameson, as for T. S. Eliot, the depersonalization of the subject is not the same as "alienation," nor does it connote loss and incapacity. It is not the "bad, perverted depersonalization" of which Adorno speaks, the "bourgeois devaluation of the individual whom one glorified in the same breath."[134] Instead, it signals a "taboo on the representation of subjectivity," which leads to a certain freedom from bourgeois notions of the "centred subject."[135] In the domain of the "centred subject," marginalization ("bad" depersonalization) guarantees the positivity and self-centered identity of the subject. Because this taboo against centeredness is most vibrantly displayed and challenged in the realm of art, we should not be surprised to find that by the end of the century it is primarily the artist-hero who seeks to unseat the bourgeois subject and who aspires to do so paradoxically by turning to some form or another of classical or, to emphasize the repetition, *neo*classical Bildung.

The modernist Bildungsroman encourages the emergence of new conceptions of self-formation concerned with evading and resisting socialization, with disharmonious social spheres, or with hybrid, ambivalent, sometimes traumatic processes of identity formation. By challenging the pedagogical assumptions of the genre—that is, by challenging the grounds on which young men and women become "viable subjects"—modernists appear to challenge the pragmatic and instrumental values the nineteenth-century Bildungsroman more or less overtly legitimizes and celebrates. For Paul Sheehan, the challenge takes the form of a deadlock: How can a narrative genre like the novel abandon humanism when narrative is so strongly linked to human motives and human desire? How can the modernist novel, with its experimental deviations from the humanist ethos, remain as a force within humanism? One answer appears to lie in the structure of the Bildungsroman, which sought at the very beginning "to demonstrate the shape of [humanistic] subjectivity." Sheehan follows Martin Swales and other critics of the Bildungsroman in finding the genre's teleology "illusory, ironic."[136] At the risk of minimizing his accomplishment (he is, after all, one of the few critics to broach the problem of a modernist Bildungsroman), I would like to suggest that Sheehan does not go far enough. Instead of describing a specifically modernist Bildungsroman, his argument invokes the classical form as a point of contrast against which modernist writers deviate in their "posthumanist" or "antihumanist" projects. In my view, the modernist Bildungsroman challenges the humanist project not, as Sheehan suggests, by rejecting or redefining Bildung but precisely by reestablishing a classical form of it as the motive force of narrative. If the modernist Bildungsroman harbors within it a conceptual throwback in its embrace of classical Bildung, it is of the sort that Adorno describes in his theory of negative dialectics when he says, "Dialectics is not only an advancing process but a retrograde one at the same time."[137] In an attempt to avoid what he perceives to be the totalizing tendencies in Hegelian dialectics, Adorno insists on the critical power of contradiction and nonidentity within dialectics. An unresolved contradiction ("nonidentity under the aspect of identity") that has "an inescapably and fatefully legal character," which is ever-present in Hegel, is of a different order than identity *as* contradiction, which is in fact what Adorno seeks in *Negative Dialectics*: the "turn toward nonidentity [that] is the hinge of negative dialectics," the "[d]isenchantment of the concept."[138] His theory of negative dialectics, though a theory of philosophy, nevertheless affords a useful tool for understanding a literary genre founded on a dialectical view of the subject and the subject's relation to the social world. In all of these respects, Adorno is an exemplary philosopher for modernism. As with so many modernist artists, his commitment to modernity is a turning away from it that is also a returning to it. Adorno's work captures and explains the paradoxical and critical nature of modernism—its wariness with respect to dialectics and its desire to refashion dialectical thinking, to recover the progressive aspects (especially concerning the subject and subjectivity) of modernity's "unfinished" project. Indeed, modernism too is an unfinished project, and the modernist Bildungsroman points this up in its openness to the very modernity from which it struggles to escape.[139] In this, the modernist Bildungsroman reflects and focuses sharply the conflicted relation between modernist artists and modernity.

Looked at in this light, the modernist return to Bildung is part of a larger critique of humanist reason and the totalizing tendencies of classical dialectics in which the human subject (and human subjectivity) is subordinated to rationalized social systems. Gellner's state-sponsored educational systems would be a case in point: the subject is formed only in the thoroughgoing process of subject formation, one that optimizes the reduplication of a "model" subject. A certain failure, anything that might give any indication of a problem with the system or with narrative, paradoxically serves as a reliable index of the system's otherwise persistent and reliable success. In modernism, we see the destabilization of this process, very much along the lines of Adorno's negative dialectics, in which "identity is the universal coercive mechanism which we, too, finally need to free ourselves from universal coercion, just as freedom can come to be real only through coercive civilization, not by way of any 'Back to nature.'"[140] We can understand Jameson's "depersonalization" as a form of negative dialectics operating within a literary aesthetics, a process in which failure is itself transvalued, given a new meaning and importance, just as Adorno's theory gives new meaning and importance to nonidentity. The motive force behind this productive failure is a "vocation for aesthetic change and new and more radical artistic practices [which] finds itself powerfully reinforced and intensified by the dawning conviction that radical change is simultaneously at large in the social world outside."[141] I believe Jameson is right to see in the dialectic of innovation and precedence the ideology of aesthetic modernism. Such a dialectic eschews the synthetic ambitions of classical modes and acquires a "negative" vocation; it substitutes a "constellation" of textual effects for the totalizing and hierarchizing structure of the classical Bildungsroman. For Adorno, as for Walter Benjamin, "constellations" are complex conceptual possibilities that elude the grip of conceptualization, and can be understood only as a mode of thought. "As a constellation, theoretical thought circles the concept it would like to unseal, hoping that it may fly open like the lock of a well-guarded safe-deposit box: in response, not to a single key or single number, but to a combination of numbers."[142] Such thought is itself a critique of idealist systems that refuse to recognize the self-referentiality of the concept, its citationality, for "Concepts alone can achieve what the concept prevents. . . . The determinable flaw in every concept makes it necessary to cite others; this is the font of the only constellations which inherited some of the hope of the name. The language of philosophy approaches that name by denying it. . . . To be known, the inwardness to which cognition clings in expression always needs its own outwardness as well."[143]

The "vocation for aesthetic change" that is for Jameson the prime motive force in modernism models Adorno's negative dialectics insofar as it "attempts by means of logical consistency to substitute for the unity principle, and for the paramountcy of the supraordinated concept, the idea of what would be outside the sway of such unity. To use the strength of the subject to break through the fallacy of constitutive subjectivity."[144] I want to emphasize that the "vocation for aesthetic change" manifests itself as a "negative" desire for self-formation that embraces disunity and disharmony; it is a mode of aesthetic consciousness that takes subjectivity as its object but not in order to *objectify* it. The aim of the modernist Bildungsroman is to put into play a Bildung process that harkens back to the classical mode, in which the goal is inner culture, but that also inevitably confronts the impossibility of either a unified, harmonious consciousness or a unified, harmonious relationship with the social world. This impossibility results, or *can result*, in a productive nonidentity that is not simply the negation of identity in which the object becomes congruent with the subject. "The less identity can be assumed between subject and object," writes Adorno, "the more contradictory are the demands made upon the cognitive subject, upon its unfettered strength and candid self-reflection."[145] The *Bildungshelden* of modernist Bildungsromane are aware of the dialectic of self and society but are equally aware of its antagonistic, interminable nature; they are aware of the way the self never finds its identity within society—not, at least, without a rem(a)inder that undermines the totalizing sovereignty of the bourgeois subject. I would argue that this awareness is one way of being situated "outside the sway" of the dialectical unities of both classical Bildung and the socially pragmatic variants that succeed it in so much cultural and political discourse.

In short, a new kind of subject is born in this immanent critique of Bildung. This new subject rediscovers the aesthetic dimension of self-cultivation and becomes conscious of the artifice of the self, which now, in this climate of revolt, constitutes the only available freedom from the so-called freedoms of bourgeois subjectivity. Nietzsche's concept of "style"—the "great and rare art" of "giv[ing] style' to one's character"—is one articulation of this freedom, as is Humboldt's theory of Bildung, in which an "aesthetics of personality" leads to the "full beauty" of character. Another is Mill's theory of individualism, in which "human life is rightly employed in perfecting and beautifying . . . man himself." In all of these conceptions of self-cultivation, the Lockean ideal of a continuous, self-identical subject—"personal identity" understood as "the sameness of a rational being"—is qualified by a principle of reflexivity which threatens continuity and self-identity. In the early twentieth century, this threat becomes palpable as aesthetic education pushes beyond the limits of giving style or beauty to character and seeks to abolish character altogether—or to assert character as pure style. This is what I think Eliot theorizes in "Tradition and Individual Talent": "The progress of an artist is a continual self-sacrifice, a continual extinction of personality. . . . But, of course, only those who have personality and emotions know what it means to want to escape from these things."[146] This revolt against the "bourgeois self" is discernible in the innovative theories of consciousness and the ego put forward by Freud. The idea that the subject or ego is a problematic, dehiscent entity, operating as much through unconscious as through conscious means, had a profound effect on how the self was portrayed in literature and how self-development was reconceived. Equally profound was the knowledge that early childhood experiences played a decisive role in sexual and social identities; this knowledge could not help but complicate the symbolic value of youth in the modernist Bildungsroman, as is evident in D. H. Lawrence's resistance to the "old stable ego of the character."[147]

In light of these revolts against personality, it should be clear that the return to Bildung in the modernist Bildungsroman is not an "innocent" return to a Humboldtian concept of self-development—a harmonious dialectical relationship in which the subject's interests coincide with the state's—nor to the kind of pragmatic socialization narrated in the nineteenth-century Bildungsroman. This return is not an absolute but a differential repetition in which the power relations between subject and society are represented as contingent and non-universal. We should speak, then, of what Foucault calls a technique of power, a specific form of power that "applies itself to immediate everyday life which categorizes the individual, marks him by his own individuality, attaches him to his own identity, imposes a law of truth on him which he must recognize and which others have to recognize in him. It is a form of power which makes individuals subjects."[148] Rather than investigate the "internal rationality" of social power, Foucault suggests that we look instead at "the forms of resistance and attempts made to dissociate [power] relations."[149] This notion of the subject in agonistic dissociation from power conforms to some extent with Giddens's view that in the "reflexive project of the self" a variety of "attitudes of skepticism or antagonism towards abstract systems may coexist with a taken-for-granted confidence in others."[150] As opposed to Althusserian approaches to the subject, which would argue for a more absolute ideological interpellation, Foucault and Giddens, like Adorno at his most hopeful, emphasize the extent to which the individual can resist institutional forms of Bildung. Such resistance "question[s] the status of the individual" and attacks any force that threatens the "right to be different" or that "separates the individual, breaks his links with others"; it amounts to a "struggle[] against the 'government of individualization.'"[151] The institutional "subject of knowledge" is to be resisted insofar as it is tied to criteria of competence, efficiency, and so on. The norms that regulate the "subject of knowledge" are bound to be both rigid and flexible: rigid insofar as they dictate the limits of individuality and flexible insofar as they permit variations within those limits. According to Foucault, the evolution of the modern state has created a complex political structure, originating in the institutions of Christianity, in which "individualization techniques" and "totalization procedures" coexist. He calls this new form of power "pastoral" and argues that it had existed within the Church for centuries until it "suddenly spread out into the whole social body."[152] The same "individualizing tactics" that Foucault finds in the twentieth century were already in place in the political theory of people like Humboldt, who claimed that the individual must be free enough to exclaim, "However closely I approach the danger of transgressing the law, yet will I not succumb."[153] The difference, of course, and it is a crucial and very obvious one, is that for modernists, beginning in the 1890s, the modes of power Foucault and other theorists of modernity describe were not merely theoretical, nor were they emergent; they were accelerating, penetrating ever deeper into arenas of social and cultural life that had hitherto been relatively untouched, inflecting the processes of self-development in new ways, pushing them toward greater viability and efficiency within institutional structures.

In this context, to say that modernist writers recuperate classical Bildung is to say that they resist the totalizing norms for self-development imposed by an advanced capitalist society. An obvious way to represent this resistance is to depict the processes of education. Resignifying classical Bildung in experimental Bildungsromane, modernist novelists enter into a immanently critical engagement with the prevailing modes of socialization and social mobility, in which dialectics serves a primarily pedagogical function. This is the point at which a literary work serves as part of a political education. According to Jürgen Habermas, dialectics is the "discourse of instruction" and "serves to introduce the student to knowledge, and of course the scientist, too, insofar as he still remains a student."[154] Developmental norms are produced in educational institutions: one is made to learn how to develop and to what end. This pedagogical orientation toward social norms is *explicit* in educational institutions, but it is also inscribed in other social institutions and in the various levels of noninstitutional social life. Throughout the nineteenth century, a form of reflexivity (in Giddens's sense) was at work: self-development was increasingly taken outside the sphere of inner culture, where pedagogy was oriented toward aesthetic education, and placed in the sphere of socialization, where the pedagogical emphasis was laid on careerism, vocation, learning to be a gentleman or a governess. The line between schooling and reflexive projects of the self became bolder as the nineteenth century passed; by the 1890s, with the novels of Hardy and Wilde, the problem of the subject was less an ontological one (having to do with what or who one is) than an epistemological one (having to do with learning how to *be* and how to *behave*). This shift, dramatically narrated in Hardy's *Jude the Obscure*, marked a decisive break from customary practices of assessing selfhood, subjecthood, personhood, *being*. In both England and Ireland, as we have seen, access to post-secondary education was uneven, with gender and class inequalities on every level, and this led to predictable developments in terms of social mobility.

As Andrew Miles and other social historians have pointed out, unequal educational opportunities for both men and women persisted well into the interwar period, with some gains made in the working and lower-middle classes at the grammar or secondary school levels, but with the middle class still dominating university study. Vocational and extension training remained throughout this period linked to credentialism (that is, to the specific requirements of a given occupation) and to self-improvement, but only on a very limited scale.[155] Hardy's Jude Fawley (from *Jude the Obscure*) and E. M. Forster's Leonard Bast (from *Howards End*) are the quintessential examples of failed Bildung projects among the working classes, young men who lacked the cultural capital and privilege required to possess what they imagined to be inner culture. The crushing blow of understanding, finally, that these requirements are decisively beyond them sends Jude and Leonard to their tragic ends. As the fate of Virginia Woolf's Mrs. Dalloway or of the Schlegel sisters in Forster's *Howards End* indicates, the successful acquisition of Bildung, such as it still existed at the turn of the century, presupposed at least a middle-class background. That clerks like Leonard and village boys like Jude and Lawrence's Paul Morel (from *Sons and Lovers*) even have a shot at a classical aesthetic education indicates the persistence of the Humboldtian ideal of making Bildung available to the "entire mass of the nation." That they are bound to fail may, sadly but inevitably, indicate the persistence of the same ideal. The "mass of the nation" becomes, in turn-of-the-century England, the sum of those who can attend university. Autodidacts like Leonard and Jude struggle alone, totally isolated within a liberal culture dedicated to the reform, education, and advancement of all people.

In Ireland the picture is even bleaker, because there were even fewer attempts at providing vocational and extension programs, leaving the seminary schools as one of the few options for young Catholic men to receive any kind of higher education. Women, of course, had fewer options still. There were some efforts on the part of nationalist groups to educate young men and women, but they were restricted to grammar and secondary levels.[156] Cardinal Newman's Catholic University provided education for a class formation for which there is no clear parallel in England. Those fortunate enough to take advantage of this opportunity were, by and large, the privileged members of the emergent Catholic middle class. A young man like Stephen Dedalus (in Joyce's *Portrait of the Artist as a Young Man*) only narrowly gains his chance at such an education despite the downward mobility of his family, while Anna Murphy (in Kate O'Brien's *Land of Spices*), who comes from a family who can afford to send her to the university, must nonetheless struggle to win scholarships in order to subvert family pressures that would steer her into a dead-end job at a bank. But these are the success stories in a country in which a substantial sector of the population in the countryside continued to live under premodern conditions, with little or no access to education beyond the primary and secondary levels. As for those in the towns and cities, in the absence of educational alternatives of the kind available in England to the working and lower-middle classes, Ireland could offer little beyond underemployment or unemployment and emigration, creating the conditions for what Albert Memmi calls "an internal catastrophe," a form of arrested development unique to colonial situations.[157] State-sponsored educational systems did little to encourage Irish Catholics to go beyond the secondary levels; the university remained, long after independence, the prerogative of the well-off middle classes. At the national school level, however, Ireland's experience was much like England's, for the mission of the educational system in the colonial period (and to some degree afterwards) was to rationalize Bildung and to produce "viable and usable human beings" for the highest reaches of state government, commerce, the military, and colonial administration.

It is my contention that in the modernist Bildungsroman, the normative modes of socialization and social mobility, which had become increasingly institutionalized throughout the nineteenth century, serve as the starting point for an immanent critique of socially pragmatic Bildung, of upward mobility, socialization, "getting on." The chief difficulty facing the modernists was to articulate alternatives in a genre whose narrative conventions were extremely conservative, in some cases little altered from the time of Goethe. In an important sense, generic failure was structurally necessary, for it was the ground and registration of the immanent critique of classical Bildung. Generic (and genetic) failure was thus the sign of a critical triumph. As Jameson points out, in a discussion of Paul De Man's theory of referentiality, what makes experimental poetry work is the reference it repudiates but which provides a ground and a contrast for what is nonreferential.[158] I think the modernist Bildungsroman functions in a similar fashion. The persistence of a conventional narrative framework associated with the classical Bildungsroman tends to highlight and underscore the ways in which modernist forms of neoclassical Bildung work, how they reconfigure aesthetic education in a climate of "depersonalized" freedom—that is to say, a climate of freedom from bourgeois "freedom" (of the sort Adorno has in mind), a new freedom in which inner culture (not by any means alienation) can take place. What Adorno says of the essay form applies to the modernist Bildungsroman: "The consciousness of the non-identity between presentation and presented material forces the [essay] to make unlimited efforts."[159] If we see, in the modernist Bildungsroman, a return to classical Bildung and, to some extent, to the thematics and structures of the classical Bildungsroman, it is not a return to origins. It is not a return at all, really, but an original performance under new conditions, perhaps one of the most dramatic examples of the modernist dictum "Make it new" or, in Adorno's words, "making an effort." Modernist Bildungsromane present a broad range of outcomes, which cannot be locked into the binomial opposition success/failure, because the social conditions in which success and failure make sense are themselves foreclosed—or, to put my point another way, the binomial categories collapse, and failure becomes an index of successful alternative representations of social and cultural subjectivities. In the nineteenth century, the Bildungsroman was the preeminent genre for representing identity formation and socialization and for developing the dominant modes of narrative closure: the realization of lost illusions and dashed expectations, the ceremonies of marriage, the sober reconciliation with one's obscure contributions to society. In the modernist period, the Bildungsroman critiques these modes of closure and offers alternatives that are open and fluid. Inner culture reveals a ground in contrariness and nonidentity, while aesthetic education seeks less the dialectics of harmony than the dialectics of resistance. From Wilde to Woolf, the Bildungsroman rises above the failure of genre and offers, in the narration of the vicissitudes of an immanent critique, the singular triumph of modernist Bildung.

Pedagogy and Power
in the Modernist Bildungsroman

Hardy and Lawrence

When Jude Fawley, in Hardy's *Jude the Obscure*, gazes off at Christminster from his vantage point atop a barn in his village, he sees embodied in distant architecture a "heavenly Jerusalem," symbol of the dream of Bildung that he has nursed, inarticulately, from the time of childhood. The narrative called into play to get Jude closer to this new Jerusalem differs dramatically from the classical form of the nineteenth-century European Bildungsroman. In part this difference is the result of the genre's transformation in an English environment, where the desire for upward social mobility has been stripped of any aesthetico-spiritual dimensions. By the 1890s, when Hardy was writing, political and social developments had resulted in an educational system in which vast numbers of students from the lower and lower-middle class, especially in rural areas, were effectively barred from higher education. Many were directed into vocational training and extension courses—a dramatic improvement over conditions at the middle of the nineteenth century, but a far cry from the "Bildung for the masses" envisioned by Humboldt. The heroes of the early modernist Bildungsroman in England aspire to recapture something like classical Bildung—the ideal of inner culture, the harmonious formation of the whole individual—but fail in a variety of ways to do so. Rather than narrating "the happiness of synthesis," as Moretti describes the Goethean prototype, the modernist Bildungsroman narrates its failure. In some cases, this failure is due to the protagonist's more fundamental failure to recognize that self-formation has become rationalized and institutionalized to such an extent that Bildung can no longer flourish except among those privileged enough to enjoy a traditional university education. At least, this is what Jude Fawley comes to think. In most cases, however, even in the ancient universities, classical Bildung was increasingly irrelevant. What was needed was technical and bureaucratic skills, not fluency in humanistic disciplines like literature, philosophy, music, theology, political theory and so on. As J.P.C. Roach notes, "The role of the universities was, in a sense, social rather than intellectual. They were devoted to producing gentlemen rather than scholars. Many of their critics employed against them the example of the German universities with their devotion to abstract scholarship, though the comparison was not an especially fair one. The German universities served an entirely different social system, in which the goal of almost all able men was a position in government service instead of, as in England, a career in an independent profession or a place in an elected Parliament and a responsible ministry."[1] In late-nineteenth- and early-twentieth-century England, Bildung was bound up with the proto-cols of socialization, which were themselves linked to the levels and limitations of class and class identity, with the result that class identity served often as an unbreachable barrier to the institutionalized cultural capital required for the "Bildung effect." But this effect had undergone dramatic changes by the late nineteenth century, leaving only traces of the spiritual apprenticeship ad-vocated by Humboldt and Goethe. The bitter irony of Jude's Bildung plot is that his ideal of self-cultivation and humanist inquiry no longer existed in the modern educational system, even in the ancient universities toward which he blindly and vainly turns for a shot at upward social mobility. As so often in the modernist Bildungsroman, though perhaps not quite so devastatingly, the subject of Bildung becomes the site of a critical negation of the self.

It is the very totality, the inexorability of failure, that draws the reader's at-tention to Jude's plight. How unlike Jude's experience is Paul Morel's, narrated in D. H. Lawrence's *Sons and Lovers*, published nearly twenty years later. Paul seeks through art to find a way to avoid the social destiny of his father and the men of his hometown and comes closest to success in the early modernist English Bildungsroman. However, it is never quite clear whether he will ever outgrow his petit bourgeois ambitions to be an illustrator. Unlike Joyce's Ste-phen Dedalus, Paul remains imprisoned in social structures, his identity and the limits of its formation dictated by the processes of socialization that have supplanted the humanist tradition of Bildung. As we will see in chapter 4, Ra-chel Vinrace in Woolf's *The Voyage Out* has a similarly frustrating experience with the Bildung process, but it is gender and not class that restricts her aspira-tions. If she fails to achieve Bildung, it is not because she has been thwarted by the class structure but because she thwarts the structure itself by refusing to be "trained" in the classical manner and, finally, by dying into her own visionary space of aesthetic harmony. It is, of course, a measure of the obstacles placed before young women that Rachel instinctively refuses normative modes of so-cial education, for she recognizes, as her predecessors in the nineteenth century typically did not, that such an education would only more firmly stymie her aspirations toward self-cultivation or, at best, orient them toward acquiescence to prevailing trends for the socialization of women of her class.[2]

If we look at the development of the English Bildungsroman from the 1890s to the end of the First World War, we see that the drive to become socialized loses its appeal, in part because it appears to be a pathway *only* to material success, a "structured, meritocratic, and bureaucratically mediated route[] into the labour market."[3] In these texts, nontraditional paths open up that were not (or could not be) opened up before, say, 1880. We find counterdiscourses of self-development, which form part of a larger struggle against tradition, a modernist agonism that appropriates history into the production of something new. In these narratives, dissension and disharmony and disintegration substitute for the unity the novel no longer constitutes in and for itself. Theodor Adorno associates such processes with a negative dialectics that alone can rescue philosophy from the "truth" of its unified and totalizing concepts.[4] As I have suggested in chapter 1, Adorno's approach to philosophy is pertinent on a number of levels for the study of literature. Early modernist English Bildungsromane like *Jude the Obscure, Sons and Lovers*, and *The Voyage Out* provide striking evidence of a recuperation of classical Bildung, which performs a key role in the negative critique of normative regimes of socialization.[5] The primary target of this critique is the classical Bildungsroman and its ideal of socially pragmatic Bildung. The failure of genre serves a critical purpose by illustrating both the instrumentalization of self-development and the strategies adopted by individuals to combat it. The modernist Bildungsroman, by creating a narrative space for new forms of classical Bildung, is as much concerned with the problems of representation as it is with the problems of socialization. No longer the privileged representation of a social world in which individuals attempt to achieve harmonious development, the Bildungsroman has become, in the 1890s, the site of a negative or immanent critique of Bildung in which strategies of depersonalization undermine the authority of the sovereign bourgeois subject, opening subjectivity to new determinations and new destinies. In describing the "dynamic of depersonalization," Fredric Jameson discerns a familiar logic: "that of nominalism and of the dialectic of universals and particulars."[6] This "dynamic of depersonalization" is a fundamental feature of aesthetic modernism and plays a prominent role in the modernist Bildungsroman.

Hardy and Lawrence express a certain range of options and alternatives to socially pragmatic Bildung that the modernist Bildungsroman is capable of modeling. In the first part of this chapter, "Wished Out of the World: Hardy's *Jude the Obscure*," I focus on the modernist Bildungsroman at an early stage of its development. The tragic structure of Hardy's Bildungsroman expresses the creative affirmation of Jude's negative Bildung. Jude discovers not only that he is blocked from the university but that the university was never intended for young men like him in the first place. From his position of internal exile, Jude rails against the system he dreamed of entering as one of its ordained priests. He and his cousin Sue Bridehead engage in a running critique of marriage and the values of humanism, which are abandoned completely by Sue in a paroxysm of penitential grief over the deaths of her children. In the end, the aesthetic education that Jude prized so highly leaves him with nothing but the will and the means to make of his own death a work of art.

In the second part, "Realizing the Self: Lawrence's *Sons and Lovers*," I focus on Lawrence's attempt to overcome the dialectical logic of humanism and the bourgeois subject. Like Adorno, Lawrence disapproved of totalistic thinking, and his novels can be read as narrative attempts to overcome the ideological unities that the realist novel purveys and to embrace nonidentity, which Adorno describes as "the secret *telos* of identification."[7] Lawrence had few models other than Hardy's *Jude the Obscure* for the kind of demolition job he wanted to perform on the "old stable ego of the character."[8] Women play decisive roles in Paul Morel's development, just as they do in Jude's. But the triangular battle that Lawrence stages between Paul and his two loves, Miriam and Clara, takes the critique of marriage and the exploration of sexual desire well beyond anything Hardy could offer. Of crucial importance in *Sons and Lovers* is the commingling of sexual desire and aesthetic education, which redefines the possibilities for Bildung for Paul as well as for the women who serve as his helpmates, lovers, and mentors. In the end, the transcendent pathway of self-development that Paul envisions dissolves in the gap between his "great expectations" and the reality of his social environment. The aesthetic education he so ardently desires remains stubbornly bound up with classical dialectical economies, and it is unclear whether he is able to evade the very socially pragmatic Bildung he claims to repudiate. Lawrence's modernist Bildungsroman, like Hardy's, thus deploys the narrative of the struggling, marginalized subject of late modernity to challenge prevailing modes of socialization: "To use the strength of the subject to break through the fallacy of constitutive subjectivity."[9] In the turn toward nonidentity, in the destabilizing oscillation between a failed aspiration toward Bildung and the representation of that failure, the modernist Bildungsroman critiques and overcomes its own dialectical harmonies.

WISHED OUT OF THE WORLD: HARDY'S *JUDE THE OBSCURE*

If the early modernist Bildungsroman in England tended to focus on the failure of the *Bildungsheld* to achieve harmony, it is because the Bildung plot in such texts remained fixed on social mobility at a time when self-development and inner culture were being defined in terms that resisted prevailing modes of socialization. The two most common manifestations of this resistance were class mobility and artistic aspiration. Patricia Alden argues persuasively for an English tradition of symbolic resistance in which the Bildungsroman flourished by representing the struggles of individuals in the lower and working classes to enter the middle class. In this tradition, which begins with midcentury writers like Dickens, the protagonist's conflict with the social world in pursuit of social mobility begins to exert reformative pressures on the Bildungsroman. The outcome of this development, according to Alden, who examines late-nineteenth- and early-twentieth-century English Bildungsromane (by George Gissing, Arnold Bennett, Hardy, and Lawrence), is that ordinary people were able to "plot their own trajectory in the social world," to become new "material for fiction." Social experience became a struggle, the resolution of which led to "some kind of adjustment to society."[10] Alden, like Martin Swales, argues that the English Bildungsroman unfolds its plot along a socioethical axis; social mobility and all of the ethical implications of such mobility take the place of aesthetic education and the more abstract spiritual goal of classical Bildung. The individual freedom of inner culture and the dialectical harmony of self-development and wholeness that the German Bildungsroman narrates and thematizes give way in the English modernist form to a general sense of alienation in the face of a bewildering social landscape: the very mobility that guarantees that the artist hero will no longer have to endure poverty or obscurity conflicts with his purely aesthetic motives. The dialectical structure of harmonious Bildung that we observe in Goethe or Humboldt does not translate well into the English context where the subject of social life experiences what Alden calls a double bind in which "success or failure in upward mobility equally preclude[s] the possibility for cultivation of the whole person."[11] The parvenu is as unlikely as the village boy to achieve classical Bildung. The kind of socialization we see in the Victorian novel—for example, the production of the "gentleman" in Dickens or Meredith—expresses this double bind in terms of shifts within and between class formations of the kind that Andrew Miles describes, shifts that altered class identity and class relations in unpredictable ways. The English Bildungsroman thus performs a peculiar dual function. On the one hand, its portrayal of social mobility and pragmatic discourses of social recruitment helps "to legitimate the ideology of individualism." In other words, the old class system no longer keeps an ambitious person down.[12] Yet, on the other hand, the *Bildungshelden* cannot help but feel contempt for the very society in which they rise up. Moral imperatives clash with social exigencies; accommodation to a social system creates the uneasy sense that they are betraying their finer, more personal ambitions. The *Bildungshelden* Alden studies are caught between their working-class roots and the bourgeois class toward which they aspire and which holds out the allure of culture. For them, the "breakdown of liberal ideology" is "an anxious, guilt-ridden personal crisis." The narration of this crisis makes the Bildungsroman a "site of conflict."[13]

What is missing in this analysis, which is otherwise insightful in its treatment of the problematic of class, is a consideration of the Bildungsroman as a specifically modernist form that seeks to recapture just that "possibility for the cultivation of the whole person" that Alden argues is precluded by concerns for upward mobility. I would therefore want to modify her conclusion and suggest that, in a context of social mobility in late modernity, success and failure are no longer relevant for the project of self-development. If these descriptive terms have any relevance at all, it would lie in gauging the protagonist's sense of an achieved aesthetic education or mode of aesthetic self-fashioning. In a social world that no longer offers predictable or reliable stages of socialization, each individual is confronted with the option of (re)forming his or her own inner culture, typically in reaction or resistance to all that lies outside that interiorized cultural sphere. It should be noted that success need not be sweet, nor failure a defeat.

Nowhere is this more true than in the experience of men like Jude Fawley who encounter a social world that no longer promises the satisfaction of a secure social position or the promise of predictable social mobility. As Raymond Williams describes it, "Society from being a framework could be seen now [the nineteenth century] as an agency, even an actor, a character. It could be seen and valued in and through persons: not as a framework in which they were defined; not as an aggregate of known relationships; but as an apparently independent organism, a character and an action like others. Society, now, was not just a code to measure, an institution to control, a standard to define or to change. It was a process that entered lives, to shape or to deform; a process personally known but then again suddenly distant, complex, incomprehensible, overwhelming."[14] Hardy's novels are famously concerned with this shift in the way society registers on the subjectivity of those who live outside the large towns and cities, specifically in rural areas that have been divested of their traditional landscapes, landmarks, practices, and social relations.[15] *Jude the Obscure* in particular is concerned with the way this shift affects the desire for Bildung, especially when that desire is conceived in terms of a classical humanist education. In this context, the gap that Alden perceives between "the promises of the Bildungsroman" and the social experience it records is as much a measure of the failure of education as it is of class mobility. Indeed, Jude's failure to achieve his educational goals is the specific indicator of his class position. Unlike urban dwellers, who could benefit from the new opportunities in social education and the civil service, Jude occupies a traditional rural space in which educational opportunities have yet to penetrate.

Hardy's Bildungsroman follows the classical model by depicting a process of formation that takes the *Bildungsheld* away from his provincial home and into the larger world beyond. It departs from this model primarily in the sense that a thematics of failure complicates and critiques the formative process. Opportunities for ambitious "poor students" like Jude Fawley were not uncommon in the nineteenth century, though resistance to the "overeducation" of the working classes redefined the nature of education for those classes, with the result that more opportunities opened up at the secondary and "vocational" levels, while advancement to the ancient universities remained foreclosed.[16] The attitude of a justice of the peace in 1807 would not have been out of place at the end of the century: "It is doubtless desirable that the poor should be generally instructed in *reading*, if it were only for the best of purposes—that they may read the Scriptures. As to *writing* and *arithmetic*, it may be apprehended that such a degree of knowledge would produce in them a disrelish for the laborious occupations in life."[17] By the time Jude sets his sights on the university, he desires far more than the rudiments of reading and writing. His aspiration toward Bildung may well have been as threatening to the social order as the aspiration of the poor to acquire basic literacy was some seventy years before. In the 1880s, at the beginning of his journey to Christminster, educational opportunities tended to confirm, when they did not determine, class divisions.[18] As Williams and others point out, the ancient universities at Oxford and Cambridge, still strongly devoted to clerical training as they had been for centuries, had become exclusive enclaves, whose students came primarily from the private grammar schools (that is, the "public schools," such as Eton, Rugby, and the like). They continued to exclude the working classes, though some opportunities existed, for example at University College London, for working-class individuals.[19] In any case, the ancient universities were not devoted to the scholarship that Jude cherished but to the clerical vocation for which he would ultimately settle. Both the ideal and the reality of Christminster finally disappoint him.

Alden believes that the ideal of harmonious self-cultivation to which young men like Jude Fawley aspire is transformed, under the pressure of material obstacles, into a "'chaos of principles' . . . in which not even the most radical compromise of aspiration permits an accommodation with the social order."[20] This is no doubt the case, but Alden does not take into account the value Jude persists in placing on the ideal of self-cultivation, which is, in her view, depreciated along with everything else concerning the individual. Jude's very perseverance and his own understanding of his failure to achieve the goal of Bildung that he sets for himself testifies not only to the high value he places on it but also to the specific mechanisms by which the modernist Bildungsroman, at this early stage of its development, thematizes depersonalization not as alienation but as aesthetic self-fashioning. "I may do some good before I am dead—" Jude says, after his return to Christminster, "be a sort of success as a frightful example of what not to do; and so illustrate a moral story. . . . I was, perhaps, afterall, a paltry victim to the spirit of mental and social restlessness, that makes so many unhappy in these days!'" (*JO* 399).[21] This sentiment, which builds slowly as Jude becomes more convinced of his failed opportunities, situates him in the modernist pantheon of heroes who recognize that their negative life experiences are not merely the result of inaccessibility of opportunity but constitute a critique of the very society that withholds access. Jude's success, as he bitterly realizes, is useful only if it teaches the salutary lesson of nonidentity freed from the ignominy of dialectical negation. The negativity in *Jude the Obscure* possesses a critical value precisely because it is not dissolved in the triumph of self-identity. The irony of Hardy's treatment here, an irony that raises the critical potential of Jude's lesson, lies in the "frightful example of what *not* to do." We might well ask what is one not to do: pursue Bildung, or pursue it fruitlessly as Jude does, by trying to gain entrance to the university? John Kucich notes this irony and identifies it as indicative of an "aesthetic consciousness" in which "the honesty of art—which must be achieved through an act of energetic resistance, given the potentials for aesthetic duplicity . . .—is constructed mainly through a series of linked negations that depend on detached observation: negations of femininity, of sexual desire, of lived experience, of social ambition, and even, in a form of ironic doubling, of art itself."[22] These negations do not add up to a positive identity; they instead assert the profound lack that motivates nonidentity. Jude's aesthetic sensibility is a function not so much of artistic production, though there is some evidence of this in his stonemasonry and in the model of Christminster that he and Sue Bridehead construct. It is rather a function of his vision of self-cultivation, his inchoate sense that even his nonidentity, his failure to harmonize with the social world, is a viable aesthetic achievement. Sue, it could be argued, suffers from an even more debilitating form of this failure, but hers, like that of so many young women who are cast in the role of instrumental helpmates in modernist Bildungsromane featuring male heroes, is not the failure to achieve Bildung, for she is not placed in the narrative position to desire or seek it. Her failure is largely the subordinate one of refusing the male hero the opportunity of attaining a harmonious, aesthetically unified ideal of himself, crucial elements of which somehow lie beyond his control.

Most critics of Hardy who invoke the Bildungsroman genre are concerned with the Jude who confronts obstacles, who is, as Alden argues, excluded from the Arnoldean cultural dispensation "by the class structure of his society, a structure deeply entrenched and on the defensive, using education as a way of maintaining a social hierarchy."[23] Penny Boumelha makes more or less the same point when she notes that *Jude the Obscure* fails to fulfill the "biographical-meritocratic mould of the English *Bildungsroman*."[24] Alden and Boumelha emphasize very important aspects of the late-nineteenth-century Bildungsroman, especially its narrative response to class structures and to the socially pragmatic meritocracy that was beginning to emerge as the dominant mode of social mobility. But what is elided here, as I have already suggested, is the crucial fact that failure, for Jude at least (as for other early modernist protagonists like Paul Morel and Rachel Vinrace), is less a question of having failed at socialization and thus at socially pragmatic Bildung than of having failed to achieve the ideal of aesthetic education at the heart of aesthetico-spiritual Bildung. It is not enough to argue that social obstacles and class structures preclude such an education; nor is it enough to speak, as H. M. Daleski does, of an "inverted Bildungsroman," in which "Jude's story leads only to nullification and self-destruction."[25] It is necessary to emphasize the ways in which Jude attempts to get around these obstacles and structures, no matter how paltry and inadequate the attempts are, for it is in the representation of such attempts that Hardy critiques the ideological superstructure of the Bildungsroman form itself. To speak of an "inverted" Bildungsroman genre does not offer such a critique but, on the contrary, reaffirms the closed dialectical structure of the form's conventional narrative dynamics and strategies of characterization.[26] What I am suggesting is that Hardy's modernist Bildungsroman resists the classical structure, in which dialectics works toward pragmatic socialization, in favor of a mode akin to Adorno's negative dialectics, in which the abjection of the subject of Bildung opens a space for the development of new subjectivities. But this resistance and this opening up can only work critically within the formal limits of the conventional Bildungsroman, for critique is dependent upon failure within these limits. The failure of genre is essential for the success of critique.[27]

That this new space is narrow and darkened by the tragic death of the protagonist does not materially alter the fact that Hardy's Bildungsroman seeks to open it up. I contend that Hardy's impassioned defense of classical Bildung survives despite Jude's failure to achieve it. It survives, metonymically, in the latter's skill at stonemasonry as well as in the Christminster cakes, but most of all it survives in the tragic architecture—as beautiful as it is appalling—of Jude's self-development. What we see in his experience is the persistence of the desire for Bildung against all odds. Indeed, Sue's style of self-negation, by contrast, cancels this desire: "You called me a creature of civilization, or something, didn't you?" she says to Jude, after he follows her and Phillotson to Melchester. "It was very odd you should have done that. . . . it is provokingly wrong. I am a sort of negation of it" (*JO* 201). Hardy is not concerned primarily with the annihilation of the self in a confrontation with intransigent social obstacles, as we see in Sue's surrender to Phillotson and marriage. Instead, I want to argue that his main concern is with a productive and critical depersonalization in which the protagonist, cut off from socially sanctioned, institutionalized modes of Bildung, enters into, without adequate mentoring, the project of self-cultivation. The classical ideal of aesthetic education and a self-sufficient inner culture stands behind Jude's conscious decision to abandon his desire to attend Christminster, to marry Arabella, to live with Sue, and, finally, to court the tragedy of his death. The much lauded tragic structure of *Jude the Obscure* can thus be regarded as the specific literary valence of Jude's "negative" Bildung.

Alden makes the point, noted by others, that Hardy saw in Jude's desire to attend Oxford (Christminster in the novel) something of his own experience.[28] This is an important point, but not one that I want to pursue. Hardy himself, in the preface to the first edition, subordinates the "tragedy of unfulfilled aims" to the "deadly war waged between flesh and spirit" (*JO* 39),[29] which indicates that he was less interested in fictionalizing his own experience (though an element of such fictionalization is evident throughout the novel) than in creating a model of self-development that would implicitly critique the chief elements of bourgeois socialization: education, vocation, marriage, mentorship, and so on. It is not surprising that the materialist argument mounted by Alden should conclude that Jude's failure is the failure of Bildung or of the Bildungsroman.

Certainly this would be the case if we were concerned primarily with social mobility as the goal of self-development. However, if we emphasize instead the dynamics of self-cultivation—that is to say, of aesthetic education—then we are in a position to understand how it persists as a viable alternative to the institutionalized forms of education and self-development which are, without a doubt, denied to Jude. We see the same tragic drive toward self-cultivation in Leonard Bast, a man who moves in the ambiguous social sphere in which the working class shades into the lower middle class. His final journey in *Howards End*, like Jude's final pursuit of Sue, is a relentless attempt to recontextualize his failures to achieve Bildung in a well-nigh deliberate act of self-destruction. In Forster's novel, however, the contrast is not with the self-abnegation of a Sue Bridehead but with the complacently cultured, middle-class Schlegel sisters, for whom self-cultivation is an entitlement and whose heritage and name call to mind the German Romantic movement out of which Bildung emerged as a cultural ideal. Long before the climax that sends him to his death, Leonard realizes how far he is from the kind of culture enjoyed by these women: "They had all passed up that narrow, rich staircase at Wickham Place," he recalls, sadly, "to some ample room, wither he could never follow them, not if he read for ten hours a day. Oh, it was no good, this continual aspiration. Some are born cultured; the rest had better go in for whatever comes easy. To see life steadily and to see it whole was not for the likes of him."[30]

The Arnoldean sentiment in this last sentence, a touchstone for the attitudes of the Schlegels, sums up the nineteenth-century cultural ideal that had developed in England and that served as a fair approximation of the goal of Bildung for the English cultural elite in the early twentieth century. Unlike Jude, who wishes to attain something like classical Bildung by attending Oxford and who is well aware of the slow grind that the acquisition of culture entails, Leonard thinks he can achieve the level of culture that the Schlegel sisters have acquired as a birthright by reading Ruskin in his spare time. "He felt that he was being done good to, and that if he kept on with Ruskin, and the Queen's Hall Concerts, and some pictures by Watts, he would one day push his head out of the grey waters and see the universe. He believed in sudden conversion. . . . of a heritage that may expand gradually, he had no conception: he hoped to come to Culture suddenly, much as the Revivalist hopes to come to Jesus. Those Miss Schlegels had come to it; they had done the trick; their hands were on the ropes, once and for all. And meanwhile, his flat was dark, as well as stuffy."[31] Leonard Bast's experience in *Howards End* testifies not only to the continued persistence of the desire for classical Bildung in early modernist Bildungsromane but also to its diffusion across geographic and class boundaries. We could say of Leonard Bast what D. H. Lawrence says of Jude: "almost the bitterest, most pathetic, deepest part of Jude's misfortune was his failure to obtain admission to Oxford, his failure to gain his place and standing in the world's knowledge, in the world's work."[32]

The opening line of *Jude the Obscure* signals the paucity of opportunities for Bildung, either in its aesthetico-spiritual or its socially pragmatic form. "The schoolmaster was leaving the village, and everybody seemed sorry." The schoolmaster represents for Jude both the social opportunities offered by education and the kind of personal mentorship that is at the core of the classical Bildungsroman. Peter Widdowson remarks that this line is a "telling indicator of [the novel's] fundamental *donnée*, for everything here is in transition and everyone in transit."[33] But the problem goes beyond the inorganic transitoriness of modern society and social institutions and touches on the status of the subject and the possibilities for self-development that exist in such a social world. "*Jude* is a novel of a loss of markings and mappings," David Musselwhite writes, in a Deleuzean reading of the "desacralized" world in which Jude moves, a world "of missing *ciphers*, of apocryphal compilations—like the *brochure* of juggled and shuffled New Testament books proposed by Sue—of massive processes of marginalization and deterritorialization and, consequently, of exile and anomie."[34] Jude begins his Bildung process in just this sort of deterritorialized social space, where Old-World cruelties "sickened his sense of harmony," the very harmony he desires from the humanist education he dreams of in faraway Christminster, the "heavenly Jerusalem" he gazes at from the roof of an old barn (*JO* 57, 60). The young Jude—"an ancient man in some phases of thought, much younger than his years in others"—is easily swayed by Vilbert, the "itinerant quack-doctor" who serves as a mentor in the absence of the schoolmaster who has so precipitously left the village (*JO* 67). It is to him that Jude entrusts his desire to learn Greek and Latin, those hallmarks of the humanist tradition at the heart of classical Bildung. But even the crushing disappointment he feels when Vilbert fails to fulfill his promise does not prevent the young man from pursuing his lofty goals. At this stage in his development, he meets material obstacles—the social distance of Christminster, the "shoddy humanity" of the quack—with a sense of desperate longing. "One thing about them," writes Lawrence of Hardy's heroes and heroines, "is that none of [them] care very much for money, or immediate self-preservation, and all of them are struggling hard to come into being. What exactly the struggle into being consists in, is the question."[35] While for Lawrence the answer is simply love, the matter is more complicated when regarded from the perspective of Jude's desire for education. Hardy's characteristic irony, in the commentary to this episode, underscores the disappointment Jude feels once he discovers that there is no "secret cipher" for the knowledge he wishes to acquire in the rarefied world of Christminster. "Somebody might have come along that way who would have asked him his trouble, and might have cheered him by saying that his notions were further advanced than those of his grammarian. But nobody did come, because nobody does; and under the crushing recognition of his gigantic error Jude continued to wish himself out of the world" (*JO* 72). From the outset, we see the dialectical tension between aspiration and social position—between "the sheer complexity of individual potentiality" and "practical reality"[36]—that defines the dynamic of the classical Bildungsroman. But in Hardy's text, the point of view is that of someone marginalized by the very pressures and processes that determine social position. Jude's wish to be "out of the world" is already fulfilled, for he is no position to enter the world of humanist learning and personal Bildung that Christminster symbolizes. The dialectical struggle in Hardy's modernist Bildungsroman, then, is between two worlds: one in which Jude feels marginalized, feels the vicissitudes of nonidentity, and one in which he would occupy a seat at the very center of Bildung. To "wish himself out" is to negate himself in one world, to experience nonidentity as such, from the imagined perspective of the other, of Christminster, where he hoped to find his true identity. It is from the imagined perspective of this "other" world that Hardy narrates Jude's tragic self-fashioning.

In the early chapters of the novel, Jude feels the weight of this world even before he has lived long in it; and in his youthful naïveté, he imagines that Christminster is sufficiently out of "the world" to provide him with relief from his many disappointments. In order to prepare himself for "the magnificent Christminster dream" (*JO* 84), he follows the path taken by Humboldt and so many others, and educates himself in Greek and Latin, naively assuming that education is classless, that his acquisition of knowledge will erase his rural origins. His first sojourn in Christminster, where he will later experience "the hell of conscious failure" (*JO* 176), begins auspiciously with a vision of all those who preceded him. Barbara Hardy has argued that visions of this sort constitute a construction of Christminster, an unstable fantasy that nevertheless marks Jude's sensibility as consciously artistic. "Jude's visions are made sensuously substantial, but they are presented as visions being formed, traditionally, individually, and plausibly but also ambiguously."[37] Poets, philosophers, theologians, statesmen, scholars, scientists—"the worthies who had spent their youth within these reverend walls, and whose souls had haunted them in their maturer age"—all parade before his awe-stricken gaze, "comrades in his solitude" (*JO* 126). At the same time, he remains unconscious of the reality of this "daunting citadel of medieval privilege and intellectual irrelevance," which was "poisoning the modern movement and conditioning the future."[38] What Andrew Radford alludes to here is the reality of a university system that refused to respond to the desires of a man like Jude Fawley who quickly discovers, "on the spot of his enthusiasm," just how far he is from the object of his desire. "Only a wall divided him from those happy young contemporaries of his with whom he shared a common mental life; men who had nothing to do from morning till night but to read, mark, learn, and inwardly digest. Only a wall—but what a wall!" (*JO* 132). The irony here, which Hardy may have felt from his own experience, is that it would have been highly unlikely that such activities, free from the taint of social position and mobility, would have taken place behind the wall. Jude's aesthetic education is a fantasy construction of disinterested scholarship and study that he hopes will lead to a rich and productive inner culture. His phantasmatic mentors are hopelessly out of place in his itinerant situation, perhaps even more so once he secures work as a stonemason. His obscurity, initially at least, lies in this sense that he has no meaning in the social context of that Bildung of which he has so long dreamed: "Knowing not a human being here, Jude began to be impressed with the isolation of his own personality, as with a self-spectre, the sensation being that of one who walked but could not make himself seen or heard." He does not blame the city itself—its impersonality, its snobbery toward working-class supplicants, its unfamiliarity. Instead he blames himself and his "obscure" origins, both of which force him to be little more than "his own ghost" among "the other ghostly presences" (*JO* 125–26).

Part of the problem is that Jude has misjudged both Christminster and his own desire to be admitted to the university. The full extent of his misjudgment can be gauged by the story he constructs while on a visit to Marygreen, his home village. One of the villagers asks him if the "seat of l'arning" was all he had expected, and Jude enthusiastically cries out, "Yes; more!" The villager remarks that he remembered Christminster as "crumbling buildings, half church, half almshouse," and Jude tells him, "You are wrong, John; there is more going on than meets the eye of a man walking through the streets. It is a unique centre of thought and religion—the intellectual and spiritual granary of this country. All that silence and absence of goings-on is the stillness of infinite motion—the sleep of the spinning-top" (*JO* 162–63). This scene is indicative of Jude's intellectual and moral confusion. Patricia Ingham argues persuasively that Jude fails "to distinguish between scholarship, religion and social advancement. . . . Similarly, [he] mixes categories, seeing in the religious titles that he covets moral worth, social status and wealth."[39] By the same token, Jude confuses the two modes of Bildung in operation in the nineteenth century: the aesthetico-spiritual one, which energized his early enthusiasm for humanist values and classical languages, and the socially pragmatic one, which had for the most part displaced the former mode in institutional settings like the university. But this confusion, like the one Ingham describes, is predicated on a more fundamental delusion that class does not matter in Christminster. Despite the fact that he has had to seek an occupation in lieu of pursuing the vocation that he desires, despite his suspicion that stonemasonry is an effort "as worthy as that dignified by the name of scholarly study" (*JO* 131), despite his sense of doubt concerning his own ability to master classical languages, despite his discovery that his first mentor is "only a schoolmaster still" (*JO* 149)—despite all of this, Jude continues to live in an "imaginative world . . . in which an abstract figure, more or less himself, was steeping his mind in a sublimation of the arts and sciences" (*JO* 163). This world comes tumbling down when, in response to his query, Tetuphenay, the master of Biblioll College, tells him, "judging from your description of yourself as a working-man, I venture to think that you will have a much better chance of success in life by remaining in your own sphere and sticking to your trade than by adopting any other course" (*JO* 167).

After Tetuphenay's rejection, Jude reverts to the type he has so long avoided: the working-class lout who drinks himself to oblivion in order to block out the world in which he no longer plays a meaningful part. In the "ancient hamlet" of his childhood, Jude awakens to "'the hell of conscious failure,' both in ambition and in love" (*JO* 176). His failed marriage to Arabella, as well as his failure to enter the university, corroborates his sense of having fallen "out of the world." He claims, "I don't regret the collapse of my University hopes one jot . . . I don't care for social success any more at all" (*JO* 177). But even in the annihilation of his worldly ambitions, he is able to rescue a morsel of hope. He will attempt to enter the Church as a licentiate. On this slender possibility, Jude embarks again on a journey founded less on any clear sense of his fitness for the task than on an obsessive drive to recover whatever he can of his aspiration to acquire Bildung.

This is a pivotal moment, one that signals the denouement of his aspiration. After he has allowed himself to succumb to drink, he finally sees the real world around him: "He began to see that the town life was a book of humanity infinitely more palpitating, varied, and compendious than the gown life" (*JO* 168). But this realization does not dampen his desire for the "gown life." His return to

Marygreen, which echoes the return of the hero to the provinces that we see in the nineteenth-century French Bildungsroman, is a hiatus rather than a terminus. He lingers there "for some long stagnant time," doing nothing "to advance his new desire, occupying himself with little local jobs . . . and submitting to be regarded as a social failure, a returned purchase" (*JO* 181). His experience underscores the interminable quality of the socialization process for young men whose class background—a semi-independent tradesman—makes it impossible for them to advance through the University system.[40] "The historical irony in which Jude is trapped," writes Terry Eagleton, "is that personal fulfillment can be achieved only by painfully appropriating the very culture which denies and rejects him as a man."[41] Hence, Jude does not give up, he does not relinquish his desire for social mobility, though he is forced to downgrade his expectations, to seek a licentiate rather than a doctorate. But it is all the same to him, since his desire to enter the Church has less to do with achieving social status—although this is an important goal for him—than with normalizing his feelings of negativity and nonidentity. Hardy's Bildungsroman from this point on is the record of Jude's attempts not so much to negate this negativity (to achieve self-identity within a properly dialectical process of socialization) as to find a satisfying way to accept and even to nurture it. In this, as in so much else that happens in the second half of the novel, Jude explores and gives shape and human dimension to the truth of nonidentity, a truth that Adorno discovers in negative dialectics: "Its motion does not tend to the identity in the difference between each object and its concept; instead, it is suspicious of all identity. Its logic is one of disintegration: of a disintegration of the prepared and objectified form of the concepts which the cognitive subject faces, primarily and directly. Their identity with the subject is untruth."[42] If we apply this insight to Hardy's Bildungsroman, which retains, like so many late-nineteenth-century classical exemplars of the form, a strong dialectical structure, we can better understand the alienating pressures that Jude must endure, the truth of his Job-like attempt to bear up under the vicissitudes of nonidentity.

In the classical Bildungsroman, success depends on the willingness of the *Bildungsheld* to overcome youthful rebelliousness and to take his or her "proper" place in the social world. In Hardy's modernist Bildungsroman, however, rebellion is precluded in any but the most sublimated, interiorized sense. Inexorable institutional obstacles enforce an absence of socially effective rebellion, and it is this absence of a healthy rebellion—which would temper the hero, making him less naïve, less vulnerable to the world he will eventually reenter—that makes Jude's situation seem so hopeless. In the meantime Sue, in an attempt to console him after his rejection by Tetuphenay, makes a category mistake similar to the one that sustained Jude's initial hopes in Christminster. She tells him, "You are one of the very men Christminster was intended for when the colleges were founded; a man with a passion for learning, but no money, or opportunities, or friends. But you were elbowed off the pavement by the millionaires' sons" (*JO* 205). Undeniably, he *is* "elbowed off" by those who occupy more privileged class positions, but it is not the case that Oxford/Christminster was intended for men like Jude. As Raymond Williams and other social historians have noted, there had been, until the middle of the nineteenth century, only token opportunities for poor and working-class individuals to find a place in the ancient universities. As the century progressed, these opportunities decreased, in part because of the opening up of new opportunities in the expanded and improved secondary schools, the new Mechanics Colleges and provincial universities, and extension programs like those connected to Oxford. Jane Mattisson makes this point in her analysis of Tetuphenay's letter: "It is indicative of Hardy's sceptical attitude to university education for the rural working class that he chose Oxford, the less forward of the two old universities, as the setting of *Jude the Obscure*, and the object of Jude's admiration. By failing to mention the excellent extension work being carried out at the University from 1878 he also emphasised the closed, traditional nature of the University. For a man in Jude's situation, University College, London, offering academic education to the middle class, would have been an infinitely more suitable choice."[43] Mattisson notes also that there were several provincial colleges, established in the 1870s, that would have served Jude as well as University College, if not better. These opportunities were hardly obscure. Edmund Gosse, in an 1896 review of *Jude the Obscure*, remarks that "the conversations of [Hardy's] semi-educated characters . . . are really terrible. Sue and Jude talk a sort of University Extension jargon that breaks the heart." He is especially critical of Sue's dialogue, concluding that "Mr. Hardy is mistaken in what he heard her say. She *could* not have talked like that."[44] Though Gosse may be wrong about how young women like Sue talked, his reference to "University Extension jargon" indicates that by 1896 such programs would have been sufficiently well established to produce a recognizable (and easily parodied) style of intellectual discourse distinguishable from that associated with the ancient universities.

Hardy's choice of Oxford does more than emphasize the problems of the university system; it allows him to create, within the conventional narrative structure of the Bildungsroman, a site of critical resistance to the institutionalization of Bildung and the exclusion of the working classes from the higher educational system. Jude's position outside the social field of Bildung, especially the socially pragmatic variety that had come to dominate late-nineteenth-century higher education, constitutes a kind of internal exile, a new subject position from which it is possible to critique the processes of socialization. Hardy's ironic treatment of Jude's Bildung process, in the prolonged denouement following his rejection letter from Tetuphenay, exploits this position, indicting not only the educational system but also that other social system that brings Jude to grief, marriage, which in the classical Bildungsroman served as a material sign of the hero's successful achievement of Bildung. The importance of marriage as a symbolic legitimation is, I submit, one of the main reasons why Hardy's critique of marriage is so closely bound up with Jude's struggle to achieve Bildung and why Sue Bridehead is so intimately connected to Christminster.

Hardy's critique of marriage takes place within the context of the more fundamental spiritual friendship between Jude and Sue, for their friendship transcends the limits of social relationships like marriage. We have already seen that for Humboldt, Bildung entails a positive influence on others: "The first law of morality is: cultivate thyself; and the second is: influence others by what thou art."[45] For him, as for Goethe, this aspect of Bildung was developed in intimate friendships with women, whose influence has been, by and large, underestimated in the literature on classical Weimar. In Goethe's *Wilhelm Meister*, a chivalric view of women prevails. Women are able, indeed obliged, to rescue men from a corrupt social world and to provide the stable ground on which an inner culture can be built. Early on in Goethe's novel, Wilhelm "decides" that fate "was extending its helping hand to him, through Mariane [his first lover], to draw him out of that stifling, draggle-tailed middle-class existence he had so long desired to escape."[46] Later on, Lothario, one of Wilhelm's mentors from the Society of the Tower, argues that involvement in such an existence deprives man of "harmony with himself," while a woman, by assuming "internal governance" of a home, "assures for her husband true independence—domestic independence, inner independence."[47]

This "inner independence" is, of course, exactly what Humboldt meant in *The Limits of State Action* when he insisted on freedom for the development of one's own inner culture: "if there is one aspect of development more than any other which owes its highest beauty to freedom, it is precisely the cultivation of character and morals."[48] The women in Goethe's novel are instrumental in securing this freedom and thus guaranteeing the cultivation of character and morals. Of course, an appropriate marriage is essential to sustaining both. Wilhelm goes through a number of possible candidates for marriage after Mariane conveniently disappears from the narrative. Natalie is the final object of his matrimonial desires, the one who bears the imprimatur of the Society of the Tower as well as of Therese, her immediate predecessor. In a letter to Natalie, Therese describes the role of women with respect to others in a context that conflates the roles of educator and wife: "'If we just take people as they are,' you once said, 'we make them worse; but if we treat them not as they are but as they should be, we help them to become what they can become.'"[49] An important qualifying point needs to be made here, for the argument presented by the Weimar theorists is not that women *create* male Bildung, but that they create a space in which men can find out what is inside themselves. Again, Therese seems to understand this well when she notes to Natalie that Wilhelm's soul-searching "is sustained by the well-intentioned but curious belief that he will receive from without what can only come from within." She goes on to say, "I know my future husband better than he does," and believes that while she "sees" him, she does not "oversee him."[50] Therese and Natalie possess a kind of domestic wisdom that complements and subserves the dominant ideology of Bildung developed by the Society of the Tower. But it is not the only wisdom available for women, as indicated by the experience of Natalie's aunt, the "noble beautiful soul" who goes into seclusion to pursue her own path to Bildung and whose confession occupies an important place within the narrative of Wilhelm's own Bildung plot.[51]

The instrumental function of women I have just described can be discerned in many English Bildungsromane of the nineteenth century, modified of course to reflect different national customs with respect to social relations and marriage. Indeed, the conception of women as spiritual helpmates—the pragmatic, frankly patriarchal, and at times misogynist motif of the "angel of the house"—is hardly limited to the Bildungsroman; it can be found in innumerable cultural discourses of the era. But Hardy's novel resists this crude gender stereotyping. Indeed, some critics have seen in Sue Bridehead a version of the Girl of the Period, an early assertion of feminism that flourished in the 1860s, largely the result of enthusiasm for the work of John Stuart Mill. Moreover, the first readers of *Jude the Obscure* may well have been reminded of a more recent upsurge of feminism, the New Woman movement.[52] We see the effects of these movements on Sue's sensitive intelligence, for she begins with a desire to serve Jude, feeling "almost an ideality" with respect to him, but she soon rises above him in the material social sphere and helps to refine his thought and to direct his destiny. She skillfully abolishes the distinction between mentor and instrumental helpmate that in Goethe is clearly drawn. Jude wonders if "to know her would be to cure himself of this unexpected and unauthorized passion" (*JO* 146). In their many conversations on religion, civilization, and marriage, she emerges as an educated, thoughtful, progressive young woman, well versed in the humanist tradition in which Jude wishes to participate. He comes to regard her as "modern," but she contradicts him: "I am not modern. . . . I am more ancient than mediaevalism, if you only knew" (*JO* 187). He will come to know it well enough, but in the meantime she behaves in a distressingly modern fashion. Her Millsean individualism and Voltairean hostility toward religion are nicely dramatized in her act of "cutting up all the Epistles and Gospels into separate *brochures* and re-arranging them in chronological order," an act that places her in the company of Ernst Renan, David Strauss, Friedrich Nietzsche, and other exponents of the "higher criticism" that was, in the late nineteenth century, challenging the divine authority of the Bible. Jude, the budding Tractarian, responds "with a sense of sacrilege" that is difficult to credit, given his ardent rejoinder to Sue: "I am not against you" (*JO* 206–7). Sue's conflation of mentor and helpmate subverts the dynamics of the Bildung process precisely by exploiting, in an innovative fashion, the virtues of its conventional subject positions. "I won't disturb your convictions—I really won't," she tells him, disingenuously perhaps, given the scene that has just passed. "But I did want and long to ennoble some man to high aims; and when I saw you, and knew you wanted to be my comrade, I—shall I confess it?—thought that man might be you. But you take so much tradition on trust that I don't know what to say" (*JO* 207).

This scene, in which tradition squares off against modernity, is devastatingly ironic, given the stakes for Jude's Bildung. Sue's intellectual background aligns her with a secular humanist tradition to which Jude aspires but which he also feels compelled to condemn; at the same time, she is connected in his mind with the essence of Christminster, which in the 1880s was still a stronghold of Anglican orthodoxy. The irony is compounded when she declaims, in terms that echo her self-description, "The mediaevalism of Christminster must go" (*JO* 204). "The implications of the symbolic association of city (intellectual promise) and Sue (sexual promise)," writes Annette Federico, "become expanded for Jude into the idea of world, of civilization itself, and woman as the representative of the more subliminal forces driving the social machinery. He identifies Sue, in particular, as a product of civilized, modern life, and her nervousness as a symptom of a general social neurosis."[53] If Federico is right, then Sue signals a pervasive crisis within modernity, but her nervousness—her "tight-strained nerves," her "quivering, tender nature" (*JO* 160–61)—is a symptom less of a general social crisis than of a personal failure to engage in self-cultivation. In this respect, Jude is well in advance of Sue, for he not only pursues Bildung, retaining much of his belief in "the patriarchal authority of ancient civilizations, the mentally balanced and male-defined worlds of Greece and Rome,"[54] but does so even when the odds are against him. By the time they are living together, he imagines Sue as a denizen of one of these worlds: "one of the women of some grand old civilization, whom I used to read about in my bygone, wasted, classical days" (*JO* 337). Not only does Sue not pursue Bildung, she is the *negation* of the "grand old civilization" that gave rise to Bildung as a cultural and personal ideal. Her gradual purging of everything associated with this ideal corresponds to a slow slide into moral hysteria; the "disembodied creature . . . tantalizing phantom" Jude had once imagined her to be, the desirable figure of pure ideality, ultimately becomes "such a mere cluster of nerves that all initiatory power seemed to have left her" (*JO* 309, 436). This is not the critical and liberatory depersonalization of modernism, which allows for the emergence of new subjectivities, but the utter annihilation of self, a gutting of inner culture in the interest of a morbid "mediaevalism," a remorse of conscience (like Joyce's "agenbite of inwit") with no hope for redemption. We see here an instance of Adorno's "bad" depersonalization, the destructive condition of bourgeois consciousness in which one experiences "a loss of identity for the sake of abstract identity, of naked self-preservation."[55]

Given that marriage symbolizes the acquisition and harmonious integration of cultural values at the heart of Bildung, it should come as no surprise that Jude tries so desperately to marry Sue. Nor should it come as a surprise that she, after her intellectual and moral about-face, should resist marrying him. Marriage is the last opportunity for Jude to acquire even the semblance of Bildung, while for Sue it is the height of hypocritical self-indulgence. That both characters are legally bound to other people who regard the bond as a more or less essential element of social life underscores the impossibility of their ever marrying each other and provides the narrative opportunities for discussion of the merits and demerits of marriage as a social institution. Much has been written about this aspect of Hardy's novel; it was, in fact, the main point of critical contention in the earliest reviews. In the wake of many famous divorce trials, not the least significant being the one involving Kitty O'Shea and Charles Stewart Parnell in 1890, Margaret Oliphant in an article entitled "The Anti-Marriage League" was quick to pick up on the salient point: *Jude the Obscure* "is intended as an assault on the stronghold of marriage, which is now beleaguered on every side. . . . the lesson the novelist would have us learn is, that if marriage were not exacted, and people were free to form connections as the spirit moves them, none of these complications would have occurred, and all would have been well."[56] Oliphant misses the point that Hardy is as skeptical of Jude and Sue's experiment in living—their unorthodox "project" of self-development—as he is of the loveless marriages that each has contracted with others. I would argue that under the conditions of late modernity, when social relations and positions had become fluid and unstable, traditions like marriage were increasingly difficult to justify or defend. Hardy recognized this and addressed the problem within a narrative context that emphasized the larger stakes: the integrity of personal Bildung under new institutional pressures.

In the context of Hardy's Bildungsroman, marriage is a symbol not of the harmonious development of inner culture and the ideal integration of the self with society but of the disharmony of loveless partnership and the disintegration of all meaningful social ties. This failure of symbolic legitimacy means that women serve not as instruments of the male protagonist's successful achievement of Bildung but as impediments to or distractions from it. On this view, Jude's Bildung is undermined from the very start, with his marriage to Arabella. Critics have made much of Arabella's sensuality, and opinion is fairly uniform on her importance in the novel as a contrast to the cerebral Sue. Daleski states the case for Arabella in a way that is both reductive and representative: "Arabella is an embodiment of female sexuality."[57] Certainly Arabella is a sensual young woman, and her sensuality and instinctiveness play an important role in Jude's Bildung plot. Peter Widdowson is one of the few critics willing to see beyond Arabella's "tarty, dimpled animalism" and to recognize that "it is her continual reappearances throughout the text which centrally drive the plot along, and also . . . that it is she who concludes it."[58] One of the ways that she accomplishes this is to determine the specific orientation of Jude's Bildung process. For example, by seducing and marrying him, she provides one of the key elements of Bildung while simultaneously undermining his successful achievement of it. In a famous passage, Jude, on the road home to Marygreen, mentally reviews what he has read and what remains to be read before he obtains his D.D. degree and the astronomical sum of five thousands pounds a year. He runs through the roster of classical figures he will study at Christminster, relishing the gravity of his aspiration toward Bildung: "Livy, Tacitus, Herodotus, Aeschylus, Sophocles, Aristophanes . . . Euripides, Plato Aristotle, Lucretius, Epictetus, Seneca, Antoninus." Interspersed in this roster are the taunting words of Arabella and her friends—"Hoity-toity!"—followed by the infamous pig's genitals, which Arabella flings at him to get his attention (*JO* 79–80).

Far from serving as a positive influence on Jude's education, far from drawing his attention to his own inner resources, Arabella instead derides his desire for knowledge and sets obstacles in his path to self-development. Jude realizes this, "faintly conscious that to common-sense there was something lacking, and still more obviously something redundant, in the nature of this girl . . . something in her quite antipathetic to that side of him which had been occupied with literary study and the magnificent Christminster dream" (*JO* 84). Arabella is not simply a young girl distracting a young man from his schoolwork. She engineers the first assault on his fantasy construction of Christminster, that "magnificent dream" that he sets up as the ideal of personal and social value. In this sense, her instrumentality is less a function of Jude's Bildung than of Hardy's critique of the social world in which he seeks it, for Hardy uses her, in Widdowson's estimation, "at once to caricature patriarchy and to distance the reader from the naturalized 'fiction' of male superiority and power."[59] The specific valence of that power, for Jude at least, is the discourse of Bildung and the humanistic and theological vocation that Christminster promises.

It is important to see Arabella's marriage to Jude as a significant event, not an accident of his youth or a mere caprice of hers. Simply put, Jude married her as part of a design over which he had no control, "as if materially, a compelling arm of extraordinary muscular power seized hold of him—something which had nothing in common with the spirits and influences that had moved him hitherto" (*JO* 87). He married because it was the "custom of the rural districts" to do so once one had "drifted so far into intimacy" (*JO* 102). As for Arabella, perhaps Lawrence was right to suggest that she may have played just the sort of instrumental role that the Bildungsroman tradition calls for: "She did a great deal for the true making of [Jude], for making him a grown man. . . . [She] brought him to himself, gave him himself, made him free, sound as a physical male."[60] This argument presupposes two things: that what Jude sought was quite different from the classical Bildung he long supposed was his aim, and that Arabella was acting from a position of strength and power. I will return to the first of these points below. As for the second, Lawrence gives Arabella full credit: "No barmaid marries anybody, the first man she can lay her hands on. She cannot. It must be a personal thing to her. And no ordinary woman would want Jude. Moreover, no ordinary woman could have laid her hands on Jude. . . . She needed a complement and the nearest thing to her satisfaction was Jude."[61] In his reading of Hardy, Lawrence tends to emphasize typology over specific characterization; but here quite the opposite is the case, for he attributes to a "mere" barmaid the kind of power and agency not typically accorded to Arabella, who is usually taken at Hardy's seemingly offhand estimation as a "female animal."

More problematic is Lawrence's assumption that Jude was after the freedom to be a sound "physical male." This conclusion, while not a misrepresentation of Jude's sexuality, nevertheless scants Hardy's clear emphasis, not to be overwritten by irony, on Jude's academic pursuits and his desire to forge an intellectual bond with Sue. With respect to the latter, Arabella plays a decisive role. "Structurally," according to James Harding, "Arabella resurfaces in and disrupts the center of Jude and Sue's relationship."[62] Jude's revelation to Sue of his marriage to Arabella inaugurates a long-running debate on marriage and its importance in their lives. Sue is indignant that Jude should be apart from his wife, in large part because he is "such a religious man." "Now if I had done such a thing," she tells him, "it would have been different, and not remarkable, for I at least don't regard marriage as a Sacrament. Your theories are not so advanced as your practice!" (*JO* 222). Following swiftly on the heels of this discussion are two important plot developments: the discovery that both have been told by family members that they are of "the wrong breed for marriage" (*JO* 224) and the news that Sue is going to marry Phillotson. Her marriage quickly becomes, as Lawrence strikingly puts it, "a submission, a service, a slavery"; in marrying him, she "consummated her own crucifixion."[63] Her remark to Jude, once she has left Phillotson, bears the hallmarks of an intellectual tradition of late Enlightenment thinkers like Humboldt and liberals like Mill: "I think I should begin to be afraid of you, Jude, the moment you had contracted to cherish me under a Government stamp, and I was licensed to be loved on the premises by you—Ugh, how horrible and sordid!" (*JO* 323). There is more going on here than a critique of state interference, however, for her reaction to Phillotson's and, by extension, Jude's desire for intimacy betrays her contradictory role in a society dominated by men. She claims the intellectual freedom to condemn marriage and divorce law, but she is caught in the undertow of the social and religious principles that underwrite both. Jil Larson describes well the double bind in which Sue is caught when she argues that *Jude the Obscure* "critiques the ideology of separate spheres and the double standards, even as it demonstrates that in their relationships with men women may appear powerful when they are actually at the mercy of inflexible patriarchal rules and ingrained assumptions about gender."[64]

Jude tries to resist such assumptions, but he cannot help thinking that women are responsible for derailing his Bildung process. "Strange that his aspiration—towards academical proficiency—had been checked by a woman, and that his second aspiration—towards apostleship—had also been checked by a woman. 'Is it,' he said, 'that the women are to blame; or is it the artificial system of things, under which the normal sex-impulses are turned into devilish domestic gins and springes to noose and hold back those who want to progress?'" (*JO* 279). Shortly after his realization that he has become "quite an imposter as a law-abiding religious teacher," he burns his books, thinking that in doing so he has ceased to be a hypocrite. "In his passion for Sue he could now stand as an ordinary sinner, and not as a whited sepulchre" (*JO* 279–80). He is half aware that he is rationalizing, that, like Philottson's, his aspirations have gone into a downward spiral, the difference being that his former mentor has made his peace with the failure of Bildung, while he seeks to create a negative form of it out of his own and Sue's despair. But despair is soon compounded by a form of emotional battery, as each torments the other with the impossibility of happiness. It is easy to see why Hardy chose "the letter killeth" as the epigraph for the novel and why he fastened on marriage as its "tragic machinery,"[65] for once Sue marries Phillotson, her relationship with Jude degenerates into a theoretical feud over the distinction between legal and spiritual marriage. Sue's critique of marriage laws, specifically the state's interference in the sphere of desire and temperament, is well made, but it is soon undermined by her fear that she and Jude have overstepped the bounds of morality by leading the state "into a false supposition" about the true state of their relations (*JO* 322). As William Davis notes, Hardy's characters seem to know a good deal about the law, "enough, at any rate, to engage in what appears to be collusion."[66] The fear that she and Jude are deceiving the state masks, but only temporarily, more troubling fears that she is deceiving God. Sue insists that Jude's marriage to Arabella is the proper one and that he should return to her (*JO* 425), but not because she feels that it signifies the harmony of his development. She is reacting in fact to the depressive atmosphere that has settled around her and Jude and that is symbolized by the figure of Father Time, Jude's son with Arabella, who echoes his father's youthful desire to "wish himself out of the world" when he laments, "It would be better to be out o' the world than in it" (*JO* 406). Sue's hysterical embrace of conformity is just another way of expressing this wish. Jude's attempt to hold out against such crushing despair—"Perhaps the world is not illuminated enough for such experiments as ours! Who were we, to think we could act as pioneers!"—is in turn crushed by Sue, who sees nothing but error in their life choices: "I slipped into my false position through jealousy and agitation" (*JO* 428).

After the death of her children, Sue returns to Phillotson, chastened and remorseful, but her suffering is ambiguous, as is her agreement finally to live with him as a wife in more than name. John Kucich notes that Sue's return and commitment to Phillotson "is compromised in its honesty not just by her own divided affections, but by the general return to middle-class respectability that she has chosen."[67] The danger is that she has come to embody not the freedom of knowledge and Christminster but the kind of pernicious interference that Humboldt warned against. Perhaps she figures forth an even darker truth, the return of what bourgeois secular freedom represses, an ancient force that purges her of all "initiatory power," the "religious fanaticism associated with hysteria or even insanity."[68] In the absence of a sense of self, of the kind of aspirations that have kept Jude focused on Christminster and then on Sue herself, self-development has been supplanted by a mere "enslavement to forms" (*JO* 482). Moreover, because she had become so profoundly associated with Jude's aspiration toward Bildung, because she had in fact displaced the original object of that aspiration, her self-annihilation must mean the annihilation of any hope that his aspiration would be fulfilled.

In a sense, though, Jude has been preparing all along for this eventuality. We can understand Arabella's continual reemergence in the narrative as evidence that he recognizes the importance of his marriage to her in terms of the overall design of his Bildung or, more accurately, of its negative nonidentical form. When Jude finds Arabella working as a barmaid in Christminster, he is made aware of the critical, even deconstructive, role she plays in his Bildung process. "Here was a rude flounce into the pellucid sentimentality of his sad attachment to Sue," he thinks to himself and then determines that he must "play a straightforward part, the law being the law," with this woman who is "in the eye of the Church one person with him" (*JO* 239). He self-consciously performs his duty to Arabella—despite her unapologetic admission of bigamy, she having remarried since leaving Jude—thereby constructing a fiction of the straightforward married man that ironically echoes his earlier realization that he was "quite an imposter as a law-abiding religious teacher." In both cases Jude's struggle to be true to his sense of himself, to the Bildung he wishes to attain, is couched in terms of an aesthetic form. Ian Gregor suggests as much when he argues that Jude's "remarriage with Arabella is a black parody of Sue's with Phillotson," one that "drives home his own personal tragedy" and "casts a harsh retrospective light on Sue."[69] That he is conscious that this form is dramatic and tending toward the deceptive does not lessen its utility in his self-development; indeed, the false role he plays as Arabella's husband, as I have indicated, proves instrumental in his pursuit of aesthetic harmony in his relationship with Sue.

Their discussions of marriage and the proper harmony that it should symbolize and sanction take place under the figurative shadow of Christminster, the "new Jerusalem" that Jude first espied from the roof of an old barn and that is later parodically reduced to Christminster cakes that he and Sue sell at the spring fair (*JO* 363, 382).[70]

The failure to be admitted to Christminster finds its negative compensations, as we have seen, in Jude's attempt to conduct an "experiment" in living with Sue (*JO* 428), an attempt to change human nature through self-mastery that resembles the "reflexive" project of the self that Anthony Giddens describes as a key feature of late modernity. The "enslavement to forms" that Jude condemns in Sue's return to Phillotson stands in diametric opposition to the aesthetic self-fashioning that Jude promotes. The tragedy, of course, is that Jude recognizes that form still enjoys its hegemony, for, as he tells Mrs. Edlin just before he dies, "Our ideas were fifty years too soon to be any good to us" (*JO* 482). It is a fitting irony that his confession is made to a woman for whom marriage was an accepted fact of life: "Matrimony have growed to be that serious in these days that one really do feel afeared to move in it at all. In my time we took it more careless" (*JO* 444). It is also fitting that he should end up with Arabella, the woman who encouraged, when she did not engineer, the repudiation of his high hopes for Bildung, dramatized in Jude's pub speech during Commemoration Day at Christminster, in which he rails against "social formulas" and presents himself as "a frightful example of what not to do . . . a paltry victim to the spirit of mental and social restlessness, that makes so many unhappy in these days!" Like his ideas about marriage, his ideas about educating the working classes are "untimely," for it would take "two or three generations to do what I tried to do in one" (*JO* 399, 398). His haranguing, like so much of his talk in the novel, is an attempt to use language to create the consistency that his life so tragically lacks. "Just as language is constituted through repetition," writes Ramón Saldívar, "so too does Jude's life acquire a narratable consistency. But the symbolic 'inscription' of Jude's desires upon the surface of Wessex as he travels its roads from Christminster to Shaston, to Albrickham and back again, constitutes only the provisional creation of meaning through a process of deferment. . . . It is always only in retrospect, however, that Jude's perceptions of those illusions of totality and stability can be organized and lived as an aesthetically coherent *meaning*."[71]

In a sense, Arabella creates the retrospective coherence that Jude so desperately seeks in his wanderings. Despite the downward spiral of his great expectations, Arabella returns and, in her own fashion, provides continuity and order for Jude's "chaos of principles" and his wayward pursuit of Bildung. Through her machinations, Jude becomes once again married, once again secured in the unhappy internal exile that has become his lot; the trajectory of the traditional Bildungsroman is short-circuited by this return and by his suicidal death march in the rain after seeing Sue one last time. Daleski's point that the "contrast between the ideal and real is . . . concretized throughout [the novel] in systematic frustration of all aspiration"[72] is nowhere more poignantly evident than in this deliberate negation of Bildung. For in his death design he not only achieves a kind of harmonious aesthetic apotheosis, "oddly swathed, pale as a monumental figure in alabaster" (*JO* 467), he also brings his Bildung plot back to its origins at the milestone from which he first espied Christminster, hard by "the spot where the gibbet of his ancestor and Sue's had stood" (*JO* 471).

Jude Fawley's attempt to transform aesthetic consciousness into some form of meaningful personal Bildung fails because he can transform neither himself nor the world around him. In the end, his wish to be "out of the world" is as much a mystification as the world itself. The tragedy of Jude's self-development calls into question both the prevailing regimes of socialization and the ideal of classical Bildung.[73] The harmonious unification of faculties and resources, the dialectical integration of inner culture with external society, that characterizes Goethean and Humboldtian Bildung and that Jude so passionately desires is finally unavailable to him—though it is, in a sense, available posthumously, in Hardy's ironic representation of Jude's "magnificent dream" of Bildung, a representation that succeeds not only in revealing the gap between Jude's "great expectations" and the reality of his social environment but in subjecting specific features of this environment (marriage and education) to a thoroughgoing critique. Lawrence takes this process a step further in *Sons and Lovers*, a novel that challenges the very foundations of the subject and subjectivity and offers more empowering strategies for negotiating the gap between classical Bildung and socialization, between the construction of inner culture and the "manufacture of viable and usable human beings."[74] If Jude Fawley could not rise to this challenge, Paul Morel, a generation later, seems more fitted to the task. It is to the narrative of his development that I now turn.

REALIZING THE SELF: LAWRENCE'S *SONS AND LOVERS*

In many ways, Lawrence's Bildungsroman is much closer to the classical tradition than Hardy's—or most other modernist's, for that matter. The trajectory of Paul Morel's development is well in line with the English tradition, despite the barrier thrown up by his coal town origins, and there is a strong emphasis on aesthetic education and marriage. What makes Lawrence's text unique, at least among early modernist exemplars, is its frank treatment of sexual desire and unorthodox intimate relationships and the critical role both play in Paul's development. This treatment has attracted the attention of many biographers, scholars, and critics, including Freudians and Lacanians, who seek to understand Lawrence's insights into human desire and the dynamics of human relationships and conversation. However, as we found with Hardy, there is relatively little critical material on Lawrence's Bildungsroman, though many critics mention either the Bildungsroman or the Künstlerroman in passing. Those who do treat the subject extensively are not interested in the generic issues I have been addressing or in the concept of Bildung. They tend to focus on the ways that *Sons and Lovers* fits into an English tradition of Bildungsromane and on the role of autobiography in the construction of Paul Morel's self-development.[75] Paul Sheehan is a notable exception to this general trend, in large measure because he focuses on Lawrence's antagonistic relation to the humanist tradition. Sheehan proceeds from a view of the form that sees it as ironized from the outset: "In the genre the hero's progress is ironised; he never finds what he sets out to find. Yet somehow, through circuitous rather than direct means, self-awareness is accomplished. . . . the mismatch between inner life and outer circumstance eventuates in the attainment of *Bildung*. In *Sons and Lovers* this both is and is not the case."[76] Social strife is countered by a conjunction of the soul with a deeper "mysterious source"; the two are "mutually harmonious, in synch with each other's inhuman authenticity."[77] This is a suggestive reading, but it tends to retain the very dialectical logic that underwrites humanist discourse and cancels any potential for an alternative to the "authenticity" of what Lawrence called "soul-sickness."[78] In other words, though Sheehan believes *Sons and Lovers* "is inimical to the *Bildungsroman*" form, his argument points us in a quite different direction: Lawrence's antihumanism ends up striking a harmonious note within a genre that has, albeit ironically, celebrated and given shape to the humanist ideal of Bildung. Still, Sheehan's reading is perceptive in its acknowledgment that Paul's Bildung is problematic and that the conclusion represents an "incipient apostasy,"[79] an ambivalent revolt, from the "essentialist" notions of subjectivity that Lawrence struggled against throughout his career.

One significant gauge of this struggle is the extent to which Lawrence's own essential "reality" has played a role in the interpretation of *Sons and Lovers*. This may be why generic readings are so often waylaid by biographical ones. There is certainly a vast amount of biographical material—Stanley Sultan claims that

Lawrence "appears to have been the subject of more biographical writing than any other English(-speaking) author of this century"[80]—and most criticism of *Sons and Lovers* makes reference at some point to it. Of special interest to the biographical critic are the remarks of Jessie Chambers, the woman on whom Lawrence based his character Miriam Leivers.[81] The relationship between author and protagonist, a relationship that has been the object of critical scrutiny since *Sons and Lovers* was first published, is neatly summed up by Michael Bell: "the equivocal relation between Paul and the author has two aspects. While the author undoubtedly has some self-vindicatory interest in Paul, Paul is at the same time the figure through whom Lawrence is struggling towards a more impersonal metaphysic of feeling and of narration."[82] Certainly this is what Scott Sanders has in mind when he suggests that Lawrence used the Bildungsroman form to work out his oedipal frustrations with his father: "for Lawrence the very act of writing a *Bildungsroman*—with its emphasis upon the development of consciousness in an isolated, artistic hero—divorced him from his father and his father's people."[83] In *Sons and Lovers* this interest in the family marks a significant generic development. The early chapters cover new ground for the Bildungsroman by narrating the social and familial preconditions of Paul's development, which is not conveyed in "complexity of action" but in an account of "the living conditions, parental attitudes, work and friendships which shape his character."[84] The personal relationships and subjectivity that Lawrence dramatizes constitute, according to Sanders, "a subjectivity permeated by social forces, which registers the stress of growing up within a working community that was being transformed by industry, the schools, and the awakening of social consciousness."[85]

At this point, we could not be farther from the pathways of classical Bildung. Critics like Sanders, influenced by Raymond Williams but lacking his depth of vision, miss that element of subjectivity that is *not* "permeated by social forces," that in fact struggles against just these forces. This is why we find so often an artist hero in the English Bildungsroman, and it is this artistic subjectivity that counts. The main point, then, is not that Lawrence may have transposed "raw" biographical material into his fiction, but that he used this material to create a new mode of representing artistic consciousness. In terms of the Bildungsroman tradition, the salient issue is not the biographical *fact* but the biographical *trope*.

Sultan's argument about Lawrence's "anti-autobiographical" style is an important one, for it corrects the critical tendency to privilege Lawrence's biography by showing, in a painstaking analysis of the early fiction, that he "subordinat[ed] self-presentation to a pragmatic concern with making effective art."[86] By the "radical transmuting of his life experience," Lawrence was able to get around the problem that arises in most realist fiction, especially the Bildungsroman: the problem of the sovereign and autonomous bourgeois subject who stands in opposition to the external world, seeking unity and self-identity in his battle with it. In a well-known letter to Edward Garnett, Lawrence made explicit his rejection of this sort of subject and his intention as a writer to "depersonalize" the characters in his novels: "that which is physic—non-human, in humanity, is more interesting to me than the old-fashioned human element—which causes one to conceive a character in a certain moral scheme and make him consistent. . . . You mustn't look in my novel for the old stable ego of the character. There is another ego, according to whose action the individual is unrecognisable."[87] Lawrence's target here is not so much the Freudian ego, though he did have his disagreements with Freudian conceptions, but the characters in realist fiction, which purport to represent human beings in all of their psychological variety and depth and in recognizable social relationships. This is not to say that a novel like *Sons and Lovers* breaks with realism, for it does not, or at least not in any decisive way.[88] What I think Lawrence insists on is jettisoning realistic characterization in favor of a new mode of *realization* by which an "other ego" can be discerned, both by other characters and by the reader. By attacking realism, of course, Lawrence is attacking the very notion of the subject as it came down to him from the dualistic tradition of Descartes and Locke, a tradition that equates being with consciousness and opposes consciousness to the external world, a tradition that came to a glorious peak in the late eighteenth century. It is ironic, therefore, that Lawrence's first concerted attack on this conception of the subject should be launched in a Bildungsroman, the genre that, in its classical form, preeminently celebrates the traditional notion of the sovereign and autonomous subject. We have here another instance of modernism's radical conservatism: if *Sons and Lovers*, like *Jude the Obscure* and other modernist exemplars, hews to the narrative conventions of the classical Bildungsroman, it does so in order to represent, with the same kind of narrative irony that we find in Hardy, the struggling emergence of a new form of subjectivity. Lawrence captures the oscillation between an outmoded conception of the stable ego and a new "unrecognizable" alternative to it, a reflexive project of the self, as Giddens puts it, that opens consciousness to new determinations but also bewilders it with the choices and conflicts entailed in the acquisition of selfhood.[89] It is just this oscillation that defines the narrative dynamics of Lawrence's modernist Bildungsroman, which, like Hardy's, depicts the subject's turn toward nonidentity within a genre that has traditionally narrated the triumph of self-identity.

The quality of *Sons and Lovers* to which many readers react in regard to Paul's identity—his intensity and his unrelenting quest to find a woman who will *realize* him—can be understood as the effect of a modernist strategy of depersonalization. I do not mean the "bad" depersonalization of which Adorno speaks and which can be described in terms of a dialectics of alienation in an industrial environment, the "instrumentalization of human beings and the mechanization of personal relationships."[90] Indeed, it is this very mode of alienation that Lawrence's modernist depersonalization seeks to remedy by seeking a mode of self-development that emphasizes artistic cultivation and realization of the self instead of the alienated dialectics of a mechanized social world. What Paul seeks is not an identity in harmony with the conventional surface of things in his hometown but rather something more enduring and more authentic, *more true*. Lawrence's fiction tends to showcase such moments; on this score, *Sons and Lovers* does not disappoint. In a long discussion with Miriam, his friend and first love, Paul tries to get across his sense of the reality of things, their vital and essential being. He uses the image of the "shimmering protoplasm": "Only this shimmeriness is the real living," he tells her. "The shape is a dead crust. The shimmer is inside, really" (*SL* 183).[91] Inner culture is scandalous and hidden away in the protoplasmic unconscious; it develops and bears fruit outside the limits of legitimate knowledge, outside the predictable circuits of dialectical harmony. It is, in a word, illegitimate. However, to speak of legitimacy and essentiality with reference to Lawrence's work is always problematic, for images like the "shimmering protoplasm" (or the blood references in *Women in Love*) can be read, quite legitimately, as symbols of spiritualized nature, of a Wordsworthian concordance of the material and the divine. But they may also call to mind the idea of the sign cut off from its legitimate context, free to create for itself a new repertoire of associations and meanings. Anne Fernihough argues that Lawrence wants it both ways: he wants art to be the embodiment of absolute truth, but he cannot resist a mode of artistic expression in which "the symbolic or organic empties the artifact of any such (transcendent) meaning."[92] Fernihough specifically links Lawrence's nondualistic conception of being to Adorno's antiessentialist notions of the subject.[93] Like Adorno, Lawrence did not approve of totalistic thinking. According to Fernihough, "They both repudiate instrumental reason in so far as it is, in their view, based on a totalitarian identity principle which reduces phenomena to its own pattern."[94] In *Sons and Lovers*, Paul is fascinated by certain aspects of industrial design and operation, but he resists the temptation to let his own subjectivity become instrumentalized. Everyone around him knows he will not last long at the factory where he lands his first job. Indeed, it is ironic that in the masculine space of industrial technology, where the blunt leading edge of dialectical thinking meets the materiality of nature, Paul discovers his susceptibility to the instrumentality of women who prepare the way and sometimes guide him on his upward path to social power. It is a further irony that the very "shimmering protoplasm" that Paul promotes in his talks with Miriam becomes strongly associated both with her and with the "unconscious self" or "great force" of a totalizing nature that he fears will annihilate his conscious identity. His fear is not ill placed, for the young artist-hero, confident that he can realize the essence of his being with the aid of women who will help him along his path toward Bildung, comes up against the intransigence of these same women, their unwillingness to be subjected to an identitarian logic in which their own nonidentity, their ineluctable otherness, is subsumed in the dialectical totality of male Bildung.

The first and, for some readers, the most important woman in Paul's life is his mother, Gertrude, who performs an instrumental function that is sustained in his relationships with Miriam and Clara.[95] One of the innovations of *Sons and Lovers*, when considered from the standpoint of the Bildungsroman, is that it presents the relationship between Paul and his mother *before* he is born and during his infancy. This prehistory of Bildung is dramatically symbolized in the famous scene in which Gertrude is locked outside by Walter, her drunken husband. She realizes that the "tall white lilies . . . reeling in the moonlight" have "penetrated her consciousness," their perfume charging the air with presence. Her consciousness in turn penetrates the unborn child she carries and breaks down the boundaries that separate consciousness from the object world. "After a time, the child too melted with her in the mixing-pot of moonlight, and she rested with the hills and lilies and houses, all swum together in a kind of swoon" (*SL* 34). Though Gertrude, melted into the "mysterious out-of-doors," forgets him for the moment, Walter hovers on the margins of this scene, drunkenly dozing in the locked house, transformed into the opposite of what Gertrude has become: he is totally objectified in his inert oblivion. Gertrude's "swooning" out of consciousness is not a renunciation of her selfhood so much as a confirmation that self and world are inextricably connected in a complex negotiation of being with the world that refuses both dialectical sublation and undifferentiated oneness.[96] For Gertrude recovers from this brief liminal moment and returns to the life of her family. As Michael Bell writes, "it is abundantly evident that Mrs. Morel's moment of oceanic swooning . . . is not a value in itself nor in any way the culmination of the emotional process." The scene thus stands as "a paradigm for more complex, and hence potentially misreadable, experiences elsewhere."[97] Regardless of its paradigmatic status, this scene is an especially fruitful starting point for considering Paul's Bildung process, which is characterized by a similar desire for an intense consciousness of the self *and* what lies beyond it as well as by a similar understanding that these two modes of being in the world need not cancel each other out in a dialectics of self-identity that defines the "incomplete emancipation" of bourgeois consciousness.[98]

Sons and Lovers, perhaps more than any other modernist Bildungsroman, situates oedipal desire in a matrix of relationships that Patricia Alden calls "sexual Bildung." According to Alden, "sex affords [Lawrence's] characters a way of attaining a full experience of individuality without costly estrangement, guilt, self-betrayal, or disillusionment." Sex functions as "a private resolution of conflicting ideologies."[99] The sexualized nature of the relationship between Paul and his mother can thus be understood as an early, formative stage in the construction of an emphatically sexual identity. At first, Gertrude's lack of love for her husband sways her to wish that Paul had not been born. This does not contradict the scene in the garden, for at that moment of "swooning," it is *her* consciousness in the child. The person-to-be, Paul Morel, is not yet a consciousness in its own right.[100] It would be merely sentimental to call "it" a "person" or this swooning feeling "love," for Gertrude's experience signifies something more important and encompassing: an understanding of and connection to an unconscious force that penetrates individual consciousness and makes it possible to experience that which exists but which is not yet in being. Lawrence, with brilliant and uncharacteristic understatement, undercuts the sentimental belief in a "stable ego" and subject of Bildung that we might be tempted to imagine already occupies Gertrude's womb. Her lack of any consciousness of a subject as such may account for her later resolution that "she would make up to it for having brought it into the world unloved. She would love it all the more now it was here, carry it in her love" (*SL* 51). The repetition of the neuter, objectivizing pronoun "it" emphasizes Gertrude's inability to conceive of the "consciousness in her child" as something that belongs to another being. It is *her* consciousness that penetrates *it*. Her belief that to her sons she was "behind them as motor force, when they grew up" (*SL* 44), can be understood as the habitual form that Gertrude's "swooning" comes to take.

She shares in their lives because in a genuine way hers has become inextricably connected with theirs below the level of conscious discernment and articulation.

There are numerous indications of this connectedness in the first part of the novel, the most famous and emblematic of which is the scene in which Gertrude, holding the infant Paul, is injured by a drawer her husband has hurled in drunken anger. "He was turning drearily away, when he saw a drop of blood fall from the averted wound into the baby's fragile, glistening hair. Fascinated, he watched the heavy dark drop hang in the glistening cloud, and pull down the gossamer. Another drop fell. It would soak through to the baby's scalp. He watched fascinated, feeling it soak in. Then, finally, his manhood broke" (*SL* 54–55). It is an important moment for Gertrude, for it marks the end of her passion for her husband and of his authority over her and her children. It is an even more important moment for Paul, because it brings to bear on his infant consciousness not only the castrating violence of the father but also the integrative blood bond with the mother. Despite these early moments of intense bonding with Paul, the early chapters are concerned primarily with Gertrude's attachment to William, her first child, whose story reduplicates the tragic Bildung process that we see in *Jude the Obscure* and *Howards End*, but without the emphasis on aesthetic education. It is a finely wrought miniature of the socially pragmatic form of Bildung that had become the norm in social and cultural narratives of formation in the period extending from the early nineteenth century to at least the 1920s. William is very ambitious, beginning work as a teacher in a night school (*SL* 70) and then heading off to London to be a clerk, the destiny of so many children of working-class families who had few other options for social mobility. His mother encourages his ambition, ever anxious for him "to develop and to bring to fruit all that she had put into him. In him, she wanted to see her life's fruition, that was all" (*SL* 77). William proves to be something of a disappointment to her, however. She is especially unhappy with his fiancée Gyp, whose elegant full name, Louisa Lily Denys Western, and pretentious behavior belie her social status as "a sort of secretary, or clerk, in a London office" (*SL* 147). Gyp is the female counterpart to William, for by the turn of the century young women were increasingly finding their way into the workforce, filling positions that would hitherto be filled by men. William defends her frivolity and spendthrift habits, but he is himself ambivalent. "Only his mother could help him now. And yet, he would not let her decide for him. He stuck to what he had done" (*SL* 162). In very short order, he succumbs to the pressures of working in London and keeping up with his fiancée, becomes fatally ill, and dies in a "dreadful paroxysm" (*SL* 166). Like Jude and Leonard Bast, William's ambition is outstripped by social conditions for which he has not been adequately prepared. Though Gyp's desires and aspirations are less cultured than, say, Sue Bridehead's or Helen Schlegel's, she nevertheless represents, in a distorted and vulgar fashion, the cultural ideal to which William aspires. In the end, however, his aspirations are not the main point; at best, he serves as a kind of object lesson to Paul and his mother about the dangers of not matching aspirations with character and ability. Lawrence drives the point home when Paul falls into a near-fatal fever after his brother's death. This is the event that allows him to "realise" his mother: "His whole will rose up and arrested him. He put his head on her breast, and took ease of her, for love." For her part, Gertrude's life "now rooted itself in Paul" and the "two knitted together in perfect intimacy" (*SL* 171).

When Paul turns fourteen, Gertrude asks the key question: "What do you want to be?" (*SL* 113). He has not got the slightest idea, so it is not surprising that his ambitions are at first determined by his relationship with his mother, who becomes the first woman to play an instrumental function in his Bildung process: "His ambition, as far as this world's gear went, was quietly to earn his thirty or thirty-five shillings a week, somewhere near home, and then, when his father died, have a cottage with his mother, paint and go out as he liked, and live happy ever after" (*SL* 114). His complacent daydream of petit bourgeois respectability—the conventional mode of advancement for men of his class, from the rural working class to the lower middle class of "service" workers—about which he has little real knowledge at this point in his life, is couched in the fantastic language of the family romance in which the love-besotted son rescues his mother from his father and lives "happy ever after."[101] The family romance is Paul's early attempt to work through his oedipal desires and to begin forming his own conception of personal Bildung, which at this early stage is conceived primarily in terms of the freedom to *take his father's place* with his beloved mother. When he and his mother make the trip to Thomas Jordan and Son, Surgical Appliances, in Nottingham, they "walked down Station Street, feeling the excitement of lovers having an adventure together" (*SL* 118). However, this fantasy is short-lived. Even before he gets the job at Jordan's, he feels himself a "prisoner of industrialism ... taken into bondage" (*SL* 114–15). After the summons from Jordan, "he seemed to feel the business world, with its regulated system of values, and its impersonality, and he dreaded it. It seemed monstrous also that a business could be run on wooden legs" (*SL* 117). At first he resists the world of commerce, finding Jordan's "an insanitary ancient place" (*SL* 128), but he soon feels at home, especially among the women workers, who appreciate his sensitive, artistic nature (*SL* 135, 138). He comes home to his mother just as a husband would, thus substituting, with his emotional and financial fidelity, for his improvident father. Paul's Bildung intertwines with his mother's displaced desire, a process that Lawrence captures in an exquisite image that exoticizes Paul's life even as it brings it down to the level of drab mundanity: "His life-story, like an *Arabian Nights*, but much duller, was told night after night to his mother. It was almost as if it were her own life" (*SL* 140).

Soon the pattern is set. "Mrs. Morel clung now to Paul. He was quiet and not brilliant. But still he stuck to his painting, and still he stuck to his mother. Everything he did, was for her. She waited for his coming home in the evening, and then she unburdened herself of all she had pondered or of all that had occurred to her during the day. He sat and listened with his earnestness. The two shared lives" (*SL* 142). Until he begins to see Miriam as a love object that would replace his emotional attachment to his mother, Paul effectively displaces his father in his mother's life. The relationship sustains Gertrude even as it begins to draw Paul closer to a sense of his own artistic abilities and aspirations. Though she is not quite conscious of it, she is preparing her son for his foray into the world, always aware of what she perceives as her failure to save William from his own tragic life choices. Alden believes that Gertrude's oedipal relationship with Paul proves instrumental in a quite unintended way: "the story of oedipal attachment does not so much replace the story of upward mobility as repeat its problematic in a different register. . . . [It] is intimately related to the story of upward mobility, for it is mother who both dreams of individuation and pushes her sons up and away in order to realize that dream."[102] What Alden slights in her reading is the role that such attachments play in Paul's aesthetic education and the way that he is able to transfer them in a relatively seamless fashion onto Miriam. The point at which Paul begins to turn from his mother to Miriam is precisely the point at which he "was just opening out from childhood into manhood" (*SL* 177). Once he begins to show interest in Miriam, he must appease his mother, continually reminding her of her singular importance in his life and art. "I can do my best things when you sit there in your rocking-chair," he tells her, and he means it, deriving from her a "warmth inside him like strength" (*SL* 190). What Miriam can provide is the assistance Paul requires in achieving the *conscious* apotheosis of his feelings, a burgeoning, as Calvin Bedient remarks, "of psychology into metaphysics."[103] In order to understand the vital significance of what he accomplishes as an artist, he will have to turn to another, to Miriam (later Clara), who grasps not only his "soul's intensity" but also its metaphysical nature and its significance for his aesthetic education.

Much of part 2 is taken up with dramatizing the roles of Miriam and Clara, who further Paul's artistic self-development and tutor him in the ways of women and sexuality. They are crucial to the development of his "[s]exual and aesthetic Bildung" (which Sheehan links to the process of "soul formation") because they perform the instrumental function of defining self-identity through a conventional dialectical negation (not to be confused with "negative dialectics"). This function is central to the classic Bildungsroman, as it is to the humanist tradition generally, a tradition in which, according to Sheehan, "women are recruited for their otherness, then 'colonised' in order to maintain the sameness of the (male) subject."[104] In *Sons and Lovers*, as in *Jude the Obscure*, we find a set of contrasting female helpmates, one abstract and sexless, the other vital and sexual.[105] This opposition is complicated, of course, by the dominant role played by Paul's mother, who is, in his experience, the first and principal sign of culture. Miriam is perhaps an inevitable first choice for Paul, because her desire to learn and be cultured reduplicates his mother's. "She could not be princess by wealth or standing. So, she was mad to have learning whereon to pride herself. For she was different from other folk, and must not be scooped up among the common fry" (*SL* 174). For Miriam, the desire to play the role of helpmate for Paul is linked to her desire to express her love for him: "If she could be mistress of him in his weakness, take care of him, if he could depend on her, if she could, as it were, have him in her arms, how she would love him!" (*SL* 174). The instrumental function she plays is crucial. She provides the emotional and intellectual stimulation that Paul requires to advance in his art. To some extent, she serves as a mentor as well as a helpmate. As Holderness argues, Miriam's idealism, her transcendent nature, "answers to Paul's original preconceptions" about women and art.[106] He gravitates toward her and soon finds her as necessary to his art as his mother still proved to be. "He was conscious only when stimulated. A sketch finished, he always wanted to take it to Miriam. Then he was stimulated into knowledge of the work he had produced unconsciously. In contact with Miriam, he gained insight, his vision went deeper" (*SL* 190). The break with his mother becomes palpable after this point. Lawrence recognized the oedipal dynamic in these scenes and claimed that *Sons and Lovers* was an attempt to dramatize the "soul-sickness" that strikes "thousands of young men in England": the overweening and oppressive quality of a mother's love for her son.[107] Paul's turn to Miriam, however, only partially accomplishes the task of breaking with his mother, for he comes to realize that she too wishes to possess him in an absolute way, that her self-sacrificing nature is in fact an assertion of her own desire in the guise of an abject surrender. Her mystical and religious urge toward sacrifice contaminates desire with shame: "there was a serpent in her Eden. She searched earnestly in herself to see if she wanted Paul Morel. She felt there would be some disgrace in it. Full of twisted feeling, she was afraid she did want him. She stood selfconvicted. . . . She felt as if her whole soul coiled into knots of shame." The "rapture of self-sacrifice" into which she falls on the heels of her shame, the desire to love Paul "as Christ would, who died for the souls of men" (*SL* 208), is reminiscent of the similar desire of Sue Bridehead for Jude Fawley. Unlike Jude, however, Paul does not misread Miriam's abstract and ethereal nature as a form of subdued passion; he regards their intimacy, with some regret, as "abstract, such a matter of the soul, all thought and weary struggle into consciousness" (*SL* 209). He longs for sexual experience, but he seems willing only to offer an intimate intellectual friendship.

What Paul does not see, blinded by his own need to discover himself mirrored in her, is that the abstraction he abhors is exactly what he fears about himself. He feels his soul "drawn out" toward Willey Farm, and he resists it, but he is nevertheless unable to avoid Miriam's vampiric power. "All his strength and energy she drew into herself through some channel which united them." In a druglike state, he feels an "intensity like madness" and finds himself discoursing with her, as is his wont. She feels the "deepest satisfaction" at these times, "fingering the very quivering tissue, the very protoplasm of life" (*SL* 232). This protoplasm, like the earlier shimmering variety, is linked to the "unconscious self" that Lawrence wished to *realize* in fiction, as opposed to the lifeless "stable ego" of realism. It is the opposite of what he saw happening in *Jude the Obscure*, in which Jude's consciousness is fed from his senses, a "continuous state of incandescence of the consciousness, when his body, his vital tissue, the very protoplasm in him, was being slowly consumed away."[108] For Lawrence, consciousness represents the true state of abstraction. "Man's consciousness, that is, his mind, his knowing, is his grosser manifestation of individuality. With his consciousness he can perceive and know that which is not himself." At its highest level, consciousness is the Absolute, a state of "perfect frictionless interaction." The greater the level of consciousness, the greater the sense of individual distinctness, of being separate from what one is not, which is what Paul desires and what proves fatal to Jude. At the outer limits of consciousness lies everything that, for Paul at least, Miriam represents, "that which is not conscious, which is Time, and Life, that is our field."[109]

It is clear that Paul has mistaken for abstraction in Miriam precisely her affiliation with the unconscious and, because he is linked "through some channel" to her, *his* affiliation with it as well. He tells her that her "unconscious self" always bids him to talk to her, to reveal the quivering protoplasm, and that he "supposes" he wants it too. In a portion of the text that was deleted by Edward Garnett from the first edition, Paul implicates himself in the very abstract unconscious that he decries: "you always do it," he tells her. "You switch me off somewhere, and project me out of myself. I am quite ghostish, disembodied. . . . A sort of disseminated consciousness" (*SL* 232). In these lines Paul articulates the Lawrentian idea of the unconscious as a natural force outside the scope of human understanding. According to Cynthia Lewiecki-Wilson, Lawrence's conception is quite different from Freud's, who saw the unconscious as a function of the psychic apparatus which expressed itself in both mental and somatic processes. For Lawrence, the unconscious pertains to "what is essentially inarticulate and nonconceptual knowledge repressed by culture." It is "material and biological; that is . . . a force outside of the subjectivity of individuals," a "source of creativity from which precognitive experience of the world provided an 'uncerebral' but rational 'form of knowledge.'"[110] This is what Paul attempts to explain to Miriam, who he thinks wants only to "fix [his] soul well in its sheath" (*SL* 233). What he is attempting to explain is what Dorothy Van Ghent calls "terminal individuality—the absolute 'otherness' or 'outsideness'—that is the natural form of things and of the uncorrupted person." It is this same terminal condition that afflicted his mother in the famous garden scene, "a typifying instance of the spontaneous identification Lawrence constantly found between image and meaning, between real things and what they symbolize."[111] By Paul's own logic, then, Miriam has no control over this paradoxically "other" individuating power, since, as he tells her, "you are what your unconscious self makes you, not so much what you want to be" (*SL* 233). Now, it seems to me that Paul, like Lawrence, wants it both ways. On the one hand, he wants to ascribe to Miriam an intention of which she is unaware, so that her desire to "sheath" his soul in hers would appear to be the work of what Sheehan calls "the cosmic will, Lawrence's soul-source coupling,"[112] not her own conscious desire. On the other hand, Paul wants to arrogate to himself the ability to *want to do* what she cannot. "We're neither of us quite normal—" he tells her, "but now I want to be, and I don't think you do" (*SL* 233). His desire must trump hers, otherwise he would have to admit that he is no less abstract than she is and that she, by the same token, is potentially no less sensual than he is. What stymies him is the inability to go the next step to physical intimacy. No wonder he feels fearful of his own "ghostishness." In other words, Miriam seeks to be instrumental against his wishes by taking him where he does not know that he wants to go (or *must* go) to be an artist. On this view, Paul would have to surrender any desire for the absoluteness of consciousness and affirm, embrace even, the disembodiment and dissemination of the conscious self. The philosophical gambit by which he means to demonstrate her unlikeness to him ends up threatening to collapse the difference between them in a radical and irreparable fashion. In other words, nonidentity threatens to overwhelm identity.

While Miriam plays an important role in the development of Paul's aesthetic education as well as in the formation of his artistic style, it becomes increasingly unclear whether she serves *only* an instrumental function and whether Paul is the only one whose Bildung process is furthered by it. For in *Sons and Lovers* the flow of pedagogical power is reciprocal, and this reciprocity signals the duplicity of Lawrence's modernist Bildungsroman, which harbors an inadvertent counterdiscourse of female development. We notice this counterdiscourse despite the sense of shame that Miriam feels in her mood of self-sacrifice and her continued willingness to be a spiritual helpmate for Paul. "Miriam was the threshing floor on which he threshed out all his beliefs. While he trampled his ideas upon her soul, the truth came out for him. She alone was his threshing floor. She alone helped him towards realisation. Almost impassive, she submitted to his argument and expounding. And somehow, because of her, he gradually realised where he was wrong. And what he realised, she realised. She felt he could not do without her" (*SL* 267). To some degree, she forces Paul to "justify himself," as when he reveals his inclination to pursue commercial design, "decorating stuffs, and . . . embroidery." He is drawn to this kind of work and tells Miriam that he has got "a passion for conventionalising things just now." Miriam, who "did not care for conventional studies," nevertheless wants to know why he would be so fascinated with the applied arts (*SL* 240). This leads him to explain the complexities of "correct geometrical line and proportion," which she ultimately comes to understand as something more than a "mere lie" to her. "There was for him the most intense pleasure in talking about his work to Miriam. All his passion, all his wild blood went into this intercourse with her, when he talked and conceived his work. She brought forth to him his imaginations. She did not understand, any more than a woman understands when she conceives a child in her womb" (*SL* 240–41). This last sentence is belied by the quite conscious efforts that Miriam takes to understand his methods and motives. That she remains unconscious of her instrumentality is perhaps a function of Paul's artistic vanity, his desire not to share the imaginative process of which she is, in fact, very much a part. Scenes like this remind the reader that the distinction between mentor and instrumental woman, which is typically clear cut in the classical Bildungsroman, is blurred in Lawrence's as it is in Hardy's. So while it is true that Paul "could not do without her," one is tempted to add that she could not do without him, for as Lawrence indicates here, Miriam is realizing the same things as Paul. Though Miriam appears principally to *react* to Paul's desire to educate her in an effort to make her instrumental to his own development, her desire to learn and to cultivate herself is as much a matter of her own willfulness.

Education thus plays a decisive role in *Sons and Lovers*, but not in the sense of representing the experiences of formal training. Formal education is available to the Morel children—Paul receives a scholarship to Nottingham High School (*SL* 78), while William goes on to teach at the night school (*SL* 70) and Annie enters the Board School (*SL* 142)—but these experiences are depicted parenthetically and do not contribute significantly to the general structure of the plot. Jerome Buckley is right, therefore, to conclude that *Sons and Lovers* is a "novel of 'education' only in the broad sense of the word" and that, "like other Bildungsromane, [it] lays much stress on the educative results of emotional experience."[113] Peter Scheckner, for his part, may also be right that characters like Paul and Miriam "attach a great value to education and culture as the means whereby they may escape the horrors of industrial drudgery."[114] However, such a motivation would entrap Lawrence's characters in an unforgiving dialectic of freedom and necessity in which freedom would always be contested and, for that reason, reduced to a mere negative state. I submit that the specific details of Paul's self-development suggest another motivation. It is an important fact that Paul comes to understand and even admire workingmen like his father and Baxter Dawes and learns to appreciate the beauty of the industrialized landscape in which their lives have been shaped. As Paul sketches the "great pit-hill," Gertrude notes that the world "is a wonderful place . . . and wonderfully beautiful." Her son responds, "And so's the pit. . . . Look how it heaps together, like something alive, almost—a big creature that you don't know" (*SL* 152). The men who work in this landscape acquire a new significance for the developing artist, one that contrasts dramatically with the hatred and shame he earlier felt for his father and the other miners (see *SL* 85, 96). "I like the feel of *men* on things, while they're alive. There's a feel of men about trucks, because they've been handled with men's hands, all of them" (*SL* 152). Paul's pursuit of Bildung cannot be grasped in terms of a materialist reading like Scheckner's, which is concerned only with "Lawrence's fluctuating attitudes toward the significance of social class as a determinant of individual development."[115] It is important to understand that Paul and Miriam turn to education and culture to escape the limitations of their own being and the kinds of options for self-development that the world offers them—and not just in Bestwood, but in London as well, as William Morel's brief tragic experience teaches them. They seek not merely to escape "industrial drudgery" but to avoid the incomplete freedom that defines and delimits the "stable ego." "In the shadow of its own incomplete emancipation," writes Adorno, "the bourgeois consciousness must fear to be annulled by a more advanced consciousness; not being the whole freedom, it senses that it can produce only a caricature of freedom—hence its theoretical expansion of its autonomy into a system similar to its own coercive mechanisms."[116] It is to prevent this fall into caricature that Lawrence represents, with almost surgical precision, Paul's relationships with Miriam and Clara, for they propel him down paths that challenge bourgeois consciousness more compellingly than would any mere repudiation of industrial horrors.

Because they imply a two-way dynamic of knowledge and education, the pedagogical thematics in Lawrence's Bildungsroman—both the informal discussions in which Paul teaches Miriam the secrets of the unconscious self and aesthetic beauty and the more formal lessons during which he teaches her French or guides her reading—deconstruct the instrumental function that Miriam is supposed to play for Paul's Bildung process by suggesting that she is less a mere helpmate than an equal who desires the same goal of self-cultivation. For Miriam, education is an "avenue of self-development and also a way of maintaining social distance: an escape and a barrier."[117] The education she gets through Paul is part of her bid for freedom, and so she requires him every bit as much as he requires her. This pedagogical desire and its demands are displaced onto Miriam's relation to nature, the perfection of which seems to require Paul's presence. When she takes him to "a certain wild-rose bush," she recognizes that he is an essential part of her experience: "till he had seen it, she felt it had not come into her soul. Only he could make it her own, immortal" (*SL* 195).[118] Passages like this one are often read as evidence of Miriam's passivity, her demoralizing subordination to the male artist's will. But do we not see here also a desire on the young woman's part to subjugate that will, to make it do *her* bidding by helping her to make the world "her own"?

To be sure, Miriam is a self-sacrificing young woman, hopelessly in love with a man who does not return that love in the same manner. He can only offer her friendship: "it's all I'm capable of—" he tells her, "it's a flaw in my makeup.—The thing overbalances to one side" (*SL* 260). But this does not prevent her from developing her own inner culture. She may be, as Sanders describes her, an "educated Cinderella," but even so, she "resents serving as drudge to her farming menfolk; like Paul she yearns to escape by the one means available to her—her mind."[119] Though she may, in time-honored fashion, serve as a help-mate to Paul, she also turns the tables and forces him to help her. Nor is this strategy a quietly subversive one, in which Miriam, like the helpless heroine of a Victorian novel, must use the weapons of mild deceit and manipulation in order to gain a measure of freedom. She is strong-willed enough to know what she wants and expresses herself accordingly. Her intransigence lies in her refusal to be "scooped up among the common fry." She wants the freedom to act: "I want to do something. I want a chance like anybody else. Why should I, because I'm a girl, be kept at home and not allowed to be anything. What chance *have* I?" (*SL* 185). She differs from women like Sue Bridehead and Clara Dawson in her belief that she can attain this freedom to act through the peda-gogical "soul communion" that she feels with a man. Indeed, she appears to be somewhat ahead of the game, in terms of what she wants for herself, for her statement "I want to do something," with its ringing tone of self-assur-ance, contrasts dramatically with Paul's cluelessness when his mother asks him, "What do you want to be?" (*SL* 113). Paul, of course, does not remain so jejune in his ambitions, but the point is that he is not alone in the struggle toward self-cultivation. In fact, one of the reasons he finds Miriam so charming is that "she was not held by conventions" and that with her "the inner life counted for everything, the outer for nothing" (*SL* 192). In many scenes, we discern in Miriam a radical aspiration toward something like Humboldtian Bildung, which is not as easy for Paul to desire, for he distrusts the inner life insofar as he associates it with undifferentiated unconsciousness in which his sense of self is lost or "sheathed" within or by another's. He strives not for unconscious-ness but for the bright singular consciousness of the artist who has succeeded in delimiting all that is not himself, a familiar preference for the modernist *Bildungsheld*. Over against Miriam's "inner life" is Paul's belief that "What we are inside makes us so that we ought to go one particular way, and no other" (*SL* 193). Where we expect to find a manifestation of the aesthetically fungible, self-sufficient inner culture of Humboldt, we find instead the "lawlike develop-ment" that Dilthey theorizes out of the more philosophically rigorous logic of Hegel. It is to Miriam's credit that she rises above Paul's ignorance of "her soul's history" (*SL* 246)—indeed, she insists upon that history even in the depths of her despair over her pointless self-sacrifice in the name of love. While she succumbs to her love for Paul and seeks only to serve him, we get a sense in this novel, more than in other modernist Bildungsromane, that the helpmate can achieve Bildung for herself. Michael Bell's query, "Is there not a suppressed Miriam voice whose story represents a crucial part of the truth about Paul?"[120] suggests that there is a vital but incompletely articulated role for Miriam to play. That she rebels and seeks her own Bildung does not preclude her continued desire to be with Paul and to serve as his helpmate. To the end, she feels the "anguished sweetness of self-sacrifice," but the feeling is only temporary, the reaction of someone whose strategy has failed. She will wait, she thinks. "When he had had enough, he would give in, and come to her" (*SL* 462–63).[121]

Miriam is not the only woman whose experience reverses the dynamics of instrumentality found in the classical Bildungsroman. Clearly Gertrude Morel is empowered by her oedipal relations with her sons. "She frankly *wanted* [Paul] to climb into the middle classes, a thing not very difficult, she knew. And she wanted him in the end to marry a lady" (*SL* 299). Though she may have believed such upward mobility to be possible for her sons, that knowledge did not prevent her own slow slide into the genteel working-class poverty that the novel describes. As we have seen, William's development is, in a sense, her "life's fruition"; his success represents "all that she had put into him" (*SL* 77). As for Paul, she shared his life "almost as if it were her own life" (*SL* 140). She pushed her sons into the world in part as a way of pushing herself into it as well. She lived through her sons vicariously in an attempt to regain through them what she was not able to gain (or what she had lost) for herself. But nothing is ever this simple in Lawrence. It would be better to say, in view of Lawrence's theory of the unconscious self, that Gertrude "sheathed" her own soul in theirs, seeking to share with them that region of life that was beyond all of them individually but that included them vitally. Once again, by an appeal to the forces of the unconscious world, women turn the tables and make men instrumental *for them*. The problem, of course, is that this appeal both robs women of agency and sets them up to take the blame for the failures of men. By "pushing men 'to rise in the world,'" Alden argues, "women use them to realize their own ambitions; the man's betrayal in leaving is then shifted on to the woman. Women, not men, are responsible for the separation and are to blame for the protagonist's feeling of estrangement."[122] In Alden's view, Lawrence punishes women for their ambition, making them responsible not only for that ambition but also for the losses incurred in providing the "motor force" behind the men who leave them behind. While this may be the case for Gertrude and to some extent Miriam, something else transpires with Clara, who is far less caught up in the relentless gender dialectic that requires such table turning in order to achieve a modicum of social and cultural capital.

With Clara, the problem of instrumentality is raised in a quite different way. As I have suggested, she does not aspire, like Miriam, to be tutored by Paul in the humanist tradition, nor does she appear to want to learn from him the better to impose her own will upon him. This pedagogical mediation is not necessary, in part because Clara is already an educated woman: "During the ten years that she had belonged to the women's movement, she had acquired a fair amount of education" (*SL* 306). As a result of her education, and her polemical attitude toward him, she is less susceptible to Paul's esoteric aestheticism. Finally, unlike Miriam, whom Paul has bracketed off from the workaday world in which he moves at Jordan and Son, Clara is fairly representative of the working- and lower-middle-class women flooding the manufacturing and service sectors at the turn of the century. Paul's attraction to her has as much to do with this aspect of her character as it does with her sexuality. His first impressions of her, upon meeting her at Willey Farm, are ambivalent; on the one hand, he is "curious" about her and finds himself drawn to her physicality; on the other hand, he takes every opportunity he can find to alienate her. "Whatever Mrs. Dawes had said, Paul would have taken sides against her. He argued that a woman was only an accessory in the labour market, and that, in the majority of cases she was a transitory thing, supporting herself alone for a year or two" (*SL* 273). Paul does not really know what he is talking about here. Women at this time had become quite important in the labor market, though they did not enjoy equal wages with men, as Clara points out. His polemical attitude toward her masks his desire, and it is not long before this desire clashes with his still quite strong need for Miriam, thus forming a "triangle of antagonism" (*SL* 289). Miriam understands Paul's desire for Clara in terms of her own disappointment. "It made Miriam bitter, to think that he should throw away his soul for this flippant traffic of triviality with Clara." Paul, however, is torn by complex emotions that he feels Miriam cannot understand. "He could not leave her, because in one way she did hold the best of him. He could not stay with her because she did not take the rest of him, which was three quarters" (*SL* 291). His mother intensifies the antagonism by reduplicating in sharply polarized, even eugenic, terms his own attitude toward the two women: "she hated Miriam for having . . . undermined his joy"; she wanted for Paul "a girl equal to be his mate—educated and strong," but "she was not hostile to the idea of Clara," who at least excited "wholesome" feelings (*SL* 300, 283).

Though Paul never quite resolves the antagonism, he does try to break his ties with Miriam, writing her a letter on her twenty-first birthday in which he speaks of their "old, worn love" for the last time and acknowledges, "You have played a fundamental part in my development." He concedes, "I might marry. . . . It would be a woman I could kiss and embrace, whom I could make the mother of my children, whom I could talk to playfully, trivially" (*SL* 292). However, despite his attempt to opt out of love with Miriam and despite the fact that he feels a "thickening and quickening of his blood" whenever he talks to Clara, he continues to feel that he belongs to his first love. Indeed, he feels this because "she was so fixedly sure, that he allowed her right" (*SL* 294). Later, they will try one last time to have the kind of relationship that Paul desires, when Miriam is left alone for a week at her grandmother's cottage. After making love to her he realizes that he is "a youth no longer" and that after their passionate moments together "there remained . . . always the sense of failure and of death" (*SL* 334). What he fears in these moments is the "sheathing" he has resisted before in their conversations about the unconscious self; for Paul, then, sex is linked with something beyond himself, something inhuman. Miriam confronts him with the fact that their relationship has always been "one long battle between us" (*SL* 341). His idealistic vision of her collapses: "All these years," he thinks, "she had treated him as if he were a hero, and thought of him secretly as an infant, a foolish child" (*SL* 342). The "test on Miriam" turns out to be a test on himself as well, and neither of them passes.

The turn to Clara, and to sexuality, represents a stage in Paul's development in which the dialectical economy of the classical Bildungsroman—the reciprocity of self and society, of inner culture and social responsibility—is translated into a sexual economy. What persists in the act of translation is the dilemma of dialectic itself, of finding balance in harmony and synthesis. As Alden puts it, "The issue . . . in the sexual arena is the same as in the social: how to achieve individuation while maintaining relatedness."[123] Aside from quickening his blood, Clara also promotes in Paul a sense of "a new self or a new centre of consciousness" (*SL* 294). She is certainly not like Miriam, emotionally vampiric and sexually repressed. But neither is she the diametric opposite. She too appears repressed, though it is easier to see what lies lurking beneath the surface: "Dowdy in dress, and drooping, she showed to great disadvantage. He could scarcely recognise her strong form, that seemed to slumber with power" (*SL* 313). She appears to Paul to have been "denied and deprived of so much" (*SL* 304), but beneath her denials he sees passion. Their physical intimacy, in which their bodies are "sealed and annealed" (*SL* 353), at first appears to reduplicate the "sheathing" of consciousness in an unconscious self to which Gertrude surrendered in the garden and to which Miriam seemed to be calling him in their quite different cerebral intimacies. "It's risky," Paul says, "or messy at any rate," and this is confirmed in the aftermath: "When [Clara] arose, he, looking on the ground all the time, saw suddenly sprinkled on the black wet beech roots many scarlet carnation petals, like splashed drops of blood. And red, small splashes fell from her bosom streaming down her dress to her feet" (*SL* 353, 355). The imagery figures a loss of virginity, but it also recalls the infant Paul's blood bond with his mother, a bond that ambivalently links violence with desire. Here, the oedipal implications that the novel has teased out of that bond are transposed onto Paul's substitute love object, while the violence hinged to desire in the earlier episode is echoed in this later moment of passion, as the bloodlike "scarlet carnation petals" break apart and fall from Clara's breast. The passage is a vivid example of the "spontaneous identification . . . between image and meaning" that Van Ghent finds in Lawrence's work, an identification in which dialectical harmony is masked by the frisson of a sexual "sheathing" in which Paul loses himself in Clara's physical being and becomes seemingly disembodied and disseminated. Perhaps he surrenders himself to her in order to overcome the "torture of nearness" (*SL* 375) that he did not seem to feel with Miriam. Paul's "service of worship," which Clara notices and accepts, ritualizes the "passional transcendence of self"[124] that he feels whenever he achieves intimacy with her.

It is in fact this very aspect of ritual that qualifies Paul's surrender to passion and that forecloses any disembodiment or transcendence of self that so many readers discern in such passages as the one in which he and Clara lie down along the canal bank: "He lifted his head and looked into her eyes. They were dark and shining and strange, life wild at the source staring into his life, stranger to him, yet meeting him. . . . What was she. A strong, strange, wild life, that breathed with his in the darkness through this hour. It was all so much bigger than themselves, that he was hushed" (*SL* 398). It is well to remember, in view of such passages, Adorno's insistence that negation in dialectics is inevitably in the service of a positivity; the "other" life that Clara represents, the "wild life" of an unconsciousness beyond her lover, is at this moment *with* him, constituting him—his being and identity—as part of a dialectical sublation within something "bigger than themselves." The language of sublation is unrelenting, as if the prose itself insisted on the consummation that Paul fears even as he courts it. Clara's dissatisfaction ("she wanted something permanent, she had not realised fully" [*SL* 398]) indicates that there is a difference between them, that the feeling of undifferentiation is just that, a feeling, one that they can savor as justification for their mutual neediness. The "great force" of which they are "blind agents" (*SL* 399)—like the "shimmering protoplasm" that subtends Paul's aesthetics—at times resembles the Hegelian *Geist*, which suggests that Paul's surrender to passion is, at bottom, a capitulation to dialectical totality. The heady feeling of undifferentiation masks a process by which the subjective will of "blind agents" is subsumed dialectically by the rational will of the "great force." In this scenario, the former is not so much dissolved in the latter as identical with it. Clara herself becomes something of a cipher in this "baptism of fire in passion" that Lawrence stages, for the process involves her only as a catalyst: "But it was not Clara. It was something that happened because of her, but it was not her. They were scarcely any nearer each other. It was as if they had been blind agents of a great force" (*SL* 399). In a similar vein, Bedient has argued that Paul's bond with women is not primarily erotic but mystical. "It is the Infinite that [Lawrence's heroes] love. They go to a woman as metal goes into a furnace, for a 'melting out.'"[125] In the alembic of sexual Bildung, Clara, the mystical woman, becomes the catalyst for Paul's aesthetic education. In a scene that looks forward to the birdgirl episode of Joyce's *Portrait of the Artist as a Young Man*, Paul meditates on the figure of Clara as she moves "with heavy grace across the foreshore." He wonders why she absorbs him and asks himself, "What is she after all? . . . what is *she*! It's not her I care for—" (*SL* 402). Her instrumentality with respect to his quest for sexual Bildung breaks down at this point; she is transformed from motivated helpmate to blind catalyst. In any case, her contribution to a classical dialectics of identity is confirmed by the dissolution of her singular nonidentity in the dialectical harmony of Bildung that Paul seeks for himself. This mode of transcendent depersonalization, in which bourgeois subjectivity is repudiated, threatens to reinscribe classical dialectics precisely at the point at which Paul exploits gender difference in the service of self-identity. It is a threat, moreover, that the narrator painstakingly and critically exposes and that Clara herself finally resists.

It does not take long for Clara to suspect the role she plays, or does not play, in Paul's search for "passional transcendence." She realizes that she has not "got" him, that she is not the *thing* that Paul is "taking" in their intimate moments. "Something just for yourself," she tells him. "It has been fine, so that I daren't think of it. But—is it *me* you want, or is it *It*?" (*SL* 407). Lawrence seeks in such moments, however much they may fail to provide Paul with the transcendence he desires, to find an alternative to the "stable ego," an unsentimental, inhuman sense of consciousness that is not merely undifferentiated or annihilated being. And while he is to be applauded for the critical potential of such attempts, it is regrettable that such alternatives are not held out for women like Clara, whose relationship with the hero continues to take on the form of a sacrifice. Like Stephen Dedalus, who constructs the birdgirl as an "envoy from the fair courts of life," Paul constructs Clara as an icon of the latest phase of his Bildung process, her passive submission to that process figuring her acquiescence to dialectical sublation. Hence, she is "licked up in an immense tongue of flame" which bore them both "onwards and upwards. Everything rushed along in living beside him, everything was still, perfect in itself, along with him. This wonderful stillness in each thing in itself, while it was being borne along in a very ecstasy of living, seemed the highest point of bliss" (*SL* 408).[126] Paul is "licked up" as well, but is he required to submit in the same way as Clara? Notice that the perfection of this blissful state lies in relation to him, *along with him*. Language once again undercuts the thematics of undifferentiation, smuggling in the self that should have been borne off on a "tongue of flame." And we cannot neglect the importance of Clara's acknowledgment that such moments of passion "held him to her" or the efforts that she makes to guarantee that they recur. She persists in playing the instrumental role that *she herself* envisions while doing whatever she can to encourage him to think that she plays a quite different role altogether. Paul is not entirely unaware of that fact that she resists the "passional transcendence" that absolutely requires her submission. And the more aware he grows, the more certain he is that they will "have to part sooner or later. Even if they married, and were faithful to each other, still he would have to leave her, go on alone, and she would only have to attend to him when he came home. But it was not possible. Each wanted a mate to go side by side with" (*SL* 405).

The break with Clara is of a much different character from the break with Miriam, in large measure because of her refusal to be the submissive instrument of his self-development. His recognition that she belongs with Baxter is more accurately a recognition that her instrumentality is valuable only within the context of the marriage bond she has already contracted with him. We see here the same problematic that bedeviled Jude and Sue in Hardy's *Jude the Obscure*, but whereas Sue invoked the bonds of marriage in a penitential fever, falling back on doctrine as an antidote to the tragic failure of her life choices with Jude, Paul seems more cynically to invoke such bonds as a way to appease a woman he has outgrown, a woman whose instrumentality has become too conventional for his tastes. He tells Miriam that Clara "never knew the fearful importance of marriage" and for that reason "developed into the 'femme incomprise'" (*SL* 361). Disregarding the importance of marriage has led to her being herself disregarded. It is the inverse of the situation Sue found herself in, for the regard in which she was held by Jude and by Phillotson was proportionate to her disregard of the importance of marriage. What is odd is that Paul would return Clara to the very situation in which he believed she was misunderstood, on the grounds that she was obligated to her husband. Referring to his own parents, Paul tells Miriam, "I believe she had a passion for him." "That's why she stayed with him. After all, they were bound to each other" (*SL* 361). Paul believes that Clara "never had it," and Miriam for her part realizes that what Paul seeks is a "baptism of fire in passion" (*SL* 362). She also realizes the propriety of his relationship with Clara when she sees him with her at his parents' house, in that "cool, clear atmosphere, where everyone was himself, and in harmony. . . . Something in their perfect isolation together made her know that it was accomplished between them, that they were, as she put it, married" (*SL* 367–68). It is an irony Paul may be incapable of appreciating that the virginal and cerebral Miriam is far more appropriate for him than Clara, at least in terms of the spiritualized instrumentality that he seeks. We have seen that in his letter to Miriam he refuses to entertain the possibility of marrying her, though he readily admits to loving her. Yet his belief that "Sex desire was a sort of detached thing, that did not belong to a woman," encourages him to think that "it would be his duty to marry Miriam" should he ever decide to marry at all (*SL* 319). His feelings for Miriam and Clara are further complicated by his oedipal relation to his mother, to whom he declares that "to *give* myself to them in marriage—I couldn't. . . . And I never shall meet the right woman while you live" (*SL* 395). His remarks about marriage are in general more self-serving and far less critical than either Jude's or Sue's. But Lawrence's presentation of his protagonist's views accomplishes the same goal: a critique of marriage insofar as it functions in the classical Bildungsroman as a symbolic legitimation of normative modes of socialization.

"What a blessed life I dreamt of with her," Lothario muses in *Wilhelm Meister*, imagining his ideal marriage to Therese, who ultimately marries the hero instead; "not the blessings of ecstatic bliss, but the joys of a secure earthly life: order in joy, courage in misfortune, concern for every little detail, and a soul able to cope with larger matters and, in due course, dismiss them. I saw in her those qualities we admire when history shows us women far superior to any men."[127] The women in Lawrence's Bildungsroman are anything but guarantors of the "joys of secure earthly life," for their passion, willfulness, intransigence, and individuality undermine the efforts of a *Bildungsheld* who seeks helpmates rather than partners. *Sons and Lovers*, like *Jude the Obscure*, ends with the women on the sidelines, unhappy and unfulfilled. But they nevertheless emerge as subjects in their own right, having undermined the dialectical instrumentality in which they would have found themselves absolutely and fatally subsumed. Lawrence's sexual politics are, of course, extremely problematic, and I do not want to suggest that his treatment of Clara and Miriam is beyond reproach. But it is difficult to find more fully realized female characters in early modernist fiction written by men, and it is well-nigh impossible to find such dynamic and critical women in the classical Bildungsroman tradition.

Can we say, then, that Lawrence's modernist Bildungsroman exemplifies the "alternative aesthetics" that critics like Amit Chaudhuri and Anne Fernihough find in his poetry, art criticism, and later novels? We can answer in the affirmative only if we keep in view a separation between thematics and narrative and posit a critical relation between them. Like Hardy's *Jude the Obscure*, Lawrence's Bildungsroman manipulates convention in such a way as to critique its own thematics; it depicts a failure at the level of achieved Bildung but represents that failure within a nearly classical narrative structure. Both writers perform an immanent critique of socialization from the standpoint of the most conventional genre of fiction. Moreover, by depicting the critical rescue of classical Bildung, they simultaneously provide a platform for resistance to socialization and an alternative to it. For the modernist Bildungsroman characteristically refashions the aesthetic education at the foundation of classical Bildung, thus providing a narrative motive for *Bildungshelden* who seek to cultivate themselves deliberately along artistic lines. Self-development as transcendence fails, for Jude and Paul, because it fails to embrace nonidentity, which is the only "position" from which the subject can acquire any agency outside the dialectics of identity. To claim nonidentity is to opt out of the negation of identity, which is the punishment of the other for being other. Nonidentity is the choice of the other, a choice made within the bounds of the dialectic but untouched by its operations, not subject to it. It is not negation, it is the refusal to be negated. It is not annihilation but a retreat behind enemy lines, which is perhaps what Paul Sheehan has in mind when he describes the "anti-humanist" position of Paul Morel at the end of *Sons and Lovers* as "incipient apostasy." Though Paul's efforts to reach beyond his own limited consciousness do not succeed in effacing the subject that makes the effort, Lawrence's representation of the process within the Bildungsroman framework acquires the force of a critique aimed at the dialectical structure of self-formation at the heart of the genre.

How, then, do we read the final moments of the novel, when Paul walks "towards the faintly humming, glowing town, quickly"? After his mother's death, his mind turns to places: "Beyond the town the country, little smouldering spots for more towns—the sea—the night—on and on! And he had no place in it. Whatever spot he stood on, there he stood alone" (*SL* 464). It is clear that he chooses life over death, the "city's gold phosphorescence" over the "darkness" of despair and suicide. But can we ever know if he is heading back to Bestwood or off to somewhere more promising? Many readers see in the conclusion a totalizing synthesis that harmonizes the individual with community (the "humming, glowing town"), a moment during with the hero achieves "undeceived self-attentiveness."[128] But what is missing from the final pages is any sense of the future trajectory of Paul's aesthetic education and artistic vocation; his grandiose theories of art and artistic apprehension are discussed and are vividly imagined throughout the novel, yet it is unclear whether he goes out to explore the wider world and make his way as an artist or simply settles down to the "applied arts" (*SL* 345) that Miriam regards as "conventionalizing" his aspirations.[129] And while the ambiguity of the conclusion is suggestive of the new subjectivities that are in the offing for Paul, it leaves the reader in the dark as to what exactly he has chosen or what will become of him. This uncertain conclusion contrasts dramatically with the closure that we find in the classical Bildungsroman and that persists till the end of the century in the tragic bleakness of *Jude the Obscure*. It is a contrast that we see again and again in the modernist Bildungsroman.

Bildung and the
"Bonds of Dominion"

Wilde and Joyce

There is a moment in James Joyce's *Portrait of the Artist as a Young Man* when Stephen Dedalus discusses his aesthetic opinions with the dean of students at his school. Stephen uses the image of a lamp to explain how Aristotle and Aquinas provide light and guidance for his own intellectual journey. This soon leads to Epictetus and his lamp and the word "funnel." Stephen, perhaps eager to trump the dean, an English convert, flourishes the native Irish "tundish." Later, in the diary entries that conclude the novel, Stephen notes that he had gotten it all wrong, that tundish was "English and good old blunt English too" (*P* 251).[1] This dialectic of discovery and betrayal, enacted at every level of speech and behavior, characterizes Stephen's aesthetic education in colonial Dublin. It is also the foundation of the aestheticism that underwrites Oscar Wilde's *Picture of Dorian Gray*. That the Catholic Joyce and the Anglo-Irish Wilde should share the same mixture of discovery and betrayal owes much to the peculiar social conditions of Ireland. In the latter part of the nineteenth century, after years of uneven modernization, three social trends marked the advent of decolonization: the rise of nationalism, the emergence of a newly empowered Catholic middle class, and the gradual disempowerment of the Anglo-Irish Ascendancy. Beginning in earnest in the 1870s, these parallel developments culminated in the Free State of 1922, that *annus mirabilis* of modernism.[2] As a metrocolony, with close geographic and political ties to England, Ireland had always enjoyed a higher degree of social and cultural assimilation than other colonies in the British Empire.[3] But at the same time, this proximity led to asymmetries in the degree to which modernization took hold in Ireland: uneven industrialization, colonial rule, nationalism, and sectarian divisions created social conditions markedly different from those in the rest of Europe and the United States. These generally unstable social conditions—the symptoms of decolonization—are well suited, as Terry Eagleton argues, for the development of modernist tendencies and movements. Moreover, Irish modernism in its Anglo-Irish form, which dominated the field until the 1920s, tended to be more conservative than European and American forms.[4] But this conservatism was often conjoined with a revolutionary energy that found expression in Gothic literature. In this chapter I will look at Wilde's and Joyce's Bildungsroman and argue that each seeks to address the problem of self-development in a colonial society but that the two proceed from radically different starting points to achieve the same end: the aesthetic education of their protagonists and the achievement of personal Bildung. That both Dorian Gray and Stephen Dedalus fail in their respective cases is an index *not* of the failure of the Bildungsroman form nor of classical Bildung. The failure of social conditions to encourage and nurture Bildung is the focus of Wilde's and Joyce's representations and of an immanent critique of the modes of socialization that had displaced and transformed classical Bildung.

It is my contention that throughout the nineteenth century, neither aesthetico-spiritual nor socially pragmatic Bildung could find a foothold in colonial Ireland, given that social conditions were inimical both to the freedom necessary for Bildung to flourish as an option for self-cultivation and to the institutions that would encourage and regulate the production of "viable" social subjects. However, the upsurge of cultural nationalism in the 1890s created a climate of creative instability which proved especially conducive to the retrieval of aesthetico-spiritual Bildung and the ideal of an aesthetic education. In part because of social and political pressures unique to the colonial situation in Ireland, Wilde and Joyce, more emphatically and more critically than their English counterparts, reinscribed the fundamental values of Bildung at the same time that they critiqued the processes of socialization that had displaced them in the nineteenth century. Their more intensive, more radical critique of Bildung produced a colonial variant of the modernist Bildungsroman. The *Bildungshelden* of English Bildungsromane, like Jude Fawley and Paul Morel, may be marginalized by their class status, but the Bildung they seek to achieve is part of a tradition of self-development and socialization that stretches back as far as the Earl of Shaftesbury, whose *Characteristics of Men, Manners, Opinions and Times* (1711) was an important early influence (in England and Germany), and that includes Coleridge, Mill, and Arnold in the nineteenth century. The critique of Bildung offered by Lawrence and Hardy is the critique of a normative discourse of development and socialization that was at the same time a native discourse, one that was intimately bound up with what it meant to be English. The critique of Bildung in a colonial setting targets an essentially foreign discourse with no normative status in colonial society. Colonial Bildung is therefore always a more or less self-conscious role-playing, in which colonial subjects find themselves in an alienated relation to the goal of classical Bildung, with effects that range from sincere imitation to subversive mimicry. George Moore's protagonist in *Confessions of a Young Man* can be regarded as an example of sincere imitation, while both Dorian Gray and Stephen Dedalus exemplify subversive mimicry in quite different but equally compelling ways. In Homi Bhabha's terms, the latter constitutes "a form of colonial discourse that is uttered *inter dicta*: a discourse at the crossroads of what is known and permissible and that which though known must be kept concealed."[5] The vicissitudes of colonial Bildung are, of course, more traumatic for Catholic Irish subjects. Lacking the "legitimate" subjectivity to enter into symbolic discourse as a fully indemnified and enfranchised subject, the Catholic *Bildungsheld* will always be something of an alien, debarred from the "mediated routes" of upward social mobility, even those limited paths available to the working and lower-middle classes in England. Throughout the nineteenth century, the Catholic majority in Ireland suffered under what amounted to penal laws, and the country was administered as a colony even though its parliament had been united with that of Britain since 1800. Indeed, Ireland at the beginning of the twentieth century was not much better off than it had been at the end of the ill-fated revolution of 1798. One difference was clear: by the 1890s, a rising Catholic middle class was opening up new opportunities for young men, especially in the urban areas. However, these opportunities were unsuited to the aspirations of an artist-hero like Stephen Dedalus.

For quite different reasons, the social conditions of Anglo-Ireland were just as unsuited to the kind of aesthete protagonist that we find in Wilde's Bildungsroman. A legacy of ineffectual rule and mutual distrust between the Anglo-Irish Ascendancy and the British Parliament resulted in a sense of estrangement and deracination that was exacerbated by the erosion, through expropriation, of the grand demesnes that symbolized Anglo-Irish rule. The resistance to socialization that we see in *Dorian Gray*, though quite different from that which we see in *Portrait*, exhibits the same frustration with a "borrowed" concept of self-cultivation and a similar recourse to a model of classical Bildung. And though they seek inspiration in different sources—Joyce finds his in the sacramental theology of the Catholic Church, Wilde in continental aestheticism and the Anglo-Irish Gothic tradition[6]—they construct Bildung plots that focus in the same critical fashion on the trauma of colonial identity. Thus the peculiar nature of colonialism in Ireland, where a proxy ruling class stands between the native Catholic population and the British Empire, produces two models of colonial Bildung, neither capable of producing harmony, autonomy, or wholeness.

In the colonial Bildungsroman, the harmony of inner and outer worlds that is the aim of the classical form is displaced and reconfigured as an *inner split*, a dehiscence in the normative concept of Bildung and its dialectical will to harmony in which the disavowed colonial subject speaks dissonantly from an open, ambivalent, nonuniversal but immanent perspective.[7] The colonial subject radicalizes the modernist strategy of depersonalization by raising the political and cultural stakes. In a negative critique of the dialectic of self-development, identity is no longer balanced and affirmed by its "other," nonidentity. Where Irish modernists differ from their English counterparts is in their willingness to depart from generic convention and in their greater success in recapturing the aesthetic dimension of classical Bildung. The Irish Bildungsroman, because it employs the defamiliarizing techniques of parody and mimicry, thus functions like the radical modern art that Theodor Adorno describes, which is hated "because it reminds us of missed chances, but also because by its sheer existence it reveals the dubiousness of the heteronomous structural ideal."[8] It is these missed chances that I want to examine in the modernist Bildungsromane of Wilde and Joyce.

Some clarification is necessary before I begin my discussion of the Irish Bildungsroman, which did not emerge as part of a larger development in Irish literary history, for there was no significant native tradition of Bildungsromane that came before. Autobiographical forms existed, of course—George Moore's *Confessions of a Young Man* is a good late-nineteenth-century example—as did biographical forms like Sydney Owenson's *Wild Irish Girl*, but neither of these forms emphasizes the concept of Bildung.[9] What we see in works like Wilde's *Picture of Dorian Gray* and Joyce's *Portrait* are instances of generic transculturation, a process by which colonial writers transform genres from an imperial culture, blending native elements with those that are retained from the "originary" genre.[10] With a form as conservative as the Bildungsroman, this has meant that a good many of the original elements—themes, characterization, plot structure—have been retained in the Irish colonial form, though there is a wide variety of variations on those retained elements. This is especially evident in the work of Joyce and Wilde. The former tends to hew closely to the line of generic conventions at the same time that he dramatizes their insufficiency for representing the experience of a colonized Catholic Irish hero who must choose exile over social integration, while the latter Gothicizes the Bildungsroman in order to illustrate a similar insufficiency for representing the experience of the Anglo-Irish aesthete whose development takes place in the cosmopolitan, transnational realms of art rather than in the institutions of colonial society. For both the Catholic Joyce and the Anglo-Irish Wilde, the Bildungsroman becomes a site of critique, the principal targets being the normative modes of self-development and the socially pragmatic form of Bildung deemed appropriate for that development.

As I have indicated in previous chapters, the socially pragmatic form of Bildung that developed throughout the nineteenth century differed significantly from the Goethean/Humboldtian variants of classical Bildung and served significantly different ideological interests. I have been arguing that the aesthetico-spiritual form of Bildung is an ideal that modernist writers seek precisely as an alternative to the socially pragmatic form. It is, in short, the key element in a negative critique of the nineteenth-century Bildungsroman, one in which the dialectical energies of normative socialization are the starting point for developing more satisfying, effective, and elective forms of Bildung. What the Irish Bildungsroman points up, among many other things, is the extent to which the recuperation of classical Bildung answers the needs of new and challenging social situations and the extent to which the Bildungsroman form continues to be resilient enough to rise to the challenge of representing these new situations.

The Anglo-Irish intelligentsia faced unique challenges in the late nineteenth century, a time when anxiety over class status reached critical levels in the wake of land acts, disestablishment of the Church, and Catholic movements of self-determination in the economic, cultural, and political spheres. For a writer like Wilde, this resulted in a displacement of development onto different, non-Irish social and cultural spaces, a kind of imaginative exile that found coded expression in a manner familiar to readers of Anglo-Irish Gothic writers like Charles Maturin, Sheridan Le Fanu, and Bram Stoker. This tradition, of which *Dorian Gray* is a key modernist exemplar, is often regarded as an index of the deracination and anxiety felt by members of a class who believed that the British parliament had undercut their authority and made it impossible to achieve ideological hegemony.[11] It also indexes a loss of innocence, for many members of the Ascendancy, like Standish James O'Grady, condemned rackrent landlordism and exploitation of the Catholic Irish and believed these to be the root causes of the Ascendancy's failure to achieve, much less sustain, hegemony.[12] The fact that the Anglo-Irish Gothic tradition so often depicts non-Irish locales should not detract from its potential to comment upon Irish matters. Though Wilde's Bildungsroman does not feature self-cultivation in an Irish context, Julia Prewitt Brown argues that Irishness figures significantly in his cosmopolitan aesthetics.[13] Joyce himself realized that Wilde's example could not be ignored, for it provided a precedent for dissent from a society that equated self-development with socialization and socialization with a repressive educational system: "the truth is that Wilde, far from being a perverted monster who sprang in some inexplicable way from the civilization of modern England, is the logical and inescapable product of the Anglo-Saxon college and university system, with its secrecy and restrictions."[14] Wilde wrote from a position of estrangement and even marginalization—the Irishman abroad—very similar to that which Joyce himself would occupy in Rome, Trieste, Paris, and Zurich. In very different ways, then, Wilde and Joyce narrate forms of colonial Bildung within the immanently critical framework of exile.

The narration of colonial Bildung challenges the "logical form of contradiction" that for Adorno and other theorists lies at the foundation of classical modes of identity formation.[15] Also implicated in this challenge are the "bonds of dominion" that (re)enforce unity as a function of a rationalized, bureaucratized society. "The absolute subject cannot get out of its entanglements," writes Adorno: "the bonds it would have to tear, the bonds of dominion, are as one with the principle of absolute subjectivity."[16] As we have seen in the previous chapter, the protagonists of the English Bildungsroman attempt to achieve personal Bildung within a society defined by a liberal humanist ethos that underwrites, at its deepest levels, the discourses of dominion, colonial and otherwise.[17] A paramount feature of this ethos, of course, is formal state-sponsored education, which, in the English tradition, is one of the chief "mediated routes" of upward social mobility. For the protagonists of the Irish Bildungsroman, education is far more problematic, tending to threaten rather than facilitate the dominant modes of socialization. Historically, education in Ireland has been a more politicized process than in England.[18] On the one hand, the National Schools sponsored by the colonial authorities were designed to repress nationalist sentiment and encourage the processes of Anglicization. On the other hand, denominational schools tended either to reverse the priorities of the National Schools or to bypass the political problem altogether and emphasize theology. In England, the division between secular and parochial education was not accompanied by a division between nationalist and colonial ideologies. Complicating this situation further is a long tradition of radical popular education that originated in the "hedge schools" of the seventeenth and eighteenth centuries and continued in the nineteenth and twentieth centuries in social organizations like the Catholic Association, the Repeal Association, Young Ireland, and the Gaelic League.[19] Joyce's *Portrait* illustrates still another complication, for the Catholic schools Stephen Dedalus attends provide him with an education that is very much in line with the classical humanist tradition. In this respect, as in others, Joyce's Bildungsroman is much more conventional than Wilde's, though Stephen's sacramentalized aesthetic preoccupations—his aspiration to become a "priest of the eternal imagination" (*P* 221)—like Dorian's aesthetic education, calls into question the adequacy of a humanist ethos for the Irish subject's Bildung process.

In Wilde's *Dorian Gray*, formal education plays no part at all, in large measure because self-development has been displaced from childhood and adolescence to adulthood; Dorian's deferred formative experiences take place as part of an informal aesthetic education conducted in a context that suggests a critique of bourgeois taste, style, education, and pedagogy. "Wilde does not follow his time in looking to institutionalized forms of education to promote self-development," writes Bruce Bashford. "Humanisms that do look to the schools clearly aspire to have the beneficial effects on society that we expect of the tradition. That Wilde does not do so raises the question of what social value he can claim for his humanism, a question that can be answered only after determining how he thinks self-development can occur."[20] Bashford's way of presenting the problem would fix the social value of Wilde's humanism, but we might well ask whether Wilde's emphasis on a form of aesthetic education that deconstructs the humanist tradition sacrifices social value for something more intrinsically personal. The fact that Wilde uses Gothic techniques to represent the Bildung process—techniques that render it monstrous and magical, inimical to the rationalist modes of inquiry and representation that are part of the humanist pedagogy at the heart of "institutionalized forms of education"—indicates that the question of the social value of Wilde's humanism is largely irrelevant. To some degree, the Gothicized and eroticized scene of Dorian Gray's aesthetic education allegorizes Wilde's own experience of marginality as an Anglo-Irishman in England, his own internal exile from the culture of Bildung. That the foundations of the aesthetics in Wilde's novel are to be found in Oxford, and in the work of Walter Pater, Wilde's teacher at Oxford, is an irony that complicates further the question of Wilde's connection to Anglo-Ireland and the Gothic irrationality he conjures up to mystify the dialectics of aestheticism.[21]

The dialectical relation between the subject of Bildung and the social world in modernists like Wilde and Joyce is transposed onto the more problematic and immanently critical relation between artist and art, with the social world falling increasingly into the category of art (or the materials for it). We have seen that for Paul Morel the essential reality of art and nature was a "shimmering protoplasm," an inner essence as opposed to an external "dead crust." Wilde and Joyce develop similar strategies by which the relationship between the subject and the social world is construed in terms of the artist's apprehension and representation of what is intrinsic or essential. Where they differ, however, is in their willingness to question the sharp difference between inner essence and outer crust. The blurring of the boundaries between representation and its object recovers something of the original dynamism of dialectics, which, as Adorno reminds us, is "literally: language as the organon of thought." The instauration of the dialectics of classical Bildung, understood in this light, "would mean to attempt a critical rescue of the rhetorical element, a mutual approximation of thing and expression, to the point where the difference fades."[22] The indeterminacy and multivalency we see in the style, narrative structure, and thematics of Wilde's and Joyce's Bildungsromane are striking illustrations of Adorno's negative dialectics—illustrations that suggest more general homologies between modernist literature and philosophy.

The oscillation and tension between failure and success, between a failed aspiration toward Bildung and the critical representation of that aspiration, that we see in the modernist English Bildungsroman is even more strikingly evident in the Irish tradition at the same historical moment. As I will show in the next chapter, there is a convergence of aims in the "high" modernist experiments of Woolf and Joyce, who sought to represent Bildung in ways that defied the integrity of generic conventions. This convergence suggests that modernism as a movement not only caught up with its Irish pioneers but generalized its strategies of negative critique and pushed style even further as a productive mode of depersonalization, producing in the process striking new strategies of self-cultivation.

AESTHETICS AND "SELF-CULTURE" IN WILDE'S *THE PICTURE OF DORIAN GRAY*

In "The Portrait of Mr. W. H.," Wilde writes of "all Art being to a certain degree a mode of acting, an attempt to realise one's own personality on some imaginative plane out of reach of the trammelling accidents and limitations of real life."[23] The development of an aesthetic theory is, for Wilde, tantamount to the development of a theory of Bildung. Yet *Dorian Gray*, often discussed in terms of the aesthetic theories that animate it, is almost never discussed as a Bildungs-roman. Neil Sammells refers briefly to it as a "peculiarly Wildean parody of the nineteenth-century *Bildungsroman*." Rather than learn who he is by experience, Dorian "tries to act out a narrative of self-definition, but ends by living one of self-destruction."[24] Charles Altieri, in the only essay to deal at length with Wilde's text as a Bildungsroman, argues that it exemplifies an "organic ideal of development," though this ideal is undermined by Lord Henry's corruption of it, which blocks the possibilities for openness to "the dialectical exchanges between the self and the world."[25] I wish to argue that such exchanges are foreclosed from the outset by virtue of Wilde's position outside the English novel tradition that includes writers like Hardy and Lawrence. Instead, his colonial Bildungsroman draws on the techniques and strategies of the Gothic tradition and the aesthetic movement to destabilize the dialectical structures of Bildung, specifically the socially pragmatic variant that dominates the English Bildungsroman. In the end, Wilde's Anglo-Irishness, his peculiar stance astride the Manichean colonial divide, gives him the critical distance from the English Bildungsroman that neither Hardy nor Lawrence was able to achieve and allows him to recover more fully the tradition of classical Bildung and, from there, to advance a radical new theory of aesthetic self-fashioning.

"The Irish son of an Irish patriot would stand at the summit of a newly de-fined, a revised and perfected, ideal of English culture, the colonial subject out-doing the occupier by capturing the history and future of culture."[26] Lawrence Danson's estimation sums up a common view of Wilde the Irishman, whose sexual and aesthetic dissidence constituted a critique of English bourgeois culture and imperial domination. However, Wilde's strategies of self-cultivation are part of a larger English tradition of progressive aesthetics and conservative social positioning that stretches from the prototypical dandy Beau Brummell to the aesthetes of the fin de siècle.[27] The chief goal of this tradition was, as Wilde puts it in *Dorian Gray*, referring to Dandyism, "to assert the absolute modernity of beauty" (*DG* 100).[28] The major influence on Wilde, at least in the 1870s and 1880s, was the aestheticism of Walter Pater, who had translated, into an English frame of reference, some of the ideas of continental aesthetes like Théophile Gautier and Charles Baudelaire. Pater was a prominent Oxford Hellenist whose work on Renaissance art was a powerful catalyst for young aesthetes. In works like *The Renaissance* and *Marius the Epicurean*, he advocated subjective materialism, a scientifically inflected humanism, which David DeLaura claims "was the imaginatively reconstructed residue of the Christian-classical synthesis after the science and skepticism of the century had taken their toll."[29] Art, according to Pater, is "always striving to be independent of the mere intelligence, to become a matter of pure perception, to get rid of its responsibilities to its subject or material. . . . Form and matter, in their union or identity, present one single effect to the 'imaginative reason,' that complex faculty for which every thought and feeling is twin-born with its sensible analogue or symbol."[30] Hellenism is the cultural context in which this aesthetic theory is most at home, for "the thoughts of the Greeks about themselves, and their relation to the world generally, were ever in the happiest readiness to be transformed into objects for the senses." Once thought has been submitted to the senses, it can be perceived according to the imaginative reason that seeks out and fulfills, either in the capacity of the creative artist or of the aesthetic critic, a "musical law." The Hellenic ideal, which Pater sought to promulgate in his criticism as well as in *Marius the Epicurean*, is one "in which the thought does not outstrip or lie beyond the proper range of its sensible embodiment."[31]

Pater was not, despite his interest in Plato's philosophy, a metaphysician; his interest was in the aesthetic dimension of life. He declared that "a taste for metaphysics may be one of those things which we must renounce, if we mean to mould our lives to artistic perfection. Philosophy serves culture, not by the fancied gift of absolute or transcendental knowledge, but by suggesting questions which help one to detect the passion, and strangeness, and dramatic contrasts of life. . . . What modern art has to do in the service of culture is so to rearrange the details of modern life, so to reflect it, that it may satisfy the spirit. And what does the spirit need in the face of modern life? The sense of freedom."[32] This ideal of artistic perfection is Humboldtian in its insistence on the freedom necessary to "satisfy the spirit." These lines, at the end of the essay on Winckelmann, prepare the reader for the book's famous conclusion, in which Pater describes the modern artistic sensibility, a form of subjective materialism that harmonizes science and aesthetics, matter and spirit, nature and poetry. Echoing early scholars like Winckelmann and Humboldt, Pater felt that the "rough, naïve sense of freedom" that he associated with ancient Greece was inaccessible to "the modern mind," which was more responsive to "the universality of natural law, even in the moral order. For us, necessity is not, as of old, a sort of mythological personage without us, with whom we can do warfare. It is rather a magic web woven through and through us, like that magnetic system of which modern science speaks, penetrating us with a network, subtler than our subtlest nerves, yet bearing in it the central forces of the world."[33] The vision of artistic perception that Pater develops in the conclusion—that experience is a "counted number of pulses" in "a variegated, dramatic life," that art offers us a "quickened sense of life" and gives "the highest quality to [our] moments as they pass, and simply for those moments' sake"[34]—aestheticizes a scientific understanding of matter. The sensation of evanescence evoked in this brilliant peroration, the sensation of finite fleeting pulses of life, is sustained within the lawlike immutability of life's forces. This is rather clearly spelled out in the opening lines, where Pater speaks of "phosphorus and lime and delicate fibres," which constitute our physical life in "a perpetual motion," biological processes that "science reduces to simpler and more elementary forces. Like the elements of which we are composed, the action of these forces extends beyond us: it rusts iron and ripens corn."[35] The "natural law" that governs our lives is echoed in the "musical law" of artistic creation and critical apprehension.

After a short period of enthusiasm for Pater's aestheticism, Wilde developed a theory of aesthetics that pursued some of the more radical implications of Pater's conclusion. In "The Critic as Artist," perhaps his most important work of criticism, Wilde elaborates on the role of the critic in relation to art, a problem that Arnold had tackled in his cultural criticism, and concludes that art must play the crucial role of protecting culture from anarchy and promoting the socially and culturally unifying powers of literature. If we accept at face value Pater's suggestion that Wilde continues the "brilliant critical work of Matthew Arnold,"[36] we must assume that Pater understood the ironic nature of Wilde's accomplishment. For Wilde's technique of argument by reversal undercuts the normative values Arnold places on art and life and gives to the critic a far more substantial and creative warrant.[37] Arnold was willing to give criticism a privileged position only in the context of a cyclical historical theory in which criticism's ascent was the effect of an attenuation of creative energy. The critic remains a critic, however influential he or she may prove to be.[38] In "The Critic as Artist," Wilde eliminated the historical structure of alternating epochs and redefined the nature of criticism, making it a primary and creative endeavor; he also rethought the nature of the relationship between criticism and works of art. The dialogue form that he used for this essay accentuates the polemical nature of his ideas about criticism and aesthetics. When Ernest remarks that "the creative faculty is higher than the critical," Gilbert, who for many readers articulates Wilde's own views, responds that the "antithesis between them is entirely arbitrary. Without the critical faculty, there is no artistic creation at all, worthy of the name" (*I* 120).[39] And he is prepared to go much further, to make the claim that is the foundation stone of an aesthetic education based on criticism: "Criticism is itself an art. And just as artistic creation implies the working of the critical faculty, and, indeed, without it cannot be said to exist at all, so Criticism is really creative in the highest sense of the word. Criticism is, in fact, both creative and independent." The critic's creative relation to art is like that of the artist to the "the visible world of form and colour, or the unseen world of passion and of thought" (*I* 136–37). It is an opportunity: "To the critic the work of art is simply a suggestion for a new work of his own, that need not necessarily bear any obvious resemblance to the thing it criticises" (*I* 144–45). In fact, Gilbert ascribes to criticism the same responsibility as the Bildungsroman: to record the harmonious cultivation of the self. The "highest Criticism, being the purest form of personal impression," refuses any external standard; it is "the record of one's own soul" and "the only civilized form of autobiography," since it deals "not with the events, but with the thoughts of one's life, . . . with the spiritual moods and imaginative passions of the mind." The critic's "sole aim is to chronicle his own impressions," while Criticism, because its "most perfect form . . . is . . . purely subjective, . . . seeks to reveal its own secret and not the secret of another" (*I* 138–40). These startling reversals in the ranking of art and criticism and the nature of the critical object are the particular effects of Wilde's ironic continuance of Arnold's critical project. For where Arnold believed that the critic should see the object for what it really is, Wilde argues that quite the opposite is the case: "the primary aim of the critic is to see the object as in itself it really is not" (*I* 144). As he argues in "The Decay of Lying" about the antimimeticism of art—"No great artist ever sees things as they really are" (*I* 46)—so he argues for the nonrepresentational aspect of criticism: "the critic reproduces the work that he criticises in a mode that is never imitative, and part of whose charm may really consist in the rejection of resemblance, and shows us in this way not merely the meaning but also the mystery of Beauty, and, by transforming each art into literature, solves once for all the problem of Art's unity" (*I* 149). In criticism, then, the critic transforms the work of art into still another work, unifying artistic creations within the contours of an autobiographical expression of the "spiritual moods and imaginative passions of the mind." The unity of art lies in the Bildung of the critic: "It is the spectator, and not life, that art really mirrors" (*DG* 3).

What occupied Wilde's attention increasingly by the end of the 1880s was the articulation of a new relationship between aesthetics and ethics, one that stressed fictionality and style rather than sincerity and substance: "Aesthetics are higher than ethics," he writes in "The Critic as Artist." "They belong to a more spiritual sphere. To discern the beauty of a thing is the finest point to which we can arrive" (*I* 214). By privileging form over content, surface over depth, Wilde's aestheticism rejected—or *appeared* to reject, for appearances are everything—the ethical and political implications of art.[40] Vivian's claim in "The Decay of Lying" that "Truth is entirely and absolutely a matter of style" (*I* 29) is the ne plus ultra of the aestheticist project. When he says, a few pages later, that "we look back on the ages entirely through the medium of Art, and Art, very fortunately, has never once told us the truth" (*I* 48), he is not contradicting himself. The "Truth" of the first statement is the secret revealed by "the cultured and fascinating liar," while the "truth" in the second is a meager reflection in the "prison-house of realism," the "cracked looking-glass" that Art at times holds up to life (*I* 28–29, 32).[41] It was to evade the latter and embrace the former that the aesthetes attempted to detach themselves from practical and conventional reality; their preoccupation with the formal and technical qualities of artistic media, as well as their distaste for art that served moral or social ends, led to a view that art is superior to action: "When man acts he is a puppet. When he describes he is a poet" (*I* 131). Art is, for Gilbert, a haven from life, for life "is a thing narrowed by circumstances, incoherent in its utterance, and without that fine correspondence of form and spirit which is the only thing that can satisfy the artistic and critical temperament." We must not "go to life for our fulfillment or our experience" but to art. "For everything. Because Art does not hurt us" (*I* 167). "From the artistic point of view, certainly," life is a failure (*I* 160). "It is through Art, and through Art only, . . . that we can shield ourselves from the sordid perils of actual existence" (*I* 168). Because "actual existence" is the realm of morality, art and the Epicurean mode of life it enables are thus immoral: "all the arts are immoral," claims Gilbert, "except those baser forms of sensual or didactic art that seek to excite to action of evil or of good. For action of every kind belongs to the sphere of ethics. The aim of art is simply to create a mood. Is such a mode of life unpractical?" (*I* 177). Well, yes, especially when the aesthetic mode is explicitly divorced from the realm of objective and practical life. The subjectivism inherent in both artistic and critical modes of expression should not be grounded in an ethics of representation, in which external nature and society stand in a heteronomous relation to the artist. These heteronomous realms continue to exist, but they become *pre*texts for both aesthetic and critical creation utterly divorced from the *con*texts of ethical action.

Wilde sought to create the self as a work of art, to live life with the freedom of art—in fine, *to create the self for its own sake*. In this, Wilde follows Nietzsche in advocating the self as a work of art outside the moral and ethical limits of the social world, in an aesthetic dimension "beyond good and evil." Wilde's early epigrams—"The first duty in life is to assume a pose; what the second duty is no one yet has found out" and "To become a work of art is the object of living"[42]—show an instinctive understanding of the reflexive subjectivity of late modernity. They also show an understanding of the paradoxical nature of the modern subject, whose chief goal is to become a work of art and exist in a realm of beauty. However, as Wilde's career as a speaker and writer make plain, this goal entails a devil's bargain with the external world, for the artist of the self inevitably places himself on the art market. This kind of apparent contradiction—neatly summed up by Regenia Gagnier as the "commodification of the dandiacal self"[43]—haunts Wilde's writing. In fact, it constitutes the "metaparadox" of the aesthetic dissidence that Wilde both exemplified and critiqued.[44]

"It is clear from Wilde's writings," Vicki Mahaffey argues, "that intellectually he never confused the realms of art and ethics; on the contrary, he insisted that life and art were essentially and necessarily incommensurable. This is also to say that art, although it is concerned with the same issues that we confront in life, enjoys an exemption from the consequences of action: art, unlike life, is reversible, subject to revision and erasure. Art's value, like that of thought, is its freedom from irreversible consequences. Art, like thought, has and must have a license for excess, unlike active life, which is necessarily hedged round by restrictions and taboos."[45] Not having confused them does not mean, however, that they were not confused or, better, inextricably interlinked in a productive and deconstructive relation. This is what I think Ellmann means when he speaks of Wilde's "higher ethics," an ethics "in which artistic freedom and full expression of personality were possible, along with a curious brand of individualistic sympathy or narcissistic socialism."[46] In fact, *Dorian Gray*, like *De Profundis* a few years later, can be read as a *re*valuation of ethical experience in which the emphasis is placed not on ethics as a radically separate sphere from aesthetics but rather on how an aesthetic education, in which ethical consequences ought not to matter, can train one properly for existence in the ethical sphere. Julia Prewitt Brown believes that Wilde's "cosmopolitan aestheticism" is not "some universalized inwardness" divorced from the external world. Though they are separate spheres, art and life are involved in a kind of distant interchange. "The so-called 'autonomy' of art—the watchword of late nineteenth-century aestheticism—is therefore the basis of its connection to life. Only by standing at a distance from life can art communicate to us 'the true ethical import' of the 'facts of life,' as Wilde insists. Art's freedom from ethics is the basis of its usefulness to us as ethical beings. Its transcendence of received morality is what forwards our own ethical discovery."[47] Understood in this way, the interconnection between aesthetics and ethics in *Dorian Gray* need not be regarded as the precondition for a "morality tale" of the simple sort noted by so many early reviewers.[48] It is the sign rather of a critical expansion of ethics that serves to open up its capacity for accommodating aesthetic experiences. Jil Larson takes this approach to *Dorian Gray*, which she reads as "an experiment in aestheticizing morality, in transforming Victorian deontology into an ethics that provides more scope for beauty and unorthodox choice."[49] Certainly Wilde himself recognized that morality had become aestheticized in *Dorian Gray* and said as much in his response to a reviewer who had claimed that Wilde "vamped up" the moral in his story. "The real moral of the story," Wilde wrote, "is that all excess, as well as all renunciation, brings its own punishment, and this moral is so far artistically and deliberately suppressed that it does not enunciate its law as a general principle, but realises itself purely in the lives of individuals, and so becomes simply a dramatic element in a work of art, and not the object of the work of art itself."[50]

What Mahaffey, Brown, Ellmann, Larson, and so many other critics of Wilde describe when they address the problematic relation of aesthetics to ethics is a form of Bildung that responds to the pressures of late modernity; it combines the deconstructive energies of modernist aestheticism with the ethical values of a conservative humanism of the sort found in classical Bildung.[51] The blurring of the boundaries between ethics and aesthetics in Wilde's Bildungsroman undermines the humanist foundation of classical Bildung even as something like a neoclassical Bildung is reinscribed in the form of a new modernist aestheticism, which is itself undermined by the Gothicized representation of its excesses. Pater's estimation of *Dorian Gray*'s Gothic effects, "its adroitly managed supernatural incidents, its almost equally wonderful applications of natural science; impossible, surely, in fact, but plausible enough in fiction,"[52] was meant to suggest the distance he had come from the vital Hellenism of his Oxford days. But Wilde goes well beyond the "applications of natural science," which suggest the very dualistic, identitarian logic that *Dorian Gray* struggles to overcome. His subversive use of the Gothic goes beyond what Julia Kristeva, referring to classical parody, calls "law anticipating its own transgression." The negative dialectics of Gothic Bildung seeks to unearth the nonidentical and the irrational as standpoints outside the normative dialectical structures of identity and rationality. It seeks the standpoint of "transgression giving itself a law."[53]

The transgressive climate of *Dorian Gray* is first discerned in the absence of certain narrative tropes—the representation of childhood, of parental influence, of education—that serve important rhetorical and thematic functions in the classical Bildungsroman and that are still viable in the Bildungsromane of early modernists like Hardy and Lawrence. Wilde's Bildungsroman opens with a young man about whom we know nothing (though we do learn about his family background from Lord Henry's uncle and from Dorian's own musings as he examines the family portraits), whose quest for Bildung has been forestalled or deferred until the point at which we meet him. However, though Wilde dispenses with any representation of early development and maturation, he remains fascinated by progressive growth, an important element of Lord Henry's New Hedonism. In fact, the representation of Dorian's Faustian bargain and the years that follow Gothicize the more conventional narrative trajectory found in classical Bildungsromane. The opening scenes, in which Dorian is the extravagantly compelling tabula rasa upon which Lord Henry and Basil Hallward inscribe their own desire, dramatize the problematic status of "self-culture," which Gilbert in "The Critic as Artist" calls the "true ideal of man. Goethe saw it, and the immediate debt that we owe to Goethe is greater than the debt we owe to any man since Greek days. . . . It was the one thing that made the Renaissance great, and gave us Humanism" (*I* 180–81). Crucial to the Goethean notion of self-culture was the figure of the mentor who assisted the hero on his journey of self-development, exerting a powerful, often mysterious and invisible, influence over him. In Goethe's *Wilhelm Meister*, the *Bildungsheld* discovers that his life has, at many junctures, been out of his control: "Perhaps it was the feeling," Wilhelm reflects, "that . . . there had been so many occasions in his life when he thought he was acting freely and unobserved, only to discover that he had indeed been observed, even directed."[54] In the end, he achieves the harmony of desire and duty that he knows is best for him. So, in a generic sense, Basil's idolatrous admiration and Lord Henry's New Hedonism are not deviations from convention but modernist variants of it. The issue, then, is not the inappropriateness of their influence but the specific nature of its effects. Basil's influence is implicit and indirect; from the comfortable distance of his unspoken idolatry, he contributes significantly to Dorian's burgeoning sense of himself as a beautiful being. What Basil cannot tell Dorian he confides to Lord Henry:

"He is all my art to me now," said the painter, gravely. "I sometimes think, Harry, that there are only two eras of any importance in the world's history. The first is the appearance of a new medium for art, and the second is the appearance of a new personality for art also. . . . But in some serious way—I wonder will you understand me?—his personality has suggested to me an entirely new manner in art, an entirely new mode of style. . . . Unconsciously he defines for me the lines of a fresh school, a school that is to have in it all the passion of the romantic spirit, all the perfection of the spirit that is Greek. The harmony of soul and body—how much that is! We in our madness have separated the two, and have invented a realism that is vulgar, an ideality that is void. . . . . Dorian Gray is to me simply a motive in art." (*DG* 14–15)

Dorian comes to represent for him an epitome of beautiful form which inspires artistic creation much in the way that the aesthetic critic takes a work of art as the starting point for a new creation of his own. This is the same function performed by Willie Hughes, the reputed inspiration for Shakespeare's plays, "whose beauty had given a new creative impulse" to the age.[55] The homoerotic valence in this "new manner in art," which Basil will later deny in favor of a more sterile and less "autobiographical" form of abstract impressionism—"Art is always more abstract than we fancy. Form and colour tell us of form and colour—that is all" (*DG* 90)—suggests that Dorian is as much a mentor to Basil as Basil is to him. But Basil is too passive, morally and aesthetically, to perform the mentoring function in the way demanded by the Bildungsroman form, even in Wilde's modernist variant of it.

Lord Henry performs this function with a vengeance. His discourse on New Hedonism is an explicit and direct, even aggressive, attempt to seduce Dorian into enjoying his own youth and beauty and to do so in a way that pleases the Epicurean fancies of both. Basil asks him not to influence Dorian—"Your influence would be bad" (*DG* 17)—but Lord Henry persists in his desire by seeming not to. "All influence is immoral—immoral from the scientific point of view" he tells Dorian.

> ". . . to influence a person is to give him one's own soul. He does not think his natural thoughts, or burn with his natural passions. His virtues are not real to him. His sins, if there are such things as sins, are borrowed. He becomes an echo of someone else's music, an actor of a part that has not been written for him. The aim of life is self-development. To realize one's nature perfectly—that is what each of us is here for. People are afraid of themselves, nowadays. They have forgotten the highest of all duties, the duty that one owes to one's self. . . . And yet—
>
> . . . "I believe that if one man were to live out his life fully and completely, were to give form to every feeling, expression to every thought, reality to every dream—I believe that the world would gain such a fresh

impulse of joy that we would forget all the maladies of mediaevalism, and return to the Hellenic ideal—to something finer, richer, than the Hellenic ideal, it may be." (*DG* 19–20)

Lord Henry's New Hedonism subordinates all human desire, aspiration, and potential to an aesthetic concern for beauty, for beautiful forms, for language detached from the tiresome realm of material reference and responsibility. But his theory of influence is fundamentally contradictory: it claims that individual human nature is teleological—"To realize one's nature perfectly—that is what each of us is here for"—but at the same time it advocates an Epicurean inter-subjectivity in which human nature can be transformed by an "other" who will "project one's soul into some gracious form, and . . . convey one's temperament into another as though it were a subtle fluid or a strange perfume" (*DG* 33). Connected with this ambition is what Gilbert in "The Critic as Artist" says about the influence of the critic, that "flawless type" who may "desire to exercise influence; but, if so, he will concern himself not with the individual, but with the age, which he will seek to wake into consciousness, and to make responsive, creating in it new desires and appetites, and lending it his larger vision and his nobler moods" (*I* 202–3). Given that Lord Henry believes Dorian to be "the type of what the age is searching for" and that he implicitly concurs with Basil's belief that Dorian is "the visible incarnation of that unseen ideal whose memory haunts us artists like an exquisite dream" (*DG* 165, 89), it is reasonable to conclude that any influence exercised on Dorian is meant to extend beyond him and to touch on the age that he thus symbolizes.

Lord Henry's theory of influence resignifies in a Gothic framework Gilbert's notion that "the more objective a creation appears to be, the more subjective it really is. . . . Yes, the objective form is the most subjective in matter" (*I* 185). What Lord Henry considers to be disinterested, objective study is really something quite different. He regards Dorian as an "interesting study," a more fit object for "the methods of natural science" than is "the ordinary subject-matter" of that field: "And so he had begun by vivisecting himself, as he had ended by vivisecting others" (*DG* 48–49). Yet earlier he described Dorian in terms that suggest a kind of insidious mode of intersubjective manipulation. "Talking to him was like playing upon an exquisite violin. . . . There was something terribly enthralling in the exercise of influence. . . . to hear one's own intellectual views echoed back to one with all the added music of passion and youth . . . ; there was a real joy in that" (*DG* 33). Lord Henry's description of his scientific interest as "vivisection" is telling, for vivisection is a form of dissection, "or other painful experiment, upon living animals as a method of physiological or pathological study."[56] Lord Henry's flagrant violation of his own stated views against influence are linked through this painful mode of observation to the figure of Victor Frankenstein, whose manipulation of the human body leads to the creation of a monstrosity.[57] Dorian is an "interesting" or "wonderful study" (*DG* 61), but he is also the raw material for Lord Henry's act of creation: "To a large extent the lad was his own creation. He had made him premature" (*DG* 49). The passive influence exercised by Basil is trumped by the active interference of Lord Henry, whose idea of intersubjectivity takes the form of aesthetic domination. Dorian seems to be aware of all this. "You have a curious influence over me," he tells him at one point, and later flippantly decries his "wrong, fascinating, poisonous, delightful theories . . . about love, your theories about pleasure. All your theories, in fact" (*DG* 45, 63). Wilde intensifies and complicates this mentorship dynamic when he has Lord Henry present the notorious yellow book to Dorian, a gift designed to draw out what is latent in the younger man's character. Dorian is fascinated by the tale of a decadent youth given over to the extravagances of sensuality and material pleasure. It is, in fact, "the story of his own life, written before he had lived it" (*DG* 99). The yellow book serves, albeit in a conventionally Gothic manner, the same function as the scroll that Wilhelm Meister receives from his mentors in the Society of the Tower on the completion of his apprenticeship. In the scroll Wilhelm sees "a picture of himself, not like a second self in a mirror, but a different self, one outside of him, as in a painting."[58] Basil's painting, which sets Dorian in relation to a different or "other" version of himself, is a Gothic repetition of this classic moment in Goethe's Bildungsroman in which the apprentice recognizes that his destiny, even the very essence of his selfhood, has been directed and formed by mysterious mentors who know him better than he knows himself.[59] The yellow book thus serves as an ironic, duplicitous sign, representing both the humanist tradition of Goethean Bildung and the Gothic resignification of it in an era of late modernity.

The Sibyl Vane subplot functions in a similar way to enable a critical reinscription of elements central to the classical Bildungsroman. Walter Pater, in his review of *Dorian Gray*, remarks of this subplot that it contributes an element of "sordid" realism to what is otherwise an emphatic protest against "so-called 'realism' in art." He refers to the "interlude of Jim Vane" and claims that "his half-sullen but wholly faithful care for his sister's honour, is as good as perhaps anything of the kind, marked by a homely but real pathos, sufficiently proving a versatility in the writer's talent, which should make his books popular."[60] This is damning with faint praise, but it does indicate a quality of Wilde's novel that has led some readers to depreciate it for stylistic inconsistency. However, what is condemned as inconsistency, when regarded as part of a critique of genre, fits well with Wilde's general concern to combat "so-called 'realism' in art." As with the Gothic elements of the novel, the melodramatic aspects of the subplot draw out the patent literariness of self-cultivation and reinforce the sense that Dorian's life is a magical fiction. We see this most vividly in the depiction of his experience with Sibyl Vane, the young actress whose charming artificiality attracts Dorian and blinds him to her humanity and his own. He loves her primarily because she is, like himself, a tabula rasa upon which others project their aesthetic desires: "One evening she is Rosalind, and the next evening she is Imogen. I have seen her die in the gloom of an Italian tomb, sucking the poison from her lover's lips. I have watched her wandering through the forest of Arden. . . . She has been mad, and has come into the presence of a guilty king. . . . She has been innocent, and the black hands of jealousy have crushed her reed-like throat. I have seen her in every age and in every costume" (*DG* 44). Sibyl, who is "more than an individual" but never herself, lives a life of artificial drama, which the narrator describes as a "bad rehearsal" (*DG* 47, 59). Lord Henry sees this aspect of her character as a positive thing: "I love acting. It is so much more real than life" (*DG* 65). But once Dorian's love has distracted her, she ceases to be a "great artist": "This evening she is merely a commonplace, mediocre actress" (*DG* 68). It is clear from Dorian's confrontation with Sibyl in chapter 7 that he has confused the two spheres of art and ethics. Ironically, what turns Dorian away from her is that *she* has suddenly learned to tell the difference; she sees that life is more meaningful than art: "You had brought me something higher, something of which all art is but a reflection." Sibyl speaks more or less the conventional wisdom about the relation of art and reality; Dorian, on the other hand, prizes artistic imitation over life and sees life as an opportunity for aesthetic experiences. He is incredibly cruel to her: "Without your art you are nothing" (*DG* 70). Curiously, Pater's review does not allude to the thematics of theatricality and self-dramatization that go along with the "homely but real pathos" of this part of the novel; but it is just in these thematics, and in the plausible but incidentally drawn scenes involving James Vane's death, that Wilde's "sordid" realism subverts itself. Far from bolstering a strategy of realism, the Sibyl Vane subplot adds a layer of antirealistic commentary to Wilde's critique of Bildung.

It is significant, as Ed Cohen points out, that Dorian's traumatic experience with the portrait of himself begins just when his relationship with Sibyl fails. "Not coincidentally . . . the famous reversal between the character and his portrait first appears to stem from the failure of the novel's only explicitly heterosexual element. By introducing the feminine into a world that systematically denies it, Dorian's attraction to the young actress . . . seems to violate the male-identified world" of Lord Henry and Basil.[61] It also violates the heterosexual ambience of romance and marriage created, however briefly, by their affair. In this sense, Dorian's relationship with Sibyl performs an important critical function by pointing out the utter inadequacy of marriage as a form of symbolic legitimation. My analysis of Hardy's and Lawrence's Bildungsromane has indicated the extent to which they too have thematized this inadequacy, though in both *Jude the Obscure* and *Sons and Lovers* marriage remains, even in its disparaged, disavowed form, a respected institution and a fulcrum for the development of the protagonists' Bildung plots. In *Dorian Gray*, however, marriage is dismissed as a troublesome social convention whose inadequacy has become the subject of Lord Henry's witty epigrams: "Men marry because they are tired; women, because they are curious; both are disappointed" (*DG* 41). But there is a serious critique behind these epigrammatic sallies, for over against the Goethean notion that a wife "assures for her husband true independence—domestic independence, inner independence,"[62] Lord Henry argues that marriage robs one of this very independence. "The real drawback to marriage is that it makes one unselfish. And unselfish people are colourless. They lack individuality" (*DG* 61). Implied in his remarks is a rejection of the idea that women can serve as spiritualized helpmates for men as they pursue their personal Bildung. Marriage is, at best, an experience, and all experiences have value. But it is nevertheless silly: "there are other and more interesting bonds between men and women. I will certainly encourage them" (*DG* 61). These other bonds are primarily those that repeat a romantic emotion and thereby convert it into art: "Romance lives by repetition, and repetition converts an appetite into an art. Besides, each time that one loves is the only time one has ever loved. Difference of object does not alter singleness of passion. It merely intensifies it. We can have in life but one great experience at best, and the secret of life is to reproduce that experience as often as possible" (*DG* 151). Lord Henry not only condemns marriage on the grounds that it is irrelevant to self-development, he advocates in its place a concept of romance that flies in the face of the bourgeois belief that emotions are unique and inimitable. This critique is bolstered by the travesty of romance and marriage that we see in Dorian's dalliance with Sibyl, particularly in the tragic view he takes of it.

The critical point here is the ease with which romance can become converted into art and the centrality of this process to self-development. As Lord Henry says, "Difference of object does not alter singleness of passion." Dorian's tragic affair with Sibyl becomes a creative opportunity, another lesson in his aesthetic education, which has been conducted all along in drawing rooms, restaurants, theater boxes, and other spaces where ordinary life becomes performance. But at the same time that Dorian is transforming his relationship with Sibyl into melodramatic tragedy, he is also asserting his absolute autonomy, his unique and superior individuality. Dorian's callousness, his maniacal self-centeredness, Gothicizes the self-sufficiency of the sovereign subject that Humboldt, Mill, and so many others regarded as the right of all cultivated individuals. It is interesting that while Wilde is creating Dorian Gray, he is expressing elsewhere a view of individualism that is, in fact, very much in line with the nineteenth-century intellectual tradition just mentioned. In "The Soul of Man under Socialism," Wilde defines individualism as a lawlike process that weds self-sufficiency to a progressive vision of self-development. "Man will develop Individualism out of himself. Man is now so developing Individualism. To ask whether Individualism is practical is like asking whether Evolution is practical. *Evolution is the law of life, and there is no evolution except towards Individualism.* Where this tendency is not expressed, it is a case of artificially-arrested growth, or of disease, or of death."[63] Lord Henry says much the same thing—"no life is spoiled but one whose growth is arrested" (*DG* 61)—while he is willfully interfering in Dorian's development. In "The Soul of Man," Wilde, employing a characteristic argument by reversal, speaks of a failure to express what is essentially a "law of life," the *un*selfishness that constitutes individuality: "a man is called selfish if he lives in the manner that seems to him most suitable for the full realisation of his own personality; if, in fact, the primary aim of his life is self-development. But this is the way in which everyone should live. *Selfishness is not living as one wishes to live, it is asking others to live as one wishes to live.* And unselfishness is letting other people's lives alone, not interfering with them. Selfishness always aims at creating around it an absolute uniformity of type. Unselfishness recognizes infinite variety of type as a delightful thing, accepts it, acquiesces in it, enjoys it."[64] It is worth noting that Lord Henry means quite the opposite when he impugns unselfish husbands for having no individuality; for him, unselfishness appears to define a *lack* of self, while Wilde in "The Soul of Man" uses the term to indicate a pleasure and confidence in the self. It is difficult to tell if Lord Henry's influence over Dorian is an attempt to pull him away from his natural path and steer him toward a "bad" unselfishness or to guide him, in the classical manner of the mentor, toward his natural path (toward a "good" unselfishness). That "The Soul of Man" was composed between the magazine and book versions of *Dorian Gray* suggests that it is meant in part as a critical commentary on Lord Henry's New Hedonism. But if Wilde critiques Lord Henry's attitudes concerning self-development, it does not necessarily follow that he means to indict the concept of Bildung itself; rather, his critique, together with the general Gothicized atmosphere of the novel, suggests that there is little reason to hope for a utopian society (like the Society of the Tower in *Wilhelm Meister*) that could sustain the classical ideal of Bildung, a society in which one could become a "perfect man"—that is, "one who develops under perfect conditions," who does not seek to rebel but desires only peace, who delivers the message of Christ: "Be thyself."[65]

Many of the ideas about self-development and "self-culture" in Wilde's work reflect the influence on him of the Oxford Hellenists.[66] Like Goethe, Humboldt, Pater, and other European intellectuals, Wilde believed that Hellenistic Greece represented the apex of Western civilization and culture. But his interest was never that of the antiquarian or dry-as-dust scholar. As Linda Dowling writes, "Wilde's invocation of Plato and Greek philosophy signals not some unproblematic triumph of modernity over the dead past but . . . a moment in those ceaseless recombinations of cultural materials in which the new or contemporary or modern most often comes to birth through some transmutation, under the pressures of history and ideology, of the old or ancient or even the archaic."[67] One could say that Wilde's modernism is best understood as a project of Hellenization, an attempt to make modern literary and dramatic works convey the emotional intimacy and ritualistic intelligence of classical Greece.[68] Ideas he had gleaned from his readings at Oxford were fundamental to his thinking about the subject and the subject's relation to society at large, but he learned quickly to reject the more pernicious aspects of the education offered at Oxford and other educational institutions, particularly the formalized mode of instruction that neglected aesthetic education or discouraged artistic expression. From the early 1880s, the time of his first lecture tour in America, Wilde had been developing his own ideas about aesthetic education, seeing it as a profoundly important element of a child's formation. In one of his early lectures, "House Decoration," Wilde claims: "The art systems of the past have been devised by philosophers who looked upon human beings as obstructions. They have tried to educate boys' minds before they had any. How much better it would be in these early years to teach children to use their hands in the rational service of mankind. I would have a workshop attached to every school, and one hour a day given up to the teaching of simple decorative arts. It would be a golden hour for the children. . . . It is a practical school of morals.

No better way is there to learn to love Nature than to understand Art.... What we want is something spiritual added to life. Nothing is so ignoble that Art cannot sanctify it."[69] This practical pedagogical scheme provides an answer to our persistent questions about Wilde's aestheticized ethics, for it is clear, in this lecture at least, that learning about art is learning about what is good and right. These are just the sort of humanist values and the kind of practical aesthetic education that Wilde advocates in the dialogues.

Despite his own successful experience at Oxford, Wilde claims in the dialogues that formal education can be an impediment to the acquisition of self-culture. Speaking of "our national stupidity," Vivian in "The Decay of Lying" remarks, "I am afraid that we are beginning to be over-educated; at least everybody who is incapable of learning has taken to teaching—that is really what our enthusiasm for education has come to" (*I* 5).[70] He believes that the "old art of Lying," which is still a part of "home education" and which is "set forth in the early books of Plato's *Republic*," should be revived by the School Board. He suggests further: "A short primer, 'When to Lie and How,' if brought out in an attractive and not too expensive a form . . . would prove of real practical service to many earnest and deep-thinking people" (*I* 50–51). However, Gilbert in "The Critic as Artist" notes: "Education is an admirable thing, but it is well to remember from time to time that nothing that is worth knowing can be taught" (*I* 111). Of course, he means nothing worth knowing can be taught in an institutional setting, for his discourse in this dialogue provides just the sort of primer that Vivian recommends. Immediately after his remark, Gilbert provides an object lesson in creative aesthetic criticism: "Through the parted curtains of the window I see the moon like a clipped piece of silver. Like gilded bees the stars cluster round her. The sky is a hard hollow sapphire." In moments like this, Gilbert demonstrates how the critic composes a work of art. He is creating a picture of what the curtained window expresses for him; he is lying, so to speak, in order to teach. The point is that education in its institutional setting amounts to little more than the dispensing of "useful information" and the forming of minds incapable of composing a scene framed in a window. When Gilbert says, "I live in terror of not being misunderstood" (*I* 111), he is expressing contempt for an educational system that has no use for "lying" or for aesthetic sensibilities, that seeks to overwhelm and conquer through rational understanding. Opposed to such a system is an aesthetic education concerned primarily with how one develops self-culture in relation to beauty, and this can best be accomplished through the mode of criticism advocated by Gilbert. The "true culture of the inner man," he claims, is the "critical and self-conscious spirit" that develops in the individual, who finally (here he quotes Plato) "will recognize and salute it as a friend with whom his education has made him long familiar" (*I* 195). Criticism is the means by which the mind can be made into "a fine instrument," but it is not to be found as a subject of study in the schools. "We, in our educational system," he tells Ernest, "have burdened the memory with a load of unconnected facts, and laboriously striven to impart our laboriously-acquired knowledge. We teach people how to remember, we never teach them how to grow. It has never occurred to us to try and develop in the mind a more subtle quality of apprehension and discernment. The Greeks did this" (*I* 209).

The reference to the Greeks links Gilbert's ideas about criticism and aesthetic education to a tradition of Hellenism that contrasts dramatically with the educational system in late-nineteenth-century England—and this despite the presence at Oxford of Pater and Benjamin Jowett, distinguished Hellenists. By and large the ancient universities had forsaken the humanist tradition and become more and more committed to the research model and a socially pragmatic form of Bildung.[71] However, by the time Wilde published the dialogues, aestheticism had produced a vibrant aesthete-dandy subculture, in which it was possible to pursue a viable literary vocation. Regenia Gagnier argues that the professionalization of the aesthete was in part the result of literary coteries, in part the result of the "increasing isolation of the university as a research institution."[72] Academic specialization opened up whole new vistas of social mobility, according to Gagnier, and Wilde's choice to write outside academia was in some ways no different, especially in the sense that it enabled him to make his commitment to art without having to endure certain social responsibilities. Another development that determined the social context against which Wilde and other late-Victorian dandies were formulating their strategies of aesthetic education was the rise of public schools as the institutional framework for the production of middle-class gentlemen. This development resulted from the wave of educational reforms after 1870 that tended to give institutional force to the class-based divisions created at the secondary level. By the time Wilde was touring America and performing his own version of the aesthete-dandy, the whole idea of the gentleman had undergone a significant transformation. "By the 1880s," Gagnier writes, "to be a gentleman one must have attended a public school (or successfully pose as having done). The public schools created the gentleman whose discontents created the late Victorian dandy."[73] This connection between gentleman and dandy is pursued throughout Wilde's work. As Erskine, the Dorian-like dandy in "The Portrait of Mr. W. H.," says of his years at Eton, "It is always an advantage not to have received a sound commercial education, and what I learned in the playing fields at Eton has been quite as useful to me as anything I was taught at Cambridge."[74] The dandy, as a social figure, was very much the "anti-gentleman," an alternative to the bourgeois subject. Ironically, by the 1890s the gentleman had become "an extremely problematic category," uncannily proximate to the dandy: "The preoccupation [in the press] with the definition and construction of the gentleman did not substantially differ from a similar preoccupation with the definition and construction of the dandy: both were commodified in the cult of personality. The gentleman was the magnum opus of the middle class, and the dandy was the repressed unconscious of mass society. An ambitious system generates its own criticism; the dandy showed the gentleman what he had sacrificed: eccentricity, beauty, camaraderie, a natural aristocracy."[75] The aesthetic education pursued by Dorian Gray articulates in the extreme what the gentleman has missed, while at the same time dramatizing the sacrifices the dandy himself has to make in an age of consumption and commodification. The barter he makes with the painting is the Gothic sign of the excess of his losses.

In *Dorian Gray*, as in the dialogues, the socialization of gentlemen is subjected to a critique that strips it of its naïve attachment to the values of nineteenth-century liberalism, specifically its attachment to any form of socially pragmatic Bildung. To fuel his critique, Wilde exploits an aspect of Bildung—its multiplicity and openness—that Humboldt himself recognized, though he was able to define it only in terms of a personality that could "transform the world in its most manifold shapes into his own solitude."[76] Alternatives to normative subjectivity proliferate in the negative dialectics of *Dorian Gray*, in which the binary play of dialectical thinking is opened up, both in terms of a multiplication of subjects (and identifications) and of the multiplication of genres. For example, Dorian's development is overdetermined by intertextual identifications with Gilbert from "The Critic as Artist," Vivian from "The Decay of Lying," Erskine from "The Portrait of Mr. W. H.," and Wilde himself, whose responses to the criticism of *Dorian Gray* find their place in the vertiginous mise-en-scène of Dorian's Bildung.[77] Dorian's aesthetic education, linked through many affiliations to the Humboldtian ideal of classical Bildung, frees him to be the "more" that he is capable of becoming, to "experience this 'more' as his own negativity."[78] The multiplicity of elements that constellates around the figure of Dorian entails an education in sensuality and aesthetics, the former more or less sublimated in the latter, though at opportune times it is provoked to a dangerous level of desublimation. The negative dialectics of Wilde's Bildungsroman nurtures a Gothicized form of Bildung—monstrous, multiple, duplicitous, non-rational, tending toward nonidentity, the undeadness of vampirism—and a form of inner culture that enjoys the unstable unity of contradictoriness that Wilde's dialecticians theorize in the dialogues.

The episode of the "yellow book," in which Dorian sees "the sins of the world . . . passing in dumb show before him," epitomizes Gothic Bildung. It signals a mood of perverse decadent pleasure that corresponds to the "scientific interest" he takes in studying the changing portrait and comparing it to his own beauty: "He grew more and more enamoured of his own beauty, more and more interested in the corruption of his own soul" (*DG* 97, 99). Dorian's perverse pleasure, like the pleasure he takes in his treasures so extensively related in chapter 11 (as notorious in its own way as the yellow book), Gothicizes the "reflexive project of the self" that Anthony Giddens describes as normative in late modernity, a project in which the subject constructs himself by actively engaging with the very cultural discourses that threaten to engulf and (to use Adorno's term) "administer" subjectivity. The "treasures" that Dorian collects "in his lovely house," in their sheer excess and the sensuousness of the language that catalogues them, are the reflexive means not of identity but of nonidentity—an opting out of normative processes of self-development. His treasures are not commodities, they are like amulets, "means of forgetfulness," like the opium and reckless sexual adventures in which he also indulges, "modes by which he could escape, for a season, from the fear that seemed to him at times to be almost too great to be borne" (*DG* 109). He fears nothing at this point so much as what he sees himself capable of becoming. To modify Wilde's formula in "The Soul of Man under Socialism," he is the *anti*-Christ in the sense that he cannot *be himself*. But he also fears what has come before, for "one had ancestors in literature, as well as in one's own race, nearer perhaps in type and temperament, many of them, and certainly with an influence of which one was more absolutely conscious" (*DG* 113). These ancestors, like the yellow book and nearly everything else in his milieu, exert their influence, inscribe their desires on the scroll of his destiny, and thereby constitute his Bildung. Dorian's fear that he is being lived by his literary and lineal ancestors—"There were times when it appeared . . . that the whole of history was merely the record of his own life, not as he had lived it in act and circumstance, but as his imagination had created it for him" (*DG* 113)—translates into a Gothic context the notion, related in "The Critic as Artist," that "the imagination is the result of heredity. It is simply concentrated race-experience" (*I* 174). Dorian's degeneration is thus more than simply the lowering of his own level of Bildung. "For the development of the race depends on the development of the individual, and where self-culture has ceased to be the ideal, the intellectual standard is instantly lowered, and, often, ultimately lost" (*I* 179). What Dorian fears, then, is not only the loss of his own soul but the loss of his humanity, which he has learned from his mentors, Basil and Lord Henry, to equate with youth and beauty.

What Dorian cannot achieve is the unity of his contradictions, which at least one of his mentors has, along with Gilbert and Vivian, learned to achieve. "The unity of the individual," Wilde writes in an early review, "is being expressed through its inconsistencies and its contradictions. In a strange twilight man is seeking for himself, and when he has found his own image he cannot understand it."[79] This sense of self seems antithetical to a classical humanism that would seek the unity of Bildung, yet Wilde does not surrender the idea of unity so much as redefine it in terms of openness and complexity, which suggests both an incompleteness and an excess of self. The Wildean self, with all of its complexities and inconsistencies, is not really a unity at all but a constellation or ensemble of unifying effects held together by an immanent critical practice that I have described throughout this study as analogous to Adorno's negative dialectics.

This ensemble of unifying effects is illustrated dramatically by the portrait that Basil paints of Dorian. The gatherings in Basil's studio, as we have seen, amount to seminars in aesthetics and artistic sensibility, where Lord Henry describes and exemplifies his theories of personality and influence. As the novel unfolds, these theories are transformed in the direction of Gothic fantasy, which underscores both their limitations and their transgressive potentialities. The material sign of this phantasmatic Gothic Bildung is Basil's portrait, which becomes both the nexus of a homosocial connection between Dorian, Basil, and Lord Henry and the physical manifestation of self-development that throws the self outside the self, but without the Goethean epiphany of social belonging experienced by Wilhelm and many of his successors in the nineteenth century. Certainly, the two aspects of the portrait's signification are intimately linked. Ed Cohen argues that "Dorian Gray is to some extent born of the conjunction between Basil's visual embodiment of his erotic desire for Dorian and Lord Henry's verbal sublimation of such desire. From this nexus of competing representational modes, Dorian Gray constitutes his own representations of identity." We see here the foundation of a dialectical process by which Dorian "transform[s] Lord Henry's verbal and Basil's visual representations" and thus enters into the "circuits of male desire."[80] Dorian recathects or reroutes the sexual energy latent in this transformative process when he realizes suddenly that the picture represents the permanence of a perfection that he possesses only fleetingly. He seeks to claim for himself the eternal beauty and youth of which Lord Henry has spoken and which Basil has represented so successfully in the portrait. "I am jealous of everything whose beauty does not die. I am jealous of the portrait you have painted of me" (*DG* 26). The wish that Dorian utters and the diabolical barter into which he enters constitute what Jonathan Dollimore calls a "perverse dynamic": "not an identity, a logic, or an economy, so much as an anti-teleological dialectic producing knowledge in opposition to destiny." The perverse dynamic, which bears a strong resemblance to Adorno's negative dialectics, "transvalues sameness, abandoning self-identity for the unstably proximate."[81] Basil and Lord Henry serve as representatives of society in the sense that their influence over Dorian spurs him on to make the perverse wish that projects his own actual physical and moral development into the proximate space of the picture. And while it is true that Basil creates the picture, Dorian conscripts it to serve as a fantasy double, thereby projecting his own natural developmental *telos* onto a presumably external object. But this object is no more external than the development it depicts, a truth that Dorian and the reader learn at the conclusion of the novel. In the wish for eternal youth, which drives the Gothic logic of the story, we see a hint of Tir na nOg, the Irish "land of the forever young" that Yeats celebrated as an ambivalent place where one is freed from sorrow but also from human community.[82] The magical quality of the portrait links it to an Irish folk tradition as well as to an Irish Gothic tradition, in both cases keeping the nineteenth-century English Bildungsroman at arm's length. In this fashion *Dorian Gray* transforms the humanist project of self-cultivation, and the Hegelian *telos* that subtends it, into a duplicitous fantasia of otherworldliness and self-destruction. This confusion about the locality of Dorian's "essence" or "soul" defines the specific modality of colonial Bildung, in which identity cannot be contained in or explained by dialectics. Containment is just what David Wayne Thomas claims is possible when he describes the paradox of Dorian's self-realization as the commingling of "willing agency and unwilled determination."[83] The problem with this claim lies in underestimating the role played in Dorian's Bildung plot by the fantastic portrait.

The image that Lord Henry wishes Dorian to see and that is captured in the portrait takes on the progressive and changeable life of the developing self. "It held the secret of his life, and told his story" (*DG* 73). Cohen argues that the painting is a "surface" for the narrative of his life.[84] However, it is in the nature of the Gothic elements that Wilde employs to reach *below* the surface, for Dorian understands—tentatively at first but later, indeed too late, with conviction—that the figure on the canvas is in fact living his life in all of its forbidden depths. David Lawler points out that Dorian's wish is the classic Gothic desire "to re-create himself, this time by bartering his soul for a life in art, appropriating the appearances of the artist's icon, while his soul animates the picture that will then begin to age."[85] It would seem, then, that Dorian becomes more than simply a spectacle of himself in a "magic mirror," as Cohen and others contend, for the Gothic logic of the story insists on the reality of the portrait.[86] "Was there some subtle affinity between the chemical atoms, that shaped themselves into form and colour on the canvas, and the soul that was within him?" Dorian asks himself. "Could it be that what the soul thought, they realized?—that what it dreamed, they made true? Or was there some other, more terrible reason?" (*DG* 76). But what could be more terrible than the possibility that a painting has a living affinity with one's soul? Perhaps that the painting *is* one's soul, and that one has thereby lost it. The mirror image would then be the "real" Dorian. The dialectical play of representation and reality, of aesthetics and ethics, founders on the confusion of terms, for the portrait, in its living dimension, "taught him to love his own beauty" but in its fictive, symbolic dimension stood as "the visible emblem of conscience" (*DG* 73–74). There is no synthesis here, no sublation of the negative into the positive, no affirmation of identity in nonidentity, for the foundering of terms constitutes a constellation of effects: the undead ghost of the unified subject (Dorian, the spectral spectator) which can be discerned only in those utterly horrifying moments when Dorian realizes that his soul, the actual ground of self-development, has been transported out of himself and can be witnessed only when he, as spectator, gazes not upon an image but upon his corporeal body impossibly alive in oil on canvas.[87] There alone does he see himself as a living form that represents both his own beauty and the terrible guilty consciousness it provokes. This haunted moment, in which the dialectic of the self favors the singular reality of nonidentity and impossible corporeality, crystallizes Dorian's aesthetic education and the Gothic Bildung that is its result.

The painting's relation to the human soul is uncanny, writes Julia Prewitt Brown. It "both preserves and annihilates [Dorian's] soul, imprisoning him in what [Walter] Benjamin would later call a 'dialectical image': near and familiar yet strange and remote, a marketable commodity yet a sacred presence, fixed yet mutable, contained yet open, dead yet alive."[88] The allusion to the peculiar status of the vampire in this last phrase alerts us to how the painting signals a moment of critical unrest within the Bildung plot. Indeed, Benjamin's "dialectical image" is a *negative* dialectical image, one that refuses the easy opposition between two poles by tending toward the negative side, the nonidentity of what is being formed in dialectical opposition, much as Dracula, who is pallid and unsociable when "passing" as a human, tends to orient his whole being toward death. This "turn toward nonidentity" is an excess of signification rather than an inversion of a signifying dialectic. The oppositions noted by Brown, while certainly discernible in the text, are destabilized by the very excess of the negative term, specifically by Wilde's Gothic treatment of the portrait. Dorian's hysterical need to keep the portrait hidden from public view stems from his fear that it will confirm his own identity or, more horrifying still, that it will not. In either case, the painting represents the draining away of his humanness. It is truly vampiric, and Dorian's realization of this fact comes hard upon the proof he receives when he finally does show it to Basil. When Basil confronts Dorian with his "bad" reputation and his "fatal" influence over other men, he remarks that he could not say he knew Dorian because then "I should have to see your soul" (*DG* 119). Dorian obliges him. Basil, taking in the horrific discovery, sees it as an "awful lesson" and implores Dorian to pray. Dorian's rapid transmutation from indifferent Epicurean, who watches the artist's reactions with the "passion of the spectator" (*DG* 121), to raging murderer signals not dialectical play but the overturning of its possibility in a monstrous travesty. As horrible as it turns out to be, his relationship with Alan Campbell, who helps him get rid of Basil's body, is very much like the relationship between Dorian and Lord Henry—only Dorian is in the dominant position. But this apparent reversal and reaffirmation of a dialectical engagement between aesthetics and ethics, in which a negative term is elevated and preserved, is undercut by the actual disposal of the body, by Basil's utter annihilation by chemical means. Dorian's apparent lack of feeling in the aftermath of Campbell's efforts indicates the extent to which he must mask the terrible failure of the dialectical energies that have hitherto motivated his self-development. He goes on with his life as if he were acting: "Perhaps one never seems so much at one's ease as when one has to play a part." He "felt keenly the terrible pleasure of a double life" (*DG* 135)—double not only in the sense that he was acting but also in the sense that he is doubled in the picture, separated from his own conscience and the consciousness of his sins.

What ends up afflicting him most horribly, however, is his memory of a past that cannot be ignored: "Memory, like a horrible malady, was eating his soul away. . . . He wanted to escape from himself," for his own personality has become a "burden" (*DG* 145, 157). Later still, he cries out that he wants a "new life" (*DG* 168). Dorian's fate underscores dramatically Wilde's critique of aestheticism, the "wild desire to live" that has devolved from being a desire for beauty to an obsession with the "one reality" of crime and ugliness. Dorian's Bildung is not a beautiful artifice "against the grain" of nature but a degradation of the natural that does not transcend it. The point at which Dorian realizes that selfhood is a burden coincides with the reemergence of James Vane, whose murderous wrath he manages to escape outside the opium den, only to encounter him in the country and witness his accidental death (*DG* 153–59). He is now safe enough to tell Henry he has "a new ideal"—"I am going to alter. I think I have altered"—and then relate his having "spared somebody." Dorian's monstrous egotism is such that he feels he can be saved by "sparing" a young girl. Lord Henry of course mocks this desire for reform: "From a moral point of view, I can't say that I think much of your renunciation" (*DG* 161). He does not wish for Dorian to spoil his life with such renunciations, and so returns to his perennial themes of beauty and youth. The younger man's aesthetic perfections save him from both excess and renunciation, or so Lord Henry would like to believe. Because Dorian has access to an aesthetic education, he could very well commit a murder, but he need not do so. "I should fancy that crime was to [the lower orders] what art is to us, simply a method of procuring extraordinary sensations" (*DG* 162). It is common for readers to believe that Lord Henry fails to see the true nature of Dorian's Bildung. But is it possible that he fails to see the devastating irony of his words? "You are the type of what the age is searching for, and what it is afraid it has found," he says to Dorian, underscoring the ambivalent conjunction of desire and fear that has haunted Dorian's relation with his own image for twenty years. "I am so glad that you have never done anything, never carved a statue, or painted a picture, or produced anything outside of yourself! Life has been your art. You have set yourself to music. Your days are your sonnets" (*DG* 165). Dorian's life has in fact been a form of art, and, strictly speaking, he has not produced a statue or any other work. But he *has been produced*, outside of himself, as a picture. This production of the self is the crux of Dorian's moral dilemma: he recognizes the dehiscence of self that has pitted him against himself, not as in a mirror but as an entirely other being. Would that this art he had become were sonnets.

In the end, the reader does not know quite how to regard Lord Henry, for all he knows is the utterly unnatural youth and beauty that Dorian has managed to retain—and which his mentor does not appear to question. He has not seen, as poor Basil did, the portrait that belies the encomiums to Dorian's sonnetlike existence. This is why Lord Henry can flatly deny that Dorian could have been "poisoned by a book": "Art has no influence upon action. It annihilates the desire to act. It is superbly sterile. The books that the world calls immoral are books that show the world its own shame. That is all" (*DG* 166). Because Lord Henry does not act out the aesthetic theories he articulates, he does not fall victim to conscience and guilt as Dorian does. But it is difficult not to speculate on Lord Henry's understanding of his young friend's motives. Certainly Dorian has dropped enough hints that his aesthetic desire entails consequences that go beyond the presumably closed circuit of that desire. Does Lord Henry really not understand the ethical crisis of aestheticism, that point at which the love of beauty must take on an ethical responsibility for action? Dorian, to his credit, comes to realize the fatality of his Faustian bargain, for he learns to despise himself precisely for the beauty "that had ruined him, his beauty and the youth that he had prayed for. . . . His beauty had been to him but a mask, his youth but a mockery" (*DG* 167–68). He learns that beauty and youth, far from granting him immortality, have burdened him with the "living death of his own soul" (*DG* 168). His awareness of this undeadness, this radical nonidentity, compels him to perform his final dramatic act of self-destruction. He is no longer himself: in the portrait all he sees is a "loathsome" and "hideous thing" that urges him to confess, to free himself from the burden of his past, to "kill this monstrous soul-life." He realizes that his pursuit of self-development has been a sham, but so too has been the "denial of self" that he tried "for curiosity's sake" (*DG* 168–69). While it is possible to read the conclusion of *Dorian Gray* as a reconstitution of wholeness and innocence of the sort typical in conventional Gothic fiction, this reading is hobbled by the fact that only the painting remains of any achieved wholeness and innocence, while Dorian lies dead on the floor, grotesquely aged and corrupted. The final image of the "splendid portrait" of Dorian "in all the wonder of his exquisite youth and beauty" is haunted by what we are asked to accept as real, a corpse "withered, wrinkled, and of loathsome visage," identifiable only by its rings (*DG* 170). Even after death, identity continues to slip into nonidentity, to rest finally in some inert thing, an attenuated sign, a dead man's jewelry.

Dorian's Gothic Bildung inscribes negative dialectics as a kind of vampirism, the undead triumphing over life *and* death. It is the symbol of that irrationality that cannot be totally contained within the matrix of the rational. "Irrationality," which is not the same as "philosophical irrationalism," according to Adorno, "is the scar which the irremovable nonidentity of subject and object leaves on cognition—whose mere form of predicative judgment postulates identity; it is also the hope of withstanding the omnipotence of the subjective concept. Like the concept, however, irrationality itself remains a function of the *ratio* and an object of its self-criticism: what slips through the net is filtered by the net." The space of the irrational is that which evades the dialectical investments of rationality *and* irrationalism, but not without bearing the imprimatur of the dialectic it has dodged. One of the "motives of dialectics" is to "usurp[] a standpoint beyond the difference of subject and object—the difference that shows how inadequate the *ratio* is to thought. By means of reason, however, such a leap will fail. We cannot, by thinking, assume any position in which that separation of subject and object will directly vanish, for the separation is inherent in each thought; it is inherent in thinking itself."[89] The painting, and Dorian's final destructive relation to it, dramatizes the triumph of irrationality. It is the triumph neither of life nor of death nor of a dialectical synthesis of the two, nor even of a third term. What triumphs is the terrifying multiplicity of nonidentity that scuttles dialectic and unleashes a potential for wild, excessive, unnamable desires. It is no wonder that Wilde sought, through revision and commentary, to veil this desire, or that he sought to lift the veil in a preface that seems to countermand prior revisions and comment.[90] The "moral" that Wilde appended to the text in his attempt to defend it—"all excess, as well as all renunciation, brings its own punishment"—ought to be read as itself an ironic reading of it. This effect was repeated again and again when he defended the novel on artistic terms in the press and in the courtroom. What is "more important than the novel itself," Gagnier writes, "is the controversy it generated, for it recapitulated the novel's themes."[91] Wilde's relationship with Lord Alfred Douglas, his testimony in court, and a host of other public performances constitute extensions of the Gothic drama narrated in *Dorian Gray*. The vertigo and duplicity produced by this Salomé-like dance of the veils are textual effects of the negative dialectic at the heart of Wilde's colonial Bildungsroman.

COLONIAL BILDUNG IN JOYCE'S
A PORTRAIT OF THE ARTIST AS A YOUNG MAN

When read in the context of the English Bildungsroman of the late nineteenth century, it is difficult not to see Wilde's *Picture of Dorian Gray* as a deliberate critique of prevailing regimes of socialization that were no longer able or willing to support the freedom of self-cultivation. We can see in this resistance something like an allegory of Anglo-Irish displacement, in which the sublimated energies of the Bildung process are refracted through an aesthetic theory that encourages transgression and nonidentity. Wilde recognized that the social demand for "viable" human beings had become transformed into a demand for marketable ones; socialization had become commodification in a process that may have been made more apparent to him by his own precarious social position as an Anglo-Irishman living in London, compelled by circumstances to sell himself. It is the fate of a metrocolonial subject uneasily poised between Irish and English identities, between colonial and imperial economies, to be sensitive to the necessity to perform subjectivity in the utter lack of any "natural" or "national" claim on it.

To some degree, this is Joyce's fate as well. The shared foundation in Bildung and aesthetic education, signaled by a common thematics of portraiture, lends Wilde's and Joyce's texts their mutual affinities, one of which is the repudiation of social conditions that offer nothing productive to their respective Bildung processes. But whereas the Protestant Wilde rejects bourgeois culture from the privileged perspective of the Anglo-Irish intelligentsia, the Catholic Joyce rejects the same culture from the point of view of the colonized subject whose subaltern position effectively places him at the lowest level of the imperial class system.

As I have argued in the introduction to this study, alongside the nineteenth-century Bildungsroman we see a general trend toward the institutionalization of the regimes of socialization within state-sponsored educational systems. Theorists of modernity as diverse as Anthony Giddens, Michel Foucault, and Ernest Gellner have pointed out that this trend created a situation in which the absolute subject of bourgeois liberal society had become a commodity, a viable product for the furtherance of the very system that produced it. This is not to say that the bourgeois subject was in any way devalued as a result of this institutionalization of its formation. On the contrary, I want to stress that this trend sustained the authority and prestige the bourgeois subject had acquired, for, after all, it transformed the modes of *production* into the modes of *self-reproduction*. But this is implicit in the logic of advanced industrial capitalism, which of necessity must replicate its managers, technicians, operators, and educators. The crises in such a system are constitutive of it, are in fact the internal evidence of advancement and self-regulation.[92] Matters were quite different in a metrocolonial situation like Ireland, where unevenness in industrial expansion and development led to a crisis situation that extended well into the postcolonial era.[93] The economic models of development that governed the prosperity of England at home were, conversely, those that devastated Ireland.[94] Vast numbers of people were excluded from those sectors of the island that were developed, while the kinds of social problems found in the developed sectors—low pay, unemployment, overcrowded housing, unsafe and unsanitary conditions—tended to be far worse than elsewhere in Europe.

In the absence of viable means of economic and social reform, the asymmetries in cultural and economic development often led to arrested or catastrophic personal development, especially among those not fortunate enough to belong to the new Catholic middle classes. These conditions, taken together with the psychological effects of colonial violence, were profoundly deleterious for the self-development of the colonial subject. Albert Memmi was among the first to theorize what he calls an "internal catastrophe," a form of arrested development unique to the colonial situation:

> The revolt of the adolescent colonized, far from resolving into mobility and social progress, can only sink into the morass of colonized society—unless there is a total revolution. . . . Sooner or later then, the potential rebel falls back on the traditional values. This explains the astonishing survival of the colonized's family. The colonial superstructure has real value as a refuge. It saves the colonized from the despair of total defeat and, in return, it finds confirmation in a constant inflow of new blood. . . . Revolt and conflict have ended in a victory for the parents and tradition. But it is a pyrrhic victory. Colonized society has not taken even half a step forward; for the young man, it is an internal catastrophe.[95]

Unreflective, passive acquiescence to imposed modes of socialization, or a failure to resist them, can lead only to a travesty of the identitarian logic of Bildung in which the colonized suffers the isolation of his own subjectivity. This process not only severs the adolescent colonized from any external, socially viable means of attaining the status of a "legitimate" subject, it in fact produces a traumatic and effectively permanent dehiscence of subjectivity.

The question at this point has to do with the structure of colonial relations. Do they constitute, as Frantz Fanon argues, a Manichean dynamic—two foes, the colonizer and the colonized, pitted against each other to the death, the colonized seeking to overtake the colonizer? Or do they compose, as Memmi believes, a dialectic of social types, in which each defines the other in a classical Hegelian manner, but which threatens constantly to devolve into the absolute polarization of Manicheism? Given that this threat is all too real, one is hard pressed to see a significant difference. What is certainly clear in both cases is the sense that colonial relations are *necessary*, the sense that the colonial subject is excluded from history by an implacable and interminable process. Colonial relations, according to Memmi, "determine *a priori*" the place of both colonizer and colonized. Within these relations, the colonizer "admits to a fundamental difference between the colonized and himself"; it is a "specific historical fact."

It is part of a "dialectics exalting the colonizer and humbling the colonized."[96] When confronted with this dialectic, the colonial subject can try either to recapture the time before colonization, what Fanon has called "the vast black abyss" of the "mystical past,"[97] or to enter into the dialectic willingly. In this latter option Memmi finds the classic dilemma of the colonized subject, one that leads to a situation in which the "first ambition of the colonized is to become equal to that splendid model [the colonizer] and to resemble him to the point of disappearing in him." A third option entails "total revolution." In any case, the self-development of the adolescent colonized is subject to historical necessities over which he has no control. Subjectivity is driven inward in the process, severed from any productive social integration; it becomes totally alienated and phantasmatic: the colonial subject "almost never succeeds in corresponding with himself."[98]

By the same token, the cultural ideals that accompany colonial domination—philosophical transcendence, white male dominance, heterosexuality, secularism, positive science, bourgeois subjectivity—very often frustrate the desires of the colonial subject. They do not represent the sociality into which an artist like Stephen Dedalus would desire to be harmoniously integrated. Humboldtian self-sufficiency seems a particularly unfeasible option. What is offered instead is a contest. Whereas classical Bildung envisions a dialectical harmony of self and society, a process of productive and rewarding intersubjectivity, colonial Bildung isolates and splits the subject, pits it against itself. Whereas socially pragmatic forms of Bildung envision a socially "viable" subject, one that can be reliably reproduced by educational systems, colonial Bildung sets up an essentially penal society, where social life and self-development are hemmed in and reshaped by restraints and taboos. In colonial Bildung, dialectics threatens to become the pathway not toward harmony, subjectivity, and viability but toward tyranny and subjection. This leads to a consciousness of nonidentity, to a condition in which the colonial subject's rage for change is directed not simply against a given norm—in this case, of Bildung or socialization—but against normativity as such. The desire for self-cultivation, which in the classical Bildungsroman is tied to aesthetic and pragmatic modes of Bildung, appears to the colonial subject as a transgression, an impossible dream. The colonial Bildungsroman, like the female form that began to flourish alongside the Goethean prototype, articulates this dream.

Joyce's *Portrait of the Artist as a Young Man*, despite its subversive strategies of critique, hews closely to generic conventions. Those few critics who speak of Joyce's Bildungsroman tend to downplay the radical critique of Bildung and direct their attention instead to his ambivalent relationship with the Bildungs-roman tradition. Breon Mitchell writes: "Part of Joyce's particular genius was the ability to draw upon the literary past and deliver it to the future in an en-riched form."[99] Jerome Buckley makes a similar claim: "Joyce sums up, even as he transforms, the traditions of the nineteenth-century Bildungsroman."[100] Buckley also situates Joyce's text within a tradition of English Bildungsromane, which is the very tradition that Joyce, like Wilde, wrote *against*. I concede, of course, that Joyce's Bildungsroman does have some affinities with the English tradition, especially with respect to the centrality of the artist's development and the *Bildungsheld*'s tendency to recruit women to perform complex instrumen-tal functions in the course of pursuing his development. Though both Stephen Dedalus and Paul Morel make principled attempts to repudiate the social "nets" that entrap them, Stephen takes the more decisive step of self-exile. And while Joyce's modernist Bildungsroman is perhaps the more successful challenge to the hegemony that the form enjoyed throughout the nineteenth century, it is a challenge that nevertheless fails on more or less the same terms that we have already seen in Hardy and Lawrence—that is, it fails *necessarily* as part of an immanent critique of the genre and of its dominant theme of Bildung. It is the paradoxical situation that Wilde savors in *Dorian Gray*, that famous critique of aestheticism decked out in the regalia of the aesthete.

In his introduction to the 1993 edition of *A Portrait of the Artist as a Young Man*, Seamus Deane argues that Stephen Dedalus is primarily known to readers at first by quotations; by the end of the novel, he is quoting himself: "the narrated Stephen becomes the narrator Stephen."[101] In terms of development, he is for the most part what he has read or, as Deane puts it, borrowed: "His idea of the soul and its relation to the body is at first a borrowed one . . . culled from the teaching of his religious superiors and later confirmed by his reading of litera-ture, especially Dante. But, worst of all, Stephen feels the threat of his borrowed culture when it seeks to co-opt him, when it tries to recruit him into its system of institutionalized borrowing, either through the vocation of the priesthood or through a commitment to Irish nationalism."[102] Deane could have added the vocation of teaching to his list of possible institutionalized forms of bor-rowing, for Stephen is frequently depicted in scenes of instruction, both as a student and, in *Ulysses*, as a teacher. Elsewhere Deane has noted that Stephen is the first intellectual hero in the history of the novel and that thinking—an "intellectual vocation"—is an important element in his narrative of develop-ment.[103] However, the experience of intellectual life that Deane describes is far

from the harmonious socialization that Fritz Martini, among a host of theorists of the genre, considers to be the raison d'être of the Bildungsroman: the
"idea of cultivation (*Bildung*) through a harmony of aesthetic, moral, rational,
and scientific education [that] had long been common property of Enlightenment thought."[104] Indeed, it is in a general thematics of dissent from this
ideological function and in a refusal of its legitimating authority that we find
the modernist impulse in Joyce's Bildungsroman. Like so many other early
modernist Bildungsromane, *Portrait* manages to retain and even emulate the
formal structures of a genre whose conceptual foundations and thematic concerns are at the same time subjected to critique and revision. Joyce does this
not primarily by altering the structure of the Bildung plot in some subversive
way but by narrating new norms of development, new scenes of acculturation
and education, that test the limits and critique the various components of the
classical Bildungsroman.

In Joyce's Bildungsroman, formal education plays a more complicated role
than it does in the Bildungsromane of Hardy or Lawrence, for its protagonist is educated in denominational schools (first Clongowes, then Belvedere
College), which had found their niche within colonial society and which offered limited access to the "natural education in conformity with the inner
development of the psyche" that Dilthey links to the classical Bildungsroman
tradition.[105] Unlike the National Schools, in which colonial students had to
choose dissent or "alienated assent" to the foreign values imposed upon them,
the denominational schools did make some appeal to national values.[106] And
while such schools offered a superior grade of education, they also exposed students to forms of eroticized pedagogical violence perhaps unique to colonial
education.[107] It is no coincidence that one of the most important incidents
in Stephen's early education conjoins violence and homoeroticism. He has already learned to take pleasure in this conjunction: "And though he trembled
with cold and fright to think of the cruel long nails and of the high whistling
sound of the cane and of the chill you felt at the end of your shirt when you
undressed yourself yet he felt a feeling of queer quiet pleasure inside him to
think of the white fattish hands, clean and strong and gentle" (*P* 45; see also
50–53). Because he believes that his punishment is undeserved, Stephen rebels
against the authority of his teachers and gains the approbation of his peers.[108]
He walks the gamut of "saints and great men of the order," thinking of the
"great men of history" whose names were as distinctive as his own. He presents
his case to the rector, then returns to his fellows who "made a cradle of their
locked hands and hoisted him up among them and carried him along till he

struggled to get free" (*P* 55, 58). The figures of Father Dolan and the rector are the masculine embodiments of Church authority, but they are also embodiments of the more general authority governing socialization. As John H. Smith has noted, the "goal" of the *Bildungsroman* is to represent "the self's developmental trajectory within the bourgeois patriarchal order and thereby to expose the structuration of (male) desire."[109] By the end of chapter 1, Stephen is able to discern a pattern of violence connected with the acquisition of knowledge and to assert himself successfully against it and, to some degree, his own desire, only to find himself still under its sway. In a characteristic reverie, Stephen curtails his own rebellion: "he would not be anyway proud with Father Dolan. He would be very quiet and obedient" (*P* 59). In this microcosm of his Bildung plot, we see that the only way out for a Catholic Irish colonial subject is to capitulate to and take a certain pleasure in the mediated route of social mobility offered by the Church.

At this critical juncture in his development, Stephen is coming into consciousness of the homosocial structure of his relations with other men, both his peers and his potential mentors.[110] His interactions with other schoolboys in chapter 2 disclose the specific pressures brought to bear in a denominational school in a colonial context. The attempt to distance himself from such interactions is comically duplicated in the role he plays in the Whitsuntide play (*Vice Versâ; or, A Lesson to Fathers*) at Belvedere College. In this play about a son who does not wish to return to school and who is granted his wish that he become his father and his father become him, Stephen is cast as a "farcical pedagogue... on account of his stature and grave manners" (*P* 73). Of course, these very qualities set some of the other boys against him. Just before the play begins, Vincent Heron hails "the noble Dedalus," that "model youth." Stephen ignores him until Heron touches on the subject of his father. "Any allusion made to his father by a fellow or by a master put his calm to rout in a moment" (*P* 76). Inexplicably, the reference to his father provokes in him a meditation on his own youth and development. A "shaft of momentary anger" at Heron passes, and he finds himself thinking of an encounter two years earlier with Emma Clery ("E.C."), whom he is to see again that night; an "old restless moodiness" permeates him and he realizes, suddenly, the "growth and knowledge of two years of boyhood" (*P* 77). As if to mark this new stage of his development, Heron parodies the role of mentor when he "playfully" strikes Stephen with his cane and forces him to "admit" to his relationship with E.C., to confirm (and affirm) the heterosocial structure of courting and being found out (*P* 77–78).

Stephen's response to this playful violence is to recite the Confiteor, the confessional prayer, which simultaneously responds to and dodges Heron's command by parodying the relation of penitent and confessor. While saying the prayer, "a sudden memory had carried him to another scene called up, as if by magic," by the playful stroke and the "familiar word of admonition: Admit" (*P* 78). The memory is of a beating he suffered by Heron and his pals, for preferring Byron over Tennyson (*P* 78–82), a memory of another kind of pedagogical violence that Joyce's Bildungsroman offers up as further evidence of the institutionalization of coercive demands on self development. As he repeats the Confiteor, he is strangely calmed "amid the indulgent laughter of his hearers," and he wonders "why he bore no malice now to those who had tormented him" (*P* 82). But far from being forgotten, "that malignant episode" is revisited and rewritten as a pivotal moment the consequences of which only now crop up, when he is safely "divested" of his anger: "He had not forgotten a whit of their cowardice and cruelty but the memory of it called forth no anger from him. All the descriptions of fierce love and hatred which he had met in books had seemed to him therefore unreal. Even that night as he stumbled homewards along Jones's Road he had felt that some power was divesting him of that suddenwoven anger as easily as a fruit is divested of its soft ripe peel" (*P* 82). This falling away of anger, figured by an image of ecclesiastical divestiture, leaves the young boy entirely helpless, his nonresistance signaling the passive and somatic nature of his sense of himself as a naked, vulnerable, violated body. The general images Stephen uses—the shaft of anger, the naked fruit—suggest a homoerotic fixation, which is strengthened by his inability to recall the object of his reputed heterosexual desire. Stephen does not forget "a whit" of the episode in which Heron serves as his confessor, but he does forget E.C., the first instrumental support of his Bildung process: "He tried to recall her appearance but could not. He could remember only that she had worn a shawl about her head like a cowl and that her dark eyes had invited and unnerved him" (*P* 82). This conversion of woman into image becomes Stephen's signature response not only to the possibility of heterosexual relations but also to the crises of self-development.

In the hypermasculine world of the Catholic boarding school, the violence meted out by Heron is connected, through the pedagogical contexts in which it takes place, with a colonial relation in which the subject is coerced into socialization. He stands in for the colonial official who demands obedience as a matter of course; his authority over Stephen reduplicates without critically reflecting upon the structures of imperial power, and all the more insidiously for being simultaneously an act of imperial coercion *and* an act of personal betrayal. Heron, then, is the personification of colonial ambivalence *that is unaware of itself as such*.[111] Nor is he aware, in his unreflective bantering, that he is in the same position as Stephen: "out of the game" of history. "Of course," writes Memmi, the colonial subject "carries its burden, often more cruelly than others, but always as an object. He has forgotten how to participate actively in history and no longer even asks to do so."[112] Heron is happy to ape the prerogatives of power. Stephen, on the other hand, recognizes that he can only know his own history, can acquire knowledge only of himself and his Bildung process, which is overdetermined, at this early stage of development, by inchoate feelings—"foreknowledge," "premonition," "intuition"—forms of proleptic self-knowledge that can appear to the adolescent only as "a strange unrest" or as "monstrous images" (*P* 64–65, 90).

The episode with Heron underscores Stephen's problematic relation to patriarchal authority. Just after leaving him, while waiting to go onstage, he imagines himself subjected to a succession of possible mentors and social authorities "urging him to be a gentleman . . . urging him to be strong and manly and healthy": a din of "hollowsounding voices that made him halt irresolutely in the pursuit of phantoms" (*P* 83–84). After the play, he runs off and collapses in nearly incoherent disappointment: "That is horse piss and rotted straw, he thought. It is a good odour to breathe. It will calm my heart. My heart is quite calm now. I will go back" (*P* 86). The trope of return links this episode with the general pattern of return inscribed in and by the narrative dialectics of the Bildungsroman form, while at the same time his "[p]ride and hope and desire like crushed herbs in his heart" remind him of the need to leave his father's world behind. In the meantime, Stephen is drawn to "horse piss and rotted straw," which acquires a positive value: "a good odour to breathe." By affirming and revaluing the sordid materiality of bestial waste, Stephen covertly affirms and revalues the "monstrosities" that are emerging within him and that are linked to the material stratum of life. This affirmation will ultimately ground an eucharistic aesthetics that transforms the "sluggish matter of the earth" into an "imperishable being" (*P* 169), but not without retaining something of that sluggish matter as a reminder of the origin of artistic apprehension.

The full import of the lesson he has learned comes home to him while on a visit to Cork with his father, who is liquidating some of the family's property at auction. What he learns is that his own path is not the one of mild "gentlemanly" heroism about which Simon Dedalus gasses on in Cork pubs with his old cronies. Gerald Peters reminds us of the fundamental importance in *Portrait* of the father as a symbolic authority: "As in the traditional process of *Bildung*, a transcendental signifier of cultural authority (i.e., the father) must be invoked at some point in order to ground the identity of self within the artificial womb of culture." Language is the means by which "to maintain a transcendental signified at the center of cultural articulation that will generate vital links between individual identity and social authority."[113] One of Stephen's first responses to this patriarchal "cultural authority," in the Christmas dinner scene, is terror at its fragility, which is linked, on the one hand, to the fall of Parnell and, on the other hand, to his father's declining fortunes (see *P* 27–39). By the time he reaches adolescence, he has learned to dismantle the language of the authority of which he stood in awe as a child. Sheldon Brivic notes that "the real value of [his] meditations on language for his development is that he is taking apart the conventional codes to grow aware of alternate possibilities."[114] He comes to understand the pathos of colonial masculinity while appearing to listen to his father relate the virtues of being a gentleman. The "growth and knowledge of two years of boyhood" (*P* 77) culminate in the discovery that his "education of the senses" is the antithesis of the socialization proffered by his father: the making of "bloody good honest Irishmen" who associate with "fellows of the right kidney" (*P* 91).

This vision of the gentleman is really retrospective wish fulfillment on Simon Dedalus's part, and Stephen later indicates how well he knows it when he "enumerate[s] glibly his father's attributes": "A medical student, an oarsman, a tenor, an amateur actor, a shouting politician, a small landlord, a small investor, a drinker, a good fellow, a storyteller, somebody's secretary, something in a distillery, a taxgatherer, a bankrupt and at present a praiser of his own past" (*P* 241). This excess of attributes, far from communicating a sense of parental authority, has the effect of diminishing the authority of the father and his ability to perform reliably as a mentor to his son. Simon's scheme to have Stephen train under Mike Flynn, who "had put some of the best runners of modern times through his hands" (*P* 61), underscores his total lack of understanding of his son's talents and ambitions.[115] The famous schoolroom scene in Cork, where Stephen reads an inscription that shocks him by naming his own "monstrous reveries," illustrates further the bankrupt potential of the Father's Law, that "artificial womb of culture." The inscription of *Foetus* on a desk, like "horse piss and rotted straw," asserts the priority and power of material nature, the Maternal-as-Real over the exhausted symbolic Law of the Father. The proximity of the inscription to the monstrosities of his own "deviant" sexual desires results not so much in epiphany as in incarnation: "the word and the vision" of his father's schooldays "capered before his eyes," and his recent "monstrous reveries came thronging into his memory" (*P* 90). This proximity confirms the degradation of all his idealizations and with them the Bildung plot in which they were instrumental. What makes such proximation "at once ineluctable and dangerous," writes Joseph Valente, "is also what gives it a specific shape, valence, and site of operations—the existence of normative power relations."[116] While his "monstrous way of life" seems "to have put himself beyond the limits of reality" (*P* 92), it also urges him to regain those limits and, by so doing, to reduplicate the normative power relations he wishes to repudiate. Thus he attempts to use the money he wins in essay contests "to build a breakwater of order and elegance against the sordid tide of life without him and to dam up, by rules of conduct and active interests and new filial relations, the powerful recurrence of the tides within him" (*P* 98). He is, in effect, attempting to make up for the inadequacy of the Father's Law ("the sordid tide of life without him"), but he also realizes that his own desires ("the tides within him") are every bit as destructive as the conventional authority he reduplicates.

One of the most significant signs of Stephen's loss of faith in the authority of the Father is his attitude toward confession. We have already seen that Stephen responds to Heron with the prayer of confession, perhaps because it represents a mode of discourse that protects him from the anarchy of his own desire as well as from the retaliatory punishment (of Father Dolan and Heron) that would regulate and normalize that desire. At this early stage in his development, Stephen does not yet realize that in turning to confession he replaces one form of desire with another and thus invites new forms of regulation and normalization.

To confess is to acknowledge, to own, to avow; it is linked etymologically to the desire to utter, to declare, to disclose, to make manifest. In theological terms, confession is "the acknowledging of sin or sinfulness," specifically "the confessing of sin to a priest, as a religious duty."[117] The confessor, acting in the capacity of a transhuman conduit, accepts the penitent's burden of sin and grants the specified penance and absolution. In the Sacrament of Penance of the Roman Catholic Church, confession prepares the penitent for the Eucharist; it is an opportunity to cleanse the soul of those deformities that outrage God in order that penance and reconciliation through the Host can proceed smoothly. It is a regulated, dialectical structure in which the confessor, who is the symbolic substitute for Christ, offers absolution to the sinful penitent on the other side of the screen.[118] Foucault's famous discussion of confession confirms what is after all a matter of explicit Church doctrine:

> The confession is a ritual of discourse in which the speaking subject is also the subject of the statement; it is also a ritual that unfolds within a power relationship, for one does not confess without the presence (or virtual presence) of a partner who is not simply the interlocutor but the authority who requires the confession, prescribes and appreciates it, and intervenes in order to judge, punish, forgive, console, and reconcile; a ritual in which the truth is corroborated by the obstacles and resistances it has had to surmount in order to be formulated; and finally, a ritual in which the expression alone, independently of its external consequences, produces intrinsic modifications in the person who articulates it.[119]

Confessional knowledge is a form of sacred self-knowledge, a truth about one-self that is given to another in a ritualized dialectical relation, with the power of truth resting in the authority of the confessor.[120] The latter's power lies in his ability to draw out the truth of desire and to reconcile the penitent with himself.[121] In "the pious practice of frequent confession," Pope Pius XII writes in the encyclical *Mystici corporis*, "genuine self-knowledge is increased, Christian humility grows, bad habits are corrected, spiritual neglect and tepidity are countered, the conscience is purified, the will strengthened, a salutary self-control attained and grace increased by reason of the sacrament itself."[122] The "genuine self-knowledge" generated in the confessional is, paradoxically, a form of disavowal, a submission of the self to the transcendent example of Jesus Christ and his earthly proxies. Moreover, the structure of orthodox confession, with its dialectical interplay of repentance and absolution, dovetails with the narrative logic of the classical Bildungsroman, with its dialectical harmony of inner culture and social responsibility. Like the mentor who guides the *Bildungsheld* along a pathway to Bildung that he has mapped out in advance, the confessor guides the penitent toward a prescribed goal of absolution.

Shortly after his failure to "build a breakwater of order and elegance," Stephen succumbs to the temptation of confession and falls into the dialectical trap of sin and salvation that the Church leaves open for him and that only later he will learn to turn to his advantage. But in order to succumb to this temptation, he must first become a sinner, which he does with considerable gusto. The "cold lucid indifference" (*P* 103) that follows upon his encounter with a prostitute at the end of chapter 2 is a prelude to a more sweeping engulfment in a characteristically Irish narrative of salvation. The reader is struck by the language of redemption in which Stephen couches his rebellion against the Church, the pride he takes in "his own sin," his "loveless awe of God" that prevents him from making a "false homage to the Allseeing and Allknowing" (*P* 104). Despite his rebellion, the consciousness of sin, like the consciousness of an interdiction, holds him in his place in a providential narrative. He is soon swept away by it. The theological fervor of Father Arnall's sermon at the retreat, intensified by the intricacies of "composition" in Loyola's *Spiritual Exercises* (1541), signals the hegemony of a sacramental discourse that cannot easily be rejected, that seeks to contain and defuse colonial Bildung by creating a transcendent space for the reconciliation of the sinful individual with the Church and God.[123]

As part of this containment, the retreat discourse cancels the coming into consciousness of sexuality. Under the influence of Father Arnall's sermon, with its exorbitant imagery and horrifying conceptions of temporal and spatial interminability, Stephen feels the full weight of a sacred interdict. Father Arnall's words, like Lord Henry's in *Dorian Gray*, are those of a vivisectionist who exerts a painful and invasive influence. "The preacher's knife had probed deeply into his diseased conscience and he felt now that his soul was festering in sin." He regrets the way he has "trampled" on the innocence of Emma, whose image appears before him now and fills him with shame. He recalls the "sordid details of his orgies," which include pornographic images and "foul long letters he had written in the joy of guilty confession" left "where a girl might come upon them as she walked by and read them secretly" (*P* 115–16). The language of exorbitance—sordid orgies, monstrous dreams, apelike creatures, joys of guilty confession—is unambiguous testimony to the subversive and profane power of an "idle mind." The image of the Virgin Mary presiding over Stephen's imaginary marriage to Emma counters the "sordid details" and monstrous desires and transforms the "joy of guilty confession" into the "happiness" of a normative heterosexual union. Stephen thus enacts in fantasy the marriage of personal desire and social expectations so often narrated in the classical Bildungsroman. The power and presence of the Blessed Virgin Mary, here as elsewhere in Joyce, fulfills the function of the absent but powerful Father who stands behind and guarantees the sacramental mysteries.[124] It is perhaps her imaginary intercession, rather than the heated rhetoric of Father Arnall, that sends Stephen on his frenzied way toward the confessional and an official disburdening, nonreciprocal and univocal, of his guilty joy.

Baffled and frightened by his own desire, Stephen takes the only recourse held out to him: "No escape. He had to confess, to speak out in words what he had done and thought, sin after sin. How? How?" (*P* 126). The question is more than rhetorical, for he is genuinely unsure how confession could facilitate the disburdening of desires that constituted his very being. He turns to confession as a means of disburdening himself of sin, but also as a way to speak to himself of what divine self-knowledge excludes: "The thought slid like a cold shining rapier into his tender flesh: confession. But not there in the chapel of the college. He would confess all, every sin of deed and thought, sincerely: but not there among his school companions. Far away from there in some dark place he would murmur out his own shame: and he besought God humbly not to be offended with him if he did not dare to confess in the college chapel: and in utter abjection of spirit he craved forgiveness mutely of the boyish hearts about him" (*P* 126). He promises to "confess all, every sin of deed and thought, sincerely." But it is unclear whether Stephen really is or *can* be sincere about his intentions to repent or about his own sensual awareness of sin. "His sins trickled from his lips, one by one, trickled in shameful drops from his soul . . . oozed forth, sluggish, filthy" (*P* 144). This language suggests a reluctant wringing out of sins, not the sincere disburdening required of orthodox confession, to say nothing of the desires that motivate sin. According to Foucault, confession in the nineteenth century had developed into a sophisticated tool for discovering hidden desires. The scope of confession had thereby altered: "it tended no longer to be concerned solely with what the subject wished to hide, but with what was hidden from himself, being incapable of coming to light except gradually and through the labor of a confession in which the questioner and the questioned each had a part to play." What is hidden is often desire, sexual curiosity, sexuality in general. A subtle ritualistic coercion, much like that of the psychoanalyst, proved necessary. "The principle of a latency essential to sexuality made it possible to link the forcing of a difficult confession to a scientific practice. It had to be exacted, by force, since it involved something that tried to stay hidden."[125] The connection between confession and scientific practices can be found in both the religious and the medical domains, as Foucault himself strongly implies without making clear distinctions between the two. His unwillingness to distinguish is purposeful, I believe, since it points up the extent to which a confessional discourse was shared by priests and doctors, who both performed a "hermeneutic function." The "one who listened" was the "master of truth": "With regard to the confession, his power was not only to demand it before it was made, or decide what was to follow after it, but also to constitute a discourse of truth on the basis of its decipherment."[126]

Stephen's confession at the end of chapter 3 is of this variety: he succumbs to a discourse of sexuality in which the confessor serves as the "master of truth." His resistance to confession, his desire to confess far from his own school, can be easily grasped as part of a ritualistic structure "in which the truth is corroborated by the obstacles and resistances it has had to surmount in order to be formulated."[127] What is decipherable from Stephen's confession is known not primarily through the scripted forms of absolution but through the forms of amendment that follow upon the sacramental ritual, the "intrinsic modifications" that Foucault argues are the result of the very act of speaking in confession. "It is the confession," Wilde notes, "not the priest, that gives us absolution" (*DG* 77). Certainly the pious practices in which Stephen engages at the beginning of chapter 4 satisfy the demand of the sacrament of penance for such modifications. More significant for the present discussion is the fact that he will outgrow the necessity for the sacramental demand, the coercive force of a confessional dialectic that reaches into the unconscious and exerts a formidable influence on the motivations and desires that indemnify self-development. He will learn to see confession as a stage in a Bildung process in which an artistic vocation ultimately sublates a religious one. The "intrinsic modifications" are reinterpreted by the colonial subject as an "internal catastrophe" similar to what Memmi describes, a remnant of a specifically Irish "colonial superstructure" that serves as a refuge from despair. It is the enduring sign, like native "traditions," of the failure of the revolt against colonial oppression.

Profane confession, by attempting to evade the "master of truth," indicates not so much a loss of faith in the necessity of absolution as a positive gain in the ability to recognize and affirm the self *in sin* rather than in sin's absolution. The "appropriation of Catholic confessional language," according to Jonathan Mulrooney, enables Stephen to see "how language creates reality."[128] Confession thus creates the conditions for a new discourse of desire and provides opportunities for dialogue and debate, for freedom of expression that the lecture hall and classroom (not to mention the orthodox confessional) do not offer. It enables the free expression of disparate and conflicting modes of knowledge, power, and desire and a critique of the sexual politics of Irish Catholic education and mentorship. An early modernist exemplar of this profane mode of confession—one that looks back for its inspiration to Augustine even as it refuses the need for absolution and reformation—is, of course, Wilde's *De Profundis*. In his confessional letter to Lord Alfred Douglas, Wilde looks unflinchingly at his past and affirms it as the only authentic course of his self-development. *De Profundis* is a confession of faith *in oneself*. Indeed, repentance is an initiation into oneself and "the means by which one alters one's past."[129] Profane confession models the nontranscendental negative dialectics of Adorno. The disburdening of tabooed or secret knowledge is reconfigured as self-knowledge, as a series of epistemological crises in which Stephen must assess both *what* he knows and *how* he has come to know it. At these crisis points confession reveals the otherness of nonidentity as nonidentical, as that which is not subsumed into the economy of essence in which nonidentity is "identified" as the nothingness of being. According to Adorno, this is what idealist philosophers from Hegel to Heidegger accomplished, even when they thought they were doing something else. Hegel, for example, "exploited the fact that the nonidentical on its part can be defined only as a concept. To him it was thereby removed from dialectics and brought to identity: the ontical was ontologized."[130] That is to say, what cannot be covered by the concept of an entity—indefiniteness—is raised to the level of concept through negation; it acquires definition as "nothingness." Adorno believes that Hegel "fails to do justice to his insight," which is that "even though the nonidentical is identical—as self-transmitted—it is nonetheless nonidentical: it is otherness to all its identifications." What I think Adorno is getting at here is that the dialectical procedures in Hegelian logic do not account for the importance of a nonidentical moment that is not completely subsumed in the expression of identity. Typically, in such logic, the nonidentical contributes, through negation, to the constitution of the identical in the standard procedures of a subjective idealism; but this does not fully negate the power of nonidentity as otherness, as that "something nonidentical" with which "there is truly no identity." What is not stressed in Hegelian dialectics, then, is the "dialectics of nonidentity," in which the "indissoluble" would attain its own concept and not be swallowed "under its general concept, that of indissolubility."[131] The idea that identity is dependent on nonidentity (on its indissoluble, nonconceptual existence outside the abstraction of reflection) gets inverted, and nonidentity is dissolved, negated in the identical.

Stephen's knowledge, which he receives by the standard mediated routes of education, is bound up with the dialectical procedures of idealistic philosophy and theology, from Aristotle to Hegel, from Aquinas to Loyola. He seeks to know in his profanation of the sacrament of penance what lies beyond dialectics or, to speak in the spirit of Adorno, what dialectics simultaneously exploits and disavows, the nonidentity of the knower and the known. In his profanation of repentance and absolution, Stephen hopes to free himself of the tyranny of Catholic identity, which, for him at least, is equivalent, in its dialectical hegemony, to the tyranny of the colonial system itself.[132]

The feeling of entrapment that Stephen feels early in his development helps to explain the temptation later to become a priest, for as a priest he could escape entrapment by controlling the situation and being the one who sets the trap for others. By the time he considers a religious vocation, however, he has rediscovered desire and expresses it now as something proximate or subjacent to confessional knowledge:

> He would know obscure things, hidden from others, from those who were conceived and born children of wrath. He would know the sins, the sinful longings and sinful thoughts and sinful acts, of others, hearing them murmured into his ears in the confessional under the shame of a darkened chapel by the lips of women and of girls: but rendered immune mysteriously at his ordination by the imposition of hands his soul would pass again uncontaminated to the white peace of the altar. . . . He would hold his secret knowledge and secret power, being as sinless as the innocent. (*P* 159)[133]

Stephen's profanation of the sacrament destabilizes the dialectic of repentance and absolution by actively exploiting the aesthetic thrills of an eroticized confessional. Of course he can hardly commit himself to overturning the structures of knowledge and belief that authorize both the thrills and the sacrament they mimic. His mimicry, like Adorno's negative dialectics, can become critical only when structure *as such* is undermined, not in a simple inversion that merely privileges the left side of the bar (for example, sinfulness/piety) nor in the assertion of a powerful new third term. Stephen's profanation of the confessor's role is predicated on a constellation of possible standpoints from which he could know nonidentity in the absence of that which polarizes it within the logic of classical dialectics.[134] This is not to privilege nonidentity, but precisely to *de*-privilege it by refusing to give it identity *as* nonidentity. Instead of inversion or reversal there is a shift of emphasis, new points from which to turn toward nonidentity, toward the "profane joy" of the artist who is absorbed in the object of his aesthetic desire, who is confused with it, whose creations are not entirely abstracted from the "sluggish matter of the earth" that inspires them (*P* 171, 169). Profane joy of this sort dissolves binaries and annihilates norms even as it complies in certain thematic ways with a dialectical operation it otherwise transgresses: it is the transvalued form of the "joy of guilty confession."

Put another way, Stephen's profane performance of the sacrament of penance is a form of "colonial doubling," in which "disavowed knowledges return to make the presence of authority uncertain."[135] The mimic scene of initiation into the priesthood ambivalently recodes and thereby reduplicates the authentic one it refuses. Like the Gothic discombobulation of the subject/object dyad in Wilde's *Dorian Gray*, the profanation of confession in *Portrait* defies the "logical form of contradiction"[136] inherent in the dialectical structure of Bildung without completely expelling that structure. Stephen's *sacramental desire* functions critically within the larger Bildungsroman structure as a principle of disharmony that models other possible standpoints from which to view the problem of self-development. It models an alternative to the normative modes of socialization for a young Catholic subject in colonial Dublin.

But it is a fragile, potentially complicitous alternative, as Joyce demonstrates when he dramatizes the moment of Stephen's temptation, the moment when he is singled out and asked about his "desire to join the [Jesuit] order" (*P* 157). It is an important moment, an offer of vocation that comes closest to fulfilling the principal requirement of the classical Bildungsroman. The aggressive tactics of his would-be mentors, depicted in detail in *Stephen Hero*, are calculated to allay any fear that he would be sacrificing his artistic freedom:

> ... the Church sent an embassy of nimble pleaders into his ears. ... They stated that it was in their power to make smooth many of the ways which promised to be rough and, by diminishing the hardships of the material nature, to allow the unusual character scope and ease to develop and approve itself. ... He had what he called a "modern" reluctance to give pledges: no pledges were required. If at the end of five years he still persevered in his obduracy of heart he could still seize upon his individual liberty without fear of being called an oath-breaker therefore. ... Make one with us, on equal terms. In temper and in mind you are still a Catholic, Catholicism is in your blood. ... You can sow the seeds in the careful furrows entrusted to you and if your seed is good it will prosper. But by going into the unnecessary wilderness and scattering your seed broadcast on all soils what harvest will you have? (*SH* 204, 206)

Here we are faced with a seemingly anomalous situation, for it is rare in colonial contexts for the disavowed subject to be taken into the fold. However, the situation Stephen describes is quite complex, for on one level the Jesuit priests speak for their order only, while on another level they mediate between the imperial domain of "proper" Bildung and the colonial terrain of education and catastrophic development. Stephen is invited to take a position of real power, which he does not underestimate as his imaginary performance of priestly duties suggests. But these duties mainly support the stasis that assimilates and stymies all development; it is an abstract, ceremonial power calculated to guarantee all the more fully the powerlessness (in political terms) of the colonial subject. The "ambassadors" from the Jesuit order offer only a compensatory fantasy of intellectual freedom that would amount to little more than a translation into orthodox terms of the heretical identity that Stephen already suspects binds him irrevocably to the Church and its interminable dialectics of repentance and absolution.[137] This scene of seduction is roughly analogous, in symbolic terms, to Wilhelm Meister's induction into the Society of the Tower or Pip's into the ranks of "gentlemen" in Dickens's *Great Expectations*. The difference lies in the Irish colonial subject's resistance to social authorities whose influence, he knows from experience, is repressive and unforgiving.

Stephen's entrapment in the discourse of salvation clarifies and rigidifies his subjection, leaving him farther than ever from the promised land of classical Bildung. What the Jesuits have promised him would short-circuit the Bildung process, shunting him off the pathway leading to the fulfillment of his artistic aspirations. There would be no journey abroad, no ameliorating rebellion from the Father and his social values, no return before it is too late. There would be only stasis and damnation, repentance and absolution, the unbearable harmony of a rigid dialectic. However, the "mild proud sovereignty" (*P* 168) that he asserts after finally refusing the call to the priesthood does not represent a successful attainment of Bildung as Goethe or Humboldt understood it—that is, an experience in which "the spirit feels itself raised above the flux of things through its perfect self-sufficiency, through the richness of its own ideas and the consciousness of its inner strength."[138] His sovereignty of self is far too brittle and tenuous—a "borrowed culture," as Seamus Deane puts it—far too much like a defense mechanism, an attempt to block out unendurable social pressures. This is why he is tempted by the prospect of a spiritual vocation in the first place.

At the threshold of initiation into the Church, Stephen demurs and rejects a destiny laid out in advance by the Jesuit order. He accepts instead an artistic vocation in the open air on the strand along Dublin Bay, among larking, naked boys and a girl bathing at the shore. The call of art comes amid a confusion of mind as Stephen moves from disharmonious rebellion to ecstatic self-affirmation. He is less self-sufficient than self-contained, a proud spirit, "a being apart in every order," an artist "elusive of social or religious orders" (*P* 161–62).[139] But though he has come to realize that "the oils of ordination would never anoint his body," he knows well the fragility of his refusal and persists in questioning it: "He had refused. Why?" (*P* 165). The answer to this question is University College Dublin, just where a traditional Bildung plot should unfold: "The university! So he had passed beyond the challenge of the sentries who had stood as guardians of his boyhood and had sought to keep him among them that he might be subject to them and serve their ends" (*P* 165). In taking advantage of the opportunity held out to him by the university, Stephen was in a small minority of Catholics who would go on to be the leaders of the Free State and the Republic. But even in this context, Stephen's experience is unusual, given the shabby genteel status of his family. His precarious position on the fringes of the emergent Catholic middle class places him in a position very much like that of Anglo-Irish intellectuals who are neither colonizers nor colonized. In the confines of the university, a Catholic intellectual with cosmopolitan tastes who does not subordinate himself to the cause of nationalism can only be, as the Gaelic Leaguer Mr. Hughes put it, "a renegade from the Nationalist ranks" (*SH* 103). Davin, the "peasant student," puts the pertinent question to Stephen: "What with your name and your ideas . . . are you Irish at all?" (*P* 202).

The Catholic University, founded in 1854 by Archbishop Cullen and headed by John Henry Cardinal Newman, had become in 1882 (the year of Joyce's birth) University College. Though still a Catholic institution, University College offered curricula more or less in line with the educational mainstream of western Europe.[140] However, Stephen's desire to attend the university has less to do with a desire for a humanist education than with his obedience to "a wayward instinct" (*P* 165) that we can trace back to his early fascination with the very processes of his own understanding: "By thinking of things you could understand them" (*P* 43). He was eight or nine years old when he solemnly thought these words, but they are now, on the brink of adulthood, as apt a description of his self-wonder as they were then. His fascination with his own consciousness, with an "inner world of individual emotions mirrored perfectly in a lucid supple periodic prose" (*P* 167), differs markedly from the experience of the pliable apprentice under the watchful authority of a secretive Society of the Tower or that of the struggling artist in the metropolis longing for success. No one presents him with a scroll of his destiny in which he recognizes a "picture of himself," nor does anyone counsel him as Balzac's Lucien Chardon is counseled: "Take refuge in a garret, write masterpieces, acquire some sort of prestige and you will have society at your feet."[141] Moreover, Stephen's refusal to embrace Irish nationalism signifies the extent to which native social authorities fail to provide, much less nurture, the freedom necessary for Bildung. The result is his rejection of both social assimilation (joining the priesthood) and revolutionary struggle (joining the nationalists). "I will not serve," he tells his friend Cranly, "that in which I no longer believe whether it call itself my home, my fatherland or my church: and I will try to express myself in some mode of life or art as freely as I can and as wholly as I can, using for my defence the only arms I allow myself to use—silence, exile, and cunning" (*P* 246–47). His famous declaration of *non serviam* and his desire to encounter experience "for the millionth time" (*P* 253) have little to do with the social world in which previous *Bildungshelden* had struggled to achieve harmony or fame; and it disallows any apprenticeship to an authority other than himself. The subjective realm of the artist's "inner world" substitutes for the inner culture of Goethe and Humboldt, which was predicated on the humanist education that Stephen to some degree resists, and protects him from a hostile external world, which increasingly inhibits his freedom of artistic expression.

Stephen's refusal of the priesthood, his obedience to a "wayward instinct"—a more refined version of what produced his "monstrous images"—is followed by an act of self-confession framed and contextualized by the antiphonic shouts of nearby naked swimming boys who attempt to conscript him into a ritual of homosocial bonding in which he is marked as a sacrifice: "Bous Stephanoumenos" (*P* 168). At this moment he achieves a kind of Gothic grandeur such as Pater and Wilde noticed in Leonardo's *La Gioconda*: "So timeless seemed the grey warm air, so fluid and impersonal his own mood, that all ages were as one to him" (*P* 168). His epiphany, the confirmation of his decision to become an artist, occurs in almost total seclusion from social life, in a space where he hears a voice from "beyond the world" calling his name:

—Stephaneforos!
His throat ached with a desire to cry aloud, the cry of a hawk or eagle on high, to cry piercingly of his deliverance to the winds. This was the call of life to his soul not the dull gross voice of the world of duties and despair, not the inhuman voice that had called him to the pale service of the altar. An instant of wild flight had delivered him and the cry of triumph which his lips withheld cleft his brain.
—Stephaneforos! (*P* 169)

The cacophony of boys' voices and the iteration of his name in a pseudo-Greek form lend the scene a certain archaic eroticism. This other voice, his own voice projected out into the world of hawks and eagles (the noblest of creatures in the Nietzschean bestiary), comes back to him, to the "altar" of himself, that inner world where he confesses himself in "lucid supple periodic prose" and where he disburdens himself of the need to hear the dull gross voices of the world. At this pivotal, liminal point, his creative imagination pliable but curiously at rest, his boyhood finally falls fully away from him. The homoerotic atmosphere, together with his aestheticization of the birdgirl immediately following, underscores the distance Stephen has traveled from the compulsory heterosexuality subtly insisted upon in most classical Bildungsromane.

As I have indicated throughout this study, women in the classical Bildungsroman serve, in a primarily instrumental fashion, to promote the advancement (or to precipitate the failure) of the *Bildungsheld*. One need only recall Mariane, Therese, and Natalie in Goethe's *Wilhelm Meister*, Madame de Bargeton in Balzac's *Lost Illusions*, Madame Arnoux in Flaubert's *Sentimental Education*, and Estella and Miss Haversham in Dickens's *Great Expectations* to envisage women as instrumental figures in determining the fate and fortune of young men. Women, in this conventional world, are the conduits of desires for power and fame; they are the rewards for success in the social world or the memory of what might have been that haunts the young man who fails to succeed. Women mark the *telos* of a journey; they legitimize hardship and, in some cases, deceit. In marriage, that sought-after social ideal, they provide a symbolic completion, an achievement of wholeness and dialectical harmony, the attainment of the "joys of a secure earthly life" celebrated in Goethe's *Wilhelm Meister*.[142] Stephen is far from interested in the kind of marriage that we find in Goethe and so many other classical Bildungsromane, the kind that would allow the male *Bildungsheld* to discover his own self-identity in harmony with woman-as-other. Paul Morel and Jude Fawley struggle with this temptation, flirting with or pursuing the option of marriage, but they inevitably discover how implausible marriage is as a means to achieve Bildung. Stephen does not, like Jude and Paul, argue about marriage, though in *Stephen Hero* he does claim that a "woman's body is a corporal asset of the State" and that in marriage she is invited to "traffic with it" (202). Instead the discourse of romance and marriage is transformed, through the artist's creation of iconic female images, into another frame of reference. Christine Froula sees this kind of dynamic at play in Stephen's relationship with E.C., a dynamic that results in the transposition of "thwarted romance from the personal (a love story) to the political (a critique of the marriage system)." His representation of her "implicitly acknowledges (albeit contemptuously, from the perspective of its designs upon him) the socioeconomic system that binds Emma into compliance."[143]

The actresses and harlots, society women and simple provincial girls who move in and out of the French Bildungsroman are part of a stratified social system; they form a crucial mechanism whereby male ambition is either tempered or eviscerated. In the English Bildungsroman, wealthy urban women and village girls, orphans and heiresses seek marriage as the most viable socioeconomic option for their own social mobility and emotional well-being. It is a measure of Joyce's progress beyond the gender dynamics of the classical Bildungsroman that, in *Portrait*, he abandons the conception of woman as an instrument of social assimilation and advancement.[144] Women like Mercedes, from Alexandre Dumas' *Count of Monte Cristo* (1844–46), come to represent for Stephen not the means to social success but the possibility of imaginative freedom; they are vaguely erotic "premonition[s]" of an "unsubstantial image" (*P* 65). Froula argues that Stephen makes Mercedes "his ideal not of a desired object but of a desired self, an animated mirror in whom he seeks himself 'transfigured.'" In his transformations of real and imagined women, he seeks a "virtual female self," an "external mirror of his own virtual femaleness," a process that entails "act[ing] out his own repressed femininity by the symbolic means his culture affords." Froula reads the scene in which he meditates on the birdgirl as critical for his artistic development, for through her "metamorphosis" he "learns how to use the symbolic law of gender to change the law of nature, to turn his lack of an actual womb into a Daedalian symbolic womb/wings."[145] Froula's reading is exceptional in its willingness to regard Stephen's "refashioning" of women as part of an aesthetic project that aims to undermine the masculinist tendencies of modernist art. What I want to emphasize is the way his fantasy world becomes a space of aesthetic creation in which he imaginatively transforms real and fictive women—Eileen Vance, E.C., Mercedes, the unnamed prostitute, the Virgin Mary, the birdgirl, the temptress of the villanelle—into a progressive series of iconic images that represent significant points along the way of his artistic self-formation. In all of this, Joyce seems to reach back to the era of Goethe, and the kind of symbolic function women played in *Wilhelm Meister*, though Stephen's intentions are not to use women to symbolize or substantiate the dialectical harmony of Bildung. If women in *Portrait* nevertheless end up serving an instrumental function, it is important to note that gendered instrumentality as such is undermined by the explicitly imaginary nature of the women in question and especially by the Gothic excessiveness of their departures from the gender norms typically depicted in the classical Bildungsroman. When, for example, Stephen is looking for a prostitute and feels "some dark presence moving irresistibly upon him from the darkness," a murmuring female presence, when "he suffer[s] the agony of its penetration" (*P* 100), we are witnessing a confounding of sexual and gender identities that inspires a sublime terror. This is clearly not the normative experience of the young *Bildungsheld*, for whom a woman is supposed to be a helpmate and selfless partner rather than a monstrous, vampiric "presence" or "batlike soul" (*P* 183) that can only derail the Bildung process. Given the catastrophic nature of colonial Bildung, it should come as no surprise that women succeed less in facilitating than in distancing Stephen irrecoverably from harmonious socialization. His mother, after all, packs him up for exile.

The iconic series culminates with the so-called birdgirl who inspires Stephen's "profane joy" (*P* 171) by reaffirming the materiality of life at the same time that she offers an aestheticized alternative to it. Like the portrait of Dorian Gray, the birdgirl represents to the young artist an otherworldly aspect of himself, one excluded or disavowed by the dialectics of socialization that he has repudiated. This "wild heart of life" is for him, as the portrait was for Dorian, a world made beautiful because he has wished it so. "She seemed like one whom magic had changed into the likeness of a strange and beautiful seabird," an "envoy from the fair courts of life" (*P* 171–72) whose principal role is to inspire a desire for beauty and freedom. She is a "likeness," sign and proof of what the naked swimming boys have already urged him toward, the affirmation of life: "Yes! Yes! Yes! He would create proudly out of the freedom and power of his soul, as the great artificer whose name he bore, a living thing, new and soaring and beautiful, impalpable, imperishable" (*P* 170). Instead of creating the possibility of social advancement or unity through marriage, as she would have done in the classical Bildungsroman, the birdgirl prepares Stephen to strike out on his solitary path: "To live, to err, to fall, to triumph, to recreate life out of life" (*P* 172). He accedes to his artistic destiny in a moment of profane joy, barely able to contain his wild desire to cry out. This is the moment of her "recreation," the transformation from flesh-and-blood girl on the strand to icon of the artist's self-realization, the precise moment when his desire to "recreate life" finds expression in a union of the masculine "indifferent dome" of the sky and the feminized "earth beneath him," a labial vortex into which he falls: "Glimmering and trembling, trembling and unfolding, a breaking light, an opening flower, it spread in endless succession to itself, breaking in full crimson and unfolding and fading to palest rose" (*P* 172).

Valente notes that the birdgirl "must enable a simplification and sublimation of Stephen's perverse desire, which is where the aesthetic framework becomes crucial. In this regard, it is important that she is not a bird woman, but a bird girl, poised in her incipient physical maturity between complete and incomplete gender differentiation."[146] Stephen's aestheticization of her responds to his own requirements not to settle on a single masculine or feminine identity. The private fiction of her rebirth confirms the new aesthetic function that women play in his Bildung plot. In Hardy and Lawrence, women play productive social roles and ultimately acquire some measure of autonomy; it is difficult to reduce either Sue Bridehead or Miriam Leivers to mere signs of the young artist's aesthetic vocation. But with the women in *Portrait* and *Dorian Gray* this is precisely what occurs, and it occurs by virtue of aesthetic theories that consign the material world, including the people in it, to the status of catalysts for artistic (re)creation. It is important to emphasize that the iconic women in *Portrait*—batgirl, birdgirl, peasant seductress, suffering mother, mysterious virgin, vague temptress—are not mimetic representations. The girl on the beach, E.C. "in the flesh," the prostitute, and any number of others who provide Stephen with a starting point for creating iconic images effectively drop out of the equation. We can more profitably accuse him (or Joyce) of not representing women at all than of representing them badly. One is reminded of J. M. Synge's response, when questioned about the "reality" of the Aran Island girls he represented in *The Playboy of the Western World*. When a reporter asked whether they had actually made love to the patricide, Synge replied, "No. Those girls did not, but mine do."[147] Like the Aran girls in Synge's play, the women in *Portrait*—especially the birdgirl and the "temptress of the villanelle"—function in purely aesthetic terms. The aesthetic theory articulated in chapter 5 provides an artistic justification for these "imaginary" women.

Stephen's theory of aesthetics and aesthetic production is typically understood in terms of Thomist theology or Neoplatonic epistemology. To be sure, it stresses the transubstantiated world-as-image, but it also curiously reinscribes the material reality of that world as an integral part of the image. What in subjective idealism would be called a "remainder" is acknowledged and even given a role to play in a negative dialectical process. Stephen begins by noting that neither tragic emotion nor beauty is to be conceived in terms of "kinetic" or improper arts—that is to say, "pornographical or didactic" arts. Wilde makes a similar claim in "The Critic as Artist": "all the arts are immoral, except those baser forms of sensual or didactic art that seek to excite to action of evil or of good" (*I* 177). For both Gilbert and Stephen, art that appeals to sexual curiosity or the desire to be instructed is fundamentally ethical and has no relevance for the apprehension of beauty. For his part, Stephen makes clear to Lynch, who threatens to undermine the seriousness of what his friend is dead serious about, that "we are just now in a mental world," an acknowledgment that aesthetic matters are not ethical ones. The apprehension of beauty, no matter how widely different the object of that apprehension may be in different cultural contexts, "induces, or ought to induce, an esthetic stasis, an ideal pity or an ideal terror, a stasis called forth, prolonged and at last dissolved by what I call the rhythm of beauty" (*P* 206). In other words, the apprehension of beauty is a universal aesthetic function. What he means by beauty is a system of relations of "part to part" or of any part to the "esthetic whole." It would appear, then, that beauty is a quality of objects or of the relations among parts that constitute an object and that there are stages of "esthetic apprehension" that coincide with these relations within the object. It is no surprise that Stephen aestheticizes women to serve as icons of his Bildung process, that he uses women, as objects of beauty, to illustrate his theory. Regardless of the culture in which a woman is deemed beautiful, there is this universal factor at work: "all people who admire a beautiful object find in it certain relations which satisfy and coincide with the stages themselves of all esthetic apprehension" (*P* 208–9). When the "satisfying relations" of the object correspond with the "phases of artistic apprehension . . . you find the qualities of universal beauty" (*P* 211).

In the paragraphs that follow, Stephen describes three phases of "esthetic apprehension," in which three states of relation are discoverable in the object: *integritas, consonantia, claritas*. In the first phase, the mind separates out the structure of the object from "the rest of the visible universe." What the mind apprehends as a single thing is an "esthetic image . . . selfbounded and selfcontained upon the immeasurable background of space or time which is not it" (*P* 212). We recognize here something like the philosophical process of abstraction by which a thing is made identical with a subjective idea of it; at the same time, Stephen emphasizes the element of nonidentity in aesthetic apprehension, what is *not* the abstract concept or "esthetic image." In the second phase, one apprehends the complex balance of parts within the object and the "rhythm of its structure." The apprehension of parts corresponds with the relation of parts in a rhythmical unity. The object is harmoniously unified, but the emphasis is on its thingness: "Having felt it is *one* thing you feel now that it is a *thing*" (*P* 212). Though the object is apprehended and conceptualized, Stephen does not lose sight of the fact that it remains, for the subject who apprehends it, still immersed in the world of objects; it carries with it, in the act of apprehension, an aspect of its materiality, its ineluctable nonconceptuality. Finally, in the last phase, the object is apprehended as internally radiant; it "is that thing which it is and no other thing." The corresponding state in the subject is that point at which the "esthetic image" is first apprehended not as the "selfbounded and selfcontained" thing set against the externality of what is not it, but rather as an image *in the imagination*. This third phase, then, is the moment of artistic creation, not of an art object but of a mental image that has effectively "recreated" an object out of the "sluggish matter of the earth." What is important to notice, for a theory of aesthetics that must maintain contact with the *thingness* of the world, is the link between the moment of aesthetic pleasure and the very workings of material nature: "The mind in that mysterious instant Shelley likened beautifully to a fading coal. The instant wherein that supreme quality of beauty, the clear radiance of the esthetic image, is apprehended luminously by the mind which has been arrested by its wholeness and fascinated by its harmony is the luminous silent stasis of esthetic pleasure, a spiritual state very like to that cardiac condition which the Italian physiologist Luigi Galvani, using a phrase almost as beautiful as Shelley's, called the enchantment of the heart" (*P* 213).

By linking Shelley and Galvani, Joyce brings together Romantic Neoplatonism and late-Enlightenment science in such a way as to suggest their compatibility. In the context of Stephen's aesthetic theory, however, the physical detail of the cessation of the frog's heart (the "enchantment" or *incantesimo* noted by Galvani)[148] tends to tilt aesthetic experience in the direction of the heart's materiality, its *thingness*. The "spiritual state" that Stephen describes coexists with a material reality that cannot be subdued by that state; indeed, the very metaphor used to describe it produces an intractable remainder, analogous to the basket "which a butcher's boy had slung inverted on his head" (*P* 212) and which serves as the starting point and exemplar, the *thing* to which Stephen alludes in his explication of the three phases of apprehension. For Kant, as for Heidegger and Lacan much later, such a *thing* is noumenal, an ungraspable fullness of presence, an aspect of reality that cannot be contained by our perceptions or by our abstract concepts.[149] It is what stands in the way of all attempts to achieve self-identity, because it refuses to be repressed or disavowed, to be taken up and preserved in a dialectical sublation (*Aufhebung*). Stephen must keep the *thing* in mind, he must account for it, for it is that which simultaneously grounds his theory of aesthetics and tacitly refuses the theoretical coherence and harmony he expounds. And I submit that this is a deliberate strategy, that he does not intend for his argument to confirm the self-identity of the artist in the apprehension of the world as object; quite the contrary, his argument keeps reminding us that there is this *thing* that is apprehended, this enchanted *thing* that makes art and aesthetic apprehension possible. This is why he has the artist disappear, for only in this way can the *thing* be sustained as an object of aesthetic apprehension. From lyric to epic to dramatic modes of artistic expression, the artist is increasingly "impersonalized"; at the same time, the "esthetic image," purified in the imagination, is then "reprojected," presumably back into the world, the region of "sluggish matter," from which the image was first derived. At this point Stephen would seem to be suggesting that the artist achieves transcendence, but his emphasis on the *thing* draws our attention back down to earth, for the whole process is grounded in materiality in relation to which the apprehending subject is "impersonalized." The moment of transcendence that so many readers discern is actually a moment of profound immanence, an intimate proximity to the *thing* itself. "The mystery of esthetic like that of material creation is accomplished. The artist, like the God of the creation, remains within or behind or beyond or above his handiwork, invisible, refined out of existence, indifferent, paring his fingernails" (*P* 215). The reader might mistake artistic apprehension for the machinations of a godlike transcendental subject, were it not for those fingernails which, like the butcher's boy's basket, ground subjectivity in a singularly ungodlike material stratum.

Stephen's theory ought to interest us on a number of levels, not the least of which is the function it performs in his Bildung plot, for in the performance of the theory we witness the making of a certain kind of modernist artist who reaffirms the materiality of the "sluggish earth" through a process of depersonalization that transforms Bildung from an aspiration toward transcendent, dialectical harmony to an affirmation of the value of the nonidentical and the nonconceptual, the enchanted *thing*, the "batlike" quality of artistic consciousness itself. By casting himself as a disappearing artist "within or behind or beyond or above his handiwork," he paradoxically attempts to grasp—as Paul Morel had done—the materiality of the external world and his own relation to it as subject in a negative dialectical relation to the world-as-object. Further, the aesthetic theory explains the process by which women are similarly transformed into images that both represent and facilitate the male artist's self-development. Stephen takes the radical step of attempting to *re*materialize women, the better to serve his critique of socialization and his own aspiration toward Bildung. Like Sibyl Vane, whose life passes "into the sphere of art" where her love becomes a sacrament offered up to Dorian Gray (*DG* 86, 83), the women in *Portrait* become images and icons of Stephen's wayward desires. As aesthetic images, women "purify and reproject" the life they embody, but they also taunt the male artist with a slight rem(a)inder of their materiality: Mercedes's "muscatel grapes," the "dark pressure" of the prostitute's "softly parting lips," the birdgirl's "long slender bare legs" and the "faint noise of gently moving water" that breaks the silence of Stephen's "profane joy" on the strand, and, most prominently, E.C.'s eyes, "dark and with a look of languor," and the "soft merchandise" of her hands (*P* 63, 101, 171, 223, 219).

It is significant, in view of his theory, that Stephen's first composition involves the creation of an aesthetic image out of the material provided by the living body and experience of E.C. That he remakes her as a kind of muse doubles her instrumentality. For Froula, "Stephen deftly accomplishes Emma's metamorphosis in the prelude to the villanelle scene." I would add that this prelude connects with the interstitial remembrances of Emma that occupy Stephen during the composition of the villanelle itself. The inspiration she provides, an eroticized vision of the Annunciation—"Gabriel the seraph had come to the virgin's chamber" (*P* 217)—and the Daedalian myth of the perdix converge "in Emma's metamorphosis into a 'simple' bird/sacred dove, not just iconographically but in the primal-word psychodynamics in play throughout Stephen's initiatory progress." E.C.'s "generic femaleness" is appropriated into his "symbolic art," a process by which she is able to model Stephen's "artist-identity."[150] The villanelle form, with its structural rigidities, both articulates and contains, in a rhetoric at once sensuous and sacred, Stephen's image of E.C., while the process of composition itself is suspended in a fluid, labial space where "liquid life" "enfolded him like water" (*P* 223). This enfolding rearticulates his surrender to desire in terms of orthodox structures of poetic and religious adoration:

> Our broken cries and mournful lays
> Rise in one eucharistic hymn.
> Are you not weary of ardent ways?

Alongside this ethereal temptress we detect another figure, a Gothicized form of materiality, of *thingness*, a trace of the "batlike soul," the inevitable vampire lover who has haunted Stephen since Eileen Vance and will continue to haunt him in the form of his mother's ghost in *Ulysses*. In a sensuous and indolent reminiscence, he recalls the "real" E.C., who is then refined out of existence in a subdued blaze of eroticism:

> And still you hold our longing gaze
> With languorous look and lavish limb!
> Are you not weary of ardent ways?
> Tell no more of enchanted days. (*P* 223–24)

The resignification of sacramental images in the villanelle, like so many of Stephen's other highly stylized, self-conscious performances, is meant to signal an attitude of refusal that is intertwined with a moment of affirmation and acceptance. The half-serious mimicry of priestly duties in chapter 4 is here a more fully invested performance of self-ordination, in which Stephen becomes "a priest of eternal imagination" (*P* 221). In the villanelle, the language of a sacramental mystery that he ostensibly rejects is used to affirm and articulate the aesthetic vocation that colors his own "ardent ways." It is an aesthetic priest who conjures up the real E.C. in the interstices of his composition and who imagines her, recalling Davin's encounter with a peasant woman, as a "batlike soul waking to the consciousness of itself in darkness and secrecy and loneliness, tarrying awhile, loveless and sinless, with her mild lover and leaving him to whisper of innocent transgressions in the latticed ear of a priest" (*P* 221).[151] The proximity of his sacramental desire to the earthly desire of the "priested peasant, with a brother a policeman in Dublin and a brother a potboy in Moycullen," recalls the butcher's boy with his basket, the intrusion of the real *thing* in the midst of his idealizations. Like the profanation of confession that opens up or disrupts the divine dialectics of repentance and absolution, Stephen's villanelle "reprojects" a purified aesthetic image while at the same articulating a material rem(a)inder that takes the form of memories within the narrative account of his artistic apprehension. "Part to part," his reminiscences of E.C.—the "daily bread of experience"—create the balanced rhythmic structure of an aesthetic image, the "radiant body of everliving life," that is expressed in the narration of the composition of the villanelle itself (*P* 221). In this sense, the villanelle is only a part of a larger aesthetic whole, which includes the material setting of its creation, the cigarette package on which it is scribbled, like the pared fingernails, serving as a metonymy of the *thingness* that both instigates and sustains the "element of mystery" (*P* 223).

In the denouement of *Portrait*, Stephen confesses to Davin and Cranly his desire to exile himself in the name of art, and his confessions are haunted by the iconic women he himself has created. To the former, he confesses his need to repudiate Ireland and its political, historical, and mythological baggage. Davin epitomizes the rural and traditional Ireland that Stephen both fears and despises. In the anthropological fiction Stephen has constructed, Davin is simple, guileless, superstitious. When he confronts Stephen, urging him to join the nationalist cause and questioning his Irishness, Stephen is quick to suggest: "Come with me now to the office of arms and I will show you the tree of my family" (*P* 202). Because Davin stands unselfconsciously for his own authenticity yet questions Stephen's, he stands "between Stephen's mind, eager of speculations, and the hidden ways of Irish life" (*P* 181). Davin's story of seduction by the peasant woman (*P* 181–83) becomes for Stephen an allegory of his own seduction by a vampiric Ireland. His rejection of nationalism is motivated by his fear that Ireland will betray and consume him as it did Wolfe Tone and Parnell. He argues "vaguely" that what is important is the birth of the soul, "a slow and dark birth, more mysterious than the birth of the body. When the soul of a man is born in this country there are nets flung at it to hold it back from flight. You talk to me of nationality, language, religion. I shall try to fly by those nets" (*P* 203). Stephen rejects nationalism—indeed, the entire Symbolic order of patriarchal authority—as an impediment to the soul's "slow and dark" *Bildung*. It is just this kind of confessional intimacy that terrorizes Davin. "I'm a simple person," he tells Stephen. "You know that. When you told me that night in Harcourt Street those things about your private life, honest to God, Stevie, I was not able to eat my dinner. I was quite bad. I was awake a long time that night. Why did you tell me those things?" (*P* 202).[152]

"Let us eke go," Cranly says, as he takes Stephen away from the verbal jousting of the boys in the college grounds. To Cranly, son of the "[s]trong farmer type" (*P* 248) that will come to dominate Irish politics after 1922, Stephen confesses a more personal reason for his exile: his failure of belief and his need to test his artistic vocation against the "great mistake" his repudiations may entail. The long scene with Cranly approximates the dynamics of official confession:

> —And you made me confess to you, Stephen said, thrilled by his touch, as I have confessed to you so many other things, have I not?
> —Yes, my child, Cranly said, still gaily.
> —You made me confess the fears that I have. But I will tell you also what I do not fear. I do not fear to be alone or to be spurned for another or to leave whatever I have to leave. And I am not afraid to make a mistake, even a great mistake, a lifelong mistake and perhaps as long as eternity too. (*P* 247)

Confession for Stephen has now become a fearless assertion of his own identity and destiny and his potential for Icarian error. In this restaging of orthodox confession, he not only announces his intentions, confessing that he is confessing, he also undermines the sacrament by unveiling what is repressed in scripted confessions and absolutions: erotic desire. Stephen is "thrilled" by the touch of his friend, and alludes to the "many other things" he has confessed to Cranly, thus creating, in the scene of disburdening, an aura of homoerotic intimacy. Knowingly transgressing against destiny, he implicitly refuses the aid of mentors and confessors who claim to know the *telos* of his journey in advance. He finds knowledge of himself in the process of willfully disrupting the dialectic of self and society at the heart of the classical Bildungsroman, repeating and deregulating its ambivalence—the same ambivalence sequestered in the history and etymology of the term "confessor." When Cranly alludes to one "who would be more than a friend," Stephen wonders: "Had he spoken of himself, of himself as he was or wished to be?" (*P* 247). When Stephen asks, "Of whom are you speaking?" he refers as much to the unstable dialectics of profane confession as to the unspeakable ambivalence of his own incompletely repressed desire.

Stephen's ambivalent sexual identity is nicely captured in a carefully poised rhetorical question worthy of Yeats which may, as some critics suggest, signal a moment of homoerotic abandonment, hovering at the brink of full confession.[153] The haunting figure of woman, who waits batlike in the shadows of Stephen's colloquy with Cranly, further destabilizes a scenario already charged with homoerotic possibilities. Shortly after Cranly invokes Stephen's mother and the certainty of "a mother's love" (*P* 241–42)—and thus of the normative relations of oedipal desire—the song of a servant girl introduces an ambiguous analogue of the instrumental woman of the classical Bildungsroman: "The figure of woman as she appears in the liturgy of the church passed silently through the darkness: a whiterobed figure, small and slender as a boy and with a falling girdle. Her voice, frail and high as a boy's, was heard intoning from a distant choir the first words of a woman which pierce the gloom and clamour of the first chanting of the passion" (*P* 244). Aside from the iconic nature of this spiritualized figure of woman, we are struck by the confusion of gender and stages of development: the "figure" has the body and voice of a boy (the normative subject of classical Bildung) but the words are a woman's. The inversion here—the male occupying the position closest to the somatic level of existence, the female occupying the position of transcendence—signals once again a space of opposition both to the teleological pulsion scripted in the classical Bildungsroman and to the repressive mechanisms of heterosocial relations of power that authorize ideological fictions of harmonious socialization. Once again, as Froula puts it, the "figural Irish woman" ends up as "another prototype for Stephen's dialectical self-fashioning."[154] In the general context of Stephen's Bildung plot, however, the multiplicity of possibilities for the "figural Irish woman" disrupts any potential for simple inversion.

Joyce ends *A Portrait of the Artist as a Young Man* with Stephen poised on the verge of leaving Dublin for Paris, already psychologically alienated from the social world in which he grew up, the network of material and emotional relations seeming less like harmonious socialization than like a trap set especially for him. While appearing to carry out the demands of the Bildung plot—going to university, considering vocations, vying with Cranly for E.C.—he increasingly confronts the "outer" world of people and objects with the indignation of his "inner world of individual emotions." By suggesting, in his grand artistic justification for exile, that the solitude attendant upon his "great mistake" will be productive of new knowledge, he revalues error as an opportunity for new knowledge about himself and the world.[155] His famous boast "I go . . . to forge in the smithy of my soul the uncreated conscience of my race" (*P* 252–53) seems paradoxically to rely on the Law of the Father, but only if we ignore the illicit and material connotations of the desire "to *forge*" a racial conscience. With this in mind, we can conceive of his boast as a promise that new knowledge is in the offing—a promise that is left hanging at the conclusion of *Portrait*. His return to Dublin after his sojourn in Paris is a parodic deconstruction of the return narrated in Goethe's Bildungsroman; in some ways, it resembles the return of the failed artist in Flaubert's *Sentimental Education*. He is no longer the young man who once boasted of his "mild proud sovereignty."

Ulysses narrates this sense of belatedness, the elegiac mood of recollecting a catastrophic youth that sputters to an end in "Proteus," again in "Scylla and Charybdis," only to end finally, again, in "Ithaca," the series repeating in a meaningless, unproductive way the futility of Bildung and of the young hero's inconclusive exile. However, Stephen's problematic colonial Bildung functions critically within Joyce's modernist Bildungsroman by pointing up the inadequacy of normative models of self-development and education that neither alleviate nor represent an "internal catastrophe," coming of age in the age of empire. Stephen's struggle with the processes of socialization, together with Joyce's struggle to represent those processes, indicates some of the problems the modernist Bildungsroman faces—not just in the colonial territories, but in the entire field of late modernity.

Bildung for Women

Joyce and Woolf

Dorian Gray, Jude Fawley, Paul Morel, Stephen Dedalus—the young men whose stories fill the pages of early modernist Bildungsromane symbolize the endurance and even supremacy of the male hero's desire to replicate, in his own destiny, the triumph of nonidentity. Such a triumph, which Adorno calls the "secret *telos* of identification,"[1] stands in defiance of all those forces that would seek to obliterate the radical difference of nonidentity in a sanctifying and transcendent dialectical harmony. These early pioneers sought to rescue classical Bildung, to aspire toward aesthetic education and self-sufficiency. The failed narratives of their aspirations, set the standard for later modernist Bildungsromane. The narrative innovations of the 1920s introduced new narrative paradigms for the articulation of neoclassical Bildung and a new roster of female *Bildungshelden*. Until the First World War, the narrative structure of the Bildungsroman had remained fairly stable, for the critique of Bildung and the creation of a space for innovative aesthetic education did not radically alter the narrative dynamics of self-development. (A notable exception, of course, is Oscar Wilde's *Picture of Dorian Gray*.) In the work of modernists like Virginia Woolf and the later James Joyce, however, the narrative structure of the Bildungsroman comes to seem increasingly untenable. And they are not alone. If we look at other English modernists in the postwar period, including D. H. Lawrence, Samuel Beckett, and E. M. Forster, or at Americans like F. Scott Fitzgerald, William Faulkner, and Gertrude Stein, we see that the representation of self-development and inner culture—that is to say, the representation of what is demonstrably classical Bildung—is no longer tied to the conventions of the Bildungsroman. Often what we find are ensemble narratives in which Bildung plots are embedded and thereby re- or decontextualized by a larger narrative structure that contains them.[2]

In the modernist texts under discussion in this chapter—the "Nausicaa" episode of Joyce's *Ulysses* and two novels of Virginia Woolf, *The Voyage Out* and *Mrs. Dalloway*—the Bildungsroman form is all but abandoned in a critique that undermines the preeminence of the male *Bildungsheld* and the subordinate, instrumental status of women in classical Bildungsromane. Entailed in this critique of the gendered subject of Bildung is a critical representation of key elements in the classical form: mentorship, vocation, and, most important of all, marriage. In *Ulysses*, the possibility of "female Bildung" is explored from the perspective of the embedded and foreshortened Bildung plot concerning Gerty MacDowell. Foreshortening is perhaps the most radical innovation in the modernist Bildungsroman. In such narrative forms, the development of inner culture is suggested through the behavior and memory of the adult subject rather than through narrative action depicting the progress from childhood to adulthood. The role of a parodic discourse in undercutting the conventions of socially pragmatic Bildung is central to Joyce's critique of the nineteenth-century female Bildungsroman. Woolf's fiction presents us with a number of ways to gauge the critical power of the modernist Bildungsroman. Her first novel, *The Voyage Out*, though published at about the same time as Lawrence's *Sons and Lovers* and Joyce's *Portrait of the Artist as a Young Man*, eschews the traditional narrative structure of the Bildungsroman in favor of a foreshortened Bildung plot encompassing several months in the life of Rachel Vinrace. I contrast this early effort with Woolf's achievement a decade later in *Mrs. Dalloway*, a complex double Bildungsroman featuring the foreshortened Bildung plot of Clarissa Dalloway, in which developmental modalities and possibilities are retrieved through memory and retrospection and in which we find embedded still another, even more radically foreshortened Bildung plot, that of Clarissa's daughter Elizabeth. What is common in all of these temporal structures is that Bildung must be inferred from present actions or through reminiscences, flashbacks, and other memorial strategies whereby the content of a more or less achieved Bildung is revealed to the reader. Such innovative forms of narrative emplotment mark a more general modernist strategy of critique that seeks, through the deconstruction of literary forms, the recuperation of modes of self-formation that could effectively combat the ideologies of the subject and subjectivity that had been, by the 1920s, consolidated within educational systems and political institutions.

Before beginning my discussion of "Nausicaa," I would like to consider briefly another modernist innovation that may be unique to Joyce's canon: the serialization of his Bildungsroman. Joyce's engagement with the Bildungsroman genre ultimately led beyond the limits of a single text to form an entirely new and different kind of *inter*text, in which self-development is narrated and *re*narrated across a series extending from the tentative sketch "A Portrait of the Artist" through the incomplete draft of *Stephen Hero* to the published text of

Portrait. Maud Ellmann calls this textual dispersal a form of "disremembering" or "scarification" that represents the devolution of identity as opposed to its coherent formation. Joyce thus creates three portraits of the artist: "a first draft, whose rejection gave rise to *Stephen Hero* and to what we regard, teleologically, as the final text. As for this last version, the indefinite article of its title suggests that it, too, may represent yet another Wordsworthian preparation to write. It is *a* portrait, not 'The Portrait.' At first, a repetition of the author's life, Joyce's autobiography seems henceforth destined to repeat itself. What can it be about self-portraiture, for Joyce as for Wordsworth, that makes them so reluctant to conclude?"[3] But *Portrait* is not the "final text" of the series, for *Ulysses* provides multiple alternatives to the closure that Stephen calls for in his invocation to Daedalus, "Old father, old artificer" (*P* 253). This serialization raises a number of questions, few of which can be posed, as Joyce discovered in *Stephen Hero*, within the generic limits of the classical Bildungsroman. His solution to one of the more pressing problems of modernity—namely, the impossibility of either harmonious inner culture or a satisfying socialization—is to create a hero who embodies the dynamism and instability of the present but who challenges the ideology of youth which (if we follow Franco Moretti) is the "specific material sign" of modernity, its "'essence,' the sign of a world that seeks its meaning in the *future* rather than in the past."[4]

In the opening episodes of *Ulysses*, Stephen is doing anything but looking to the future, despite his high-handed rejection of revivalist historicism and his embrace of "the loveliness which has not yet come into the world" (*P* 251). Like Frédéric Moreau in Flaubert's *Sentimental Education*, he has returned to the scene of his "innocence" and seems to ask, as Frédéric does, "Do you re-member?"[5] When Joyce opens *Ulysses* with a scene in the martello tower, a ruin from the era of Napoleon, whose invasions of German territories essentially put an end to the glory days of classical Weimar, he invokes the Society of the Tower in Goethe's *Wilhelm Meister*, but in a context of dispossession, usurpation, and colonial subjugation that is far from the kind of ideal society Goethe envisioned in his Bildungsroman. In many other intertextual moments like this, *Ulysses* resonates in a dissonant, dissatisfied way with the Bildungsroman tradition. Leaning on a parapet of the tower, Stephen thinks of his inglorious past behavior with his mother, mulling over his refusal to take the Eucharist, Yeats's "Who Goes with Fergus?" running through his head as a reminder, if the reader needed one, that his triumphant boast at the end of *Portrait* to create the conscience of his race has failed because his race appears already to have created him. Stephen is haunted by the past throughout *Ulysses*, which accounts for his desire to escape it by opting out of history altogether. This does not mean, as we have seen, that Stephen has "forgotten how to participate actively in history and no longer even asks to do so."[6] Quite the contrary, his desire to be free of history at this point is predicated precisely on his memory of it, his vivid perception of history as "a nightmare from which I am trying to awake" (*U* 34).[7] The irony, of course, is that he is supposed to be teaching history to the schoolchildren in his charge, but he is capable only of offering them incoherent fragments of the humanist tradition that failed to support his aspirations toward Bildung. The young pedagogue who sees nothing amiss in swerving from history to poetry to riddles to silence in the "Nestor" episode instinctively (if half consciously) undermines the ideological aims of the history lesson he is supposed to be teaching. As his ineffectual mentor, Mr. Deasy, blithely predicts, "you will not remain here very long at this work. You were not born to be a teacher, I think" (*U* 35). Stephen's failure as a teacher reflects his failure as a student, however much he thinks of himself as a "learner." His aesthetic education amounts to a handful of epiphanies and, as we discover in "Proteus" and "Aeolus," a slight imitation of a Douglas Hyde poem:

> On swift sail flaming
> From storm and south
> He comes, pale vampire,
> Mouth to my mouth. (*U* 132; see also 47–48)

The easy slide from "mouth to my mouth" to the letter on foot and mouth disease that Deasy has commissioned him to deliver to the *Freeman's Journal* is not lost on him: he is the "bullockbefriending bard" (*U* 132), caught up in the nostalgia and romanticism of the very colonial world he wishes to escape.

In "Scylla and Charybdis," the problem of Bildung is raised anew in the context of a discussion in which Stephen reveals to a group of Anglo-Irish revivalists his views on Shakespeare, views that thinly veil his own attempts to evade the nightmarish effects of literary history. The episode begins in medias res with a reference to Goethe: "And we have, have we not," asks Best, the Quaker librarian, "those priceless pages of *Wilhelm Meister*? A great poet on a great brother poet" (*U* 184). The brother poet here is Shakespeare, who is held up by the revivalists as the epitome of a national bard. At key moments in Goethe's Bildungsroman, Wilhelm and his mentors discourse on Shakespeare, who was immensely influential in late-eighteenth-century German intellectual circles. Of special interest is *Hamlet*, which Wilhelm persuades the director of his dramatic troupe to perform. He is drawn to Hamlet, whose "troubled mind expresses itself with strong emotion": "I also believed that I was really getting into the spirit of the part by somehow myself assuming the weight of his profound melancholy and, beneath this burden, following my model through the strange labyrinth of so many different moods and peculiar experiences."[8] Wilhelm is clearly attracted to the depth of character he discovers in Hamlet, which betokens the "problematic elusiveness" and the tension between "the sheer complexity of individual potentiality" and "practical reality" that Martin Swales attributes to the hero of the classical German Bildungsroman.[9] It is, unfortunately, a set of character traits that the German people fail to comprehend. When Serlo, the director of the troupe, suggests cuts in *Hamlet* so that it will play better, he blames "the sorry state" of German theater.[10] It is in just this context of national culture that Goethe's Bildungsroman seeks its justification for advocating an aesthetic education, for the nation needs young men like Wilhelm, who will improve the general state of culture. When Mr. Best makes his remark about "those priceless pages," he sets up an ironic contrast between the Weimar nationalism figured in *Wilhelm Meister* and the revivalist nationalism figured in *Ulysses*. The contrast is not meant to favor Stephen's Anglo-Irish interlocutors.[11] Stephen's theory of Shakespeare is a brilliant performance of his own resistance to both literary history and the oedipal nightmare that would make him beholden to the symbolic order of language, the "legal fiction" of paternity he repudiates in his desire to become, like Shakespeare, the "father of all his race, the father of his own grandfather, the father of his unborn grandson" (*U* 207–8). His Shakespeare theory recapitulates, in a deconstruction of literary history, the triumphant boast at the end of *Portrait*, only now the "old artificer" is his own alienated, colonized subjectivity. Stephen's catastrophic colonial Bildung reconstitutes itself in an immanent critique of Shakespeare and the consoling but false dialectics offered up by the revivalists, which are summed up in the episode by a variety of dualisms from Plato to the "auric egg" of George Russell, whose brand of mysticism, like Yeats's, glamorized the dialectics of Bildung that Stephen has tried so hard to fly past.[12]

When Stephen speaks of banishment and usurpation in Shakespeare, he refers to the "note of banishment, banishment from the heart, banishment from home" (*U* 212), which is entirely consistent with the colonial Bildung enunciated in subsequent episodes of *Ulysses*, culminating again and again until he disappears from the narrative in "Ithaca," his Bildung plot left in permanent abeyance.

"Buildung supra Building": The Subject of Empire in Joyce's "Nausicaa"

Stephen's story is not the end of the story of Bildung, for Joyce presents another story in "Nausicaa," which moves the critique of Bildung and the Bildungsroman to an entirely different level. This layering and building up of significations and representations in *Ulysses* looks forward to "Bygmester Finnegan," that "master builder" in *Finnegans Wake* of whom Joyce wrote: "during mighty odd years this man of hod, cement and edifices in Toper's Thorp piled buildung supra buildung pon the banks for the livers by the Soangso."[13] The humanistic notion of Bildung as inner culture developed through dialectical harmonies is transformed in modernist texts like *Ulysses* into the notion of "Buildung" as multiple and (de)constructed subjectivities.[14]

Joyce's treatment of Gerty MacDowell exemplifies high modernist experimentation with forms of embedded and foreshortened Bildung plots. Wilde had anticipated this innovation in his displacement of Bildung onto a period of adulthood and in his problematization of "youth" as the privileged sign of modernity, though *Dorian Gray* nevertheless relies on an extended developmental process—Dorian's transformation into art—that effectively inverts and Gothicizes the classical model. Joyce continues this critical tradition with his representation of a young Irish Catholic woman whose aspiration toward Bildung is doubly threatened by colonial disavowal and by the commodification of desire. In his use of parody, Joyce calls our attention to the pernicious effects of the dialectics of self and society at the heart of the classical Bildungsroman, especially the bourgeois conception of marriage and domestic harmony. Through the performativity of style he also figures the residue, an uncontainable remainder, the evidence of "something" that refuses to be captured in the conceptualizing dynamics of dialectics. Gerty is this "something," a function of Joyce's parodic style, a recalcitrant subject whose resistance to dialectics models the negative dialectics of Adorno when he writes: "Nonconceptuality, inalienable from the concept, disavows the concept's being-in-itself. It changes the concept."[15]

Joyce himself once said to Frank Budgen, apropos the reception of his new character Leopold Bloom introduced in the forth installment of *Ulysses*, first published in 1918 by *Little Review*: "I have just got a letter asking me why I don't give Bloom a rest. The writer of it wants more Stephen. But Stephen no longer interests me to the same extent. He has a shape that can't be changed."[16] Part of the reason Stephen's shape "can't be changed" is that it is locked within the conceptual limits of Bildung and the narrative limits of the Bildungsroman.

Stephen's story in *Ulysses*, as we have seen, is that of a young man deeply embittered by having been rejected by the very "race" whose conscience he thought, only a year before, he could create, "in the smithy of my soul." Throughout *Ulysses* he wavers between embracing the classical ideal of Bildung and its totalizing dialectical harmonies and rejecting both in a creative exile from social determinations. In a similar fashion, Gerty evades the magnetic power of these poles and exists instead as a wavering between them, a wavering that marks the critical power of colonial Bildung. More radically than in *Portrait*, Joyce confronts in "Nausicaa" the problem of colonial discourse and employs, as he had not in that earlier text, parody as a mode of immanent critique, an imaginative resistance to imperial discourses of power. Gerty MacDowell's story is part of Joyce's ongoing attempt to change the shape of Bildung, in this instance by parodying the conventions of the female Bildungsroman, especially as it had developed in the popular literature of the nineteenth century. Joyce's parodic appropriation of the style and tone of Maria Cummins's *Lamplighter* (1854), a popular novel of female development, illuminates the problems of young women subjected to a discourse of Bildung that emphasizes quietist piety, moral perfection, and marital security. Though Cummins's novel makes significant breaks with the classical Bildungsroman tradition, it remains committed to a concept of socially pragmatic Bildung deemed appropriate for young women. This commitment is certainly a target of Joyce's parodic critique. However, a more significant target is the novel's ideological warrant, the way it structures the colonial subject's desire for subjectivity and harmonious social integration along the lines of what Frantz Fanon calls "a borrowed aestheticism" and "a conception of the world which was discovered under other skies."[17]

It will be useful to look briefly at some theories of parody in order to understand better Joyce's treatment of *The Lamplighter* in "Nausicaa." The classical parodic text is based on a clearly identifiable antecedent text. Its primary modes are satire, ridicule, mockery; it masters the style of the antecedent text and, to some degree, pays homage to it, at the same time that it calls attention to its faults, its aporias, its naïveté.[18] It creates literary value because it targets other texts, its authority to do so grounded in an unexamined assumption of authority over those texts. Linda Hutcheon draws on poststructuralist theories of differential repetition to redefine parody as an intertextual process of "transcontextualization," "an integrated structural modeling process of revising, replaying, inverting" that takes place between two texts.[19] And while she claims that it functions as "an 'auto-critique' of discourse in its relation to reality," she quickly reminds the reader that there is "no necessary correlation" between the self-criticism of parodic discourse and "radical ideological change."[20] Julia Kristeva's theory is similarly suspicious of any normative or orthodox relation to an antecedent text. The parodic text, in her estimation, refuses to engage in the "pseudo-transgression" characteristic of "a certain modern 'erotic' and parodic literature." Such texts "operate according to a principle of law anticipating its own transgression. It thus compensates for monologism, does not displace the 0–1 interval, nor has anything to do with the architectonics of dialogism, which implies a categorical tearing from the norm and a relationship of nonexclusive opposites."[21] Something like this is suggested in Jean Baudrillard's notion that modern art "can parody this world, illustrate it, simulate it, alter it; it never disturbs the order, which is also its own."[22] Kristeva, following M. M. Bakhtin, prefers the mode of the carnivalesque, a form of parodic discourse that does not rely on an "incestuous" binarism in which parody reaffirms the social and artistic values embedded in an antecedent text. The carnivalesque, which is the mode of the polyphonic novel, is not a law anticipating its own transgression but is "transgression giving itself a law."[23] It is this notion that Fredric Jameson has in mind when he compares modernist and postmodernist parody and argues that the latter is really pastiche or "blank parody": "a neutral practice of . . . mimicry, without any of parody's ulterior motives, amputated of the satiric impulse, devoid of laughter and of any conviction that alongside the abnormal tongue you have momentarily borrowed, some healthy linguistic normality still exists."[24] By creating its own law, critical parody ceases to depend on the law of a prior text, much less on its priority.

Many critics identify parody as one of Joyce's signature modernist strategies.[25] In Stephen Heath's reading of Joyce, this practice is called plagiarism, "a copying that fixes no point of irony between model and imitation, that rests, in this respect, in a hesitation of meaning." The hesitation of meaning, the aporia created by the author's uneasy relationship with tradition, converts parodic appropriation into theft: the "continual appropriation and fragmentation, the purloining that defines Joyce's writing."[26] Patrick McGee's understanding of parody in "Nausicaa" involves a similar transgression of the laws of writing. For him, Joyce "is reproducing the literary man's nausea, he is rewriting the style of another that both seduces and repulses him." McGee goes on to suggest, "The law that distinguishes good from bad writing, the law of Joyce's signature, has been transgressed by the force of his parody, by an antistyle that anticipates postmodern pastiche."[27] The often unstated conclusion of such readings is that *Ulysses*, by virtue of its deconstructive parodic impulse, is a postmodern text, narcissistic instead of critical, a hall of mirrors.[28] Advances in postcolonial theory suggest that in Joyce's colonial texts parody ceases, really, to be parody at all and begins to approximate what Homi Bhabha calls mimicry, a "mode of colonial discourse" that is "constructed around ambivalence," in which the authority of that discourse is permanently disturbed, split between "two disproportionate sites": "the colonial scene as the invention of historicity, mastery, mimesis or as the 'other scene' of *Entstellung*, displacement, fantasy, psychic defense, and an 'open' textuality." Mimicry is the fatal flaw of colonial discourse, "the representation of a difference that is itself a process of disavowal."[29] The ambivalence of mimicry—"almost the same, but not quite"—ruptures and unsettles colonial discourse, which is always, for Bhabha, fraught with the fatal contradiction of its own conditionality. Colonial discourse disavows colonial subjects through "discriminatory identity effects" in order to establish its authority. Mimicry reverses the process of disavowal inherent in "colonial representation and individuation" and permits "'denied' knowledges" the opportunity to "enter upon the dominant discourse and estrange the basis of its authority—its rules of recognition." This "violent dislocation," for Bhabha, is "the conditionality of colonial discourse," a "strategic displacement of value" along a metonymic pathway that produces "the signifier of colonial mimicry as the affect of hybridity."[30]

In the context of the Bildungsroman, this affect of hybridity is the sign of an immanent critique of Bildung, specifically of the dialectical structure that subtends it. Joyce's parodic or mimic strategies insist that the limits of critique fall within the classical structure. "The limit of immanent critique," writes Adorno, "is that the law of the immanent context is ultimately one with the delusion that has to be overcome."[31] The delusion, of course, is the ideal of harmonious socialization at the heart of the classical Bildungsroman, both the aesthetico-spiritual and the socially pragmatic variants. Gayatri Spivak's description of such an immanent context—an "inaccessible blankness circumscribed by an interpretable text"—is particularly apt in a discussion of an intertextual parody that would avoid the tendency of dialectics "to hide the relentless recognition of the Other by assimilation."[32] Mimicry and hybridity, a "text-inscribed blankness" within a colonial discourse riven by contradiction and aporias: these are the textual effects of colonial discourse, effects that I believe are discernible in "Nausicaa." To read Gerty MacDowell as the subject of empire is simultaneously to reveal her as the subject of colonial Bildung. In this reading, Gerty emerges less as a pawn of discursive hegemony than as a subject reconstituting traditional narratives of development in order to speak for herself—"everything speaks in its own way," as Bloom himself puts it (*U* 121)—even if what she speaks is "colonial nonsense," "productive of powerful, if ambivalent, strategies of cultural authority and resistance."[33]

In the context of a parodic representation, the question of the female subject of colonial Bildung intersects with other more general questions of representing subjectivity. A dominant view among Joyce critics is that "Nausicaa" reflects the powerful influence of ideology on identity formation. Thomas Richards, for example, argues that female subjectivity constitutes "a specific site of advertised spectacle" determined by "a commodity language," "the filtration into language of the commodity in its ubiquitous and liquid modern form." According to Richards, Gerty's relationship with the world is mediated by "manufactured objects" that "hover free," creating a "veil of commodities with which she finally lives in symbiosis."[34] On this view, culture industries translate the dialectics of Bildung into the unforgiving terms of commodification. Garry Leonard argues, in a similar way, that subjectivity is "an effect rather than a given" and femininity purely a construct inseparable from the commodity language that defines it. "In essence, Gerty packages her body in a manner that advertises the culturally accepted norm of 'femininity.'"[35] In Richards's reading, Gerty retains a level of subjectivity—the human agency required to endow things with "human energy" or "personality"—that Leonard's Lacanian analysis strips away. By suggesting that "it is not that products have 'personality,' but that Gerty's 'personality' is a product," Leonard claims to invert Richards's argument that her narrative is "a climatized display of the docile coexistence of commodities which [she] has invested with human energy."[36] Patrick McGee's analysis of the episode generalizes these observations. He argues that Gerty is entirely assimilated into a system of signs in which her desire is confounded with the abstract desire of signification. Thus "Gerty desires desire itself"; she "desires the symbol of a symbol, a metonymy—a symbol whose structure is ambivalent, a symbol from which she derives a pleasure in the play of ambivalence, in the production of the other's uncoded desire or jouissance."[37]

These "arguments from construction" pose unique problems for a critique of colonial Bildung. Rajeswari Sunder Rajan, speaking of the representation of the "new" Indian woman, writes that "if we are to avoid the cultural determinism that follows from the argument from construction, we must also locate the liberatory space for resistance that it allows (from the premise that what is 'made' can be 'unmade' or made differently)."[38] For Sunder Rajan, as for Spivak, resistance is all the more urgent when the subject of theory is the female subaltern. When postcolonial intellectuals seek to "speak to" (rather than for) the "historically muted subject of the subaltern woman," they must "*systematically* 'unlearn[]' female privilege."[39] With respect to the representation of Indian women, both Sunder Rajan and Spivak insist upon the necessity of a critique of gender construction that does not lead to the creation of a "new orientalism."[40] By the same token, it is equally important that the colonial subject not become the pretext of a new "claim to authenticity" with respect to the authority of the "ethnic voice" that Sara Suleri associates with "a great enamorment with the 'real.'"[41] The colonial subject tends to exemplify more dramatically the problem of identity because identity is always something that must be fought for, retrieved, even invented. Identity is thus always about discovery, transformation, imaginative creation. As Bhabha puts it, drawing on a Lacanian formulation of the subject, "the question of identification is never the affirmation of a pre-given identity, never a self-fulfilling prophecy—it is always the production of an 'image' of identity and the transformation of the subject in assuming that image."[42]

Joyce's "Nausicaa" addresses these issues of subjectivity and ideological inscription from the standpoint of an immanent critique of a young Irish Catholic woman's investments in the discourses of late modernity, specifically those emphasizing self-development and self-improvement. Gerty MacDowell represents in a striking and dramatic way the dual nature of such investments, for while she appears to be a passive subject of social and cultural discourses, she is obviously responding creatively to those discourses, exemplifying Anthony Giddens's notion that the subject of late modernity engages in a reflexive project of the self. According to Giddens, *self-identity* "is not something that is just given, as a result of the continuities of the individual's action-system, but something that has to be routinely created and sustained in the reflexive activities of the individual."[43] Self-development is thus a process of constantly revising and negotiating identity within rapidly shifting and changing discursive contexts. The emphasis, therefore, should not be on whether we find Gerty to be a representation of discourse or of an essential subjectivity—to be a function of style or of mimesis—but on whether representation clarifies the nature of her Bildung plot. "A person's identity is not to be found in behavior," writes Giddens, "nor—important though this is—in reactions of others, but in the capacity *to keep a particular narrative going*."[44]

Consider the following oft-quoted passage: "Gerty was dressed simply but with the instinctive taste of a votary of Dame Fashion for she felt that there was just a might that he might be out. A neat blouse of electric blue, selftinted by dolly dyes (because it was expected in the *Lady's Pictorial* that electric blue would be worn). . . . She wore a coquettish little love of a hat of wide-leaved nigger straw contrast trimmed with an underbrim of eggblue chenille and at the side a butterfly bow to tone. . . . Her shoes were the newest thing in footwear" (*U* 350). For readers who wish to see Gerty as merely a site of commodity spectacle or an "economy of signs," the language of fashion constitutes entirely her subjectivity; she would exist only as an identity mediated by a discourse of fashion. I do not wish to argue against the reality of mediation, only to insist that such mediating discourses constitute opportunities for an immanent critique of the dialectical structure of socially pragmatic Bildung, particularly that variety of it that targets young women. As Judith Butler argues, "to claim that the subject is constituted is not to claim that it is determined; on the contrary, the constituted character of the subject is the very precondition of its agency."[45] In Joyce's critique of Bildung, Gerty achieves just this form of agency; her self-representation mimics the discourse of female development and improvement, and by so doing she becomes a subject aware of and, to some degree, in control of a complex system of discourses that constitute but do not necessarily determine self-identity.

The question I wish to pursue here is the extent to which such an awareness and control constitute a critical engagement with Bildung as it is represented in the nineteenth-century female Bildungsroman. Gerty's awareness of herself begins with the kinds of discursive mediations that focus, as we have seen, on fashion and personal appearance. In this context, identity is a function of a reflexive response to attitudes generated by popular novels, fashion magazines, advertisements, folk wisdom, superstition, and gossip. For many critics, Gerty's identity is entirely composed of such attitudes. "Gerty's plumes are borrowed ones," writes Fritz Senn. "She is composed of traits assembled in a technique of collage and montage, in keeping with the chapter's art, painting. Stereotypes have replaced judgment and discrimination, attitudes to life fall into readymade categories."[46] However, such discourses do not determine her essentially, they determine a specific performance, a self-fashioning that she does not always recognize as such. But, insofar as such performances grant her a level of reflexive control over cultural discourses, she possesses agency. Critics who impugn the subject for adopting "attitudes" all too often imply, as does C. H. Peake, that an essential self is being obscured, that beneath the "oversweetened mess" of discourses that cluster around Gerty, "the dry facts of [her] real situation occasionally emerge, and the vulgarities of her undoctored self erupt," revealing "the essence of her consciousness."[47] But the point is not to insist that Gerty strip away cultural determinations and expose an essential selfhood; rather it is to acknowledge the mediating contexts of modern life and seek to gain control over the processes of reflexivity that alone (at least according to theorists like Giddens and Butler) guarantee social agency. It is through such attempts to acknowledge and gain control over the "reflexive project" of identity ("build-ung supra buildung") that she is able to compensate for her status as a colonial subject. Out of colonial inferiority she elevates herself to a level of culturally sanctioned beauty and irresistibility; she basks in what she imagines to be "the love that might have been, that lent to her softlyfeatured face at whiles a look, tense with suppressed meaning, that imparted a strange yearning tendency to the beautiful eyes, a charm few could resist" (*U* 348). And while some critics fail to find agency in such clichés, it is possible to see here an attempt at self-representation that Margot Norris has linked to the "phantom narrator" of "Nausicaa": a voice "constructed by Gerty's imagination to produce the lan-guage of her desire, the hypothetical discourse of her praises that she fears no one will ever utter."[48] She thus produces a critical narrative perspective that attests less to the spectacle of advertising than to an enabling mimicry of a language that is otherwise inadequate to represent colonial Bildung.

It goes without saying that Peake's assumption of an "undoctored self" be-speaks a conception of "authentic" subjectivity—"a great enamorment with the 'real'"—that is potentially as pernicious as the argument from construction. An argument like McGee's or Norris's, by privileging the "oversweetened mess" of a marginalized and alienated ("doctored") subject, inverts the ethical polari-ties of Peake's reading. McGee argues that "Gerty makes her mark from time to time, *in the text*, as the voice marginalized by, even as it attempts to break through, the dominant style of the first half of 'Nausicaa.' We hear this voice as the sign of Gerty's class, her social and economic situation, both limiting and reinforcing her desire."[49] McGee asserts the impossibility of a subject position outside the libidinal economy in which Gerty can be located or identified only as "desire desired." So too does Jules David Law, who is concerned with the circuitry and circulation of desire in which "feminine subjectivity is clearly staged only in order to be reappropriated by, or relocated within, masculine subjectivity."[50] Law goes further than McGee and many other critics of "Nausi-caa" who focus on Gerty's marginalization within patriarchal culture in that he articulates the mechanisms by which that culture inscribes female subjectivity and desire as natural and, therefore, inevitable. Of particular interest is Law's analysis of what can only be described as latent orientalism in the use made of "the East" as an orientation and origin of the natural against which "the West"

is defined as culture, as repetition and difference. And while his reading emphasizes the possibility of a "deconstruction of binary themes," the "massive cultural
system of hierarchical differentiation, with its implications of origin and error,
remains."[51] Though Law, like other critics of "Nausicaa," does not link these "binary themes" to the structure of dialectics in Bildung, it is exactly this link that
Joyce dramatizes when he contextualizes Gerty MacDowell's self-development
within a tradition of the female Bildungsroman.

Maria Cummins's *Lamplighter*, the immensely popular American novel most
often adduced as the specific antecedent text of Joyce's parody, participates in
this tradition. That this tradition is not mentioned in the critical literature on
"Nausicaa" may be due to the fact that critical emphasis is typically placed on
stylistic borrowings and thus on the generic form most commonly associated
with the sentimental style.[52] It seems to me that if Joyce parodies (or, better,
mimics) Cummins's novel, his target is not a style of discourse but a discourse of
development, which stands behind "Nausicaa" as a model of socially pragmatic
Bildung available to Gerty as part of a constellation of discursive mediations.
This discourse of development shares some affinities with the traditional male
Bildungsroman. As Nina Baym points out in her introduction to *The Lamplighter*, Cummins's novel "shows awareness of the formative role of the early
years and begins its story in childhood." However, it differs in some fundamental ways from the male tradition, primarily in its focus on gender and the social
opportunities open to women, in its concern "with the formation of character
in the old-fashioned sense of strengthening within individuals particular traits
that are deemed admirable," and in its concern with "those responsible for wom-
en's upbringing."[53]

To some extent, *The Lamplighter* challenges crucial elements of the classical
Bildungsroman. Most important, it revalues female experience (and the dialectical structure of its representation) and reroutes the journey of development
through domestic channels, circumventing almost entirely the social spaces in
which the male hero of the classical Bildungsroman cultivates Bildung. For Gertrude Flint, Cummins's hero, the opportunities of dialectical development are
nullified in the pursuit of religious and moral training, primarily at the hands
of her friend and guardian Emily Graham. Gertrude's unselfconsciousness and
apparent passivity have earned her the opprobrium of those who see her as a
hapless victim of patriarchal morality. However, as some critics have pointed
out, when held up against contemporary female Bildungsromane—especially
Susan Warner's *Wide, Wide World*, which many regard as the original of Cum-

mins' poor imitation—*The Lamplighter* features a much stronger, more resilient, and ultimately more independent female hero than one usually finds in
sentimental fiction.[54] Though outwardly conventional, Gertrude nevertheless
practices a brand of Christian love and humility ("the power of Christian humility, engrafted into the heart,—the humility of *principle*, of *conscience*"[55])
that implicitly criticizes the more authoritarian variety preached by the male
characters in the novel. And her endearing regard for her childhood friend
Willie Sullivan and for the mysterious stranger who turns out to be her long
lost father not only reaffirms the morality she has embraced since childhood
but also reestablishes the broken family that was the cause of her hard life.
These elements of domestic harmony supplant the world-historical dialectic of
Bildung that underwrites the Goethean narrative of development. Moreover,
the moral benignity of Gertrude's character has an effect on Willie that causes
him to reject the women who could have become instruments in his successful rise to power, thereby short-circuiting one of the principal mechanisms of
the classical Bildung plot. This is a very subtle maneuver on Cummins's part,
for Willie, on his way to becoming a successful imperialist working in India,
has the opportunity, once he returns to Boston, of wooing and marrying his
employer's daughter. That he does not do so and that he finds his way instead
into Gertrude's domestic circle signals an important revision of the classical
Bildungsroman.

It is in Gertrude's relations with men that we find the most telling contrasts
with Gerty MacDowell. Of particular importance is Philip Amory, who appears to Gertrude at first as a dark mysterious stranger and who promotes in
her feelings of pity and a vague sexual anxiety. We are struck with the erotic
quality of her relationship with Philip; but as he comes increasingly under her
moral tutelage, it becomes clear that her regard for him is entirely in keeping
with her "humility of conscience." Nevertheless, the relationship raises questions about the authority figures in the classical Bildungsroman. In the latter,
the figure of the mentor (often a father or father figure) typically guides and
advises the hero, functioning both as the authority against which he rebels and,
symbolically subsumed or transformed into social institutions, as the authority
to which he ultimately capitulates. In Cummins's text, this authority is initially
wielded by the kindly and almost childlike lamplighter, Trueman Flint. Moral
and religious guidance is provided by women, and the male authorities in her
life, including the disguised and returned father, turn out to be largely irrelevant or ineffectual. It is in this displacement and reduction of male authority

and in the rise to power of the female *Bildungsheld* that we can best discern the generic resistance of *The Lamplighter* and its relevance for "Nausicaa."

Kimberly Devlin has suggested that Gerty MacDowell undermines the un-selfconsciousness of the romance heroines she emulates by revealing her artful-ness and her awareness of Leopold Bloom's attentions. This may be true, but if we follow Leonard and Richards, we find that the difference between the two indicates less a fundamental contrast than a suppressed similarity, for both women act *in the service of* specific discourses of femininity. Gerty's difference from Gertrude is only apparent, for her artfulness is implicated in a conven-tional behavior that Bloom recognizes and associates with dancers, actresses, and other generalized social types. Both women are prisoners of gender typolo-gies, and both use conventional behaviors (Gerty's artfulness, Gertrude's piety) in order to optimize their participation in cultural discourses of development and self-improvement. Where Gerty most strongly differs from Gertrude is in her willingness to take artfulness to the limit of exhibitionism.

What is the nature of this exhibitionism? It begins with the invocation of a fairy tale: "No prince charming is her beau ideal to lay a rare and wondrous love at her feet but rather a manly man with a strong quiet face who had not found his ideal" (*U* 351–52). Gerty's domestic aspirations reveal the extent to which her desires are determined by expectations that are far from "unreal" but that are not quite realistic, given her social status, her age, and her lack of "a good educa-tion" (*U* 348). By subtly portraying Gerty as a resourceful, young working-class woman with dreams of entering the solid middle class, Joyce underscores the paucity of a desire downgraded from the level of fantastic unreality to that of quite ordinary unavailability. The pathos of her desires lies both in her willing-ness to settle for a "mere man" (*U* 352) and in the unbridgeable distance between that man and herself.

As a result, the expectation of prince charming is parodically transformed into the expectation of bourgeois marriage, represented by Gerty's desire for "a nice snug and cosy little homely house" (*U* 352). Her idealization of mar-riage reveals the patently subordinate and instrumental nature of a woman's role with respect to her husband. Her fantasies generally are part of a discourse that prepares women for the marriage market, which Andrew Miles claims was the dominant option in the nineteenth century for young women who sought social mobility.[56] For a colonial subject like Gerty, this option would still be an important if not an inevitable or achievable one. Beneath the conventional expectation of a bourgeois marriage, however, lies the temptation of a potentially dangerous attraction to an unknown man on the beach, an attraction that mimes, through a constellation of narrative perspectives, the sincere but abstract morality of the nineteenth-century female Bildungsroman. For the incestuousness that never rises above the subliminal level in *The Lamplighter* here becomes the dramatic focus of the episode. Devlin argues that Gerty's attraction to the paternal "manly man" implies an ambivalent, incestuous desire for the male figure who seems to have so much power over her.[57] To this reading I would add that Gerty's ambivalence is the sign of her desire to comfort (and perhaps reform) a father figure; it combines conventionality and its subversion in a way that deeply upsets the moral rectitude of Cummins's Bildungsroman and lends a forbidden sexual potency to the implied critique of the dialectical substructure of the classical Bildung plot. In this process, the "manly man" who earlier called to mind the image of a consoling father becomes a "foreigner" with "dark eyes and . . . pale intellectual face," which was "wan and strangely drawn" and which "seemed to her the saddest she had ever seen" (*U* 357, 356). Of this mysterious stranger—whose face held "the story of a haunting sorrow" that Gerty "would have given worlds to know" and who "couldn't resist the sight of the wondrous revealment half offered" (*U* 357, 366)—she knows nothing.

In scenes like this, Gertrude's description of her father is mimicked by Gerty's vision of Bloom. On first seeing Philip Amory, before she has been introduced, Gertrude notes: "His features were rather sharp, but expressive, and even handsome; his eyes, dark, keen and piercing, had a most penetrating look," while his smile "made him look so handsome, and yet so melancholy."[58] Her language is reduplicated, though more salaciously, in Gerty's discourse: "One moment he had been there, fascinated by a loveliness that made him gaze, and the next moment it was the quiet gravefaced gentleman, selfcontrol expressed in every line of his distinguishedlooking figure" (*U* 361). Unlike Gertrude, who is discomfited by Philip's gaze—he had "a pair of eyes whose earnest, magnetic gaze had the power to disconcert and bewilder her"[59]—Gerty relishes Bloom's, molding its raw, palpable force into the romanticism of her expectations. In the process, his onanistic attentiveness is misread as the sign of a secret affinity. His gaze is imperious and imperializing; but Gerty takes hold of the orientalizing discourse of the "dark stranger" and exploits its sexual charge as part of her own self-representation.[60] In her gaze we find a mimicry of the Hegelian moment of recognition—both the slave's recognition of the master and the impossible recognition of the slave by the master. She not only mimics the discourse of domesticity but enters into a hybridizing critique of the Bildungsroman, for by frankly engaging Bloom's erotic gaze she both displaces the authority of the father/master who guides and legitimizes the Bildungsroman hero and dislodges herself from the sphere of a symbolic instrumentality.

Her freedom, however, is tenuous and temporary, in large measure because it depends on the supplementary economy of Joyce's representation. According to Jacques Derrida, the supplement "harbors within itself two significations whose cohabitation is as strange as it is necessary."[61] In "Nausicaa," these two significations are shared out between Gerty and Bloom. On the one hand, Gerty invokes Bloom as the principle of pure addition; her representations of him—the "manly man," the "thorough aristocrat," the dark stranger—are additions to his essence, "a plenitude enriching another plenitude, the *fullest measure* of presence."[62] For Bloom, on the other hand, Gerty is a dream image, a phantasm: "O. Pity they can't see themselves. A dream of wellfilled hose" (*U* 368). She functions in the manner of the Freudian dreamwork, a reality cut off from any demonstrable presence. She resembles the other signification of the supplement, which "adds only to replace. It intervenes or insinuates itself *in-the-place-of*; if it fills, it is as if one fills a void. If it represents and makes an image, it is by the anterior default of a presence."[63] The duplicitous logic of supplementation breaks down the harmonious synthesis of dialectics that constitutes identity as *self*-identity; it forestalls sublation of the otherness of nonidentity into the plenitude of what is identified and identifiable. If Bloom objectifies Gerty in his representations, hoping to dissolve her otherness within a stable binary—"Pretty girls and ugly men . . . Beauty and the beast" (*U* 369)—she counters with her own discursive agency. But her freedom to act is limited by the social context in which she finds herself, a context in which colonial, nationalist, and religious discourses strongly influence self-development. As Adorno asserts, referring to the limits of individual freedom, "Freedom is a moment . . . in a twofold sense: it is entwined, not to be isolated; and for the time being it is never more than an instant of spontaneity, a historical node, the road to which is blocked under present conditions."[64] Gerty's foreshortened Bildung plot is the narrative form of this spontaneity, a brief moment of agency that expresses the freedom of both her social identity *and* her "untamed" nonidentity: "Only if one acts as an I, not just reactively, can his action be called free in any sense. And yet, what would be equally free is that which is not tamed by the I as the principle of any determination."[65] "Nausicaa" thus brings to light and celebrates the nonidentity of the female subject of Bildung at the same time that it critiques the threat to the freedom of nonidentity represented by the socially pragmatic Bildung inscribed in texts like Cummins's *The Lamplighter*.

There is still another way in which "Nausicaa" furthers Joyce's critique of the Bildungsroman tradition, for intertextual connections to *Portrait* and to other episodes in *Ulysses* reconfigure the episode as a repetition or rewriting of Stephen's Bildung plot. For example, a significant parallel exists between Stephen's meditation on the materiality of nature in "Proteus" and Bloom's erotic ramblings in "Nausicaa." Fritz Senn has described the parallel between "Proteus" and "Nausicaa" in perceptual terms: "Cognition through vision is connected with Aristotelian 'diaphane' in 'Proteus,' the sensual leering in 'Nausicaa' with transparent stockings."[66] And while Bloom marshals some of the same concepts that preoccupy Stephen (the cyclicity of nature, the repetition of history), the parodic reduction of context in "Nausicaa" further underscores the untenable position in which Stephen finds himself, a position that clearly marks the failure of classical Bildung in a colonial context. Stephen's position is that of the hero for whom there is no chance for harmonious development. But this is less a problem of knowing his place in the social world than of knowing *with certainty* if there is a world beyond his "inner world of individual emotions" (*P* 167). By the end of "Proteus," Stephen has decisively turned his back on the "ineluctable modality of the visible" (*U* 37); his search for the "[s]ignatures of all things" (*U* 37) has led him to the point of a disabling boredom with the sensible world. Watching the "writhing weeds lift languidly and sway reluctant arms," hearing the rhythmic "wavespeech" of the sea (*U* 49), he experiences the futility of eternal recurrence: "To no end gathered: vainly then released, forth flowing, wending back: loom of the moon" (*U* 49–50). His artistic vision—"We walk through ourselves . . . always meeting ourselves" (*U* 213)—compensates for the loss of the sensible world. Bloom, however, because he is not preoccupied with abstract philosophical solutions to the mystery of perception, does not require such high-handed consolations. His frame of reference is erotic, quotidian, even banal: "Dew falling. Bad for you, dear, to sit on that stone. Brings on white fluxions. . . . Might get piles myself" (*U* 376). Stephen's pedantic tactile experimentation—"Limits of the diaphane. . . . If you can put your five fingers through it, it is a gate, if not a door. Shut your eyes and see" (*U* 37)—is parodically reduced to Bloom's frankly erotic desire "to be that rock [Gerty] sat on" or the "[h]appy chairs" under the girl graduates in the library (*U* 376). Bloom and Gerty inhabit and mimic the space Stephen occupied earlier in "Proteus." And when we recognize that in "Proteus" Joyce was already beginning to mimic himself, to cast an interrogative eye upon the procedures of the Bildungsroman that had led Stephen, in *Portrait*, to the point of triumphant self-assertion, we are confronted with a productive and parodic repetition, a generic resistance constituted by vertiginous narrative possibilities, layering "buildung supra buildung."

I will conclude with a final example of this dizzying process. As I argued in the previous chapter, Stephen's experience with the birdgirl in *Portrait*, which symbolizes his induction into the priesthood of eternal imagination, corresponds with the moment in the classical Bildungsroman when the hero achieves harmonious integration of self and society. The birdgirl, aestheticized and elevated as an icon of secular redemption, resembles figures like Mariane and Natalie in Goethe's *Wilhelm Meister*, whose instrumentality serves the male hero's rise to power. The highly charged symbolic encounter in *Portrait*—the birdgirl as "angel of mortal youth and beauty, an envoy from the fair courts of life" (*P* 172)—becomes in "Nausicaa" an anonymous erotic interlude, a moment of onanistic gazing that both repeats and fulfills Bloom's thwarted moment in "Lotus-eaters": Gerty has, after all, "[m]ade up for that tramdriver this morning" (*U* 368) who had blocked his view of a woman in silk stockings.[67] His idea of woman combines soft-core pornography with questionable wisdom about the nature of female sexuality: "*Lingerie* does it. Felt for the curves inside her *deshabillé*. Excites them also when they're. I'm all clean come and dirty me" (*U* 368). By association, Gerty and the woman in silk stockings have become interchangeable objects of voyeuristic desire, pornographic stars like those in the "Mutoscope pictures in Capel street: for men only" (*U* 368). Both women "suffer" the gaze of men; and it is on this voyeuristic gaze—imperializing, colonizing—that the critical power of "Nausicaa" hangs, for it is through Bloom's gaze that Joyce critiques Stephen's aestheticism by reconstituting it as the colonial discourse that it disguises.[68] "Nausicaa" repositions Gerty as a subject of colonial Bildung whose resistance to discourses of development (and the dialectical sublation of nonidentity within that discourse) produces a hybrid, immanently critical text that exposes the "ambivalence at the source of traditional discourses on authority," as Bhabha puts it, and "enables a form of subversion, founded on the undecidability that turns the discursive conditions of dominance into the grounds of intervention." In "Nausicaa," the socializing functions performed by the classical Bildungsroman are disrupted and revised by the female colonial subject, "the discriminated subject" who, in the ambivalence of mimicry, is transformed into "the terrifying, exorbitant object of paranoid classification—a disturbing questioning of the images and presences of authority."[69]

Although it dwells only on the momentary meditations of Bloom and Gerty, "Nausicaa" nevertheless invites us to begin rethinking the problem of Bildung and to see parody and mimicry as the principal modes of representing development in the colonial Bildungsroman. Gerty MacDowell, lame avatar of Stephen's birdgirl, is the material sign of this possibility, the sign of the disabling ambivalence of colonial Bildung.

"What a lark! What a plunge!": Woolf's Critique of Bildung

Joyce's representation of Gerty MacDowell's foreshortened Bildung plot is in part a critique of Maria Cummins's Bildungsroman, but "Nausicaa" itself does not constitute a female Bildungsroman. In fact, it is debatable that *The Lamplighter* would satisfy theorists of the female Bildungsroman, for they would likely regard it as a sentimental popularization of the classical form, despite its representation of a potentially empowered female subject. As many critics and theorists have argued since the early 1980s, when Elizabeth Abel and her colleagues published *The Voyage In: Fictions of Female Development*, the female Bildungsroman differs from the classical tradition in fairly substantial ways, while adhering to it in other, equally substantial, ways. In the most radical formulations, female development ceases to resemble Bildung at all, while in other more conventional ones, it retains a connection to Bildung, though that connection is often defined by critique and contestation. In almost all cases, the thematics of the Goethean Bildungsroman, which are rooted in the concept of autonomous subjectivity and in the harmonious and dialectical integration of that subjectivity with the external world, are differentiated as male from a thematics of feminist resistance to them. For the editors of *The Voyage In*, this resistance takes a programmatic form:

> The fully realized and individuated self who caps the journey of the *Bildungsroman* may not represent the developmental goals of women, or of women characters. Female fictions of development reflect the tensions between the assumptions of a genre that embodies male norms and the values of its female protagonists. The heroine's developmental course is more conflicted, less direct: separation tugs against the longing for fusion and the heroine encounters the conviction that identity resides in intimate relationships, especially those of early childhood. The deaths in which these fictions so often culminate represent less developmental failures than refusals to accept an adulthood that denies profound convictions and desires.[70]

Abel and her colleagues isolate two main narrative patterns in the female Bildungsroman: the narrative of apprenticeship, which "adapts the linear structure of the male *Bildungsroman*," and the narrative of awakening, which "frequently portrays a break . . . from marital authority" and "may be compressed into brief epiphanic moments." The first pattern tends to concern the fortunes of women in the social world (*Jane Eyre* is a classic example of a Bildungsroman following this pattern), while the second tends to depict internal changes, "flashes of recognition [that] often replace the continuous unfolding of an action." The editors suggest that Kate Chopin's 1899 novel *The Awakening* and Woolf's *Mrs. Dalloway* are good examples of this second pattern, as is a male-authored text like Flaubert's *Madame Bovary*.[71] In both patterns, we are likely to find internal tensions and shifts in the relative position of plot levels, for example, "a disjunction between a surface plot, which affirms social conventions, and a submerged plot, which encodes rebellion," or "between a plot that charts development and a plot that unravels it." We are also more likely to find that women characters are "more psychologically embedded in relationships," especially with other women, a situation that complicates the traditional relationship of mentor to apprentice.[72]

Marianne Hirsch has identified a pattern that appears to be a variant of the apprenticeship narrative, one that she calls "spiritual *Bildung*." She traces this pattern as far back as *Antigone*, but regards the "Confessions of a Beautiful Soul," book 6 of Goethe's *Wilhelm Meister*, as a paradigmatic modern version of it. Hirsch perceives in the narrative of spiritual Bildung a "lack of 'harmony' between the outer and the inner life," a "dichotomization that propels man outside and confines woman inside," and declares, "Woman's exclusively spiritual development is a death warrant." This is clearly evident in "Confessions of a Beautiful Soul," where spiritual Bildung is situated "squarely on one side of the dialectic that defines the German *Bildungsroman*." This dialectic—defined, as we have seen, by the interaction of self and society, inner and outer experience, reflection and action—becomes, in the narrative of spiritual Bildung, overbalanced in the direction of a nearly suffocating inwardness and self-reflection. Unlike the main narrative of *Wilhelm Meister*, which "finds itself uneasily poised between the two poles of this dialectic, the 'Confessions' demonstrate the rewards and the dangers of being locked into one."[73] The dangers are typically figured in terms of death or an absolute estrangement from society; the rewards are often tied to the embrace of proscribed experiences and states of consciousness. There is a strong emphasis in such narratives on the pre-oedipal phase of development, "characterized by fusion, fluidity, mutuality, continuity and lack of differentiation, as well as by the heroines' refusal of a heterosexual social reality that violates their psychological needs." For this reason, gender proves to be "even more fundamental than national tradition in determining generic conventions."[74] Though Hirsch does not discuss spiritual Bildung in Adornean terms, the description she offers of the lopsided dialectical investments made by female *Bildungshelden* reminds us of the dangers and rewards of the turn toward nonidentity in many modernist Bildungsromane.

By the 1990s, feminist critics had built substantially on the work of *The Voyage In* and continued to argue for a separate tradition of representing female development. One of the most telling signs of a radical repositioning of theory with respect to the Bildungsroman tradition was Susan Fraiman's insistence, in 1993, that the term "female Bildungsroman" is itself problematic. "Perhaps this is the time to jettison once and for all the notion of a 'female *Bildungsroman*' — by uncoupling these two terms to release our discussion of female developmental fiction from so much Goethean baggage and relinquish the appeal to any single, authoritative because originary, novel of formation, whether female or male." Fraiman's readings of nineteenth-century novels make some of the same thematic and structural points found in *The Voyage In*, but they belong within a much broader literary historical context. "Instead of reconceiving the genre in terms of the different road taken by the female individual, I suggest we locate its multiple narratives within a larger, cacophonous discourse about female formation." In her analyses of "plural formations," she reveals the way that social determinations undermine any notion of an "'integrated' selfhood" and the way that class, nationality, and race make it impossible to speak of "a uniform fiction of female development."[75] What Fraiman calls "the novel of self development" seeks to represent different trajectories of self-formation that have also been discussed in terms of "self-awareness" or "initiation" or "awakening." Another way of addressing Fraiman's concern is to argue that what is often referred to as the "female Bildungsroman" constitutes a unique movement within literary history that can be understood either as a creative and critical reaction to the male-oriented discourse of Bildung, which we can trace to the late eighteenth century and writers like Mary Wollstonecraft, or as a tradition that has no substantial relation, reactive or otherwise, to those discourses, but develops out of other forms of auto/biographical or confessional discourses written by women in a tradition extending back at least to the medieval period and the mystical writings of St. Theresa of Avila and Julian of Norwich.[76] The problem with this reading of literary history, of course, is that it reinscribes the very gender and genre differences that a writer like Virginia Woolf seeks so brilliantly to overcome, for her novels do not so much discover a separate space of female self-development as occupy a common space that is seen in a radically different fashion from the men who share it. It is this common space seen from a radically different perspective that I want to explore as the basis of Woolf's critical modernist Bildungsroman.

In the classical Bildungsroman featuring a male protagonist, Bildung entails the coming into social existence of the self in a dialectical process involving reflexive interactions and accommodations with society. In the female Bildungsroman, this process is complicated by the fact that the very society that ought to permit such accommodations delimits or represses the process of self-development even before it starts. That is to say, it delimits or represses the idea of female self-development *on principle*. Nevertheless, as I suggested in the introduction, the nineteenth-century female Bildungsroman is a fair index of the critical potential of the classical form and, to a limited degree, looks forward to the modernist Bildungsroman.[77] But whereas the female Bildungsroman is to some degree hobbled by the politics of gender, which render it largely reactive and subordinate, Woolf's radical feminist Bildungsromane refuse these limitations even as they reclaim and reconfigure classical, aesthetico-spiritual Bildung to serve the developmental needs of women seeking to escape the pernicious effects of the socially pragmatic Bildung so often reserved for them. The recovery of Bildung, without any attempt at "repristination" (to use Adorno's term), can be made to serve a progressive and critical intention on the part of modernist artists. Susan Stanford Friedman makes the point that Woolf's "deconstruction of phallogocentric forms of 'identity,' 'subjectivity,' and 'authority,'" though an important part of her feminist project, does not define it absolutely; "her experimentalism does not eliminate these concepts as much as it forges new forms of them suited to women."[78] Friedman argues that the "assertive agency" in Woolf's work requires a more complex theoretical model than poststructuralism. My contribution to the imagining of such a model is to suggest that this assertiveness extends to Woolf's employment of the Bildungsroman genre. I argue that her work is perhaps the most compelling evidence in support of my claim that the modernist's strategy of reinhabiting the Bildungsroman form and destabilizing its dialectical structure is the ideal condition for the progressive and critical instauration of Bildung. For this reason, I want to consider her work as part of the "mainstream" Bildungsroman tradition rather than as part of a separate movement outside it. I believe that doing so situates Woolf's feminism and her critique of Bildung at the center of a literary tradition that would otherwise marginalize her work and contributes further to the revaluation of women's experience that her novels so richly explore.

Woolf's critical modernist Bildungsromane focus our attention on the failure of both major forms of Bildung: the aesthetico-spiritual variety in *The Voyage Out* and the socially pragmatic form in *Mrs. Dalloway*. In both of these novels, Woolf narrates the resistance of the nonidentical element of dialectics to being swept up into the fullness of self-identity. In their meditations on the failure of Bildung or on the alternatives to it that evolve out of that failure, Woolf's *Bildungshelden* exemplify the triumphs of disharmony and dialectical instability. Like Joyce's "Nausicaa," Woolf's novels refuse the uncritical adoption either of classical Bildung or of an alternative to it that is somehow gendered female. This is not to say that female Bildung does not exist, only that in Woolf's texts female self-development exists as a struggle within, and a critique of, a concept that originated in the discourse of men.[79] I would also like to emphasize that Woolf's modernist Bildungsromane, because of their critical orientation, open up possibilities for the representation of female development that simply did not exist before. In this respect, she is in advance of eighteenth- and nineteenth-century women writers, who lacked social and political contexts for literary protest, as well as of early modernists like Hardy and Lawrence, whose critique of the form did not address in any concerted way the problem of gender and female development.[80] I also want to suggest that Woolf's texts, especially *Mrs. Dalloway*, do more than register internal changes and "flashes of recognition," that in fact such effects are part of a critique that implicates social and cultural contexts at the same time that they illuminate the inwardness of the subject. In other words, Woolf's texts challenge the very basis of the distinction between inward and outward and thus the very basis of a binary or dialectical (en)gendering of narratives of self-development. By addressing the critical problem of gender and focusing on female experience within the context of the Bildungsroman and its ideological core, classical Bildung, Woolf perhaps more than any other modernist writer calls into question the fundamentally patriarchal authority—characterized by compulsory heterosexuality and its sociocultural imprimatur, marriage—of classical Bildung and subjects its dialectics of self and society to a negative critique that is itself the starting point, and the critical context, of Bildung for women.

Woolf's first novel, *The Voyage Out*, expresses her "discovery of the inner life as fictional material,"[81] but it also records her ambivalence with respect to the Bildungsroman tradition, for in this text she presents what is quite patently a story of development that features a protagonist who does not develop—at least not in the sense implied by classical Bildung. Rachel Vinrace, the protagonist of *The Voyage Out*, embarks on one of her father's ships for the South American seaport of Santa Marina, where she spends a few months among the town's English sojourners. She becomes engaged to Terence Hewet, one of the young Englishmen there, and almost immediately falls ill and dies. In this relatively foreshortened plot, we can discern the principal contours, as well as the principal failures, of Rachel's Bildung. Some critics, notably Rachel Blau DuPlessis, regard the problem as an ambivalence concerning the kind of story Woolf wishes to tell, for *The Voyage Out* "draw[s] on the traditional concerns of love plots—the production of newly joined heterosexual couples—and of quest plots—the *Bildung* of the protagonist."[82] Others, like Patricia Juliana Smith, ask the pertinent question: "what is the purpose of a bildungsroman in which the heroine has so little chance to develop to any very meaningful end, save the rejection of marriage?"[83] I believe that Woolf's use of the Bildungsroman form is crucial, for it is the generic context of an immanent critique of Bildung; her text seeks to discover, through the narration of Rachel's stymied development, whether Bildung is possible for women outside the limits set for them by a subordinate, instrumental role in which marriage presupposes a state of trained readiness to serve as helpmates for men. Though, as Susan Stanford Friedman argues, *The Voyage Out* enables the expression of Woolf's own Bildung, it is the representation of Rachel's failure that in the end carries the full weight of critique.[84]

"It was with a view to marriage that [a woman's] mind was taught," Woolf writes in *Three Guineas*. "It was with a view to marriage that her body was educated. . . . all that was enforced upon her in order that she might preserve her body intact for her husband."[85] *The Voyage Out* narrates this education of the body within a narrative structure that embeds a foreshortened Bildung plot within a larger quest-narrative that emphasizes the gender dissymmetry involved in acquiring Bildung and highlights the possibility of two alternatives: Rachel can either appropriate the cultural means to Bildung and accommodate her desires to those means or she can reject any attempt at accommodation and thus lose any chance at Bildung. All of this assumes what is common in the criticism, that Bildung is gendered male and that women must either give in or give up hope. Certainly, Woolf wants to undermine any simplistic, gendered identification of Bildung with maleness, and she does so in part by drawing our attention to traditional gender typologies in her treatment of Terence Hewet's and St. John Hirst's influence on Rachel's education, especially insofar as they link education to marriage. We see the critical force of Woolf's treatment almost immediately in her treatment of Rachel's sexual education. Until the time she meets her aunt Helen, Rachel's education, as DuPlessis puts it, has been in "chastity and avoidance such that any kind of sexual awakening is repulsive and destabilizing." This destabilizing effect is particularly marked in her brief relationship with Richard Dalloway, whose response to her "yearning for education . . . has, with a depressing swiftness, been reduced to sexuality."[86] For Suzette Henke, Dalloway's seductive gestures "point to the phallomorphic engulfment of the female subject by heterosexual scripts of courtly love and romantic infatuation."[87] But given his disquisitions on the state and his quasi-scientific faith in mechanism, we can add a number of other scientific and humanist "scripts" that attempt to engulf Rachel's aspiration toward Bildung. The social education of Rachel's body is as much determined by a long tradition of scientific discourse, in which "the material female body became the object par excellence of taxonomic study," as it is by the "softer" literary and philosophical discourses of the humanists at Santa Marina.[88]

Though some critics argue that *The Voyage Out* is a failed Bildungsroman, the focus on Rachel's education locates it squarely in the Bildungsroman tradition. Friedman, for example, places Woolf's novel in this tradition on the grounds that "like all *Bildungsromane* . . . [it] is fundamentally pedagogical, motivated by the protagonist's education into the ways of the adult world."[89] Rachel's education is, as the narrator herself points out, inadequate. "The way she had been educated, joined to a fine natural indolence, was of course partly the reason" for her shifting among a variety of intellectual pursuits, "for she had been educated as the majority of well-to-do girls in the last part of the nineteenth century were educated. Kindly doctors and gentle old professors had taught her the rudiments of about ten different branches of knowledge. . . . But there was no subject in the world which she knew accurately" (*VO* 31).[90] Rachel is, according to Friedman, the precursor of Woolf's "common reader" who is positioned "outside the system of reading represented by the classics and embodied by the university men"; her reading is "a scrapbag of disparate fabrics most consistently represented by 'the moderns.'"[91] Her flirtation with humanist studies is in keeping with the kind of education available to women at the turn of the century. She is at the borderline between two eras: one in which young women acquire only those cultural attainments that would enable them to become better wives and mothers and one in which they are free to aspire to the kinds of education and vocations that were traditionally the sole objects of male Bildung. Because she is, as DuPlessis so plainly puts it, a "mid-nineteenth-century girl heroine in a twentieth-century context,"[92] her educational options are either too little too late or, given her academic preparation, too much too soon. Rachel's education, as John McCombe points out, is tragic in the level of its inadequacy; her "thirst for self-knowledge" is undermined by the belatedness of what instruction, academic and otherwise, she does receive: "Rachel's questions are asked too late in her life and are the product of an education which teaches her very little and grants too much time for idle contemplation."[93] Like other critics who note this inadequacy, he places the emphasis primarily on Rachel's lack of access to the educational institutions that have trained men like Hewet and Hirst. This is certainly to the point, but McCombe's claim that Rachel's education "grants too much time for idle contemplation" unwittingly underscores a complexity that is often overlooked. If we consider the issue from the standpoint of the Bildungsroman tradition, we find that contemplation is valued highly when it is the occupation of male heroes like Wilhelm Meister, Frédéric Moreau, Paul Morel, or Stephen Dedalus; indeed, insofar as the male *Bildungsheld*, especially in the modernist period, resists a bourgeois vocation that would prescribe a set schedule for practical labor, "idle contemplation" emerges as a subversive outlet for creative energy. Those around Rachel tend to distrust her contemplative moments thinking of music or literature or history, because these moments lie outside the dialectical field of productive *reactions* to educational or social norms. Understood as actions, however, they lie outside normativity as such, even as they take their content from the materials that structure education and social discourse. Thus Rachel reads Gibbon and Cowper, not to become a well-rounded humanist, but to become better acquainted with her own desires. What she discovers through the humanist tradition, however, is precisely *what she is not*. It is just this paradoxical situation both inside and outside the dialectical field of Bildung and humanist aspiration that makes the position of the female *Bildungsheld* so difficult to interpret from the standpoint of the classical tradition, unless this standpoint is understood not as a norm but as a point of departure, a point of turning toward the nonidentical *as such*. For when it is understood outside the economy of self-identity, the nonidentical is always both inside and outside, always that which is disavowed as well as that which must be acknowledged and affirmed, always something more and something less than a subject. People are human, writes Adorno, "only where they do not act, let alone posit themselves, as persons. . . . The subject is the lie, because for the sake of its own absolute rule it will deny its own objective definitions.

Only he who would refrain from such lies—who would have used his own strength, which he owes to identity, to cast off the façade of identity—would truly be a subject."[94]

What is so dangerous for Rachel is not that she has too much time on her hands but that she is prey to mentors who wish to give shape and purpose to her contemplative moments, to situate them within the dialectics of Bildung in which they would acquire a productive and properly reactive dimension. However, she is not the passive victim that she might at first appear to be. It is possible, I think, to read her relationships with her mentors as instances of an immanent critique of the "subject that lies."[95] For while she eagerly picks up the works of novelists and historians, learns the works of the great European composers, and tries to understand Richard Dalloway's discourse on its own terms, she is also aware that her would-be mentors' liberal humanism, a "native" tradition that had evolved out of the thought of Bentham, Mill, Arnold, and others, is subtly misogynist and overly rational. She senses that it would ultimately exclude her, deprive her of the status of an autonomous and enfranchised subject, would try in fact to subsume her into a totalizing and dialectical framework in which she would perform her expected instrumental role. For David Bradshaw, Rachel is sufficiently prepared to critique these oppressive modes of socialization from the perspective of a feminist liberal humanism. Bradshaw argues that Woolf sustains a "native liberal" tradition "through [an] implicit critique of Hegelian political theory,"[96] especially as it is embodied in Dalloway's description of the state as a machine in which some citizens "fulfil more important duties; others (perhaps I am one of them) serve only to connect some obscure parts of the mechanism" (*VO* 69). The problem is less the specific role played by individuals than the mechanized nature of society and the state that emerges as the sum of the individual parts—a problem that Rachel understands intuitively, as is evident from her inability to square the image of society as a machine with "a lean black widow, gazing out of her window, and longing for someone to talk to" (*VO* 69). The widow signifies for Rachel not a social "organism" but a subjectivity, a person with a mind and affections; she looks forward to Mrs. Hilbery, the "old lady opposite," who signifies for Clarissa Dalloway the "privacy of the soul" (*MD* 126–27).[97] Rachel's example of the widow and her defense of her individuality are important features of Woolf's critique of Dalloway's mechanistic statism. According to Bradshaw, Woolf's portrayal of female characters serves a critical function by literalizing the figurative discourse of neo-Hegelians like Bernard Bosanquet, whose work in the early twentieth century had become, in Peter Nicholson's estimation, "a classic statement of the idealist view of politics" and thus a leading rival of liberalism and democracy.[98] It is in this context that Bradshaw can call Woolf a "dissident political thinker."[99]

Dalloway's view of the mechanized state finds its corollary in his attitude toward Rachel's life prospects. "I should imagine that you were a person with very strong interests," he tells her. "Of course you are! Good God! When I think of the age we live in, with its opportunities and possibilities, the mass of things to be done and enjoyed" (*VO* 79). Rachel's reply—"You see, I'm a woman"—is meant to undercut the false enthusiasm that even she detects in his encomium to modernity. But while she is insightful enough to detect a false note, she does not see the full extent of Dalloway's design, which is to force her, by means of a sudden sexual advance, to become an obscure part in the mechanism of his desire. His rough kiss is not only a lesson in sexuality, it is also a paradigm of mentorship. It seeks to draw out and shape Rachel's desire according to a regime of socialization in which Rachel is a subordinate, sexualized object. But Dalloway is not the lone villain. "If she is forced by Dalloway and beset by an internalized ideology, Rachel is also coerced by her 'good' mentors."[100] I would amend slightly DuPlessis's observation and say that she is coerced into mentoring relationships with people who do not recognize that she has already made substantial intellectual and artistic investments. In terms of the Bildungsroman tradition, Rachel is quite literally surrounded by mentors of all kinds. Her chief male mentors are her uncle Ridley Ambrose, whose immersion in Greek culture and literature signifies the enduring power of a humanist tradition that goes back to the Renaissance and runs through Winckelmann, Humboldt, and Pater, and Hewet and Hirst, who represent the humanistic tradition of male Bildung as modified in England's ancient universities and the social cliques centered in Cambridge and Bloomsbury. Unlike Leonard Bast in Forster's *Howards End*, Rachel does not try to achieve Bildung in a headlong rush; she is aware of the time and labor involved and is in a much better position, despite her relative isolation before her voyage, to benefit from the cultural capital possessed by her uncle and her new friends in Santa Marina. The key question is how relevant all this is to Rachel's aesthetic education and her aspiration toward Bildung, especially since both are so often defined by competing female mentors.

Rachel's aunt Helen is her first substantial female mentor, a woman who complicates the gender dynamics at the heart of classical Bildung. After Rachel tells her about Mr. Dalloway's kiss, Helen decides that "she would very much like to show her niece, if it were possible, how to live, or as she put it, how to be a reasonable person. She thought that there must be something wrong in this confusion between politics and kissing politicians, and that an elder person ought to be able to help" (*VO* 89). By deciding to mentor Rachel, she dramatizes the paradoxical position of many female educators at the turn of the century, for she acts both as an intimate friend and as an emissary of the liberal humanist tradition dominated by men.[101] In her role as a teacher, Helen brings into Rachel's frame of reference the values of mentorship and augments, through her example and encouragement, the aesthetic education that Rachel has long been conducting on her own. "Rachel is a fine pianist," Marianne DeKoven reminds us. "Woolf has developed her piano playing throughout the novel as the locus of her modernist heroinism, her capacity for profound, difficult, unconventional, authentic behavior and expression."[102] With seemingly little effort, Helen accomplishes the most important goal of all, at least from Rachel's perspective. Having been told by Helen that she can "go ahead and be a person on your own account," Rachel experiences an epiphany: "The vision of her own personality, of herself as a real everlasting thing, different from anything else, unmergeable, like the sea or the wind, flashed into Rachel's mind, and she became profoundly excited at the thought of living" (*VO* 90). But Helen's intentions become complicated, and at variance with Rachel's desires, once she is enlisted by Willoughby Vinrace, Rachel's industrialist father, to perform a quite specific pedagogical task. He would like Helen to educate his daughter in such a way that she may become a dutiful surrogate for the wife he has lost. In short, he wants her to become a "Tory hostess": "I should be very glad," he tells Helen, "if you could see your way to helping my girl, bringing her out,—she's a little shy now,—making a woman of her, the kind of woman her mother would have liked her to be" (*VO* 93). He gestures at a photograph of Rachel's mother, as if it were the image rather than the real woman that was to be the model of his daughter's makeover. Helen agrees to this plan "even if she ha[s] to promise a complete course of instruction in the feminine graces," though she does not see the wisdom of thinking his daughter could ever be a Tory hostess. Her aim now is to socialize Rachel in such a way that she can feel free among men. In a letter to a friend back in England, she writes that she would like for "a young man to come to my help; someone, I mean, who would talk to her openly, and prove how absurd most of her ideas about life are. Unluckily such men seem almost as rare as the women" (*VO* 105). She believes that through conversation Rachel can overcome her own shyness and overcome the barriers that prevent her from feeling equal to the men around her. "Talk was the medicine [Helen] trusted to, talk about everything, talk that was free, unguarded, and as candid as a habit of talking with men made natural in her own case." She offers

Rachel books and tries to discourage "too entire a dependence upon Bach and Beethoven and Wagner" (*VO* 137). Despite her efforts to turn her niece's interests toward nineteenth-century European literary classics, Rachel continues to prefer modern writers. In the long run, Helen does not believe her influence will be persuasive: "people always go their own way—nothing will ever influence them" (*VO* 183). In these sentiments we detect something of Lord Henry Wotton's attitude toward Dorian Gray, though in Helen's case there is no ironic subversion that would make her especially culpable for Rachel's "fall." If Helen errs, it is because she thinks that influence could have any effect at all. "Helen's plan for Rachel's education," writes DuPlessis, "which extends fraternal male bonding to a genial brother-and-sisterhood, attempts, in a flash, to provide a solution to the woman question so commonsensical as to be almost flatfooted: men should treat women as they treat men."[103] Rather than wait for a young man to come along to help Rachel, she enlists one of the men who have already shown some interest in her: "D'you know," she tells Hirst, "I believe you're just the person I want . . . to help me to complete her education? . . . Why shouldn't you talk to her—explain things to her—talk to her, I mean, as you talk to me?" (*VO* 182–83). To her credit, Helen comes to doubt whether Hirst is "the person to educate Rachel," in large measure because she comes to regard her as "a live if unformed human being, experimental and not always fortunate in her experiments." Hirst, though brilliant, would submit Rachel to a scholastic regime rather than encourage her "capacity for feeling" (*VO* 233).

Woolf was well aware of the difference in educational opportunities available to men like Hewet and Hirst and to young women like Rachel. Responding ironically to her brother's and his friends' efforts at poetry, Woolf wrote that "there is much to be said surely for that respectable custom which allows the daughter to educate herself at home . . . preser[ving] her from the omniscience, the early satiety, the melancholy self-satisfaction which a training at either of our great universities produces in her brothers."[104] Hirst, with his belief that Gibbon is the true test of a woman's education, expresses the common view: "It's awfully difficult to tell about women," he says to Rachel, "how much, I mean, is due to lack of training, and how much is native incapacity" (*VO* 172). Hirst's statement about the "training" of women in the humanist tradition, which implies standards of competence and credentialing, uses the rhetoric of socially pragmatic Bildung. In an earlier era, he might have used the language of "separate spheres," which posits wholly different Bildung processes for men and women. This gender differentiation lies behind Goethe's decision to embed the "Confessions of a Beautiful Soul" within the larger narrative of *Wilhelm Meis-*

ter, for it substantiates and legitimizes the spiritual Bildung of women without making explicit the essential social subordination of their experience. It is the same model of gender differentiation that we find in the discourse of the "angel of the house," in which women are granted moral superiority and domestic authority in order to mask this same social subordination. Rachel's unwillingness to enter into the dialectical relation in which she would play a predetermined role with respect to the humanist tradition is dramatized in the lesson she takes away from Gibbon, whose "book of the world" (*VO* 196) echoes the sense of privileged expectation bound up in male Bildung that Franco Moretti sums up in the phrase "the way of the world." What Gibbon offers is less a scholarly knowledge of Roman history than a specific level of cultural capital, the attainment of which serves as an entrée to social discourses of power. The "book of the world" is in fact the *way* of the world, at least the way taken by Ridley Ambrose, who tries to impress upon his niece the importance of the canon of great literary works, but especially the Greeks: "But what's the use of reading if you don't read Greek? After all, if you read Greek, you need never read anything else, pure waste of time" (*VO* 192). Ridley, like Hirst and, to a lesser extent, Hewet, represents the Humboldtian ideal of humanism, in which an aesthetic education in classical culture is the foundation of personal Bildung. This point is driven home again and again in the narrator's frequent descriptions of scholarly activity and the scholarly life, of men and women surrounded by books, "talking about philosophy and God" (*VO* 174).[105]

Rachel's desire to read Gibbon is in part motivated by a desire to know more about this ideal. But a more pressing motivation is a general "excitement at the possibilities of knowledge," which open before her upon reading Gibbon and which lead her characteristically to one of those "idle moments" that reveal the hidden realities of her own emotions. She "sought the origins of her exaltation, which were twofold and could be limited by an effort to the persons of Mr. Hirst and Mr. Hewet. Any clear analysis of them was impossible owing to the haze of wonder in which they were enveloped. She could not reason about them as about people whose feelings went by the same rule as her own did, and her mind dwelt on them with a kind of physical pleasure such as is caused by the contemplation of bright things hanging in the sun. From them all life seemed to radiate; the very words of books were steeped in radiance" (*VO* 197). Despite the best efforts of her young friends—Hirst, for example, "thought that almost everything was due to education" (*VO* 183)—Rachel refuses to be educated. This does not mean, of course, that she devalues humanist learning; on the contrary, she finds Gibbon's words to be "so vivid and so beautiful."

But her appropriation of Gibbon, which necessitates her putting him aside in order idly to contemplate what has inspired her in his words, initiates a different form of learning, one that results in *self*-knowledge. "Unconsciously" she walks about, "her body trying to outrun her mind," engrossed by "a great yellow butterfly." The lesson she takes away from Gibbon is not about history but about love: "What is it to be in love?" Rachel demands (*VO* 197). A reader could be forgiven for thinking that she is simply alluding to Hewet and her growing affection for him. But what actually happens here is that she has come upon the connection, intrinsic to the classical Bildungsroman, between humanist knowledge of the way of the world and the marriage plot that just at this point begins to take shape as a motivation for the novel's action. Rachel recognizes this connection, sees that what Hirst and Hewet have in mind is the conquest of what Woolf will call, in *Mrs. Dalloway*, the "privacy of the soul." It is for this reason that Rachel tucks Gibbon under her arm and returns home, "much as a soldier prepared for battle."[106]

Many critics read *The Voyage Out* in terms of a marriage plot or, as it is sometimes called, the "two-suitor plot," which involves "the protagonist coming of age by distinguishing Mr. Right from Mr. Wrong."[107] These critics often insist that Woolf challenges the "either/or" trap of "phallogocentric dualism" duplicated in the institution of bourgeois marriage.[108] This dualism consists, presumably, of legal union and compulsory heterosexuality on the one hand and of some form of "spinsterhood" or deviant sexuality on the other. However, what often happens in readings of Woolf's *female* Bildungsroman is the inscription of a choice between another set of options: between classical and spiritual Bildung or, more radically, between marriage and death. The difference lies in the valuation of the second term in each set, spiritual Bildung and death. I have indicated above that spiritual Bildung is an ambivalent achievement, involving certain rewards but also certain dangers, insofar as "exclusively spiritual development" leads to social isolation and death. It is, as it were, a necessity born out of a desire for freedom or, as Hirsch puts it, a "creative response to impoverishing and diminishing social circumstances."[109] As for the value of death, we all too often read that Rachel Vinrace's death defiantly marks her refusal to be socialized, to have her body and desires regulated by a masculinist appropriation of her identity in marriage. There can be no denying that Rachel confronts this duality in her own experience, but I want to suggest that in Woolf's narrative representation of it, death does not form a dualism with life but subverts dualism altogether. This transformation begins with Rachel's critical orientation toward the Bildung process itself, a process in which marriage functions as a microcosm of the larger dialectical unities required in normative regimes of development and socialization. It is marriage *as such*, the negotiations and accommodations within the relationship, that represents "phallogocentric dualism," not the choice between marriage and something outside of it. In Woolf's Bildungsroman, this "something" outside is always a remainder or an excess with respect to marriage; death is not one choice out of two on offer, it is the radical form of a condition of nonidentity that defeats the "twoness" of dialectical structures and choices, that defeats *the* choice by the creation of another choice.

The models for marriage, like the models for mentoring, are abundant in *The Voyage Out*. The British colony at Santa Marina, with its numerous couples and couples-in-the-making interacting in relative isolation, provides Rachel (and the reader) with an extraordinary perspective on modern modes of romance and marriage. Older couples—the Ambroses, the Elliots, the Thornburys—proffer durable models for normative married relationships, while the coming together of Susan and Arthur illuminates the ambivalent dynamics of courtship. Susan's engagement comes as a violent blow, something that happens *to* her: "She was struck motionless . . . and her heart gave great separate leaps" on hearing Arthur's declaration of love. The moment, while strange and unsettling, also has the effect of settling her: "So then, it had actually happened to her, a proposal of marriage" (*VO* 154). Susan's subsequent responses to her own engagement illustrate how profoundly the desire to normalize her relationship determines her worldview. She becomes busy with "benevolent plans for her friends, or rather with one magnificent plan . . . they were all to get married—at once" (*VO* 201). In the dialectical structure of marriage, two individuals integrate and synthesize their desires and demands in a way that accommodates them to society, which in turn sanctions a union that provides a symbolic legitimation of social values. An ideological tautology of this sort tends to expand, for, like the imperial society of which they are members, a married couple like Susan and Arthur become missionaries who seek to convert those around them to the state in which they have found their own socially sanctioned happiness. It is this form of conversion, in fact, that Clarissa Dalloway finds so damaging to the "privacy of the soul," because it seeks to amalgamate individuality within a social unity. It is Susan, not Mrs. Dalloway, who advertises the normative ideal: "Marriage, marriage, that was the right thing, the only thing, the solution required by everyone she knew." All the aberrant states that people, especially women, can experience—"discomfort, loneliness, ill-health, unsatisfied ambition, restlessness, eccentricity"—are traceable "to the fact that they wanted to marry, were trying to marry, and had not succeeded in getting married" (*VO* 201). In these stark terms, we see the cruel and unforgiving dialectical economy of marriage, in which harmony is the achieved state and disharmony is evidence of the fruitless attempt to achieve it. One's relation is always *to* marriage, there is no standpoint outside of it, even in death, for then one simply dies unmarried.

The scenes depicting the courtship and engagement of Hewet and Rachel present the reader with another example of this dialectical structure, but one in which Rachel struggles with the all but inevitable outcome. What she struggles against is a situation in which her education, under the auspices of others, is merely a preparation for the normative socialization offered by marriage. Ridley Ambrose speaks from the perspective of the norm when he tells his wife, "Young gentlemen don't interest themselves in young women's education without a motive" (*VO* 220). Rachel seems to understand this more clearly, and thus seems to resent it, once her attachment to Hewet becomes more apparent to her. Thus, when Hewet asks if she likes the Gibbon she has been reading, she responds that she does not, for "the glory which she had perceived at first had faded." She tells Hewet, "It goes round, round, round, like a roll of oil-cloth"—a telling image in view of the circular logic of legitimation that marriage performs by virtue of its dialectical syntheses. Where Gibbon once represented for Rachel a possibility of self-knowledge, he now signifies a *social* relation of power in which knowledge is the prerogative of the husband-to-be. That she meant "Hewet alone to hear her words" about Gibbon suggests that her opinion is no longer part of a larger social discourse. When Hirst overhears and asks what she means, she is "instantly ashamed of her figure of speech, for she could not explain it in words of sober criticism" (*VO* 226). Her relationship with Hewet has already imputed to her the insobriety of opinion that will require the influence of a temperate, "masculine conception of life." For Hewet, this conception is all about the economic role he plays in marriage: "I've got between six and seven hundred a year of my own," he tells Rachel (*VO* 240), but this is not an assertion of his personal freedom from the expectations of society, which is what Woolf means when she claims that a woman requires "money and a room of her own."[110] Rather, it is a confirmation and embodiment of those expectations. By the same token, Hewet's uncertainties about marriage are the sign not of any critical attitude toward marriage as such but of his frustration over Rachel's apparent reluctance to embrace the idea of marrying *him*; "he did not know what she felt, or whether they could live together, or whether he wanted to marry her, and yet he was in love with her" (*VO* 283). His confusion masks his disappointment that he has incomplete power over her, and it does not dissipate until he feels that she is completely involved in the social rituals involved in the "marriage plot."

These rituals are depicted as taking place haphazardly and with a certain lack of emphasis. On the jungle expedition, much analyzed by critics, Hewet does not really propose to Rachel; instead they fall into an incantatory repetition of phrases—"'We love each other,' Terrence said. 'We love each other,' she repeated" (*VO* 316)—that mimes the rituals of marriage and gives to their mutually ambivalent attraction the aura of an achieved state of engagement. In the days following, they are unsure of themselves; Rachel asks, "Am I in love—is this being in love—are we to marry each other?" and Hewet wonders, "What's happened? . . . Why did I ask you to marry me? How did it happen?" (*VO* 327, 329). Helen's role in these events is highly ambiguous. She appears both to desire Rachel for herself and to oversee the marriage plot with Hewet, as is evident in the infamous tumble in the grass in which Helen wrestles Rachel to the ground and appears at once to possess her sexually and to pin her down for Hewet's delectation. There have been many fascinating readings of this episode—the published version as well as various draft forms—most of which focus on Helen's homoerotic desire.[111] What I want to emphasize here is the way in which Helen's desire for Rachel is determined by Hewet and the machinations of male Bildung. The two of them loom over Rachel as she lies shaking and panting on the grass, "two great heads, the heads of a man and a woman, of Terence and Helen" (*VO* 330). Homoerotic desire is sublimated in the imperative of a normative heterosexual romance, just as the "[b]roken fragments of speech" that Rachel hears falling on her from above resolve themselves into coherent words "of love and then of marriage" (*VO* 331).

After the "strange day in the forest when they had been forced to tell each other what they wanted," Hewet and Rachel's engagement becomes "slightly strange to themselves" (*VO* 338). Hewet focuses on the role he feels he needs to play, which helps him to answer the question, "How did it happen?" It happened because he was meant to play a social role that authorizes his patriarchal authority over Rachel, whom he seeks to place in a subordinate position. He asserts his privilege within a division of domestic labor—Rachel writes invitations, Hewet works on his novel (*VO* 344)—and identifies her in relation to what she is not: he tells Helen in Rachel's hearing that "she's a person of no conceivable importance whatever, not beautiful, or well dressed, or conspicuous for elegance or intellect, or deportment," then says to Rachel, "A more ordinary sight than you are . . . except for the tear across your dress has never been seen" (*VO* 359). Her failure to be important and beautiful means that she not only fails to measure up to the standards of the "masculine conception of life" but fails even to conform to the standards of femininity. In marriage, her nothingness would confirm his importance, but only because he is totally oblivious to the real nature of the woman he claims to love. The point is driven home emphatically when he quotes the representation of marriage in a contemporary novel he is reading, in which one of the characters does not realize "at the time of his marriage . . . the nature of the gulf which separates the needs and desires of the male from the needs and desires of the female" (*VO* 345). Hewet does not comprehend that the novel he derides precisely mirrors his own situation. It is in reference both to the novel and to Hewet's own words that Rachel responds with her cry, "Why don't people write about the things they do feel?" When Hewet attempts to understand "the things people do feel" and sits Rachel down and looks at her, what he sees is an unbeautiful woman whose thinking is lost on him. This is what he believes he likes, this quality of her face that "makes one wonder what the devil you're thinking about" (*VO* 346–47). He tells her of his fear, that there are moments "when, if we stood on a rock together, you'd throw me into the sea." Rachel repeats the phrase, but excludes him from the image, thinking, "To be flung into the sea, to be washed hither and thither, and driven about the roots of the world—the idea was incoherently delightful." By excluding him, she envisions herself alone in a nonrational, nondialectical space, a pre-oedipal imaginary realm. In a curious repetition of the tumble in the grass with Helen, Hewet struggles to subdue a "mermaid" who undermines "an order, a pattern which made life reasonable" (*VO* 347–48).

It is just this order, this pattern that reasserts itself, at least until Rachel falls ill and upsets permanently the dialectics of heterosexual romance by refusing its terms of mental and physical health. Like Septimus Warren Smith in *Mrs. Dalloway*, Rachel falls ill not in order to negate the norm of "divine proportion" but to step outside the norm itself, to seek some other perspective from which she can know herself and her place in the world. I do not think that Woolf means to suggest that illness and death are preferred states of being; they are rather figures for what lies outside the dialectical structures of Bildung, in which identity is confirmed and bolstered by what one is *not*, by nonidentity. This might explain the reference to Milton's *Comus* at precisely the moment when Rachel first exhibits symptoms of her illness. What Woolf emphasizes with the Miltonic allusion is not the masculine authority of literature and language but the presence of "Sabrina fair" who is ultimately disruptive of that authority. It is another inscription of the dangerous mermaid within the discourse of male power.

"Sabrina fair," for DeKoven, "suggests the Kristevan impossible dialectic, the Irigarayan opening of the equalizing vaginal passage *between* the paternal and the maternal."[112] In her invocation of feminist theory, DeKoven alludes to an immanent critique of dialectical structures, specifically those associated with the marriage plot so essential to the classical Bildungsroman. The "Irigarayan opening," or something approximating to it, is frequently invoked when analyzing the otherworldly element of Rachel's death experience. "She was completely cut off, and unable to communicate with the rest of the world, isolated alone with her body" (*VO* 384). Rachel's sense of disconnection from the world around her, the Gothic phantasmagoria of her visions and dreams, with "little deformed women sitting in archways playing cards, while the bricks of which the wall was made oozed with damp" (*VO* 386), the unreality of the people who attend her—all of this suggests to many readers a rejection of the conventional world of romance and marriage, of knowledge and Bildung. DuPlessis asserts a popular view when she writes, "Death becomes Rachel's protest against marriage and sexuality as her sole aim, against the change of a *Bildung* into a marriage plot, which powerful figures who resemble Woolf's family demand."[113] Some critics, however, see Rachel's death in terms of a much broader repudiation of Western culture and knowledge. By dying, Rachel transgresses "the ordered coordinates of the Newtonian universe, by departing from the block of matter that so essentializes her: her body."[114] An opposing view is that Rachel's death is a defeat and that she is "killed off" because she cannot negotiate the gap between art and life. "Rachel's engulfment in the interpenetrating books of words and life is a negative model for Woolf," writes Friedman, "a mode of reading that she 'kills off' with Rachel's death and replaces with her persona of the 'common reader.'"[115] Such readings, however, are committed to the terms of a dialectical structure of engagement: her death is opposed to the life she could not or would not endure. But her death is not an opposition, it is an opting out. It is telling that Rachel identifies those who nurture her as "tormentors" who can think only in terms of whether she is alive or dead; they torment her with a seemingly inevitable either/or choice, but she chooses not to choose. They "thought that she was dead, she was not dead, but curled up at the bottom of the sea" (*VO* 397–98). Like Dorian Gray, she is "undead," occupying the disavowed position of the nonidentical, of the other who has chosen no longer merely to serve the instrumental function of negation. As wife, daughter, niece, student, Rachel can only foresee the surrender of her identity to those who would profit by that surrender. As something "not dead," but presumed to be dying, she exists alone, under guard, in the painful knowledge of her own nonidentity.

Alone, but under guard, Rachel must contend with a social world that cannot tolerate the irrational repudiations represented by her illness and "undeadness"; she must contend with the fact that "every now and then someone turned her over at the bottom of the sea" (*VO* 398). Her own choice to opt out of the dialectic of romance and marriage, of conventional bourgeois existence generally, is co-opted in turn by those who require her surrender in order to bolster their own identities. Nowhere is this more clearly the case than when Terence, at the moment of her death, "turns her over at the bottom of the sea" and translates her opting out into the perennial option of classical Bildung. "So much the better—this was death. It was nothing; it was to cease to breathe. It was happiness, it was perfect happiness. They had now what they had always wanted to have, the union which had been impossible while they lived. Unconscious whether he thought the words or spoke them aloud, he said, 'No two people have ever been so happy as we have been. No one has ever loved as we have loved'" (*VO* 412). Terence conscripts Rachel into a happiness that she always doubted and rewrites their life together so that it conforms to the convention of a harmonious union. Rachel may repudiate Bildung, but her "tormentors" foist it back upon her posthumously. It is significant that the novel ends with bourgeois life falling back into place, the reinstatement of a social order in which marriage is a refuge from chaos. Rachel may lie at the bottom of the sea, but her Bildung plot carries on without her, in other lives and other marriages, haunted perhaps by the fact that she is down there, somewhere, curled up, dying but "not dead."

Woolf's representation of Clarissa Dalloway is in some ways an attempt to explore how women might evade the dialectics of romance and marriage without opting out or dying. Moreover, it implies that the classical Bildung plot, with its emphasis on youth and education, tells only part of the story. In *Mrs. Dalloway*, we cannot speak of the Bildungsroman genre, only of Bildung effects that are conveyed through other novelistic strategies, specifically a temporal foreshortening of developmental history that produces an epitome of developed character. Clarissa's Bildung plot is discerned through retrospection and inference, in much the same way that psychoanalysis retrieves the historical foundation of neurotic symptoms. According to Elizabeth Abel, Woolf employs a "radically foreshortened notion of development, condensed for Freud into a few childhood years, focused for Woolf in a single emotional shift. Both narratives eschew the developmental scope traditionally assumed by fiction and psychology . . . and both stress the discontinuities specific to female development."[116] I will return, at the conclusion of this chapter, to Abel's unwillingness to see this foreshortening in terms of Bildung and the Bildung tradition. For now, I want to emphasize her insight concerning Woolf's attention to the discontinuities of female development, which she argues, following Woolf's own lead, are part of a larger critique of realist fiction.[117]

The foreshortened and embedded Bildung plots in *Mrs. Dalloway* are situated within a radical new form of narrativity that "evade[s] the tyranny of sequence by reshaping time as depth."[118] I am referring to the famous technique of "tunneling," which allows Woolf to "tell the past by installments, as I have need of it": "how I dig out beautiful caves behind my characters: I think this gives exactly what I want; humanity, humour, depth. The idea is that the caves shall connect and each comes to daylight at the present moment."[119] The "beautiful caves" constitute the temporal and spatial nexus in which Clarissa's "exquisite moment" in the past with her childhood friend Sally Seton—when Sally "kissed her on the lips" and offered her "a diamond, something infinitely precious" (*MD* 35)—brushes up against the present moment. It is also the moment in which Septimus Warren Smith, utterly unknown to Clarissa, doubles for her and fulfills her by making the impossible choice of death. DuPlessis describes Woolf's double-edged innovation as a technique that not only creates "an inner alliance" among characters but "may also mute critique by showing that connections of the heart can occur despite differences in gender and status."[120] The impulse to create "inner alliances" offers another level of critique, one that is far from muted, for the technique of "beautiful caves" undercuts the authority of a socially pragmatic Bildung in which self-development is rationalized and regulated by institutions. At the same time, this technique serves the ends of the aesthetico-spiritual variant in which inner culture presupposes both the sovereign autonomy of a self that exists in splendid self-sufficiency with respect to others and the possibility of a negative dialectical relation with the social world that does not come at the expense of individuality. In Woolf's novel, the narrator guarantees an approximation to this dialectical relation, one in which memory sustains the difference between two dialectical poles by orienting the process toward individuals (both characters and narrator) who remember. J. Hillis Miller has argued that *Mrs. Dalloway* "depends on the presence of a narrator who remembers all and who has a power of resurrecting the past in her narration." This power is dependent on the fundamental conflation of character and narrator. "In the depths of each individual mind" the relationship between the two becomes reciprocal. Indeed, Miller says, "In the end it is no longer a relationship, but a union, an identity."[121] I take issue with his formulation here, his emphasis on union and identity, for if we regard the relation of character and narrator as a strategy of sustaining individuation, then the whole process turns toward the very *non*identity that refuses to confirm through negation the harmony and wholeness of *self*-identity.

Miller's analysis is an attempt to resolve a dilemma that has concerned Woolf's readers from the beginning: the persistence of the individual even as narrative valorizes universalizing (or collectivizing) experiences that as a rule sublate (when they do not annihilate) individuality. However, his conclusion that *Mrs. Dalloway* "seems to be based on an irreconcilable opposition between individuality and universality" suggests the frustration of a dialectical operation which, ideally, seeks a state of totalizing reconciliation. In fact, Miller's general description of Woolf's narrative syntax—the novel is organized around "contrary" movements, "so that down and up, falling and rising, death and life, isolation and communication, are mirror images of one another rather than a confrontation of negative and positive orientations of the spirit"—points to the kind of discombobulation of dialectical harmonies that we have seen already in Wilde, where mirroring and doubling destabilize the identitarian dynamics ("negative and positive orientations") of normative regimes of socialization. Even Woolf's sentences, with their oscillation between the past of the characters and that of the narrator, confound any harmonious relationship between them or, on a symbolic level, between the self and the social world of parliaments and omnibuses. This "structural element," so fundamental to Woolf's narrative art, is the "one final twist which reverses the polarities once more, or rather which holds them poised in their irreconciliation."[122]

It is difficult to say whether this "poise" is not, finally, a resistance to dialectical harmony, for Miller's analysis of "undecidability" in *Mrs. Dalloway* is concerned with where union might exist (within or outside the text), not with an "assertive agency" (as Friedman puts it) that might undermine the concept of unification altogether. I contend that there is just this sort of agency in Woolf's novel, one that requires the "privacy of the soul" to which Woolf returns again and again in her fiction. In *Mrs. Dalloway*, the soul's sequestration is represented in a number of ways that indicate its fundamental importance for Clarissa's Bildung process. Perhaps the most important is the attic room to which Clarissa retreats, "an emptiness about the heart of life," where women can "put off their rich apparel" (*MD* 31). In the privacy of this room she recalls the "exquisite moment" with Sally Seton, a moment that takes on the substance of a thing that cannot be abstracted, that cannot be thought but is instead brought back to vivid life. She constitutes herself in a provisional union with others, on the condition that her selfhood be inviolable, sequestered in her attic room, away from a more total and more permanent union outside her control. We see something similar near the end of the novel, when Clarissa disappears after hearing of Septimus's death. She goes into "the little room where the Prime Minister had gone with Lady Bruton," a room now empty save for the "impress" of the two former occupants. "There was nobody. The party's splendour fell to the floor, so strange it was to come in alone in her finery" (*MD* 183–84). She thinks of Septimus's sacrifice, the young man who "made her feel the beauty; made her feel the fun" (*MD* 186). In these domestic interiors, the soul's privacy is not only protected, it is nurtured and educated; Clarissa learns to appreciate the beauty of the moments she had shared with Sally and of the life that she has lived since then. What she fears most are modes of unification—love, religious conversion, mental health—that would destroy the individual soul. Like Rachel Vinrace, who seeks to protect the "widow in black" from Richard Dalloway's mechanistic state, Clarissa is drawn to protect the singular individuality of Mrs. Hilbery, the "old lady opposite," from the "odious Kilman [who] would destroy it" (*MD* 126–27) and from doctors like Sir William Bradshaw who invade by "forcing your soul," who are "obscurely evil . . . capable of some indescribable outrage" (*MD* 184).

What is at stake throughout *Mrs. Dalloway* is the freedom to be oneself or, more precisely, the freedom to recreate oneself, for the precious memorial moments experienced in the "privacy of the soul" have an aesthetic dimension. Moreover, Clarissa is not alone in having such aesthetic experiences. Early in the novel, Peter Walsh follows a girl along the streets of London, an "escapade" in which he invents himself as a "romantic buccaneer, careless of all these damned proprieties." His fantasy overlaps with memories of Clarissa in a singular half-fictive moment that epitomizes Bildung: "And it was smashed to atoms—his fun, for it was half made up, as he knew very well; invented, this escapade with the girl; made up, as one makes up the better part of life, he thought—making oneself up; making her up; creating an exquisite amusement, and something more. But odd it was, and quite true; all this one could never share—it smashed to atoms" (*MD* 53–54). Peter's "exquisite amusement" with this "made up" girl, like Clarissa's "exquisite moment" with Sally, characterizes the aesthetic component of personal *Bildung* in a modernist context. The essential condition for these exquisite experiences is the freedom from interference. Clarissa asks herself, "Had she ever tried to convert anyone herself?

Did she not wish everybody merely to be themselves?" (*MD* 126). The desire for self-formation in isolation, which Miller describes as "a desire to take possession of . . . continuities, to actualize them in the present,"[123] has two important implications. First, it indicates that the Humboldtian ideal of individual freedom can no longer be guaranteed and nourished by the community. Second, it indicates that there is perhaps a greater freedom to be enjoyed in the kind of "unselfishness" that Clarissa desires and that Wilde describes in "The Soul of Man under Socialism" when he writes that "unselfishness is letting other people's lives alone, not interfering with them. Selfishness always aims at creating around it an absolute uniformity of type. Unselfishness recognizes infinite variety of type as a delightful thing, accepts it, acquiesces in it, enjoys it. It is not selfish to think for oneself."[124] The freedom to "make oneself up," to enjoy an "infinite variety of type" in oneself and others, is a defining characteristic of the modernist Bildungsroman. It is an important element in Joyce's *Portrait*, where Stephen Dedalus learns to assert his "mild proud sovereignty," and it is the fundamental principle of aestheticism that Wilde Gothicizes in *Dorian Gray*. It is also the hidden spring of Rachel's vision of "herself as a real everlasting thing, different from anything else, unmergeable, like the sea or the wind" (*VO* 90).

One of the themes that connects *The Voyage Out* to *Mrs. Dalloway* and that connects Woolf's fiction in general to the historical project of Bildung is what Franco Moretti calls "the 'aesthetic' dimension of everyday life," a theme that he derives from Goethe's presentation of aesthetic education in *Wilhelm Meister*.[125] For Woolf's characters, aesthetic education is a function of an orientation toward the immediacy of life. Peter Walsh gives this idea a quintessential expression: "there was design, art, everywhere; a change of some sort had undoubtedly taken place" (*MD* 71). As Ellen Bayuk Rosenman suggests, no aspect of reality lacks an aesthetic dimension. Mrs. Hilbery, for example, "distant, anonymous, and finally invisible in the dark, evokes this potential of the outside world to be made into art, the negative capability of reality itself."[126] This unregulated, provisional, fortuitous *and feminist* sense of an aesthetic education lies at the heart of Woolf's modernist Bildungsromane. Her representation of Clarissa marks an advance on the failure of Rachel to achieve the aesthetic education she pursued but could not sustain. Clarissa succeeds because she eschews altogether the scholarly humanism represented by men like Ambrose, Hewet, and Hirst, and acquires her aesthetic education in everyday life: "In people's eyes, in the swing, tramp, and trudge; in the bellow and the uproar; the carriages, motor cars, omnibuses, vans, sandwich men shuffling and swinging; brass bands; barrel organs; in the triumph and the jingle and the strange high singing of some aeroplane overhead was what she loved; life; London; this moment of June" (*MD* 4).[127] Clarissa believes intuitively that "beauty and life are to be shared, even though she can share them only imperfectly."[128] For example, she "cared much more for her roses than for the Armenians . . . but she loved her roses (didn't that help the Armenians?)" (*MD* 120). Woolf's point is similar to Wilde's: a sense of the beauty of life tends to improve the value of life; and since roses are the only flowers Clarissa can "bear to see cut," they become part of an arrangement, part of an aesthetics of everyday life, "rescued" from the external world. Though Clarissa cannot articulate her belief in beauty in the same way as Wilde, though she cannot theorize her aesthetic orientation to life, it is much the same in substance: art answers to the soul more satisfyingly and more faithfully than life. Of special relevance here are Wilde's earliest statements on the aesthetics of everyday life, which occur, appropriately, in the essay titled "House Decoration": "What we want is something spiritual added to life. Nothing is so ignoble that Art cannot sanctify it."[129] Clarissa's roses, made a part of her own house decoration, are the sign of an artistic attitude that wishes to ennoble and spiritualize life; they are all she can offer to the Armenians: one person fewer persecuting and oppressing others, one person more who recognizes beauty in life and not death and ugliness. Clarissa's aesthetic appreciation of her roses is part of a more general aesthetic framework of self-development in which the roses become an extension of herself, a part of herself that is able to come into contact with the external social world. In the moments of aesthetic pleasure in *Mrs. Dalloway*—her house decoration, the preparation for the party, the party itself—we see the external manifestations of a Bildung process that otherwise takes place in the privacy of Clarissa's soul. As Lucio Ruotolo puts it, her "willingness continually to revise her relationship to the extended world of past and present challenges all who surround her to similar acts of re-creation. Her reconstituted moments challenge the presumptive formulations of an age that rarely questions itself."[130]

Woolf's text simultaneously privileges the beauty of the object world (what Adorno calls "objective definitions") and resists the abstract and unifying totality of a socially pragmatic Bildung in which aesthetic education would amount to a history of art or, at best, the acquisition of knowledge about the forms of art. Though lacking its dialectical harmony, Clarissa's aesthetic education resembles that advocated by Weimar theorists like Schiller and Humboldt. As I have suggested above, Clarissa is not alone in achieving such an education; Peter Walsh also aspires toward and achieves something very much like it. So too does Septimus Warren Smith. Unlike Clarissa, whose enjoyment of the "here, now, in front of her" (*MD* 9) is inextricably linked to a life of privilege, Septimus experiences a crystallization of things as they are that is all the more dangerous because he sees the unspeakable horror beneath the façade of civilized life: "this gradual drawing together of everything to one centre before his eyes, as if some horror had come almost to the surface and was about to burst into flames, terrified him" (*MD* 15). Still, his sense of the connectedness of things resembles both Rachel's and Clarissa's "healthy" aesthetic joy in life: "But they beckoned; leaves were alive; trees were alive. And the leaves being connected by millions of fibres with his own body, there on the seat, fanned it up and down; when the branch stretched he, too, made that statement. . . . Sounds made harmonies with premeditation; the spaces between them were as significant as the sounds. A child cried. Rightly far away a horn sounded. All taken together meant the birth of a new religion." The bird on a railing sings "freshly and piercingly in Greek words" (*MD* 22–24). Septimus discovers in the utter disordering of his rational faculties the "supreme secret": "first that trees are alive; next there is no crime; next love, universal love" (*MD* 67). In this discovery, there is an aesthetic basis and truth, one that is no different from what Clarissa and Peter discover in the privacy of their souls, in their "exquisite moments" of recollection: "all of this, calm and reasonable as it was, made out of ordinary things as it was, was the truth now; beauty, that was the truth now. Beauty was everywhere" (*MD* 69). Just after one of his visits to the doctors, Septimus has his "great revelation": he hears his dead friend Evans speaking from "behind the screen" and mutters, "Communication is health; communication is happiness" (*MD* 93). Near the end, just before he plunges out the window, Septimus realizes the aesthetic texture of his life in a jumble of associated images that represents his attempt at communication: "Now for his writings; how the dead sing behind rhododendron bushes; odes to Time; conversations with Shakespeare; Evans, Evans, Evans—his messages from the dead; do not cut down trees; tell the Prime Minister. Universal love: the meaning of the world. Burn them! he cried" (*MD* 147–48). Though clearly suffering from paranoid delusions, Septimus resembles other young men, like Jude Fawley and Leonard Bast, whose Bildung plots have been foreclosed by a society that cares little for their cultural aspirations and that, in any case, leaves open no "mediated routes" by which they may be pursued.[131]

Septimus resembles his predecessors also in his problematic relation to the institution of marriage, which, as I have stressed throughout this study, is a cornerstone of most normative regimes of socialization. On this point Septimus differs radically from Clarissa, who remains securely tethered to the social world through her marriage to Richard. Marriage does not function as a stabilizing force for Septimus; indeed, he "became engaged one evening when the panic was on him—that he could not feel" (*MD* 86). For him, marriage is far from the ideal and harmonious state of "domestic independence, inner independence" recommended by Goethe.[132] It is instead a last-ditch effort to save his sanity, and it does not work.[133] For Clarissa, however, marriage is a more complicated and complicitous condition; while it submits her to the often unforgiving dialectics of socialization, it also provides her with comfort and security (specifically, her attic room) as well as an outlet for her creative energy. Nevertheless, her attitude toward marriage and her desire for women together mount a critique against the institution of marriage that Septimus does not even consider. I think this significant difference in the role marriage plays for these two characters, who are in so many other respects doubles for each other, is a function of gender and of genre. For in the Bildungsroman tradition, marriage is always a positive move for men, an enduring symbol of their successful achievement of Bildung. In the modernist Bildungsromane of Lawrence and Hardy, as we have seen, marriage is a predominant issue. For Jude Fawley, marriage figures as a potentially stabilizing force that is denied to him, while for Paul Morel the issue is more complex, as he rejects marriage to Miriam Leivers but also suggests that marriage may play its traditional role. He tells Miriam that if he marries he will marry someone he can "kiss and embrace," can "make the mother of [his] children" (*SL* 292). For the women in these novels, marriage signifies a surrender rather than a completion of the self. And while the issue of marriage is raised in Woolf's Bildungsromane in a similar fashion—that is, in terms of self-surrender—the outcome for the women in *The Voyage Out* and *Mrs. Dalloway* is markedly different. As we have seen, Rachel neither advocates marriage nor surrenders herself to it; nor does she reject it in the principled manner of Sue Bridehead. Her death negotiates the terrain of a third option beyond the choice of rejection or acceptance. To some extent, Clarissa Dalloway plays the role that Rachel's father wished his daughter to play, the domestic helpmate of a member of Parliament. Even if this were the full extent of the case, it represents an advance in generic and literary historical terms, for *Mrs. Dalloway* could be said to represent the Bildung of an instrumental helpmate within a narrative context that virtually excludes the male *Bildungsheld*.

But, of course, this is not the full extent of the case, for in Woolf's representation, marriage is also a contested social institution, the site not only of a struggle against normative socialization but also of a complex form of autonomy.[134] Clarissa resists the dialectical pull of marriage, which would restrict her to a merely subsidiary and binary relation to her husband's social and "inner" independence—restrict her, in other words, to the status of a "speculum," the blank screen on which he defines himself. In *A Room of One's Own* Woolf states: "Women have served [for] centuries as looking-glasses possessing the magic and delicious power of reflecting the figure of man at twice its natural size. Without that power probably the earth would still be swamp and jungle." Moreover, if a woman "begins to tell the truth, the figure in the looking-glass shrinks; his fitness for life is diminished. How is he to go on giving judgement, civilising natives, making laws, writing books, dressing up and speechifying at banquets, unless he can see himself at breakfast and at dinner at least twice the size he really is?"[135] Luce Irigaray, in a critique of the role played by women in the constitution of male subjectivity, elaborates on Woolf's insight about women's instrumentality: "Is [woman] the reverse of the coin of man's ability to act and move around in the physical world we are calling 'place'? Is she unnecessary in and of herself, but essential as the nonsubjective sub-jectum? As that which can never achieve the status of subject, at least for/by herself? Is she the indispensable condition whereby the living entity retains and maintains and perfects himself in his self-likeness?" For Irigaray, man's knowledge of himself, the development of his subjectivity, always takes place in specular relations: he defines his essence by finding himself (the "self-same" in Irigaray's idiom) in objects. Nowhere is this process more pronounced than in the relations of men and women, for in woman man finds the ideal speculum: a smooth, silent surface on which his own image can be created. Within this relation, woman is incapable of reflecting herself, of constituting herself *as subject*. Woman becomes a "faithful, polished mirror, empty of altering reflections. Immaculate of all auto-copies. Other because wholly in the service of the same subject to whom it would present its surfaces, candid in their self-ignorance."[136] Clarissa feels this emptiness as absence in relation to her husband and family: "She had the oddest sense of being herself invisible, unseen; unknown; there being no more marrying, no more having of children now, but only this astonishing and rather solemn progress with the rest of them, up Bond Street, this being Mrs. Dalloway; not even Clarissa any more; this being Mrs. Richard Dalloway" (*MD* 10–11). The void of woman, her emptiness, is the primal materiality that Irigaray locates as the paradoxical locus of male essence and subjectivity. As Diana Fuss puts it, summarizing Aristotle, "a woman does not *have* an essence, she *is* Essence."[137] In this sense, woman is mere matter, the nonessential ground of Essence; because she "threatens every minute to shake the present certainties of the subject [she] *must not be allowed any power of specularization*."[138] The void of woman is thus a passive medium which cannot reflect (upon) itself.

It is precisely to self-reflection that Clarissa is granted access, paradoxically enough, within the relation of marriage, a relation that succeeds in destabilizing from an immanent perspective a dialectical structure in which woman as nonidentical, pure Essence serves only to guarantee the essential self-identity of a man. Adorno claims that "the mistake in traditional thinking is that identity is taken for the goal." For as we have seen, "Nonidentity is the secret *telos* of identification."[139] By this I think Adorno means that the tendency in traditional thinking, whether it is about logic or social institutions, is to fasten on to the abstract result of a process of identity in which nonidentity (the object in its concreteness and individuality, its "nonessential Essence") is simply subsumed in the perfection of "self-likeness." This object, however, this concrete "thingness," can be construed as a remainder, some "thing" in excess of the abstract process that purports to subsume it. "It is the part," says Adorno, "that can be salvaged." Nonidentity must be freed from its role in identitarian dialectics: "Emancipated from that measure, the nonidentical moments show up as matter, or as inseparably fused with material things."[140] What both Adorno and feminist thinkers like Irigaray and Fuss are attempting to theorize is the nondialectical possibility of subjectivity, a possibility that must emerge from within dialectics only because the subject has in fact constituted dialectical relations from the beginning. Rachel Bowlby describes this emergence with respect to the female subject when she argues that Clarissa's meditations on her "exquisite moment" with Sally Seton and on her broken engagement with Peter Walsh should not be read as expressions of regret at having married Richard Dalloway. They reflect rather on the choice itself and how it "made way for the idealization of the two other lovers thereby given up." What appears to be the stabilizing structure of marriage is, in Clarissa's case, a "risky balance of subjectivity" in which her meditations on past possibilities open up dialectics to the "effect of harmony, itself dispersed across three approximations."[141] Clarissa recalls "the purity, the integrity, of her feeling for Sally" which was "not like one's feeling for a man. It was completely disinterested, and besides, it had a quality which could only exist between women, between women just grown up" (*MD* 34). The point at which the young male *Bildungsheld* is about to strike out into the world to pursue his vocation marks for young women like Clarissa and Sally the beginning of what is, for them, the true Bildung process: the "secret *telos*" of their own identities, outside the boundaries of the marriage plot that at the time takes the form of "a catastrophe." Peter Walsh's intrusion upon their "soul's privacy" signifies this catastrophe. "The moment of exclusive female connection is shattered," writes Elizabeth Abel, "by masculine intervention, a rupture signaled typographically by Woolf's characteristic dash."[142] In a similar manner, in the present time of the narration, Peter interrupts Clarissa as she is mending the dress she will wear to the party, just minutes after recalling his past interruption. She feels at first the impulse to hide the dress, "like a virgin protecting chastity, respecting privacy." As they get past the first few awkward moments, she reflects on the possibility he represents: "Now of course, thought Clarissa, he's enchanting! perfectly enchanting! Now I remember how impossible it was ever to make up my mind—and why did I make up my mind—not to marry him?" (*MD* 40–41). She soon recalls precisely why: Peter would have to know everything, would have to be with her at every moment, while Richard gave her the privacy she required, represented most obviously by her separation from him in her attic room. For some critics, the choice of Richard over Peter was like that of Hobson: a free choice, but an only choice. For DuPlessis, such a choice is a matter of choosing the lesser of two evils, for Clarissa's marriage "was a resistance to [Peter's] possessive and jealous love, his sexual and psychic colonization."[143]

While I agree with DuPlessis that Peter is possessive and colonizing, I think that to regard her marriage to Richard in terms only of a resistance to Peter understates Clarissa's "assertive agency," her ability and willingness to critique the institution that inhibits her on one level but allows a paradoxical opening up of opportunities on another level. Her agency resides primarily in her ability to destabilize the dialectical expectations of marriage and thus of the subject position of the female *Bildungsheld*. Her "risky" subjectivity, especially with respect to her desire for Sally Seton, models an alternative that Rachel Vinrace, for example, could not imagine, a subjectivity that confronts the pleasures of unity and the "soul's privacy" with a curious and self-possessed composure, holding them, in Miller's phrase, "poised in their irreconciliation." Clarissa embodies this poise as well as its fragile, composite nature. She "is both perfectly conventional in her role as lady and hostess and, at the same time, a misfit," writes Bowlby. "*Mrs. Dalloway* is all about the fact that she is still unresolved in a choice apparently completed a generation before.... Like Mrs. Ramsey [from Woolf's *To the Lighthouse*], to all appearances a model of maternal equilibrium, she is in reality anything but 'composed,' except in the sense of being put together from disparate parts."[144]

Bowlby's reference to Clarissa's "maternal equilibrium" suggests another vantage point from which we might consider Woolf's resistance to the classical Bildungsroman. What makes *Mrs. Dalloway* so innovative, according to Bowlby, is that "the heroine is the woman of fifty and not her eighteen-year-old daughter on the brink of courtship."[145] I would like to add that Elizabeth Dalloway is also on the brink of a vocation, the point at which the classical and early modernist Bildungsroman alike tend to posit the culmination of Bildung. Moreover, the fact that her dramatically foreshortened Bildung plot is not the focus of the novel suggests either Woolf's frustration with the Bildungsroman form and the concept of Bildung it narrates or her decision to situate the young woman's aspirations toward Bildung within the context of a narrative focusing on a day in her mother's life, a strategy that Joyce employs in *Ulysses* when he contextualizes Stephen's and Gerty MacDowell's Bildung plots within the sprawling narrative of Leopold Bloom's odyssey. Like Joyce's, Woolf's modernist experiment resists the narrative structure of the classical Bildungsroman while at the same time appropriating the aesthetic dimension of classical Bildung for the everyday experience of women in late modernity.

We do not know much about Elizabeth. The narrator's description suggests a pale, mysterious, budding youth: she "was dark; had Chinese eyes in a pale face; an Oriental mystery; was gentle, considerate, still. . . . at seventeen, why, Clarissa could not in the least understand, she had become very serious; like a hyacinth, sheathed in glossy green, with buds just tinted, a hyacinth which has had no sun" (*MD* 123). She is later described as being "like a lily . . . by the side of a pool" (*MD* 193). These associations with flowers both idealize her youth and minimize her capacity as a social subject. Such descriptions remind us of Rachel, but there is a significant difference between the two young women. Rachel is suspended between two choices: an endless sojourn under the care of ineffectual mentors and mother substitutes or marriage to Hewet. Her haphazard studies lack the discipline of university training, while her musical talents, though substantial, are not directed toward a career in performance or composition. Elizabeth, however, is afforded different sorts of educational and social experiences, a glimpse of which we get in her relationship with her governess, Doris Kilman. Clarissa's animosity toward Kilman is violent: "This woman had taken her daughter from her! She in touch with invisible presences! Heavy, ugly, commonplace, without kindness or grace, she know the meaning of life!" (*MD* 125). But Miss Kilman is an educated woman: "She had her degree. She was a woman who had made her way in the world. Her knowledge of modern history was more than respectable" (*MD* 132). She represents a class of women who, in the early twentieth century, were able to take advantage of opportunities in education and to fulfill at least some of their aspirations toward the kind of vocation that marks the achievement of classical Bildung. As a governess, however, her "way in the world" remains circumscribed, and she is well aware of it. Her affection, perhaps her love, for Elizabeth, ameliorates the bitterness that might otherwise convert her self-awareness into an accusation against her charge. Like Helen Ambrose, though more effectively because more substantially educated, Kilman models social potentiality and promotes Elizabeth's ambitions: "every profession is open to the women of your generation," she tells her, and Elizabeth thinks "she might be a doctor. She might be a farmer. . . . She might own a thousand acres and have people under her" (*MD* 136). The city of London itself, the bustle of the Strand especially, can also be adduced as substantial provocations to a young woman who "would like to have a profession. She would become a doctor, a farmer, possibly go into Parliament if she found it necessary, all because of the Strand" (*MD* 136). Elizabeth's aspirations invert the situation faced by Rachel, whose father wishes her to be merely a helpmate for him as he pursues his own ambitions to stand for Parliament. She does not shrink from the social world because, unlike Rachel, she is not afraid of the accommodations she may have to make to be a part of it. She is excited at the prospect of people "busy about their activities, hands putting stone to stone, minds eternally occupied not with trivial chatterings (comparing women to poplars—which was rather exciting, of course, but very silly), but with thoughts of ships, of business, of law, of administration"—just the sort of vocations typically reserved for the male *Bildungsheld*, particularly those featured in the socially pragmatic English Bildungsroman. She is "determined, whatever her mother might say, to become either a farmer or a doctor. But she was, of course, rather lazy" (*MD* 137). It is difficult to tell whether this last sentence is Elizabeth's judgment or the narrator's, but in any case, it has the effect of undercutting the decisiveness of her observations.

Bowlby draws our attention to a complex paradox at work in Elizabeth's desire for Bildung and social mobility. On the one hand, Kilman is the "origin of her ideas of female aspiration," and for this reason Elizabeth's attachment to her is in defiance of her mother.[146] On the other hand, her mother has herself made the point that the Dalloway family is filled with illustrious women: "Abbesses, principals, head mistresses, dignitaries, in the republic of women" (*MD* 138). What are we to make of this curious rebellion? How could Elizabeth's professional aspirations constitute an escape from women like her mother who are "supporters of professions for women"?[147] Could it be that Clarissa's sense of the "republic of women" is, for her daughter, too cloistered, too limited, too much a relic of a time when women served what amounted to subordinated, domestic roles in the public sphere? Her feelings of freedom and stimulation on the Strand suggest a wider field of opportunity for her own ambitions, a field entered "like someone penetrating on tiptoe. . . . she was a pioneer, a stray, venturing, trusting" (*MD* 137). Moments after thinking of the Dalloway family's "tradition of public service," Elizabeth "penetrated a little further in the direction of St. Paul's," moving outward from the gendered frame of reference of her mother's sense of public service. The noise and bustle of the city are, in a liberating and empowering way, neutral, neutralized: "She liked the geniality, sisterhood, motherhood, brotherhood of this uproar" (*MD* 138). However, as Bowlby argues, "Elizabeth's destiny is far from certain in either its evaluation or its outcome": her predicament offers a choice between two incompatible options, "the centres of masculine power" and "a 'trivial' femininity as the object of male admiration."[148] This predicament is dramatized in the novel's penultimate scene, in which Elizabeth stands by her father—"one can see they are devoted to each other" (*MD* 194)—and presides over the party in a manner similar to that which Mr. Vinrace might have imagined for himself and Rachel. It is an ambiguous image, one that suggests both Elizabeth's vocational options (she may take up the ambitions of her father) and the danger of falling into an instrumental role (she may become a "Parliamentary wife"). This vignette of Elizabeth and her father is rendered even more complicated when we see it as preparatory to the small triumph of Clarissa's reemergence after her brief meditation on the death of Septimus. The half-known excitement that Peter has felt throughout the day crystallizes at this point. "It is Clarissa," he says. "For there she was" (*MD* 194). Elizabeth's ambiguous Bildung throws into relief Clarissa's tremendous personal authority, her "assertive agency," even as it forces us to reevaluate that authority and agency in the light of her daughter's potential repetition of her own Bildung process.

Woolf's representation of Clarissa's and Elizabeth's mutually embedded Bildung plots attests to a significant departure from the tradition of the Bildungsroman—indeed, from the realist novel generally, as Woolf and other modernists would have understood it in the 1920s. One thing to which this mutual embeddedness testifies is the complexity of the relations between mothers and daughters, which has a particularly subversive resonance in any discussion of the Bildungsroman. The problem hinges on identification, the daughter having to suffer what Abel describes as a "catastrophic repression of her 'masculine' desire for her mother."[149] I have been arguing that the problem of identification in *Mrs. Dalloway*, as in "Nausicaa," is one of identification within a bourgeois conception of marriage and domestic harmony. As we have seen in Joyce's depiction of Gerty MacDowell, identity is fantasy formation, a cultural production of which Gerty is half aware, but which Joyce presents as part of a larger parodic critique of a culture industry that commodifies the subject and (re)produces her as "viable" for the marriage market. I think Woolf is interested in resisting (though not through parodic representation) the same phantasmatic process of commodification in which desire is reduced, in an acceptable social relation like marriage, to the dialectics of identity in which there is no remainder, no "something" that evades the social relation, no "exquisite moment" that exceeds the present by infusing it with all of its pungency and immediacy, that shatters one's sense of identity, of *self*-identity, by reminding one of what one *is not*. Nonidentity, within the normative social relation, is of the positive sort that (re)kindles identity and preserves it against all that is not it (against itself, really), all that threatens it in the darkness that surrounds it. As normative, it reinforces the symbolic order, what Lacan calls the Name of the Father, which intercedes in and forecloses the enjoyment of that "something," that jouissance, that unnegated negative moment of the dialectical relation. The origin of this process, in the Freudian tradition of psychoanalysis, is, of course, the oedipus complex, and it is in relation to this complex that normative resolutions to the problem of development are worked out not so much "by" the subject as through the dialectics of subjectivity.

It is in this context that I wish to return to Abel's reading of *Mrs. Dalloway*, specifically her explanation of how Woolf orchestrates the resolution of Clarissa's problematic development. Abel reads this development primarily in terms of a resistance to the oedipus complex, which, in the case of girls, "defines the moment of acculturation as a moment of obstruction."[150] She concludes that Woolf's response to the Freudian masterplot is to "subtly revis[e] the terms of the opposition": rather than have Clarissa choose between mother and father, between Sally Seton and Richard Dalloway, she constructs a narrative situation of doubling in which another person, Septimus Warren Smith, takes on the burden of choice, redefined as a choice between life and death. Through the agency of Septimus's death, which Clarissa interprets "in her private language of passion and integrity," she "completes the developmental turn initiated thirty years before."[151] It is a brilliant reading of a difficult aspect of Woolf's novel, but unfortunately it tends to leave open the question of dialectical harmony to which the choice itself, in either one of its forms, boils down. On the one hand, Clarissa accedes to the compulsory harmony of heterosexual union with Richard and thereby plays a largely subordinate role in another's Bildung plot; on the other hand, she enters into a mystical compact with a stranger who makes the impossible choice of death that stands for the choice Clarissa could have made had she made a life with Sally Seton in rebellion against all social expectations:

"Death was defiance. Death was an attempt to communicate" (*MD* 184). Abel argues that Woolf privileges the latter, the mystical compact whereby Clarissa accedes to a symbolic resolution of her intractable relation to the past: "Through Septimus, Woolf recasts the developmental impasse as a choice between development or death. By recalling to Clarissa the power of her past *and* the only method of externalizing it, Septimus enables Clarissa to acknowledge and renounce its hold, to embrace the imperfect pleasures of adulthood more completely."[152]

Certainly Woolf intended for Septimus to be indispensable to the novel's action. "And this I certainly did mean," she wrote in a letter to Gerald Brenan, "that Septimus and Mrs. Dalloway should be entirely dependent upon each other."[153] The issue I would like to raise with respect to Abel's reading is whether Clarissa, in her connection with Septimus, resolves (or "acknowledges" or "renounces" or "embraces"—all forms of positive negation) an incomplete development or whether she recognizes, through his experience of madness and suicide, a conscious choice to preserve the very thing that haunts her about her "exquisite moment" with Sally Seton, the very "thing," the diamondlike treasure that she fears she may lose amid the chatter of her bourgeois life with Richard: "A thing there was that mattered; a thing, wreathed about with chatter, defaced, obscured in her own life, let drop every day in corruption, lies, chatter. This he had preserved. Death was defiance" (*MD* 184). It is this "thing," which could not be accommodated by medical science or the humanist tradition of Shakespeare, that Clarissa and Septimus have in common. It is also what Clarissa has in common with Stephen Dedalus, whose Eucharistic aesthetics preserve a remainder, a "thing" that links what is imperishable to its origin in the "sluggish earth." For Clarissa and Septimus, the link is to relationships with people who are, in different ways, lost to them. It is perhaps for this reason that critics discuss the relation between them in terms of a doubling that displaces or resignifies madness and homoerotic desire.[154] Certainly, the contexts of madness and homoeroticism are relevant to the figuration of this "thing," which exceeds the scope of a dialectical mode of rational thinking that sanctions only heterosexuality and marriage as acceptable social relations. Also relevant is the related context that would have Doris Kilman serve as a foil for Clarissa's "lesbian panic."[155] My point is not that Abel misreads Woolf's strategy of representing development; in fact, I am indebted to her perceptive psychoanalytic reading of *Mrs. Dalloway*, for it suggests a compelling justification for Woolf's strategy of a "foreshortened notion of development." I want instead to suggest that some of the implications of Abel's reading, which assiduously avoids any mention of Bildung, can be productively contextualized within a modernist critique of Bildung and the Bildungsroman tradition. It is my contention that Clarissa seeks not to resolve the aporias of development on which she meditates throughout the day, but rather to acknowledge and even affirm the very "thing" that has prevented resolution from happening. If we look instead at the dynamics of *irresolution*, we cannot help but see, in the relationship between Septimus and Clarissa, a subversive, Gothicized version of the self-identity encoded in the Bildungsroman tradition. As in Wilde's *Dorian Gray*, we find in *Mrs. Dalloway* a split subjectivity in which the doubled or mirrored self exceeds the boundaries of the unified sovereign subject. "To declare that Septimus is Clarissa's double," writes Daniel Ferrer, "is to say that there exists between them a mirror symmetry (they are at once almost the same and completely different), and it is also to admit that the strangeness of the 'mad' character takes its origin from a familiarity not recognized as such."[156]

The relationship between Clarissa and Septimus is uncanny in a way similar to the relationship between Dorian Gray and his painted self, uncanny in that it evokes the comforting sensation of familiarity as well as the disturbing sense of seeing oneself entirely separated from oneself. What is Gothicized here, as in Wilde's Bildungsroman, is the positive sense of doubling that Wilhelm Meister feels when he reads the scroll of his destiny: "a picture of himself, not like a second self in a mirror, but a different self, one outside of him, as in a painting." I want to emphasize here that for Goethe, as for the classical Bildungsroman generally, such self-splitting is finally the sign of the harmoniously socialized subject (and therefore not a true splitting at all), for immediately following this sentence, the narrator notes: "One never approves of everything in a portrait, but one is always glad that a thoughtful mind has seen us thus and a superior talent enjoyed portraying us in such a way that a picture survives of what we were, and will survive longer than we will."[157] What differs in *Mrs. Dalloway* is that Septimus resists, as totally as Dorian Gray, this self-sustaining doubling, resists the social pressures that would define him in terms of acquiescence in the vision of mental health advocated by Sir William Bradshaw. For Sir William, "divine proportion . . . made England prosper," reined in the lunatics and the depressed, and "made it impossible for the unfit to propagate their views until they, too, shared his sense of proportion" (*MD* 99). Proportion propagates proportion, a formula entirely in line with its inverse, Sir William's belief that "unsocial impulses" are "bred more than anything by the lack of good blood" (*MD* 102).[158] If we accept the arguments of Abel and others that Clarissa is doubled by Septimus in order to resolve her stymied self-development, then we must also accept that she is put to the same test as Septimus, only the idea of proportion is displaced by *its* double, the dialectical harmonies of heterosexual marriage. Clarissa's identification with Septimus is not the seamless, proportionate, dialectical one of self-identity, inscribed in classical Bildung as the redoubled and redoubtable social subject, the viable, reproducible, *happily married* subject. It is something both less and more than this, a disproportionate identification, in which enough exists for resemblance but not enough for identity. To be sure, Septimus's suicide "was her disaster—her disgrace," but she remains behind, alive and able to appreciate what he threw away, aware also that while she "was never wholly admirable," "[s]he felt somehow very like him" (*MD* 185–86).[159] In her ambiguous identity with Septimus, askew like the faulty registering of a color reproduction, Clarissa finds relief, perhaps, from the unrelenting demands on her to harmonize with herself; but more than anything else, she reacquires that "thing" she has not yet lost, the part of herself that cannot be harmonized or subsumed within the (re)production of herself as a social subject, the "thing" she felt Sally had given her and that links her back, via the "beautiful caves" that annihilate time and space, to the "exquisite moment" they continue to share.

Clarissa's pursuit of Bildung is not the "accomplished synthesis" of a circular dialectics, the "union of contradictory moments" in which nonidentity is affirmed through identity.[160] What we see in *Mrs. Dalloway*, rather, is the narrative expression of a mode of negative dialectics, an expression that is not concerned with union understood as resolution but with the justice of an irresolution that does not unite (at least not in terms of a seamless circle), that leaves the compelling "thing" that one dies for out in the open. What Clarissa discovers in her relationships with Septimus, Peter Walsh, her daughter Elizabeth, even Doris Kilman is not the comforting resolution that might make her past less of a burden to her or a missed opportunity. What they offer is the reality of radical otherness, of that "thing" which cannot be exhausted in normative social relations, that nonidentity which is, as Adorno puts it, "the secret *telos* of identification." It is just this secret that the modernist Bildungsroman narrates: the triumphant and critical failure to achieve Bildung that we see from Hardy to Woolf and that, to varying degrees, we continue to see "after modernism."

Conclusion

The Janus Face of Modernism

Throughout this study I have argued that the Bildungsroman is emblematic of certain tensions and contractions within modernism, that it is an exemplary genre for the representation of subjectivity, subject formation, and the relationship of the subject to modern social formations. If we look at the epoch in which modernism arose and defined itself (circa 1890–1940), we see the development of Bildung extending from an uneasy attachment to a traditional dialectic to an almost complete disavowal of dialectics and its utopian dream of totality. In this context of evolution and critical disavowal, the modernist return to classical Bildung is a return with a difference, for the classical conception, its dialectical structure the focus of an immanent critique, could now be used as a defense against the rationalizing and dehumanizing tendencies of the pragmatic form that had emerged in the mid-to-late nineteenth century. The modernist hero is able to recuperate his or her own experiences as part of a productive process of self-development that is predicated, ironically, on the fundamental elements of classical Bildung: aesthetic education, mentorship, marriage, and self-sufficiency. As we have seen, the latter is especially difficult for the modernist *Bildungsheld* to attain, but it is necessary to aspire toward it nevertheless, for self-sufficiency is the necessary condition for a successful aesthetic education. Of course, as the experiences of artist heroes like Paul Morel and Stephen Dedalus bear out in very different ways, self-sufficiency does not mean solipsism or isolation. It is rather an ethical frame of mind that entails a readiness to turn toward one's inner resources, one's inner life, in order to critique and restructure social relationships. One need not be an artist to strive for self-sufficiency or to acquire an aesthetic education, as the experiences of Jude Fawley, Rachel Vinrace, and Clarissa Dalloway demonstrate; indeed, these characters point up the necessity for both self-sufficiency and aesthetic education as crucial elements of subjective and social freedom. However, this freedom, as Theodor Adorno has written, is problematic and by no means unlimited or permanent: "it is entwined, not to be isolated; and for the time being it is never more than an instant of spontaneity, a historical node, the road to which is blocked under present conditions."[1] All of these characters experience this limited freedom and enjoy equally limited benefits. The dangers are dramatically conveyed in the fate of Dorian Gray, but even his fate has a progressive and critical dimension, for it constitutes the central lesson of Wilde's ethical aesthetics. That the hero's aspiration toward Bildung might end in failure or even death does not call into question the necessity of that aspiration. Instead, it paves the way for a new understanding of Bildung and a new mode of social and cultural critique.

Modernism embraces certain elements of modernity, especially innovative technologies of artistic production and reproduction, while rejecting rationalization, standardization and the totalization of "mass" or popular culture. The general tendency toward recuperation of the "classical" that I have been describing is born of this rejection and is essential to an understanding of modernism's radical conservatism. As many theorists of modernism and modernity have demonstrated, this conservatism does not preclude innovations in style, character, narrative point of view, expressive form, and emplotment—the whole ensemble of techniques that critics like Fredric Jameson identify as aesthetic modernism. Indeed, one of the paradoxes of modernism is that its conservatism serves the progressive end of subverting bourgeois culture. Many of the features of modernist literature and art are innovative precisely because they are reactions to contemporary social conditions that reflect a dehumanized, rationalistic, and instrumentalized world. It has been my contention that the modernist Bildungsroman, because it employs one of the most conservative literary forms in order to test the limits of form, preeminently models these innovations in an immanently critical fashion. Further, one of the implications of my argument is that immanent critique, an important part not only of Adorno's work but of so many contemporary critical theorists, was already an integral part of modernist artistic production, a point that Adorno himself makes again and again.[2]

The modernist Bildungsroman combats the identitarian philosophy at the heart of a bourgeois ethics of socialization defined by a pragmatics of self-formation in which the subject acquires identity through a process that sublates or incorporates what Adorno calls nonidentity, the "negative" element of dialectical processes. As I have illustrated in chapter 1, both the socially pragmatic and the classical aesthetico-spiritual form of Bildung embody a dialectical process, but while the classical form depends on aesthetic education and self-sufficiency to form a harmonious integration of self and society, the socially pragmatic form relies on institutional structures of education and social mobility together with commodified forms of individualism to form a similar, though less "spiritualized," harmony. And while some intellectuals in England, like John

Stuart Mill, advocated a benign form of socially pragmatic Bildung, the general trend throughout late modernity has been toward social engineering, toward "quality control" in "the manufacture of viable and usable human beings."[3] The recapture by modernist artists of classical Bildung is an expression of an ethics of the self that regards identity as a radically conflicted site in which the subject is at odds with his or her own reluctant dreams of harmonious integration with the social world. The negative dialectical process that I have borrowed from Adorno to illustrate this site of conflict underscores the rewards of embracing the *non*identical, accepting and affirming that which is not subsumed into the totalizing design of the *self*-identical: the objective, the object, the "thing" that serves so often in modernist literature as the sign of what cannot be subsumed in classical dialectics. The knowledge of objects can be attained only by giving up the illusion that subjective reason can attain knowledge through concepts that strive to designate what objects are in their actuality. "[T]he empirical substance of dialectics," writes Adorno, "is not the principle but the resistance which otherness offers to identity. Hence the power of dialectics. The subject too is hidden in dialectics, since its real rule brings forth the contradictions, but the contradictions have filtered into the object. If we attribute dialectics to the subject alone, removing contradiction by contradiction, so to speak, we also remove dialectics by broadening it into a totality. The system was the source of Hegel's dialectics, not its measure."[4] As Adorno points out, the agonistic journey toward the nonidentical starts out from a standpoint of identity, for the subject who lives the truth of his being, who does not deny the objective element (the material strata, the disavowed difference and otherness of the self) that an identitarian philosophy would subsume as a constituent part of self-identity, this subject "use[s] his own strength, which he owes to identity, to cast off the façade of identity."[5]

Anthony Giddens, Michel Foucault, and other theorists of modernity have offered alternative definitions of this process of identity formation, and their visions of the self as a "reflexive project" or a locus of "individualizing tactics" affirm what we find in the work of Adorno: the self is nonidentical, it stands in opposition to social forces that would seek to define selfhood and subjectivity in terms of harmony and dialectical totality. In this study I have argued that modernist writers were aware of these alternatives to bourgeois socialization and that their experimental Bildungsromane modeled both the possibilities of nonidentity and the failure of the Bildungsroman form to represent these possibilities adequately.[6] I have argued that this failure should be regarded as a critical success when viewed from the standpoint of genre, for the narration of failure provides an important lesson, one that we see in other forms across many different manifestations of modernism in the arts: the failure of form leads to its rehabilitation under new conditions of engagement. The postcolonial *Bildungsroman* especially, despite undergoing significant transformations, remains committed to the idea of the self, often found in modernist works, as a deeply ambivalent, internally split subject fighting against a hostile world, a subject who, in the solitude of fantasy and dream, formulates new meanings and destinies for the nonidentical.

Generally speaking, it is difficult to deny the efficacy of the Bildungsroman form in the later twentieth century, for it has proved profoundly useful in the representation of postmodern and postcolonial subjectivities. As in the modernist Bildungsroman, the lesson of form is accompanied by the recuperation of a classical mode of self-development, one that is modified to reflect current conditions of late modernity, but that retains the crucial emphases on aesthetic education and self-sufficiency and the freedom that guarantees both. As Wilhelm von Humboldt, one of the theorists of Bildung in classical Weimar, wrote, "spontaneity . . . is fostered by freedom." Only in conditions of freedom can the "inner life of man . . . unfold its strength and beauty" and this inner life "would become the ultimate object of [man's] activity."[7] In the modernist Bildungsroman, as in the postcolonial and even the postmodern forms, the hero may fail to socialize, may fail to acquire the freedom necessary for Bildung, but does not fail to be singularly and successfully human. It is my belief that the modernist recuperation of classical Bildung is one of the most significant and far-reaching innovations of an aesthetic that was famously summed up by Ezra Pound: "Make it new."

The modernist critique does not only look backwards for its innovations. Many of the novels under examination in this study raise new questions about the future of the form, some of which are addressed in the postmodern and postcolonial traditions. For example, does the modernist Bildungsroman enact symbolic legitimations that have more to do with some *future* or otherwordly dispensation—"the loveliness which has not yet come into the world," as Stephen Dedalus puts it (*P* 251)—than with the world as it exists in the present? Does the sense for beauty displace the energy of youth as the sign for modernity, as Wilde's *Picture of Dorian Gray* suggests?[8] Or, bearing in mind Woolf's achievement in *Mrs. Dalloway*, can we speak of a shift in which belatedness and middle age come to characterize modernity? These questions all point in the same direction, toward a genre revivified by a critical vocation. In mounting a successful critique of socialization within the failure of a genre, the modernist Bildungsroman unveils its Janus face. Despite the radical turn toward nonidentity and the near annihilation of the subject, it produces new "technologies of the self" and advances new solutions to the problems of identity and society, new harmonies to accommodate the new ways of new worlds.

Notes

INTRODUCTION: THE PATHWAYS TO INNER CULTURE

1. Definitions of the term *Bildungsroman* vary, but most commentators agree that it should be distinct from other narrative forms of development, the most common of which are *Entwicklungsroman* and *Erziehungsroman*. The former concerns personal development but does not emphasize self-discovery or the formation of personality—in short, it does not emphasize Bildung; the latter concerns education in the narrow sense, usually resulting in the "pedagogical novel." The term *Künstlerroman* refers to a novel dealing with the formation of the artist. While some of the works I discuss in subsequent chapters may be usefully described using one of these terms (for example, Hardy's *Jude the Obscure* has been called an Erziehungsroman and *Portrait of the Artist as a Young Man* has been called a Künstlerroman), my main concern in this study is the concept of Bildung and how it is transformed in modernist texts. For more on these distinctions, see Tennyson, "The *Bildungsroman* in Nineteenth-Century English Literature."

2. Most book-length studies are devoted to the German or the European tradition; some of these will be mentioned below. Two important works on the English tradition are Buckley, *Season of Youth*, and Alden, *Social Mobility in the English Bildungsroman*. Neither focuses on the concept of Bildung and neither explores the specific features of *modernist* Bildungsromane. Buckley's work stands behind much discussion of the English Bildungsroman, which for him is a relatively unproblematic genre through the mid-twentieth century. In his view, the English Bildungsroman is strongly determined by autobiographical elements and tends to emphasize the socially pragmatic theme of socialization rather than a thematics of aesthetico-spiritual inner culture. Important work on the female Bildungsroman in England is included in Abel, Hirsch, and Langland, *The Voyage In*. Critical attention to Bildungsromane featuring female, gay and lesbian, and non-European *Bildungshelden* has steadily increased since the rise of feminist and cultural-studies approaches to literature. I believe that the interest in identity and subject positions drives recent interest in the Bildungsroman genre.

3. I will discuss the relation of this emergent late modernity to modernism and to the tradition of the Bildungsroman in greater detail in chapter 1.

4. Many recent critics of the Bildungsroman do not in fact emphasize the idea of Bildung, choosing instead to concentrate on structural, thematic, and contextual features of literary texts. For example, Moretti's influential *The Way of the World* is concerned primarily with problems of realism, narrative structure, and the sociology of the text. Minden in *The German Bildungsroman* "offers a definition of the genre based on the peculiarities of the texts themselves, not on the idea of *Bildung*" (1). A notable exception

in recent years is Redfield, whose *Phantom Formations* explores the same European traditions as Moretti but emphasizes the problematic nature of the concept of Bildung from a point of view informed by Gadamer's hermeneutics. My study proceeds from the assumption that Bildung is fundamentally important for understanding the genre, especially its rehabilitation in the twentieth century.

5. Eagleton, *Heathcliff*, 276. See also Jameson, *A Singular Modernity*, pt. 2.

6. Jameson, *A Singular Modernity*, 74. I will return to this conception in chapter 1.

7. Adorno, *Negative Dialectics*, 141. The epigraph to this chapter comes from page 277 of this work.

8. Adorno, "Cultural Criticism and Society," 32–33.

9. See Moretti, *Way of the World*, and Redfield, *Phantom Formations*.

10. A significant exception is the critical work on Bildungsromane written by women. According to Abel, Hirsch, and Langland, "While the *Bildungsroman* has played out its possibilities for males, female versions of the genre still offer a vital form. Women's increased sense of freedom in this century, when women's experience has begun to approach that of the traditional male *Bildungsheld*, finds expression in a variety of fictions. . . . the novel of development has become, in Ellen Morgan's words, 'the most salient form of literature' for contemporary women writing about women" (*The Voyage In*, 13; for Morgan, see "Humanbecoming"). It is also the most "salient" form for many colonial and modernist writers as well.

11. J. Smith, "Cultivating Gender," 216.

12. I say "so-called" in view of Fraiman's persuasive argument, in *Unbecoming Women*, that the term "Bildungsroman" is too freighted with masculinist and logocentric assumptions to be of much use in designating the experience of women in nineteenth-century English fiction. Hence her use of the term "novel of development." Theories of the female Bildungsroman generally tend to emphasize "coming of age" or "awakening" rather than Bildung, with resistance to the cultural assumptions behind Bildung constituting an important part of the experience. I discuss these matters more fully in chapter 4.

13. In the interests of clarity, let me emphasize my use of terms: in the phrase "classical Bildung" the word "classical" refers to the aesthetico-spiritual form of Bildung developed by people like Goethe and Humboldt. In this form of Bildung, the emphasis is laid on self-cultivation and the self-sufficiency of inner culture. Opposed to this classical form is the socially pragmatic form, which emphasizes social mobility and social success. To some extent this is an evolutionary process whereby the aesthetico-spiritual form develops into the socially pragmatic one, but it is important to add that Bildung is always socially pragmatic to some degree and that the classical form of it subordinates pragmatic socialization to the more important value of aesthetico-spiritual development. Conversely, the socially pragmatic form retains, in many instances, a residual connection to aesthetics. When used in the phrase "classical Bildungsroman," the word "classical" refers to the eighteenth- and nineteenth-century tradition, regardless of the

form of Bildung that underwrites individual novels. In both cases, the word "classical" signals a coherent concept and/or tradition that stands in opposition to "modern" social and textual practices. The modernist Bildungsroman, then, is not part of the classical tradition of the genre even though, according to my main argument, it attempts to recuperate the ideal of classical Bildung.

14. On the concept of transculturation, see Lima, "Decolonizing Genre." I will return to this topic in chapter 3. A related term is "autoethnography"; see Pratt, *Imperial Eyes*, and Castle, *Modernism and the Celtic Revival*. Autoethnography, in Pratt's formulation, is a form of transculturation "in which colonized subjects undertake to represent themselves in ways that *engage with* the colonizer's own terms . . . in response to or in dialogue with . . . metropolitan representations" (7).

15. Redfield, *Phantom Formations*, 65. Redfield continues: "The notion of the *Bildungsroman* . . . has no existence apart from either the post-Romantic history of aesthetics, or the aesthetic formalization that this 'genre' takes as its content—in the guise, of course, of the formation of a specific, anthropological subject."

16. Sammons suggests that another possible English translation of the term "Bildungsroman" is "novel of acculturation," but he admits that it is not altogether satisfactory ("Missing Bildungsroman," 231).

17. Moore, *Confessions of a Young Man*, 231.

18. I follow Eric Hobsbawm's argument that the nineteenth century begins in the revolutionary period that closes the preceding century; see the "Overture" to his *Age of Empire*.

19. Moretti, *Way of the World*, 5.

20. Ibid.

21. This phrase sums up the dialectical poles of the Bildungsroman. See Hardin's introduction to *Reflection and Action*. The dialectical structure of the nineteenth-century Bildungsroman is strongly influenced by Hegel, whose *Phenomenology of Mind* traces the kind of dialectical development pattern found in so many classical Bildungsromane.

22. Moretti, *Way of the World*, 68.

23. Habermas, *Discourse of Modernity*, 64.

24. Though less familiar to English readers, Christoph Martin Wieland was an important early influence on Weimar humanists. His *Geschichte des Agathon* is treated by some scholars as the first Bildungsroman. See Bruford, *Classical Weimar*, and Swales, *German Bildungsroman*. This has not prevented a consensus favoring Goethe's *Wilhelm Meister*.

25. Blackall, afterword, 384.

26. Goethe, *Wilhelm Meister*, 301.

27. Ibid., 309–10.

28. Ibid., 373.

29. Dilthey, "Friedrich Hölderlin," 336. Dilthey's analysis of the Bildungsroman was instrumental in the formation of the modern definition of the form.

30. Ibid., 320, 336.

31. Bruford, *Tradition of Self-Cultivation*, 55.

32. Kontje, "The German *Bildungsroman* as Metafiction," 148. See also Kontje's *Private Lives in the Public Sphere*.

33. Goethe, *Wilhelm Meister*, 364.

34. Swales, *German Bildungsroman*, 5.

35. Ibid., 20. Arnds argues in a similar vein: "In Goethe's prototype of the *Bildungsroman* genre the protagonist's successful *Bildung* corresponds largely to the Hegelian dictum according to which the hero undergoes a socialization process without entirely having to give up his own individualism. At the end, a totality between the individual and society is achieved" ("Boy with the Old Face," 224).

36. Swales, *German Bildungsroman*, 29.

37. Ibid., 34.

38. Thomas Mann articulated this view in 1916: "There is a type of novel that is, to be sure, German, typically German, legitimately national in character, and that is the highly autobiographical Bildungsroman and novel of development" (qtd. in Hardin, *Reflection and Action*, xv). Howe follows Mann in positing a strong German origin for the form and the dominance of an autobiographical or confessional element, and sees the latter as dominant in the English Bildungsroman (*Wilhelm Meister and His English Kinsmen*, esp. 6–9, 14). Buckley's "Autobiography" and *Season of Youth* also emphasize the autobiographical aspect of the form.

39. Sammons, "Missing Bildungsroman," 230.

40. "This is a genre, and a predominant one at that—a category into which we can, on inspection, admit only *Wilhelm Meister* and maybe two and a half other examples?" (ibid., 237). Amrine, however, would disallow *Wilhelm Meister* because it fails to satisfy the very generic criteria that have developed out of it ("Rethinking the Bildungsroman," 126).

41. Sammons, "The Bildungsroman for Nonspecialists," 28–29.

42. Sammons, "Missing Bildungsroman," 239.

43. Redfield, *Phantom Formations*, 64. I take issue with what I see as an attempt to regard failure as part of a larger totalizing, even dialectical structure. In my Adornean reading, failure is always the sign of something that destabilizes totalization and harmonious dialectics.

44. Stendhal, *Scarlet and Black*, 77.

45. Moretti, *Way of the World*, 94–95.

46. In "Ideology and Ideological State Apparatuses," Althusser argues that "ideology 'acts' or 'functions' in such a way that it 'recruits' subjects among the individuals (it recruits them all), or 'transforms' the individuals into subjects (it transforms them all) by that very precise operation which I have called *interpellation* or hailing and which

can be imagined along the lines of the most commonplace everyday police (or other) hailing: 'Hey, you there!'" (174).

47. Ibid.

48. Moretti, *Way of the World*, 130.

49. Balzac, *Lost Illusions*, 60.

50. Ibid., 60.

51. Ibid., 649.

52. Ibid., 650.

53. Moretti, *Way of the World*, 75.

54. Flaubert, *Sentimental Education*, 96.

55. Ibid., 97.

56. Ibid., 382–83.

57. Moretti, *Way of the World*, 178.

58. Flaubert, *Sentimental Education*, 418.

59. Adorno, *Negative Dialectics*, 148.

60. Swales, *German Bildungsroman*, 164.

61. Moretti, *Way of the World*, 185.

62. Ibid., 200–201.

63. Ibid., 203.

64. The problem of social mobility in nineteenth-century England will be addressed more fully in the next chapter. On class-based social conflicts, see E. P. Thompson, *The Making of the English Working Class*; Hollis, *Class and Conflict*; Dentith, *Society and Cultural Forms*.

65. Meredith, *The Ordeal of Richard Feverel*, 9.

66. Ibid., 414–15.

67. Meredith, *The Egoist*, 44, 56.

68. Moretti, *Way of the World*, 214.

69. G. Eliot, *Middlemarch*, 613.

70. Moretti, *Way of the World*, 217.

71. Ibid., 218.

72. On the idea of a "fearful" education, see Gilbert and Gubar, *Madwoman in the Attic*, 275–78.

73. Rowe, "'Fairy-born and human-bred,'" 70.

74. Brontë, *Jane Eyre*, 86.

75. See especially Fraiman, *Unbecoming Women*.

76. Moretti, *Way of the World*, 35.

77. Sheehan, *Modernism, Narrative, and Humanism*, 5–6.

78. Adorno, *Negative Dialectics*, 85–86.

79. Ibid., 147.

80. Ibid., 154.

81. Here I adopt Adorno's notion that the principle of barter is "the identifying prin-

ciple of thought," but that the "ideal of free and just barter," which is the aim of negative dialectics, is "to date . . . only a pretext" for totalitarian thought and politics (see ibid., 147).

82. See the section "Logic of Disintegration," ibid., 144–46.

83. Ibid., 144.

CHAPTER I. MODERNITY, MODERNISM, AND THE IDEA OF BILDUNG

1. The question of the "subject" is, of course, vexed. I want to indicate here that in this and succeeding chapters, I use the terms "self" and "subject" (and its cognates) more or less interchangeably. However, context will, I hope, indicate clearly when I wish to emphasize the "subject" as *the subject of institutional power*. Terms like "self-development," "self-formation," and "self-cultivation" are used as rough translations of the German *Bildung* and are used quite intentionally to invoke the idea of "inner culture" as the German Enlightenment thinkers defined it.

2. Martini, "Bildungsroman—Term and Theory," 5. Further discussion of the term *Bildung* can be found in Bruford, *Tradition of Self-Cultivation* and *Classical Weimar*, esp. 1–12, 36–37, 418–25, and app. "Culture and Related Ideas from Cicero to Herder," 432–40. See also Sweet, *Wilhelm von Humboldt*, 1:51–52.

3. Humboldt, *Limits of State Action*, 81.

4. Sweet, *Wilhelm von Humboldt*, 1:52.

5. Jameson, *The Political Unconscious*, 19–20. Sheehan makes a similar point, emphasizing the conflict at the center of the Bildungsroman: "its 'repressed unconscious'—reconciliation of the nonextension of mind (the human) with the extension of matter (the nonhuman)—is replayed in modernist fiction through narrative: finding a space for the 'inhuman' (antinarrative) within the ostensibly 'human' (narrative)" (*Modernism, Narrative, and Humanism*, 14).

6. Giddens, *Modernity and Self-Identity*, 14–15. Other important figures whose work has informed my understanding of the concept of modernity include Theodor Adorno, Jürgen Habermas, and others in the Frankfurt School, Anthony Cascardi, Michel Foucault, Fredric Jameson, Charles Taylor, Douglas Kellner, and Jean-François Lyotard.

7. For a discussion of humanism as a "theme" or "set of themes," see Foucault, "What Is Enlightenment?"

8. Locke, *Essay Concerning Human Understanding*, II.xxvii.9. All of chapter xxvii is relevant to the concept of self that remained highly influential well into the nineteenth century.

9. See, for example, Loptson, "Locke, Reid, and Personal Identity," esp. 56–57, and Behan, "Locke on Persons and Personal Identity."

10. Loptson, "Locke, Reid, and Personal Identity," 58–59.

11. Bakhtin, "*Bildungsroman*," 17–19. The biographical novel, says Bakhtin, has four subcategories: "the naive old (still classical) form of success/failure and, subsequent-

ly, works and deeds; the confessional form (biography-confession); the hagiographic form; and, finally, in the eighteenth century the most important subcategory . . . the family-biographical novel" (17).

12. Dilthey, "Friedrich Hölderlin," 335.

13. Swales, "Irony and the Novel," 62.

14. Bruford, *Classical Weimar*, 223–24. The citation from Herder is quoted on 213.

15. Goethe, *Wilhelm Meister*, 246. On the "beautiful soul" and its influence on the development of the female Bildungsroman, see Hirsch, "Spiritual *Bildung*."

16. Blackbourn, *Long Nineteenth Century*, 34.

17. Minden, *The German Bildungsroman*, 40. Minden points out that the "Confessions" section was based on Goethe's "personal acquaintance with Susanna Katharina von Klettenberg, an intensely religious pietist friend of his own mother" (40). Also of interest in this context is his relationship with Charlotte von Stein. The editor of the Princeton edition of *Wilhelm Meister* does not know what to make of the "Confessions," leaving open the question whether or not it is a transition to the last two books of the novel; see Blackall, afterword, 381–82.

18. Hirsch, "Spiritual *Bildung*," 31, 32.

19. Giddens, *Modernity and Self-Identity*, 54.

20. Ibid., 52; see also 75–80.

21. Ibid., 53.

22. There are many examples of this tendency toward narrative in modernity. Foucault, in *The Order of Things*, provides something like a narrative of ruptures or moments within modernity. Lyotard's analysis in *The Postmodern Condition* of the "grand narratives" of modernity, especially those that arose in the Enlightenment, has been very influential. Also important is Danto's *Narration and Knowledge*, which explores the fundamental narrative nature of knowledge in modernity. Jameson, in *A Singular Modernity*, also emphasizes the narrativity of modernity, calling attention specifically to the nature of modernity as a "narrative category" (40). In this context, asking whether the subject or subjectivity exists is the wrong sort of question; the issue is not the ontology of the subject but rather its "figuration" within narrative (55–57). Continuity of the subject would not be possible, in Jameson's contra-Lockean view, since narrative representation, especially in the late modern period, is dominated by rupture, repetition, and "allegorical" reduplication (see esp. 99–118).

23. Jameson, in a reading of Foucault's *Order of Things*, has suggested a way to view the eighteenth century as a "pre-modern moment within modernity as such," thus allowing us to see both the strange and the familiar aspects of the age. "The pre-bourgeois (seventeenth- and eighteenth-century) moderns are thus already modern and yet at one and the same time not yet so: the thinkers of the classical period are no longer part of some traditional world, and yet they are not fully admissible to what we recognize as the broad daylight of full modernity as the nineteenth and twentieth centuries lived and experienced it" (*A Singular Modernity*, 74).

24. See Goethe, *Wilhelm Meister*, bk. 8, esp. chap. 1.

25. For an in-depth discussion of Goethe's administrative and cultural activities, see Bruford, *Classical Weimar*, chaps. 2–3, 5.

26. Goethe, qtd. in Bruford, *Classical Weimar*, 134. Bruford translates: "O Weimar, a special fate was dealt out to you, to be, like Bethlehem, small and great! You are the talk of all Europe, for your genius and wit, or for your follies."

27. Not everyone in these privileged classes enjoyed economic freedom and security, however. Schiller, for example, was the son of a military officer and abandoned the security of the military life in order to be a writer (see Bruford, *Classical Weimar*, 320–29). Later, once he moved to Weimar, he had to supplement his meager salary as a university lecturer by writing and editing. His experience differed markedly from the well-paid Goethe and the independently wealthy Humboldt. Yet all three men, and many in similar situations, possessed a great deal of cultural and social capital that was not available to the lower and artisan classes, as well as to many in the middle classes who lacked higher education.

28. Moretti, *Way of the World*, 208. A visitor to Weimar in 1796 noted that the Landesindustriecomptoir (center for local industries) "has indeed for some time acquainted the people of Weimar with the word industry" (qtd. in Bruford, *Classical Weimar*, 69). The Landesindustriecomptoir was set up by F. J. Bertuch in 1791 "as showrooms and advertising agency for Weimar craftsmen, and a clearing house for orders for this kind of goods," but also included a publishing house and a "'geographical institute,' where young people trained at the School of Drawing made maps and terrestrial globes" (ibid., 299, 306). Goethe supported and lectured at the School of Drawing and contributed to journals published by Bertuch.

29. Blackbourn, *Long Nineteenth Century*, 55.

30. Ibid., 57.

31. See ibid., 57–70.

32. Bruford makes 1806 the end date for his study of classical Weimar.

33. Blackbourn, *Long Nineteenth Century*, 79.

34. Goethe, *Wilhelm Meister*, 171.

35. Bruford, *Tradition of Self-Cultivation*, 17. Bruford quotes a fragment of one of Humboldt's unpublished essays from 1793 on the theory of Bildung.

36. Letter to Karoline von Humboldt, qtd. ibid., 23.

37. Nietzsche, *The Gay Science*, sec. 290.

38. Humboldt, *Humanist without Portfolio*, 399.

39. M. Cowan, introduction, 12–13.

40. Sweet, *Wilhelm von Humboldt*, 1:127.

41. Letter to Georg Forster, February 1790, qtd. ibid., 1:84.

42. Ibid.

43. Bruford, *Classical Weimar*, 276.

44. See Sweet, *Wilhelm von Humboldt*, 1:170–71.

45. Letter to Körner, October 27, 1793, qtd. ibid., 1:162.

46. Sweet, *Wilhelm von Humboldt*, 1:107.

47. Bruford, *Tradition of Self-Cultivation*, 4–5.

48. Ibid., 5. Humboldt's letters to his wife and other women provide a rich account of his early ideas about Bildung; see 1–28 and Sweet, *Wilhelm von Humboldt*, 1:51–52, 73–72. On Goethe's relationship with Charlotte von Stein, see Bruford, *Classical Weimar*, 153–71, and J. Williams, *The Life of Goethe*, 19–20.

49. Bruford, *Tradition of Self-Cultivation*, 8.

50. Humboldt, *Limits of State Action*, 20–1.

51. Ibid., 19.

52. Goethe, *Wilhelm Meister*, 307.

53. Humboldt, *Limits of State Action*, 37.

54. Ibid., 16.

55. Humboldt, *Limits of State Action*, 43. See chaps. 4–6.

56. Ibid., 116.

57. Ibid., 98.

58. J. W. Burrow in Humboldt, *Limits of State Action*, xxxi.

59. Humboldt, *Limits of State Action*, 76–77, 16, 19.

60. Ibid., 30.

61. Sweet, *Wilhelm von Humboldt*, 1:52. Sweet quotes Humboldt.

62. Mill, *On Liberty*, 267.

63. Humboldt, *Limits of State Action*, 130.

64. Sweet, *Wilhelm von Humboldt*, 2:54–56. Sheehan states that Humboldt "did more than anyone else to establish the concept of *Bildung* in an institutional context" (*Modernism, Narrative, and Humanism*, 2); see also Bullock, *Humanist Tradition*, 99. Lyotard traces the development of "grand narratives of knowledge" to the University of Berlin and Humboldt's advocacy of a curriculum dedicated to "'the spiritual and moral training of the nation'" (*Postmodern Condition*, 32).

65. Humboldt, qtd. in Sweet, *Wilhelm von Humboldt*, 2:44.

66. Humboldt, qtd. ibid., 2:48.

67. Ibid., 2:42.

68. Lyotard, *Postmodern Condition*, 33. Lyotard discusses Humboldt's role in developing a "*Bildung*-effect" that reconciles two discourses—one that answers only to truth and one that governs "ethical, social, and political practice"—within "a single threefold aspiration: 'that of deriving everything from an original principle' (corresponding to scientific activity), 'that of relating everything to an ideal' (governing ethical and social practice), and 'that of unifying this principle and this ideal in a single Idea' (ensuring that the scientific search for true causes always coincides with the pursuit of just ends in moral and political life). This ultimate synthesis constitutes the legitimate subject" (32–33). Lyotard quotes from Humboldt's memoranda on university education.

69. And not just in Germany, but throughout Europe and in the United States; see Ashby, "Idea of a University," and Flexner, *Universities*.

70. Bruford, *Classical Weimar*, 421.

71. Hegel, *Philosophy of History*, 41–42, 49.

72. The limits of Bildung apply equally to the individual and to the state, insofar as the latter is regarded as a historical agent. The "determinate National Spirit [conceived of as an individual entity] is only *one* individual in the course of world history" (Hegel, *Philosophy of History*, 56).

73. Sweet, *Wilhelm von Humboldt*, 2:61.

74. Letter to Count Alexander von Dohna, May 9, 1810, qtd. ibid., 2:64.

75. Moretti, *Way of the World*, 75.

76. On the influence of Goethean Bildung in Victorian England, see DeLaura, "Heroic Egotism."

77. Tennyson, "*Bildungsroman*," 141.

78. Carlyle, *Past and Present*, 202.

79. Tennyson, "*Bildungsroman*," 141.

80. DeLaura, "Matthew Arnold and Culture," 9. On Arnold's relation to Goethe, see DeLaura, "Arnold and Goethe."

81. DeLaura, "Matthew Arnold and Culture," 7.

82. Arnold, "Function of Criticism," 265, 267, 271.

83. The same qualities that had disturbed so many of Arnold's early critics were precisely those that attracted early modernist writers later in the century. DeLaura notes that Arnold was put off by Swinburne's "extravagant praise" of his *Poems* (1867). "What the midcentury critics had so deplored in Arnold, Swinburne now converted into virtues" ("Matthew Arnold and Culture," 9–10).

84. Pecora, in "Arnoldean Ethnology," argues that Arnold's cultural criticism was more substantial and progressive than modernists and postmodernists often give it credit for being. He claims that it looks forward to the problems of cultural relativism and diversity encountered in the late twentieth century.

85. Goodlad, *Victorian Literature and the Victorian State*, 2.

86. Qtd. in R. Williams, *Culture and Society*, 61. Though Coleridge may not have been directly influenced by Humboldt, his ideas on culture were certainly influenced by the work of classical Weimar; see Bruford, *Classical Weimar*, 199, 398.

87. Mill, *On Liberty*, 262, 264.

88. Humboldt, *Limits of State Action*, 69.

89. Mill, *On Liberty*, 272, 262.

90. Ibid., 263.

91. Ibid., 265–66.

92. Ibid., 266.

93. See note 41.

94. Goodlad, "Beyond the Panopticon," 540. The concept of "specific rationalities" comes from Foucault's "The Subject and Power," 210.

95. Moretti, *Way of the World*, 213.

96. Ibid., 185.

97. Miles, *Social Mobility*, 177–78; see chaps. 3–4 for detailed analyses of data regarding trends in mobility and the factors affecting these trends.

98. Miles, *Social Mobility*, 174; see also 145–75 ("Marriage Markets and Women's Role") and 183–87. There are many studies on the opportunities for women in domestic, rural, and other forms of labor. See, for example, Gomersall, *Working-Class Girls*; Verdon, *Rural Women Workers*; M. Cohen, *Professional Domesticity*.

99. Miles, *Social Mobility*, 189.

100. Ibid., 179.

101. W. E. Forster, whom Gladstone appointed vice-president of the Committee of Council on Education, sponsored the Education Act of 1870, which was in part motivated by the recognition that British industry required a more technically trained workforce.

102. Humboldt, *Limits of State Action*, 19.

103. See, for example, Marx and Engels, *The German Ideology*, 53–55.

104. On the ancient universities, see Ashby, "Idea of a University"; Flexner, *Universities*, 245; Roach, "Victorian Universities," *Secondary Education in England, 1800–1870*, and *Secondary Education in England, 1870–1902*; R. Williams, *Long Revolution*, 125–55. For a brief general discussion of education in Victorian England, see Heyck, "Educational." My discussion of education in nineteenth-century England is informed by these texts. I discuss this topic further in chapter 2 in the context of Hardy's and Lawrence's Bildungsromane.

105. Newman, *Fifteen Sermons*, 282. On Newman's educational philosophy, see his *Idea of a University*, esp. 74–93.

106. On this conflict in Newman's thinking about liberal education, see DeLaura, *Hebrew and Hellene*, 75–77, 322–24.

107. Arnold, *Schools and Universities*, 229.

108. *Oxford University Extension Gazette*, qtd. in Ingham, *Gender and Class*, 171.

109. Ingham, *Gender and Class*, 171. Ingham quotes from *University Extension Congress, London 1894: Report of the Proceedings*. Another complicating factor was "the isolation of the university as a research institute" (Gagnier, *Idylls of the Marketplace*, 12–13).

110. Gellner, *Nations and Nationalism*, 38, 28.

111. Ibid., 35–36.

112. Ibid., 37–38.

113. On uneven development, see Eagleton, *Heathcliff*, esp. 273–319. For an analysis of Ireland's relation to British imperial modernization, see Hechter, *Internal Colonial-*

ism. Critics of Joyce have advanced the idea of semicolonialism to explain the problem of uneven development; see Attridge and Howes, *Semicolonial Joyce.*

114. On the Land Acts, see Solow, *The Land Question and the Irish Economy,* and Bew, *Land and the National Question in Ireland.*

115. Eagleton, *Heathcliff,* 277.

116. See Castle, *Modernism and the Celtic Revival,* and Mattar, *Primitivism, Science, and the Irish Revival.*

117. K. Miller, "Distortions of Post-Modern Ireland," 12.

118. Akenson, *Irish Education Experiment,* 387.

119. On the impact of the hedge schools in the eighteenth and early nineteenth centuries, see Adams, "Swine-Tax and Eat-Him-All-Magee."

120. Foucault, "The Subject and Power," 222–23, 218.

121. Ibid., 218–19. A few pages later, Foucault speaks of the "relative autonomy" of "scholastic or military institutions" (223).

122. Ibid., 219.

123. Ibid., 221.

124. Giddens, *Modernity and Self-Identity,* 32.

125. Ibid., 21.

126. Humboldt, qtd. in Sweet, *Wilhelm von Humboldt,* 2:48.

127. Giddens, *Modernity and Self-Identity,* 21.

128. Ibid., 83–84.

129. Horkheimer and Adorno, *Dialectic of Enlightenment,* 11–12. For a nuanced rejoinder to Horkheimer and Adorno and a critique of the classical "Kantian" Enlightenment and its continuance to the present day, see Cascardi, *Consequences of Enlightenment.*

130. Jameson, *A Singular Modernity,* 28.

131. On the sense of the past in modernism, see Longenbach, *Modernist Poetics of History*; Perl, *The Tradition of Return*; L. Williams, *Modernism and the Ideology of History*; on innovation, see Jameson, *A Singular Modernity,* esp. 119–28.

132. Jameson, *A Singular Modernity,* 157. A related theory of modernist aesthetics can be found in Eagleton, *Ideology of the Aesthetic.*

133. Habermas, "Modernity versus Postmodernity."

134. Adorno, *Negative Dialectics,* 278, 279.

135. Jameson, *A Singular Modernity,* 131–34.

136. Sheehan, *Modernism, Narrative, and Humanism,* 22. See also Redfield, *Phantom Formations.*

137. Adorno, *Negative Dialectics,* 157. There are those who believe that Adorno misreads Hegel's theory of dialectics, a critique of which constitutes a significant portion of *Negative Dialectics.* Gibson, for example, in "Rethinking an Old Saw," sees Hegel as far less totalizing and imperialistic than Adorno, following Lukács, believes him to be.

138. Adorno, *Negative Dialectics,* 5, 6, 12, 13.

139. The modernist Bildungsroman thus reinforces Bakhtin's theory of the novel, especially his claim that the novel is always open to the contemporary moment. See *Dialogic Imagination*, esp. chap. 1, "Epic and Novel."

140. Adorno, *Negative Dialectics*, 147.

141. Jameson, *A Singular Modernity*, 134–35. Jameson draws on Perry Anderson's theory of modernism as situated within "the force field of several distinct emergent currents in late nineteenth-century European society" (134), including industrialization, isolation of the arts, and radical social change. I want to note that while I find this reading suggestive, it does not attend to the "specific rationalities" that would help us understand the nature of subject formation in the modernist period and the role of the Bildungsroman in representing the processes of formation.

142. Adorno, *Negative Dialectics*, 163.

143. Ibid., 53.

144. Ibid., xx. See also Adorno's discussion of "immanent critique" in "Cultural Criticism and Society."

145. Adorno, *Negative Dialectics*, 31.

146. T. S. Eliot, *Selected Essays*, 7, 10–11.

147. D. H. Lawrence, *Letters*, 2:183.

148. Foucault, "The Subject and Power," 212. On the problem of self formation, see Foucault's *Technologies of the Self*.

149. Foucault, "The Subject and Power," 211.

150. Giddens, *Modernity and Self-Identity*, 23.

151. Foucault, "The Subject and Power," 211–12.

152. Ibid., 213–15.

153. Humboldt, *Limits of State Action*, 116.

154. Habermas, *Theory and Practice*, 79. Habermas notes that "there can hardly be any doubt that for Aristotle science does not in principle, or for systematic reasons, depend on the employment of dialectics, but uses it only for pedagogic purposes" (79).

155. On credentialism, see Miles, *Social Mobility*, 167, 183–84.

156. For example, Padraic Pearse's St. Enda's School, just outside Dublin, which was a training ground for young boys before and during the Easter Rising. See Pearse, *A Significant Irish Educationalist*.

157. Memmi, *Colonizer and the Colonized*, 99. Fanon's work is relevant on this point as well. See the case studies in *The Wretched of the Earth*.

158. Jameson, *A Singular Modernity*, 106–18.

159. Adorno, "The Essay as Form," 105.

CHAPTER 2. PEDAGOGY AND POWER IN THE MODERNIST BILDUNGSROMAN: HARDY AND LAWRENCE

1. Roach, "Victorian Universities," 131.

2. George Eliot's *Middlemarch* provides an important exception in the nineteenth

century. Dorothea recognizes the paralyzing effects of the kind of education Casaubon represents and refuses it. But rather than death, Dorothea embraces her passion for Ladislaw and the obscurity of what lies "behind the scenes."

3. Miles, *Social Mobility*, 179.

4. See Adorno, *Negative Dialectics*, esp. pt. 2.

5. Though not, strictly speaking, a Bildungsroman, E. M. Forster's *Howards End* does shed light on the ideal of classical Bildung as it is practiced by the Schlegel sisters and as it is pursued by Leonard Bast.

6. Jameson, *A Singular Modernity*, 137–38.

7. Adorno, *Negative Dialectics*, 149.

8. D. H. Lawrence, *Letters*, 2:183.

9. Adorno, *Negative Dialectics*, xx.

10. Alden, *Social Mobility*, 1.

11. Ibid., 4.

12. Ibid., 5.

13. Ibid., 12.

14. R. Williams, *English Novel*, 13.

15. See Radford for a discussion of Hardy's attempt to compensate for the absence of folkloric "survivals" (*Survivals of Time*, 184–206).

16. See R. Williams, *Long Revolution*, 134–44.

17. Qtd. ibid., 135.

18. Though set in the 1880s, the picture of education presented in the novel belongs to the 1860s and 1870s, the era of the Taunton Commission and Forster's Education Act; see Dougill, *Oxford in English Literature*, 193, and Mattisson, *Knowledge and Survival*, 380.

19. See R. Williams, *Long Revolution*, 137–47; Flexner, *Universities*, 203–8; Wardle, *English Popular Education*, 26–36. On University College London, see Mattisson, *Knowledge and Survival*, 90–91. Mattisson, chaps. 1 and 2, provides an extensive discussion of education in Hardy's time and in the Dorset region.

20. Alden, *Social Mobility*, 66.

21. All parenthetical references to *Jude the Obscure* (*JO*) are to the 1978 Penguin edition, edited by C. H. Sisson.

22. Kucich, "Moral Authority," 237.

23. Alden, *Social Mobility*, 57.

24. Boumelha, "'A Complicated Position for a Woman,'" 244.

25. Daleski, *Paradoxes of Love*, 183.

26. Despite the ease with which critics describe Hardy's novel as a Bildungsroman, astonishingly little has been written on the subject. Giordano concludes that Hardy's text is a "satire on the *Bildungsroman*, a kind of anti-*Bildungsroman*" ("*Jude the Obscure* and the Bildungsroman," 589). Arnds makes a similar argument, though he grounds it in the German tradition of Hegel and Goethe. In Hardy's *Antibildungs-*

roman "the protagonist's development leads to the exact opposite of *Bildung*. . . . A happy ending that reflects the fulfillment of the Hegelian aesthetic principle no longer comes about" ("Boy with the Old Face," 224). Levine notes that the "bleak, inevitably destructive direction of Jude's life . . . is not at all characteristic of the bildungsroman" (*Dying to Know*, 204). In this conclusion Levine follows Buckley's argument in *Season of Youth*. He goes on to suggest that the form is nonetheless "an excellent narrative vehicle" for the "Cartesian system of negotiating the world" that he sees in Hardy's novel because the Bildungsroman form tends "to end in accommodation to the embodied world" with all of its instabilities (204). Here he follows Moretti's argument in *The Way of the World* in seeing the English form as seeking such accommodations.

27. According to Adorno, negative dialectics repudiates the very tradition that must in any case be preserved: for "philosophy's methexis [participation] in tradition would only be a definite denial of tradition. Philosophy rests on the texts it criticizes" (*Negative Dialectics*, 55).

28. See Buckley, *Season of Youth*, 164–68; Alden, *Social Mobility*, 50–56; Pinion, *Hardy the Writer*, 152–68. Widdowson notes that Hardy "strenuously denied" that *Jude the Obscure* was autobiographical (*On Thomas Hardy*, 172) and refers us to T. Hardy, *Life and Work*, 252, 274, 392.

29. In a letter to Edmund Gosse, Hardy similarly deemphasizes "the labours of a poor student to get University degree" in order to draw attention to "the tragic issue of two bad marriages, owing in the main to a doom or curse of hereditary temperament peculiar to the family of the parties" (*Letters*, 2:93).

30. Forster, *Howards End*, 42.

31. Ibid., 38–39.

32. D. H. Lawrence, *Study of Thomas Hardy*, 50.

33. Widdowson, *On Thomas Hardy*, 177.

34. Musselwhite, *Social Transformations*, 146–47.

35. D. H. Lawrence, *Study of Thomas Hardy*, 20.

36. Swales, *German Bildungsroman*, 29.

37. B. Hardy, *Thomas Hardy*, 68, 60.

38. Radford, *Survivals of Time*, 186. See also Dougill, *Oxford in English Literature*.

39. Ingham, *Gender and Class*, 168–69.

40. On Jude's class background, see Eagleton, "The Limits of Art," 62–64. Eagleton cites Hardy's essay "The Dorsetshire Labourer" (*Longman's Magazine*, July 1883) to illustrate a situation in which the semi-independent tradesman class "was being decimated by economic depression, increased social mobility and growing industrialization" (62). Miles, in *Social Mobility*, largely confirms Hardy's judgment. See chapter 1 of this study for a short discussion of Miles's work.

41. Eagleton, "The Limits of Art," 64.

42. Adorno, *Negative Dialectics*, 145.

43. Mattisson, *Knowledge and Survival*, 90–91. On the difficulties of gaining admission to the ancient universities, see Ingham, *Gender and Class*, 168–71.

44. Gosse, review of *Jude the Obscure*, 388.

45. See note 41 to chapter 1.

46. Goethe, *Wilhelm Meister*, 16.

47. Ibid., 277.

48. Humboldt, *Limits of State Action*, 81.

49. Goethe, *Wilhelm Meister*, 326.

50. Ibid., 326.

51. At one point the "beautiful soul" confesses that the thought of an intimate relationship with a man makes her "tremble," and she remarks, "The thought of marriage inevitably has something frightening about it for a moderately discerning young girl" (ibid., 224).

52. On the Girl of the Period, see Gittings, *Young Thomas Hardy*, 93–95. On the New Woman, especially in relation to Hardy's work, see Boumelha, *Thomas Hardy and Women*; Wood, *Passion and Pathology*, chap. 4, esp. 199–214; Larson, *Ethics and Narrative*, 44–63. For useful general studies of the New Woman, see Ledger, *The New Woman*, and Richardson and Willis, *The New Woman in Fiction and Fact*. On Sue's feminism, see Blake, "Sue Bridehead."

53. Federico, *Masculine Identity*, 113. Kucich makes the point in a slightly different way when he argues that "Jude's love for Sue is continually mediated by his awareness of symbolic social hierarchies, by the parallels between Sue's 'pureness' and the ideals embodied in social stations above his own" ("Moral Authority," 230).

54. Federico, *Masculine Identity*, 117.

55. Adorno, *Negative Dialectics*, 279.

56. Oliphant, "The Anti-Marriage League," 382.

57. Daleski, *Paradoxes of Love*, 189. See Ingham, who argues that "Arabella and Sue serve to determine each other's meaning" (*Gender and Class*, 178).

58. Widdowson, *On Thomas Hardy*, 179–80. We can read the Arabella-Jude connection as an updated version of Wilhelm Meister's dalliance with Mariane, who also threaded her way through her lover's future life, leaving him with a son to care for.

59. Ibid., 182. Widdowson's skepticism about Hardy's critical intentions with respect to Arabella are echoed by Harding: "On the one hand the novel posits Sue as a New Woman, and on the other it miraculously creates a space for Arabella even though Hardy can never quite accept her presence and can only present her in a negative, denigrated and vulgar light" ("Arabella's Missile," 105).

60. D. H. Lawrence, *Study of Thomas Hardy*, 106.

61. Ibid., 102.

62. Harding, "Arabella's Missile," 102.

63. D. H. Lawrence, *Study of Thomas Hardy*, 109, 114.

64. Larson, *Ethics and Narrative*, 50.

65. See Hardy's preface, *JO* 41. Jude himself begs Sue not to be unmerciful: "Sue! we are acting by the letter; and 'the letter killeth'!" (*JO* 468).

66. W. Davis, *Thomas Hardy and the Law*, 143.

67. Kucich, "Moral Authority," 231.

68. Wood, *Passion and Pathology*, 209.

69. Gregor, "An End and a Beginning," 55. On Hardy's desire to express Jude's end as "unequivocally and inherently tragic," see 58.

70. "The most pathetic instances of icons that express the gap, rather than the connection, between worshipper and sacred images," Weinstein contends, are just these models of Christminster (*The Semantics of Desire*, 128n2).

71. Saldívar, "Spirit of the Law," 612–13.

72. Daleski, *Paradoxes of Love*, 183. Cf. Eagleton, who notes the dialectical relation between ideality and reality ("The Limits of Art," 64).

73. In Buckley's view, Hardy "has successfully adapted the form of the Bildungsroman to the true and proper ends of tragedy" (*Season of Youth*, 185). It seems to me that the two literary forms are incommensurate, and that the most we can say is that the failure of Bildung is itself a tragedy.

74. Gellner, *Nations and Nationalism*, 37–38.

75. See Alden, *Social Mobility*, 97–128, and Buckley, *Season of Youth*, 204–24. Beards is one of the few critics to diverge from the autobiographical trend; in "*Sons and Lovers* as Bildungsroman" he sees *Sons and Lovers* as a traditional Bildungsroman concerned with vocation, mating, religion, and identity. While these are all important elements in Lawrence's text, they do not constitute a general definition of the form, which is precisely what Beards claims is the case. Pinkney notes that *Sons and Lovers* is a Künstlerroman, and a traditional one, at that. In his view, Lawrence's novel "sustains the ambition of totality but raises it one level, containing it entirely in the aesthetic rather than the phenomenal realm: subject and object now converge when the fledgling artist can write the work which presents him or her to us" (*D. H. Lawrence and Modernism*, 32). We see something of this "aesthetic totality" in Jude's deliberate construction of a "magnificent dream" and, at a still higher level, in Hardy's representation of the Bildung process. Finally, while it is certainly appropriate to refer to Lawrence's text as a Künstlerroman, its emphasis on the general problematic of Bildung warrants the more inclusive term.

76. Sheehan, *Modernism, Narrative, and Humanism*, 110. On the ironic nature of the Bildungsroman, see Redfield, *Phantom Formations*.

77. Sheehan, *Modernism, Narrative, and Humanism*, 110.

78. D. H. Lawrence, *Letters*, 1:477.

79. Sheehan, *Modernism, Narrative, and Humanism*, 111.

80. Sultan, "Lawrence the Anti-Autobiographer," 226. The most recent biographies include Worthen, *D. H. Lawrence: A Literary Life* and *D. H. Lawrence: The Early Years*; D. Ellis, *D. H. Lawrence: Dying Game*; Sagar, *Life of D. H. Lawrence*.

81. See Chambers, *D. H. Lawrence*. Michael Bell in *D. H. Lawrence: Language and*

Being, 40, suggests that Chambers's memoirs are as useful for understanding Lawrence and Paul as they are for understanding Miriam.

82. M. Bell, *Language and Being*, 46.

83. Sanders, *Major Novels*, 22. Jeffers makes much the same point when he claims that Lawrence had a "self-confessed therapeutic reason" for turning to the Bildungsroman: "the need to 'shed his sickness,' to work through his own obvious mother-obsession and apparent fatherlessness by refracting them in the characters of a *Bildungsroman*" ("'We Children Were the In-Betweens,'" 293). Jeffers alludes to a letter in which Lawrence writes that "one sheds one's sicknesses in books—repeats and presents again one's emotions, to be master of them" (*Letters*, 2:90). I note without comment the curiously utilitarian motives here ascribed to authors in shaping their fiction.

84. Sanders, *Major Novels*, 27.

85. Ibid., 58–59. On the social history of Lawrence's text, see R. Williams, *Culture and Society*, 202–7, and Holderness, *History, Ideology, and Fiction*, 130–58. Holmes, in "Social Origins," has called into question Lawrence's working-class background, strongly suggesting that he was at least in the lower middle class during most of his upbringing.

86. Sultan, "Lawrence the Anti-Autobiographer," 226.

87. D. H. Lawrence, *Letters*, 2:183.

88. On the problematic aspect of the realism in *Sons and Lovers*, see Pinkney, *D. H. Lawrence and Modernism*, 27–36.

89. For Giddens, see *Modernity and Self-Identity*. Lewiecki-Wilson notes that *Sons and Lovers* "presents the growth of a subject as a struggle-in-relation, where the outcome is never assured, and the very concept of 'self' is built out of conflict with another" (*Writing Against the Family*, 70).

90. Sanders, *Major Novels*, 56–57.

91. All parenthetical references to *Sons and Lovers* (*SL*) are to the Cambridge edition (1992; repr. Penguin, 1994), edited by Helen Baron and Carl Baron.

92. Fernihough, *Aesthetics and Ideology*, 38.

93. Referring to Lawrence's "project of modernist aesthetics," Fernihough argues: "Art is seen by Lawrence to be *both* a site of conflict *and* the one refuge from instrumentality, the one place in which ideologies can be expressed and tested without the risk of disastrous consequences in the practical world" (ibid., 45, 188). Fernihough, and also Chaudhuri in *D. H. Lawrence and "Difference,"* articulate a view of modernist aesthetics very much in line with what we find in the work of Jameson, Eagleton, and other theorists of modernism and modernity influenced by Adorno and the Frankfurt School.

94. Fernihough, *Aesthetics and Ideology*, 42.

95. See Holderness, who notes that Gertrude is "a primary instrument" in the formation of Paul's "individuation" (*History, Ideology, and Fiction*, 140).

96. The phrase "dialectical sublation" translates the Hegelian term *Aufheben*, a pro-

cess of canceling that raises up and preserves what is canceled. It is the characteristic movement of Hegelian dialectic.

97. M. Bell, *Language and Being*, 44, 43.

98. Adorno, *Negative Dialectics*, 21.

99. Alden, *Social Mobility*, 99. Discussion of psychoanalytic issues is quite common in criticism of Lawrence. For a useful study that reviews the relevant material, see J. Cowan, *D. H. Lawrence: Self and Sexuality*. Cowan stresses the significance of the dyadic mother-child nature of the oedipal conflict in Lawrence: "Despite the obvious activation of oedipal feelings in the split between sexual and spiritual love in Paul Morel, Lawrence's emphasis throughout much of his work on the dangers of merger versus respect for otherness . . . does not derive from triadic oedipal conflicts, but from the dyadic relationship of mother and child" (19). For a Lacanian approach to psychoanalytic issues, see Ingersoll, *D. H. Lawrence, Desire, and Narrative*. The foreword to *Sons and Lovers*, with its unorthodox reading of the gospel of St. John, gives Lawrence's imprimatur to oedipal readings: "John, the beloved disciple, says, 'The Word was made Flesh.' But why should he turn things round? The women simply go on bearing talkative sons, as an answer. The Flesh was made Word." Lawrence concludes the foreword pointedly, saying, "The old son-lover was Oedipus" (*SL* 467, 473).

100. Ingersoll reads this passage in terms of the "pre-natal antecedent" of jouissance, the "limitless joy" that the "subject-to-be-Paul" enjoys in the mother's womb. The narrative then attempts to recover this experience (*D. H. Lawrence, Desire, and Narrative*, 37). While this is a suggestive reading, it privileges the male "subject-to-be" over the female subject "in being."

101. According to Freud, such fantasies serve as a "fulfillment of wishes and as a correction of actual life." They express the desire of the individual for liberation from parental authority or the desire for parents of a higher social standing. They also express the uncertainty of the father's authority and the certainty of the mother's: "*Pater semper incertus est*, while the mother is *certissima*" ("Family Romances," *Standard Edition*, 9:238–39; see also "Moses an Egyptian," *Standard Edition*, 23:10–15). See Leweicki-Wilson, who discusses the family romance in *Sons and Lovers* as a function of capitalist ideology (*Writing Against the Family*, 92–95).

102. Alden, *Social Mobility*, 109. Holderness agrees that Gertrude pushes them, but argues that by doing so she "pushes them into isolation, separateness, individuality." Paul is led into a "position of isolated singleness where he is wholly dependent on his mother" (*History, Ideology, and Fiction*, 147). I would argue that this very "individuality" and "singleness" is what enables Paul to form himself, not so much in alienation from his background but in critical and even creative opposition to it.

103. Bedient, *Architects of the Self*, 118.

104. Sheehan, *Modernism, Narrative, and Humanism*, 107, 109.

105. Jeffers succinctly, if flippantly, sums up the critical consensus with his description of Miriam and Clara as Paul's "antithetical girlfriends" ("'We Children Were the

In-Betweens,'" 302). See also Jeffers, "End of Sex." Pinkney believes Miriam "has been much misunderstood . . . not just by critics but by the text itself" and stresses her emotionalism against her "fastidiously virginal" intellect (*D. H. Lawrence and Modernism*, 33–34).

106. Holderness, *History, Ideology, and Fiction*, 151.

107. D. H. Lawrence, *Letters*, 1:477.

108. D. H. Lawrence, *Study of Thomas Hardy*, 119.

109. Ibid., 42, 55.

110. Lewiecki-Wilson, *Writing Against the Family*, 74, 85.

111. Van Ghent, *The English Novel*, 247–49.

112. Sheehan, *Modernism, Narrative, and Humanism*, 109.

113. Buckley, *Season of Youth*, 206.

114. Scheckner, *Class, Politics*, 34.

115. Ibid., 23.

116. Adorno, *Negative Dialectics*, 21.

117. Alden, *Social Mobility*, 101.

118. See Scheckner, who claims that "Miriam cultivates religious and aesthetic sensibilities that will insulate her from the coarseness of the world around her; nature, too, becomes such a refuge" (*Class, Politics*, 38).

119. Sanders, *Major Novels*, 45.

120. M. Bell, *Language and Being*, 37.

121. Pinkney argues that Miriam represents "a formidable principle of anti-realism," an "external threat to the novel's realist ambitions and internal scapegoat for its own failure to achieve them." The threat to realism, which Pinkney regards as both "sexual and generic," must be expelled by the novel's fundamentally realistic commitments (*D. H. Lawrence and Modernism*, 36–37). I do not think Miriam is so easily expelled, nor does she seem to be quite the threat to realism that Pinkney believes her to be. If we understand the realism of *Sons and Lovers* to be specifically determined by the Bildungsroman form that organizes its effects, then Miriam's continued presence in the novel testifies to that very realism, which has been determined in important ways precisely by her instrumental function in Paul's Bildung process.

122. Alden, *Social Mobility*, 104.

123. Ibid., 109–10.

124. M. Bell, *Language and Being*, 46.

125. Bedient, *Architects of the Self*, 121.

126. It is ironic that Paul feels the same sense of being "pure instinct" when fighting Baxter that he feels with Clara, further evidence that her instrumentality entails a total submission of her own selfhood to the furtherance of his communion with the "great force."

127. Goethe, *Wilhelm Meister*, 286.

128. Sheehan refers here to the opinion of Lawrence's "humanist defenders" (*Modernism, Narrative, and Humanism*, 111).

129. I must therefore take issue with Beards's conclusion that Paul's future is "assured" (*"Sons and Lovers* as Bildungsroman," 215).

CHAPTER 3. BILDUNG AND THE "BONDS OF DOMINION": WILDE AND JOYCE

1. All parenthetical references to *A Portrait of the Artist as a Young Man* (*P*) are to the Viking critical edition (1964; repr. Penguin, 1977), edited by Chester G. Anderson.

2. See North, *Reading 1922*, which explores this year as a pivotal one for aspects of modernist culture, including innovations in literature, philosophy, art, and science.

3. On the concepts of "metrocolonialism" and "metrocolonial subjectivity," see Valente, *Dracula's Crypt*, esp. chap. 3, "The Metrocolonial Vampire." See also Hechter, *Internal Colonialism*, on the concept of Ireland as the "Celtic fringe" of the British Empire.

4. Many critics speak of modernism and Irish literature and culture, but relatively few have addressed the issue of a distinctly Irish form of modernism and/or modernity. See Eagleton, *Heathcliff*, esp. 282–303; Castle, *Modernism and the Celtic Revival*; Nolan, *James Joyce and Nationalism*; Deane, *Strange Country*; A. Davis, *A Broken Line*; N. Miller, *Modernism, Ireland*.

5. Bhabha, *Location of Culture*, 89.

6. For a good general discussion of the Gothic tradition, see Botting, *Gothic*. Punter's *Companion to the Gothic* offers a wide variety of essays on various topics.

7. The term "dehiscence" means both a splitting open along a natural line *and* the discharge of contents in the act of splitting.

8. Adorno, *Negative Dialectics*, 95.

9. Bakhtin regards the biographical novel as a precursor to the Bildungsroman. As I noted in chapter 1, he characterizes it as a realistic form that includes "the total life process," which he describes as "limited, unrepeatable, and irreversible." The hero of biographical discourse "lacks any true process of becoming or development" (*"Bildungsroman,"* 17–18).

10. For "transculturation," see Lima, "Decolonizing Genre." Though her emphasis is on postcolonial texts, I believe it to be a fruitful concept for talking about colonial Irish writers.

11. On the colonial dynamics of Anglo-Irish identity and the failure to achieve ideological hegemony, see Eagleton, *Heathcliff*, and Castle, "Ambivalence and Ascendancy."

12. See O'Grady, "Ireland and the Hour" and *All Ireland*.

13. J. Brown, *Cosmopolitan Criticism*, 24–25.

14. Joyce, "Oscar Wilde: Poet of 'Salomé,'" 204.

15. The complexities and contradictions of the dialectical structure of identity formation under colonialism have been discussed at length by Frantz Fanon and Albert Memmi. Both see the problem as an instance of dialectical processes frozen into a "Manichean" framework in which the colonizer and the colonized are pitted against each other in a polarized struggle for dominance. The Anglo-Irish intelligentsia undermined the Manichean framework. Its position with respect to the colonized Catholic majority and the British imperial state was complicated by shared interests and loyalties but also by flashpoints of conflict. We see this in the history of nationalist movements like the Irish Literary Revival and the Gaelic League. Wilde, like W. B. Yeats, J. M. Synge, and others, was in a unique position to criticize the dominant ideologies of colonialism and nationalism. On Manicheism and colonial relations, see JanMohamed, "The Economy of Manichean Allegory" and *Manichean Aesthetics*.

16. Adorno, *Negative Dialectics*, 48, 50.

17. Said and other postcolonial theorists have taught us how essential the empire was to the social world depicted in mainstream English fiction; see *Culture and Imperialism*, esp. chap. 2.

18. On the history of education in Ireland, see Akenson, *Irish Education Experiment*; Barr, "University Education"; Corcoran, *State Policy*; Daly and Dickson, *Popular Literacy*; McElligott, *Secondary Education in Ireland*.

19. On the hedge schools, see Adams, "Swine-Tax and Eat-Him-All-Magee." On the tradition of popular education, see O'Connell, *People Power*; R. Davis, *The Young Ireland Movement*; Grote, *Torn Between Politics and Culture*. Also of interest are the essays on education and historiography in McBride, *Reading Irish Histories*.

20. Bashford, *Critic as Humanist*, 107.

21. The irony deepens when we compare Wilde's experience at Oxford with the "mediaevalism of Christminster" that Jude Fawley endured.

22. Adorno, *Negative Dialectics*, 56.

23. Wilde, "Portrait of Mr. W. H.," 152. See also "The Critic as Artist": "art springs from personality" (Wilde, *Intentions*, 159).

24. Sammells, *Wilde Style*, 60. Tyson is even less helpful in her estimation: "an odd kind of bildungsroman" ("Caliban in a Glass," 105).

25. Altieri, "Organic-Humanist Models," 220, 222.

26. Danson, *Wilde's Intentions*, 6. On Wilde's Irishness, see Kiberd, *Inventing Ireland*, 35–50, and McCormack, *Wilde the Irishman*.

27. On the history of the dandy, see Moers, *The Dandy*. For a good summary of this history and discussion of Wilde's place in it, see Gagnier, *Idylls of the Marketplace*, chap. 2.

28. All parenthetical references to *The Picture of Dorian Gray* (*DG*) are to the Norton critical edition (1988), edited by Donald L. Lawler.

29. DeLaura, *Hebrew and Hellene*, 340.

30. Pater, *The Renaissance*, 108–9.

31. Ibid., 163, 165.

32. Ibid., 183–84.

33. Ibid., 184–85.

34. Ibid., 188, 190.

35. Ibid., 186.

36. Pater, "Mr. Oscar Wilde," 352.

37. On reversal arguments in rhetorical dialectics, see Bashford, *Critic as Humanist*, 65–66.

38. Arnold's theory of alternating epochs of concentration and expansion, of critical and creative development, can be found in "The Function of Criticism at the Present Time."

39. All parenthetical references to "The Decay of Lying" and "The Critic as Artist" are to the Brentano's edition (1905) of Wilde's *Intentions* (*I*).

40. Larson draws our attention to a general cultural context for Wilde's project of aestheticized ethics: the ethos of the late nineteenth century was "marked not by a deontological escape from self or a paradoxically strong-willed refusal of choice but instead by anxious yet flexibly ethical searching, an openness to the surprising and unusual, and an ambivalence poised between regard for Victorian morality and attention to the ethical relevance of that which lies beyond morality's authority" (*Ethics and Narrative*, 31–32; see also 39).

41. Joyce no doubt had this passage in mind when he had Stephen Dedalus point and say, "It is a symbol of Irish art. The cracked lookingglass of a servant" (*Ulysses* 6).

42. Quoted in R. Ellmann, *Oscar Wilde*, 310–11.

43. Gagnier, *Idylls of the Marketplace*, 7. See also Waldrep, who argues that "Wilde's performative abilities . . . helped not only to put him in a situation where he could shine for the purposes of networking for his projects, but went further to transform conversation into an opportunity to use autobiography and self-promotion to entice the public into buying him" ("Economics and Performance," 116).

44. Ruddick uses the term "metaparadox" to describe the resemblance between *Dorian Gray* and "the poisonous books [in the decadent tradition] that the story supposedly warned against" ("'Peculiar Quality,'" 128).

45. Mahaffey, *States of Desire*, 42.

46. R. Ellmann, *Oscar Wilde*, 305.

47. J. Brown, *Cosmopolitan Criticism*, 30, 75. Brown cites Wilde's *Intentions*. In a footnote, she cites one of Wilde's American lectures in support of her point: "By keeping aloof from the social problems of the day . . . [art] more completely realises for us that which we desire. For to most of us the real life is the life we do not lead" (122n11; see Wilde, *Miscellanies*, 256).

48. Walter Pater, in his review of *Dorian Gray*, commended Wilde's fantastical representation of Dorian's development but thought that the "dainty Epicurean theory" of the novel did not quite measure up to the neo-Hegelian telos of his own Epicurean

worldview: the "complete though harmonious development of man's entire organism." What is missing is the "moral sense": what Wilde's heroes "are bent on doing as speedily, as completely as they can, is to lose, or lower, organisation, to become less complex, to pass from a higher to a lower degree of development" ("Mr. Oscar Wilde," 352–53).

49. Larson, *Ethics and Narrative*, 93.

50. Wilde, *Letters*, 265–66. The first clause of this quotation is repeated in a letter to the editor of the *St. James's Gazette*, sent just four days prior to this one; see *Letters*, 258–59. The earlier letter explains the moral explicitly in terms of the punishments meted out to the central characters of the novel. In this letter Wilde concedes, perhaps facetiously, that the moral is an "artistic error"; however, he goes on, "It is the only error in the book" (259). It was to this letter that the reviewer to whom Wilde responds was, in his turn, responding in his review.

51. Thomas argues that a "logic of liberal agency" subtends the indeterminacies and vertiginousness of Wilde's text, one that is privileged by "historical materialist and broadly poststructuralist theories" (*Cultivating Victorians*, 158–60). Gillespie's *Oscar Wilde and the Poetics of Ambiguity* is a good recent example of the tendency to read for Wilde's "disposition for indeterminacy" (58). Many other critics take one form or another of this view; see, for example, E. Cohen, "Writing Gone Wilde"; Dollimore, *Sexual Dissidence*; Mahaffey, *States of Desire*; Nunokawa, *Tame Passions of Wilde*; Sammells, *Wilde Style*.

52. Pater, "Mr. Oscar Wilde," 354. Pater's appreciation for Wilde's supernatural effects may be an appreciation for his own dark side, as Riquelme suggests: "Wilde responds to Pater by projecting the dark implications of Pater's attitudes and formulations in a mythic Gothic narrative of destruction and self-destruction" ("Oscar Wilde's Aesthetic Gothic," 610). In a similar vein, Lawler argues that Wilde chose the Gothic mode for *Dorian Gray* in order "to deconstruct [his] own aesthetic philosophy of life as represented in his stories and essays of the late eighties and nineties" ("The Gothic Wilde," 261).

53. In her discussion of parody, Kristeva makes the distinction I have alluded to here between two forms of transgression; see *Desire in Language*, 71. I return to the subject of parody in chapter 4.

54. Goethe, *Wilhelm Meister*, 309–10. Dickens's *Great Expectations* is a good example of this kind of mentorship from afar, for Pip's ascension to the status of gentleman is engineered by the transported felon Magwich.

55. Wilde, "Portrait of Mr. W. H.," 208.

56. *Oxford English Dictionary*, s.v. "vivisection." It is also defined as a form of "animal experimentation, esp. if considered to cause distress to the subject" (*Webster's New Collegiate Dictionary*).

57. Riquelme sees Lord Henry as an "avatar of Victor Frankenstein, who produces an ugly, destructive double of himself" ("Oscar Wilde's Aesthetic Gothic," 616).

58. Goethe, *Wilhelm Meister*, 309.

59. A similar repetition of the Goethean scroll occurs in "The Portrait of Mr. W. H.," where Shakespeare's sonnets reveal the narrator's own soul to him: "it seemed to me that I was deciphering the story of a life that had once been mine, unrolling the record of a romance that, without my knowing it, had coloured the very texture of my nature.... I felt as if I had been initiated into the secret of [a] passionate friendship" (210). The narrator recalls seeing a mummified body of a young girl in Egypt, who clutched "a scroll of yellow papyrus" in her hand: "How I wished now that I had had it read to me! It might have told me something more about the soul that hid within me, and had its mysteries of passion of which I was kept in ignorance" (212). These instances are among many that link this story to *Dorian Gray* and to the thematics of Gothic Bildung.

60. Pater, "Mr. Oscar Wilde," 352.

61. E. Cohen, "Writing Gone Wilde," 82.

62. Goethe, *Wilhelm Meister*, 277.

63. Wilde, "Soul of Man," 284–85; Wilde's emphasis. Bashford sees here a link to Wilde's early essay "The Rise of Historical Criticism," which combines Enlightenment rationalism, natural science, and Hegelian historicism in order to argue for a "*telos* internal to human nature, one whose gradual emergence instantiates a larger 'law of life'" (*Critic as Humanist*, 145).

64. Wilde, "Soul of Man," 285; Wilde's emphasis.

65. Ibid., 262, 263.

66. On Wilde's Oxford training, see Smith and Helfand, *Oscar Wilde's Oxford Notebooks*, and Bashford, chap. 6. On Oxford Hellenism, see Dowling, *Hellenism and Homosexuality*, 62–86.

67. Dowling, *Hellenism and Homosexuality*, 4.

68. Joyce makes a similar point in his parody of English Hellenism, part of the opening "Telemachus" episode of *Ulysses*. "God, Kinch," Buck Mulligan says to Stephen Dedalus, "if you and I could only work together we might do something for the island. Hellenise it" (7).

69. Wilde, *Miscellanies*, 289–90. See "The Portrait of Mr. W. H.," where Wilde speculates that "acting seems to have formed part of the ordinary education" in the Elizabethan era at the public schools and the ancient universities (192).

70. Lord Henry remarks of Lord Grotrian, "He atones for being occasionally somewhat over-dressed, by being always absolutely over-educated" (*DG* 140). But Gilbert in "The Critic as Artist" asserts, "We live in the age of the overworked, and the under-educated; the age in which people are so industrious that they become absolutely stupid" (*I* 177). The point is not that Wilde is inconsistent, but that education in formal settings, whether one gets too little or too much, is a poor preparation for life or for art.

71. Cambridge, "a sort of educational institute," as the narrator of Wilde's "Portrait of Mr. W. H." describes it, was primarily known for its emphasis on science, while Ox-

ford, according to Erskine in the same story, was a school where students "dawdle over literature" (216). On the undoing of the "English Athens," see Dougill, *Oxford in English Literature*.

72. Gagnier, *Idylls of the Marketplace*, 12.

73. Ibid., 90. For a brief survey of research on the gentleman, see 90–98.

74. Wilde, "Portrait of Mr. W. H.," 155.

75. Gagnier, *Idylls of the Marketplace*, 91, 98.

76. Humboldt, *Humanist without Portfolio*, 399.

77. Wilde's notorious identification with the characters in his novel—"it contains much of me in it. Basil Hallward is what I think I am; Lord Henry what the world thinks me; Dorian what I would like to be—in other ages perhaps" (R. Ellmann, *Oscar Wilde*, 319)—complicates the dialectical logic of the Bildung process in *Dorian Gray* and creates a space for critical speculation on the reflexive project of self-development in late modernity.

78. Adorno, *Negative Dialectics*, 151.

79. Wilde, "Some Literary Notes," 389.

80. E. Cohen, "Writing Gone Wilde," 76, 79.

81. Dollimore, *Sexual Dissidence*, 229–30, 15. Within such a dynamic, "the outlaw turns up as inlaw, and the other as proximate proves more disturbing than the other as absolute difference" (124).

82. See Bourke, "Hunting Out the Fairies," 39, 42. Bourke refers us to Davis Oakley, who "finds Wilde's debt to Irish folk narrative most apparent in *The Picture of Dorian Gray*, noting that 'folklore and myth form the basis and structure of the novel, setting it apart from other works of the same genre in the English language'" (42). See also Edwards, "Impressions," 58–59. In *Wilde's Use of Irish Celtic Elements*, Upchurch provides an exhaustive discussion of the Irish motifs in *Dorian Gray*.

83. Thomas, *Cultivating Victorians*, 174. Thomas's formulation is developed out of a reading of a line in *De Profundis*: "To be entirely free, and at the same time, entirely dominated by law, is the eternal paradox of human life that we realise at every moment" (*De Profundis*, 123).

84. E. Cohen, "Writing Gone Wilde," 82.

85. Lawler, "The Gothic Wilde," 251.

86. Discussions of the portrait as a "mirror function" that constructs otherness and identity are common in criticism of *Dorian Gray*. In addition to Ed Cohen, see Allen, *Sexuality in Victorian Fiction*, 110–36; Jaffe, *Scenes of Sympathy*, 158–79; Nunokawa, "Homosexual Desire" and *Tame Passions of Wilde*, 71–89.

87. See Riquelme, "Oscar Wilde's Aesthetic Gothic," 624–27, for a discussion of the "undead" quality of the portrait in relation to Pater's description, in *The Renaissance*, of Leonardo's *La Gioconda* (97–99).

88. J. Brown, *Cosmopolitan Criticism*, 81.

89. Adorno, *Negative Dialectics*, 85.

90. Ruddick believes that the 1891 version of *Dorian Gray* veiled the homoeroticism of the 1890 Lippincott version, while the preface was a defensive maneuver. Wilde, according to Ruddick, should have "dropped all veils and written a realistic novel about the predicament of the sexual invert, in which the protagonist would clearly be seen to be corrupted by the constraints forced upon him by society, rather than by his own unnatural desires or by contamination by such external elements as the poisonous 'yellow book'" ("'Peculiar Quality,'" 131). On Wilde's response to the reviews of *Dorian Gray*, see Danson, *Wilde's Intentions*, 130–39.

91. Gagnier, *Idylls of the Marketplace*, 51. Gagnier's influential reading of *Dorian Gray* is premised on the significance of audience response and the market for the text itself. For further discussion of the reception of Wilde's novel, see Danson, *Wilde's Intentions*, and Small and Guy, *Oscar Wilde's Profession*.

92. W. Brown, *Politics Out of History*, 71–72. On the general problem of crises in capitalist societies, see Habermas, *Legitimation Crisis*, and O'Connor, *Accumulation Crisis*.

93. On economic and social development in Ireland, see Crotty, *Ireland in Crisis*, and Littleton, *From Famine to Feast*. On Ireland's relation to English national development, see Hechter, *Internal Colonialism*.

94. Eagleton illustrates the economic disparities between Ireland and Britain in his reading of Emily Brontë's *Wuthering Heights* (*Heathcliff*, 1–26). Also relevant are the essays in Attridge and Howes, *Semicolonial Joyce*.

95. Memmi, *Colonizer and the Colonized*, 99.

96. Ibid., 38–39, 25, 79.

97. Fanon, *Black Skin, White Masks*, 16. See also his *Wretched of the Earth*, 237.

98. Memmi, *Colonizer and the Colonized*, 140.

99. Mitchell, "*A Portrait* and the *Bildungsroman* Tradition," 74. Mitchell does not go beyond suggesting that there is an "antitraditional" impulse in *Portrait* that coexists with its more conventional elements (73).

100. Buckley, *Season of Youth*, 226. All of the work on Joyce's Bildungsroman, apart from my own, is from the period 1940–76. Harry Levin in *James Joyce* seems to have been the first to read *Portrait* as a Bildungsroman. He writes: "The theme of [Joyce's] novel is the formation of character; its habitual pattern is that of apprenticeship or education; and it falls into that category which has been distinguished, by German criticism at least, as the Bildungsroman" (41). See also the early studies by Beebe, "Joyce and Stephen Dedalus" and *Ivory Towers and Sacred Founts*, 3–18. Beebe reads *Portrait* in the tradition established by Goethe's *Wilhelm Meister* and thus has no trouble classifying it as a classical Bildungsroman. For a comparison of *Portrait* and Flaubert's *L'Education sentimentale*, see Cross, *Flaubert and Joyce*, 35–67. Wallace, in "'Laughing in Your Sleeve,'" argues that Joyce uses the Bildungsroman genre in order to parody the romance-comedy genre.

101. Deane, introduction, xvi.

102. Ibid., xviii.

103. Deane, *Celtic Revivals*, 75–76.

104. Martini, "Bildungsroman—Term and Theory," 5.

105. Dilthey, "Friedrich Hölderlin," 335–36.

106. On the idea of "alienated assent" as a pedagogical strategy in colonial and post-colonial contexts, see Spivak, "The Burden of English."

107. Certainly colonial conditions encourage this kind of eroticized violence in the schools. A powerful example can be found in George Lamming's *In the Castle of My Skin*.

108. Valente argues that by virtue of a "recursive symmetry, if not equity," Stephen's punishment is not entirely undeserved, because his inadvertent participation in "homoerotic indulgences" takes root in his unconscious, "where the thought or wish can stand for the deed and carry the same transgressive force" ("'Thrilled by His Touch,'" 55).

109. J. Smith, "Cultivating Gender," 215.

110. On homosociality, see Sedgwick, *Between Men*, esp. 21–27. The drives of homoerotic desire can be expressed in a number of ways. One of the most commonly discussed is the triangular structure of homosocial relations in which a woman (or a discourse of "woman") mediates desire between men. Homosocial desire tends either toward institutionalized forms of homophobia or toward alternative modes of self-development that involve "changes in men's experience of living within the shifting terms of compulsory heterosexuality" (134). Rubin, in "Traffic in Women," offers an anthropological interpretation of the "triangular desire" discussed by Sedgwick that emphasizes the role of women in economic exchanges between men. On the way homosociality and homosexuality function in Joyce's texts, see the essays collected in Valente, *Quare Joyce*.

111. Were he aware of his own ambivalent relation to colonialism, Heron might have been able to practice a form of critique that Homi Bhabha calls "colonial mimicry": a "mode of colonial discourse" that is "constructed around ambivalence," that speaks from "two disproportionate sites" (*Location of Culture*, 108). I will return to the concept of mimicry in chapter 4.

112. Memmi, *Colonizer and the Colonized*, 92.

113. Peters, *The Mutilating God*, 67–68.

114. Brivic, "Gender Dissonance," 462.

115. Stephen is certainly not interested in conventional schoolboy heroics, as his dismissal of Heron as a "sorry anticipation of manhood" indicates (*P* 83).

116. Valente, "'Thrilled by His Touch,'" 48.

117. *Oxford English Dictionary*, s.v. "confession."

118. Though historically the "confessor" referred to one who confesses his or her faith publicly, and though in contemporary dictionaries "confessor" covers "one that confesses" and "a priest who hears confession," Church practice is to reserve the term

for the priest who hears confession. See *New Catholic Encyclopedia*, 4:141–42, and *Oxford English Dictionary*, s.v. "confessor."

119. Foucault, *History of Sexuality*, 1:61–62.

120. It is worth noting that the modern mode of penance, particularly the notion of a private or secret confession in which the priest is sworn not to reveal "confessional knowledge," is generally thought to be of Celtic origin; see *New Catholic Encyclopedia*, 4:132.

121. Ibid., 4:134.

122. Qtd. ibid., 4:133.

123. On the "Ignatian spiritual model," and its significance for Stephen's sacramental identity, see Mulrooney, "Politics of Confession," 170–71.

124. In *Ulysses* Stephen points out this ruse of the Church: "On that mystery [the "mystical estate" of fatherhood] and not on the madonna which the cunning Italian intellect flung to the mob of Europe the church is founded and founded irremovably because founded, like the world, macro- and microcosm, upon the void" (207).

125. Foucault, *History of Sexuality*, 1:66.

126. Ibid., 1:67.

127. Ibid., 1:62.

128. Mulrooney, "Politics of Confession," 169.

129. Wilde, *De Profundis*, 164, 179.

130. Adorno, *Negative Dialectics*, 119.

131. Ibid., 120.

132. In *Stephen Hero*, Stephen remarks: "The Roman, not the Sassenach, was for him the tyrant of the islanders" (53). In *Portrait* and *Ulysses*, however, he clearly sees the Sassenach (the English) as equally capable of tyranny. Subsequent references to Joyce's *Stephen Hero* (*SH*) are to the New Directions edition (1959), edited by John J. Slocum and Herbert Cahoon.

133. It was just this sort of erotic intimacy that led to the creation of the confessional "box." Lowe-Evans relates that in the sixteenth century Saint Charles Borromeo, nephew of Pius IV, was assigned the task of "cleaning up" confession: "Taking into consideration all the real and potential sexual exploitation inherent in the confessional situation, Borromeo decided that a fail-safe must be created. He therefore designed a 'box' wherein confessions could be heard without threat to the chastity of priest or penitent" ("Sex and Confession," 575).

134. "Every analysis of a judgment takes us to a subject and an object, but this fact does not create a region beyond those moments, a region that would be 'in itself.' The analysis results in the constellation of those moments, not in a third that would be superior, or at least more general" (Adorno, *Negative Dialectics*, 105).

135. Bhabha, *Location of Culture*, 120.

136. Adorno, *Negative Dialectics*, 48.

137. Stephen's recognition of his heretical identity, muted in *Portrait*, is clearly ar-

ticulated in *Stephen Hero*: "But, during the formation of his artistic creed, had he not found item after item upheld for him in advance by the greatest and most orthodox doctor of the Church [i.e., Aquinas] and was it anything but vanity which urged him to seek out the thorny crown of the heretic while the entire theory, in accordance with which his entire artistic life was shaped, arose most conveniently for his purpose out of the mass of Catholic theology?" (205).

138. Humboldt, *Limits of State Action*, 59. Cf. Manganiello, who argues that Stephen is a "prime specimen of the self-sufficient individual whose ambition is to beget a new race in his own image and likeness" ("Reading the Book of Himself," 159).

139. In *Stephen Hero*, his self-image is that of a neopagan Nietzschean solitary who flings "disdain from flashing antlers" (35).

140. On the history and curriculum of University College, see Barr, "University Education." On Stephen's experience, see Muller, "Education of Stephen Dedalus."

141. Balzac, *Lost Illusions*, 186.

142. Goethe, *Wilhelm Meister*, 286.

143. Froula, *Modernism's Body*, 67.

144. On Stephen's attitude toward girls and women, specifically the way in which E.C. serves "primarily as a means to fulfill Stephen's own needs," see Church, "Adolescent Point of View." Also important on E.C. is Scott, "Emma Clery in *Stephen Hero*." On Stephen's misogyny, see Henke's chapter "Stephen Dedalus and Women" in *James Joyce and the Politics of Desire*, though I disagree that Stephen's attitudes toward women are misogynistic; on this point, cf. Froula, *Modernism's Body*, esp. pt. 1, "Initiation."

145. Froula, *Modernism's Body*, 47–48, 50, 59.

146. Valente, "'Thrilled by His Touch,'" 63.

147. J. M. Synge, *Evening Mail*, January 29, 1907, repr. in Kilroy, *The "Playboy" Riots*, 24.

148. See Anderson's note to this passage in his edition of *Portrait*, 536.

149. Fachinelli writes that "the Thing is 'at the centre of the significant relations in which the unconscious organizes itself,' but only insofar as it is excluded, foreign to the self, even though being at the very heart of it, the seat of intimate exteriority or 'exterioracy.' Further, the Thing is that part of the real (the real as a whole: the real of the subject, and the real outside it) which suffers from the signifier; or, in other words, the 'incidence of the signifier on the psychic real.' The text overflows with repeated approximations, as though trying to grasp—while at the same time making ungraspable—what seems inaccessible, lost forever and never lost, to be re-found but, yet, unfindable.... Here Lacan's thought keeps bumping into the Thing—it bolts, draws near and pulls away by means of glimpses of oblique or anamorphic thought which both alludes and eludes" ("Lacan and the Thing"; Fachinelli quotes from Lacan's *Ethics of Psychoanalysis*). On the "Thing" and its relation to the tradition of Hegelian and Kantian philosophy, see Žižek, *Tarrying with the Negative*.

150. Froula, *Modernism's Body*, 61–63.

151. Stephen uses nearly identical phrasing to describe the peasant woman who attempts to seduce Davin: "a type of her race and his own, a batlike soul waking to the consciousness of itself in darkness and secrecy and loneliness and, through the eyes and voice and gesture of a woman without guile, calling the stranger to her bed" (*P* 183).

152. For further discussion of Davin, especially his role in Stephen's "anthropological fictions" about Ireland, see my *Modernism and the Celtic Revival*, 192–202.

153. See, for example, Valente, "'Thrilled by His Touch.'"

154. Froula, *Modernism's Body*, 69.

155. See the "Scylla and Charybdis" episode of *Ulysses*: "A man of genius makes no mistakes. His errors are volitional and are the portals of discovery" (190).

CHAPTER 4. BILDUNG FOR WOMEN: JOYCE AND WOOLF

1. Adorno, *Negative Dialectics*, 149.

2. The phenomenon of an embedded Bildung plot occurs in a wide range of high modernist novels, a short list of which might include *Women in Love*, *A Passage to India*, *Absolom! Absolom!* and *The Making of Americans*.

3. M. Ellmann, "Disremembering Dedalus," 191. Friedman, in "(Self)Censorship," argues that this textual series constitutes a "composite" text that can be read in terms of unconscious desire and repression. Crump charts the changes in Stephen's aesthetic theory through the same series in "Refining Himself out of Existence."

4. Moretti, *Way of the World*, 5, quoting Erwin Panofsky.

5. Flaubert, *Sentimental Education*, 418.

6. Memmi, *Colonizer and the Colonized*, 92.

7. All parenthetical references to *Ulysses* (*U*) are to the Modern Library edition (1961, repr. Vintage, 1990).

8. Goethe, *Wilhelm Meister*, 128. See also bk. 4, chaps. 3, 13, 16.

9. Swales, *German Bildungsroman*, 164, 29.

10. Goethe, *Wilhelm Meister*, 177.

11. See Platt, *Joyce and the Anglo-Irish*, and Castle, *Modernism and the Celtic Revival*, 219–23.

12. On the problem of Shakespeare and dialectics in "Scylla and Charybdis," see Klein, "Speech Lent by Males." On the literary history of Shakespeare that Stephen deconstructs, see McCombe, "Besteglyster and Bradleyism."

13. Joyce, *Finnegans Wake*, 4. "Soangso" refers to Hwang Ho, the Yellow River of China.

14. One could make a similar claim for "Penelope." I have chosen "Nausicaa" for analysis because it raises the issues of female subjectivity and Bildung in terms of a parodic critique of a specific tradition of nineteenth-century female Bildungsromane.

15. Adorno, *Negative Dialectics*, 137.

16. Budgen, *Making of "Ulysses,"* 105.

17. Fanon, *Wretched of the Earth*, 222.

18. For a summary of this tradition, see Hutcheon, *A Theory of Parody*, 30–49. For a discussion of parody from a historical perspective, see M. Rose, *Parody*.

19. Hutcheon, *A Theory of Parody*, 11.

20. Ibid., 82.

21. Kristeva, *Desire in Language*, 71.

22. Baudrillard, *Political Economy of the Sign*, 110.

23. Kristeva, *Desire in Language*, 71.

24. Jameson, *Postmodernism*, 17. Margaret Rose, in "Parody/Post-Modernism," argues that Jameson's concept of "pastiche" can be questioned once we recall that the term "is found by Jameson in the writings of Thomas Mann and Adorno" and that theorists of parody often refer to Mann's *Dr. Faustus* (Jameson's source for the term "pastiche") as an example of parody "representing a sympathetic attitude to the text or work being imitated" (51). She also suggests that Foucault may be a better theoretical guide for a critical parody that would "challenge reality."

25. Karen Lawrence, for example, reads *Ulysses* in terms of an "odyssey of style" that moves from "norm to parody, from the psychology of the characters to . . . the consciousness of the book" (*Odyssey of Style*, 14). Riquelme holds a similar view. Speaking of the episodes in the second half of *Ulysses*, he states: "By means of parody, Joyce extends and intensifies the debunking of style that has already been taking place" and "sharply differentiates the styles in the latter half [of *Ulysses*] from the earlier ones" (*Teller and Tale*, 208).

26. Heath, "Ambiviolences," 42.

27. McGee, *Paperspace*, 89, 95.

28. This conception of postmodern discourse as narcissistic is worked out extensively in Hutcheon's *Narcissistic Narrative*.

29. Bhabha, *Location of Culture*, 108, 86. For a discussion of Bhabha's theory of colonial discourse, see 66–84.

30. Ibid., 112, 114, 120. Parry has noted that hybridity does not produce "a copy of the colonialist original, but a qualitatively different thing-in-itself"; what she calls exorbitation occurs "when the scenario written by colonialism is given a performance by the native that estranges and undermines the colonialist script" ("Problems in Current Theories," 43–4).

31. Adorno, *Negative Dialectics*, 182.

32. Spivak, "Can the Subaltern Speak?" 294.

33. Bhabha, *Location of Culture*, 132.

34. Richards, *Commodity Culture*, 206, 216–17. See also Ochoa, "Advertising Narcissism."

35. Leonard, "The Virgin Mary and the Urge in Gerty," 4–5.

36. Ibid., 4; Richards, *Commodity Culture*, 217.

37. McGee, *Paperspace*, 90, 92.

38. Sunder Rajan, *Real and Imagined Women*, 130.

39. Spivak, "Can the Subaltern Speak?" 295.

40. Spivak, "Poststructuralism," 222. On the problem of the production of a specifically Third World Woman as a singular monolithic subject in feminist scholarship, see Spivak, "Can the Subaltern Speak?" 296, and Mohanty, "Under Western Eyes." Richards seems to engage in this kind of theoretical production when he refers to Gerty MacDowell, near the end of his account, as a "third-world consumer gravitating in the orbit of the first-world manufacture" (*Commodity Culture*, 247). I say "seems" because Richards is otherwise careful to establish the specifically Irish nature of Gerty as a "common reader" of advertisements (see 222, 238).

41. Suleri, "Woman Skin Deep," 760, 762.

42. Bhabha, "Remembering Fanon," 117.

43. Giddens, *Modernity and Self-Identity*, 52.

44. Ibid., 54.

45. Butler, "Contingent Foundations," 12.

46. Senn, "Nausicaa," 295.

47. Peake, *James Joyce*, 243, 245.

48. Norris, "Modernism, Myth, and Desire," 39.

49. McGee, *Paperspace*, 90.

50. Law, "'Pity They Can't See Themselves,'" 220.

51. Ibid., 237. On orientalism, see 235–37. Said distinguishes between latent and manifest orientalism. The former is "an almost unconscious (and certainly an untouchable) positivity" in basic assumptions about the Orient—"its eccentricity, its backwardness, its silent indifference, its feminine penetrability, its supine malleability"—while the latter consists of "the various stated views about Oriental society, languages, literatures, history, sociology, and so forth" (*Orientalism*, 206). Developments in the latter frequently go forward without change in the former. See also 222–24.

52. On Joyce's parody of sentimental romance novels, see French, *The Book as World*, 157–58; Goldberg, *The Classical Temper*, 141; K. Lawrence, *Odyssey of Style*, 119–22; Peake, *James Joyce*, 245; Riquelme, *Teller and Tale*, 208. The presence of a specific antecedent text has led some critics, like Karen Lawrence, to argue that "Nausicaa" exhibits an "obvious stable irony" that "narrows the scope of the parody" deployed elsewhere in *Ulysses* (*Odyssey of Style*, 122).

53. Baym, introduction, x–xi. Richards, *Commodity Culture*, 296n6, cites evidence of the popularity in England in 1904 of Cummins's novel, and presumably that evidence applies to Ireland. In some ways *The Lamplighter* is more "British" than American. Partly this a structural effect. For example, Baym draws attention to the British sources for many of Cummins's epigraphs and links *The Lamplighter* to a British tradition of moral and ethical development, particularly as it applies to women. See appendix "The Epigraphs" in Cummins, *The Lamplighter*, 423–33.

54. Bauermeister, "Reconsidering the Recipes," 23–25.

55. Cummins, *The Lamplighter*, 73.

56. See Miles, *Social Mobility*, chap. 7, "Marriage Markets and Women's Role."

57. Devlin, "The Romance Heroine Exposed," 395.

58. Cummins, *The Lamplighter*, 258, 267.

59. Ibid., 266.

60. Here I would have to disagree with Law's conclusion that while Bloom experiments with self-objectification, "Gerty conceives of self-objectification as a goal" ("'Pity They Can't See Themselves,'" 226). In his view, Gerty's desire is, finally, contained and domesticated by the patriarchal context in which it arises. But this conclusion effectively negates the other possibility Law himself suggests when he poses the question of the relationship between sight and touch in Gerty's erotic fantasies and suggests that she is "trying to inhabit a new subjective space." While I take Law's general point, that Gerty's desire is uncertain, his conclusion—based on a distinction that he admits may be a "transparent Bloomian fantasy" (225–26)—would disallow this "new subjective space," which we could identify as the space of an immanent critique of socially pragmatic Bildung.

61. Derrida, *Of Grammatology*, 167.

62. Ibid., 167.

63. Ibid., 144–45.

64. Adorno, *Negative Dialectics*, 219. All of pt. 3, chap. 1 ("Freedom"), is relevant to this point.

65. Ibid., 222.

66. Senn, "Nausicaa," 292. Other critics have noted the parallel between "Proteus" and "Nausicaa"; see, for example, Groden, *"Ulysses" in Progress*, 45; Kenner, *Ulysses*, 100–101, 104–6.

67. On the relationship between *Portrait* and "Nausicaa," see Kenner, *Ulysses*, 104–6; Maddox, *Assault upon Character*, 79–83; Senn, "Nausicaa," 284–86; C. Smith, "Twilight in Dublin."

68. For an analysis of Bloom's voyeurism and "cinematic spectacle," see Sicker, "'Alone in the Hiding Twilight.'"

69. Bhabha, *Location of Culture*, 112–13.

70. Abel, Hirsch, and Langland, *The Voyage In*, 10–11.

71. Ibid., 11–12.

72. Ibid., 12.

73. Hirsch, "Spiritual *Bildung*," 26, 32–33.

74. Ibid., 27.

75. Fraiman, *Unbecoming Women*, 12–13. See also L. Ellis, *Appearing to Diminish*.

76. On the auto/biographical and confessional trends, including "life writing," see Donnell and Polkey, *Representing Lives*; S. Smith, *Subjectivity, Identity, and the Body*; Smith and Watson, *De/Colonizing the Subject*.

77. Hirsch notes that the male heroes of Künstlerromane find a solution similar to what female heroes find in their experiences of spiritual Bildung: "Similarly dissatisfied

and led to withdraw into the inner life, [these] male heroes find a solution that saves them from the heroines' death, the solution of art which is virtually unavailable to the young woman in the nineteenth-century novel. The story of female spiritual *Bildung* is the story of the potential artist who fails to make it" ("Spiritual *Bildung*," 28).

78. Friedman, "Scenes of Reading," 105.

79. The difficulties Woolf experienced writing *The Voyage Out*, specifically the difficulties of critiquing a patriarchal culture and of creating a female character whose developmental process would not succumb to the lure of marriage, testify to women's struggle against and within the tradition of the Bildungsroman. On the composition of *The Voyage Out*, see DeSalvo, *Virginia Woolf's First Voyage*, and Friedman, "Spatialization," 119–34.

80. To be fair, both Hardy and Lawrence do present young women in a more progressive light than did the male authors of nineteenth-century Bildungsromane, but the experience of these women remains subordinated to that of the young men whom they persist in serving in largely instrumental capacities.

81. Paul, *Victorian Heritage*, 53.

82. DuPlessis, *Writing beyond the Ending*, 47. See also Cooley, "'The Medicine She Trusted To,'" and P. Smith, "'The Things People Don't Say,'" 138–39.

83. P. Smith, "'The Things People Don't Say,'" 128–29. DeKoven calls *The Voyage Out* a "female bildungsroman in which the young protagonist cannot pass alive the obstacle of marriage in a patriarchal culture" (*Rich and Strange*, 85). Ruotolo concurs, echoing an argument common among critics of modernist literature: "Reversing the usual format of the *Bildungsroman*, Woolf offers a heroine who will not grow into the world as it is constituted" (*The Interrupted Moment*, 21). For Friedman, the Bildungsroman represents a point on a "vertical axis" of generic conventions invoked in Woolf's text ("Spatialization," 109, 121, 123).

84. Friedman makes the provocative point that *The Voyage Out* "simultaneously narrates a failed *Bildung* for its protagonist and inscribes a successful *Bildung* for its author" ("Spatialization," 109). Successful Bildung, for Woolf herself, is a "'writing cure' in which the transferential scene of writing gradually constitutes a new subjectivity" (127). See also Friedman, "Scenes of Reading," 115–17.

85. Woolf, *Three Guineas*, 38. See Barrett, "Unmasking Lesbian Passion," 146–47, for a discussion of the link between the feminist movement and Woolf's rejection of marriage.

86. DuPlessis, *Writing beyond the Ending*, 50.

87. Henke, "De/Colonizing the Subject," 103.

88. Myers, "Victorian Science," 300. Myers suggests that Woolf critiques "a scientific method centered on controlled observation, classification, and inductive reasoning" (298), largely because it medicalizes and regulates female sexuality, containing it in the domestic sphere and in the institution of marriage.

89. Friedman, "Scenes of Reading," 105. Froula, in "Out of the Chrysalis," makes a

similar argument about the role of education in Rachel's narrative of initiation. For both Friedman and Froula, Bildung designates not the classical concept of Goethe and Humboldt but rather a conception of awakening and initiation that structures the female Bildungsroman. Like many other critics of *The Voyage Out*, both also lay heavy stress on the correspondences between the text and Woolf's life.

90. All parenthetical references to *The Voyage Out* (*VO*) are to the Oxford University Press edition (1992), edited by Lorna Sage.

91. Friedman, "Scenes of Reading," 118.

92. DuPlessis, *Writing beyond the Ending*, 49. Paul argues that *The Voyage Out* remains connected in significant ways to the Victorian novel tradition through theme, technique, and its orientation toward social criticism (*Victorian Heritage*, 53–77).

93. McCombe, "No 'Tempest' in a Teapot," 284.

94. Adorno, *Negative Dialectics*, 277.

95. Ruotolo believes that Rachel's discontent and intellectual inconsistency are a "critique of culture" of which those around her, especially Helen, are unaware (*The Interrupted Moment*, 23).

96. Bradshaw, "Vicious Circles," 184.

97. All parenthetical references to *Mrs. Dalloway* (*MD*) are to the Harcourt Brace Jovanovich edition (1990).

98. Nicholson, *British Idealists*, 198, qtd. in Bradshaw, "Vicious Circles," 183.

99. Ibid., 190. There is a growing body of work that sees *The Voyage Out* in terms of social critique. Of particular importance are those that see Woolf as critical of modern science (Myers, "Victorian Science") and of colonialism (DeKoven, *Rich and Strange*, and McCombe, "No 'Tempest' in a Teapot").

100. DuPlessis, *Writing beyond the Ending*, 51.

101. See Peterson, "Harriet Martineau's *Household Education*."

102. DeKoven, *Rich and Strange*, 132. DeKoven goes on to say that "*The Voyage Out* is of course a *künstlerroman*."

103. DuPlessis, *Writing beyond the Ending*, 49.

104. Froula, "Out of the Chrysalis," 76, cites this passage from Quentin Bell's biography *Virginia Woolf*, 1:205, and notes that the name of Rachel's father's ship, *Euphrosyne*, was also the title of "a collection of uninspiring poetry" produced by her brother Thoby and his Cambridge friends (89n18).

105. See, for example, the descriptions of Hirst at the university (*VO* 174–75, 230–31), of Ridley's book-strewn study (*VO* 191), and of Miss Allan hard at work "correcting essays upon English literature," her writing table "piled with manuscript" and "heaps of dark library books" (*VO* 200, 294).

106. For Froula, Rachel prepares to "*writ[e]* into history what Gibbon . . . has left out: among other things, women's history" ("Out of the Chrysalis," 78).

107. Cooley, "'The Medicine She Trusted To,'" 71.

108. DeKoven, *Rich and Strange*, 134.

109. Hirsch, "Spiritual *Bildung*," 26, 31.

110. Woolf, *A Room of One's Own*, 6.

111. Most critics agree that Woolf toned down the erotic action and tone of the passage as she moved through successive drafts, though they do not always agree on the value, for literary or social criticism, of Woolf's revisions. See, for example, DeKoven, *Rich and Strange*, 129–31; Friedman, "Spatialization," 128–32; Froula, "Out of the Chrysalis," 79–81; P. Smith, "'The Things People Don't Say.'"

112. DeKoven, *Rich and Strange*, 134. DeKoven alludes to the feminist practice of Julia Kristeva and Luce Irigaray. See also Low, "'Listen and Save.'"

113. DuPlessis, *Writing beyond the Ending*, 52.

114. Myers, "Victorian Science," 302.

115. Friedman, "Scenes of Reading," 121. See also DeKoven, who reads the death scene in terms of an "ominous" pre-oedipal imaginary and a passive, defeated return to a womblike "death vault" (*Rich and Strange*, 137–38).

116. Abel, *Fictions of Psychoanalysis*, 36.

117. On Woolf's critique of realism, see "Mr. Bennett and Mrs. Brown" and "Modern Fiction."

118. Abel, *Fictions of Psychoanalysis*, xvi.

119. Woolf, *Writer's Diary*, 59. On the relation of this "tunneling" technique to narrative, see J. H. Miller, "Virginia Woolf's All Souls' Day."

120. DuPlessis, *Writing beyond the Ending*, 60. See Childs, who argues that "Woolf tunnels in order to gain access to the caves in which her characters hide—betraying the same fear of darkness that Foucault finds in the Gothic novel" (*Modernism and Eugenics*, 55); Childs then quotes Foucault: "imaginary spaces" (e.g., "mountains and forests, caves, ruined castles and terrifyingly dark and silent convents") that resemble "the negative of the transparency and visibility which it is aimed to establish" ("The Eye of Power," in *Power and Knowledge*, 154).

121. J. H. Miller, *Fiction and Repetition*, 178, 181.

122. Ibid., 183, 185, 198.

123. Ibid., 192.

124. Wilde, "Soul of Man," 285.

125. Moretti, *Way of the World*, 208.

126. Rosenman, *The Invisible Presence*, 91.

127. For Paul, the ambivalent unity of such descriptions is suggested by Woolf's innovative use of the semicolon, which "separates more than a comma and joins more than a period"; "in her vast collation of thoughts and external phenomena, her semicolon simultaneously emphasizes the unity of life and the quidditas of all the things that comprise it" (*Victorian Heritage*, 148). It is characteristic of the modernist Bildungsroman to duplicate at the level of style the critique of dialectical harmonies that we see at the thematic and narrative levels.

128. Ibid., 146.

129. Wilde, *Miscellanies*, 289.

130. Ruotolo, *The Interrupted Moment*, 111.

131. On "mediated routes" to social and cultural advancement, see Miles, *Social Mobility*, esp. chap. 8.

132. Goethe, *Wilhelm Meister*, 277.

133. On the catastrophic nature of marriage for men like Septimus, see Barrett, "Unmasking Lesbian Passion," 152–53.

134. Barrett argues: "The novel's scathing depictions of heterosexuality in marriage demonstrate Woolf's lesbian-feminist critique of this institution" (ibid., 147).

135. Woolf, *A Room of One's Own*, 60.

136. Irigaray, *Speculum*, 165, 136.

137. Fuss, "'Essentially Speaking,'" 76.

138. Irigaray, *Speculum*, 181.

139. Adorno, *Negative Dialectics*, 149.

140. Ibid., 149, 193.

141. Bowlby, *Feminist Destinations*, 89, 96.

142. Abel, *Fictions of Psychoanalysis*, 32. As Clarissa uncovers "a diamond, something infinitely precious," a "radiance burnt through, the revelation, the religious feeling!—when old Joseph and Peter faced them: 'Star-gazing?' said Peter" (35–36).

143. DuPlessis, *Writing beyond the Ending*, 58.

144. Bowlby, *Feminist Destinations*, 93.

145. Ibid., 87.

146. Ibid., 86.

147. Ibid., 83.

148. Ibid., 87.

149. Abel, *Fictions of Psychoanalysis*, 36.

150. Ibid., 32.

151. Ibid., 38–39. Rosenman makes a similar point: "As Clarissa's double, Septimus acts out in exaggerated form her sense of unity and fusion, bringing to the surface the hidden subtext of fatal regression which, like the problem of female immanence, has been carefully displaced" (*The Invisible Presence*, 90).

152. Abel, *Fictions of Psychoanalysis*, 40.

153. Woolf, *Letters*, 3:189.

154. See, for example, Barrett, "Unmasking Lesbian Passion," 152–54; Boone, *Libidinal Currents*, 193; DuPlessis, *Writing beyond the Ending*, 57–58; Ferrer, *Madness of Language*, 8–39; Paul, *Victorian Heritage*, 139–42; Rosenman, *The Invisible Presence*, 89–91; Whiteley, *Knowledge and Experimental Realism*, 174–79.

155. See Barrett, "Unmasking Lesbian Passion," 159–61, and Boone, *Libidinal Currents*, 193–98.

156. Ferrer, *Madness of Language*, 13. Ferrer discusses Woolf's autobiographical *Mo-*

ments of Being and the repeated images of the self in a mirror, especially its horrifying and inhuman double; see 14–16.

157. Goethe, *Wilhelm Meister*, 309.

158. On the link between Bradshaw's theories and the eugenics movement, see Childs, *Modernism and Eugenics*, 51–6.

159. Rosenman notes that in light of Septimus's suicide, his "act of absolute integrity," Clarissa's parties and "the decorative, accommodating femininity which they express, seem impotent." She goes on to suggest that the "myth of femininity" "rescues and restores her when she contemplates [Mrs. Hilbery,] the old woman next door" (89). The same myth also rescues and restores the "decorative" aesthetics that contribute so much to Clarissa's sense of beauty in the world.

160. Adorno, *Negative Dialectics*, 157.

CONCLUSION: THE JANUS FACE OF MODERNISM

1. Adorno, *Negative Dialectics*, 219.

2. See, for example, "Trying to Understand *Endgame*" and the essays in *Prisms*.

3. Gellner, *Nations and Nationalism*, 37–38.

4. Adorno, *Negative Dialectics*, 160–61.

5. Ibid., 277.

6. Adorno links such possibilities to the ineluctable reality of objects: "The means employed in negative dialectics for the penetration of its hardened objects is possibility—the possibility of which their reality has cheated the objects and which is nonetheless visible in each one" (ibid., 52).

7. Humboldt, *Limits of State Action*, 37.

8. See Moretti, *Way of the World*, introduction, for a discussion of the idea of youth as the sign of modernity.

Works Cited

Abel, Elizabeth. *Virginia Woolf and the Fictions of Psychoanalysis*. Chicago: University of Chicago Press, 1989.

Abel, Elizabeth, Marianne Hirsch, and Elizabeth Langland, eds. *The Voyage In: Fictions of Female Development*. Hanover, N.H.: University Press of New England, 1983.

Adams, J.R.R. "Swine-Tax and Eat-Him-All-Magee: The Hedge Schools and Popular Education in Ireland." In *Irish Popular Culture, 1650–1850*, edited by James S. Donnelly Jr. and Kerby A. Miller, 97–117. Dublin: Irish Academic Press, 1998.

Adorno, Theodor W. "Cultural Criticism and Society." In *Prisms*, 17–34.

———. "The Essay as Form." In *The Adorno Reader*, edited by Brian O'Connor, 91–111. Oxford: Blackwell, 2000.

———. *Negative Dialectics*. Translated by E. B. Ashton. New York: Seabury Press, 1973.

———. *Prisms*. Translated by Samuel and Shierry Weber. Cambridge, Mass.: MIT Press, 1981.

———. "Trying to Understand *Endgame*." In *Notes to Literature*, translated by Sheirry Weber Nicholsen, edited by Rolf Tiedemann, 1:241–76. New York: Columbia University Press, 1991.

Akenson, Donald H. *The Irish Education Experiment: The National System of Education in the Nineteenth Century*. London: Routledge and Kegan Paul, 1970.

Alden, Patricia. *Social Mobility in the English Bildungsroman: Gissing, Hardy, Bennett, and Lawrence*. Ann Arbor, Mich.: UMI Research Press, 1986.

Allen, Dennis W. *Sexuality in Victorian Fiction*. Norman: University of Oklahoma Press, 1993.

Althusser, Louis. "Ideology and Ideological State Apparatuses." In *Lenin and Philosophy, and Other Essays*, translated by Ben Brewster, 127–86. New York: Monthly Review Press, 1971.

Altieri, Charles. "Organic-Humanist Models in Some English Bildungsroman." *Journal of General Education* 23 (1971): 220–39.

Amrine, Frederick. "Rethinking the Bildungsroman." *Michigan Germanic Studies* 13.2 (1987): 119–39.

Arnds, Peter. "The Boy with the Old Face: Thomas Hardy's Antibildungsroman *Jude the Obscure* and Wilhelm Raabe's Bildungsroman *Prinzessin Fisch*." *German Studies Review* 21.2 (1998): 221–40.

Arnold, Matthew. *Complete Prose Works*. Edited by R. H. Super. 11 vols. Ann Arbor: University of Michigan Press, 1960–77.

———. "The Function of Criticism at the Present Time." In *Complete Prose Works*, 3:258–85.

———. *Schools and Universities on the Continent*. Vol. 4 of *Complete Prose Works*.

Ashby, Eric. "The Future of the Nineteenth Century Idea of a University." *Minerva* 6.1 (1967): 3–17.

Attridge, Derek, and Marjorie Howes, eds. *Semicolonial Joyce*. Cambridge: Cambridge University Press, 2000.

Bakhtin, M. M. "The *Bildungsroman* and Its Significance in the History of Realism (Toward a Historical Typology of the Novel)." In *Speech Genres and Other Late Essays*, translated by Vern W. McGee, edited by Caryl Emerson and Michael Holquist, 10–59. Austin: University of Texas Press, 1986.

———. *The Dialogic Imagination: Four Essays*. Translated by Caryl Emerson and Michael Holquist. Edited by Michael Holquist. Austin: University of Texas Press, 1981.

Balzac, Honoré de. *Lost Illusions*. 1837–43. Translated by Herbert J. Hunt. Harmondsworth, U.K.: Penguin, 1971.

Barr, Colin. "University Education, History, and the Hierarchy." In *Reading Irish Histories: Texts, Contexts, and Memory in Modern Ireland*, edited by Lawrence W. McBride, 62–79. Dublin: Four Courts Press, 2003.

Barrett, Eileen. "Unmasking Lesbian Passion: The Inverted World of *Mrs. Dalloway*." In Barrett and Cramer, *Virginia Woolf: Lesbian Readings*, 146–64.

Barrett, Eileen, and Patricia Cramer. *Virginia Woolf: Lesbian Readings*. New York: New York University Press, 1997.

Bashford, Bruce. *Oscar Wilde: The Critic as Humanist*. Madison, N.J.: Fairleigh Dickinson University Press, 1999.

Baudrillard, Jean. *For a Critique of the Political Economy of the Sign*. Translated by Charles Levin. St. Louis, Mo.: Telos Press, 1981.

Bauermeister, Erica R. "*The Lamplighter*, *The Wide, Wide World*, and *Hope Leslie*: Reconsidering the Recipes for Nineteenth-Century American Women's Novels." *Legacy* 8.1 (1991): 17–28.

Baym, Nina. Introduction to Cummins, *The Lamplighter*, ix–xxxi.

Beards, Richard D. "*Sons and Lovers* as Bildungsroman." *College Literature* 1 (1974): 204–17.

Bedient, Calvin. *Architects of the Self: George Eliot, D. H. Lawrence, and E. M. Forster*. Berkeley and Los Angeles: University of California Press, 1972.

Beebe, Maurice. *Ivory Towers and Sacred Founts: The Artist as Hero in Fiction from Goethe to Joyce*. New York: New York University Press, 1964.

———. "Joyce and Stephen Dedalus: The Problem of Autobiography." In *A James Joyce Miscellany*, edited by Marvin Magalaner, 2nd ser., 67–77. Carbondale: Southern Illinois University Press, 1959.

Behan, David. "Locke on Persons and Personal Identity." *Canadian Journal of Philosophy* 9 (1979): 53–75.

Bell, Michael. *D. H. Lawrence: Language and Being*. Cambridge: Cambridge University Press, 1992.

Bell, Quentin. *Virginia Woolf: A Biography.* 2 vols. London: Hogarth Press, 1972.

Bew, Paul. *Land and the National Question in Ireland, 1858–82.* Atlantic Highlands, N.J.: Humanities Press, 1979.

Bhabha, Homi K. *The Location of Culture.* London: Routledge, 1994.

———. "Remembering Fanon: Self, Psyche, and the Colonial Condition." In *Colonial Discourse and Post-Colonial Theory,* edited by Patrick Williams and Laura Chrisman, 112–23. New York: Harvester Wheatsheaf, 1993.

Blackall, Eric A. Afterword to Goethe, *Wilhelm Meister's Apprenticeship,* 381–87.

Blackbourn, David. *History of Germany, 1780–1918: The Long Nineteenth Century.* 2nd ed. Oxford: Blackwell, 2003.

Blake, Kathleen. "Sue Bridehead: 'The Woman of the Feminist Movement.'" *Studies in English Literature, 1500–1900* 18.4 (1978): 703–26.

Bloom, Harold, ed. *Thomas Hardy's "Jude the Obscure."* New York: Chelsea House, 1987.

Boone, Joseph Allen. *Libidinal Currents: Sexuality and the Shaping of Modernism.* Chicago: University of Chicago Press, 1998.

Botting, Fred. *Gothic.* London: Routledge, 1996.

Boumelha, Penny. "'A Complicated Position for a Woman': *The Hand of Ethelberta.*" In Higonnet, *Sense of Sex,* 242–59.

———. *Thomas Hardy and Women: Sexual Ideology and Narrative Form.* Totowa, N.J.: Barnes and Noble, 1982.

Bourke, Angela. "Hunting Out the Fairies: E. F. Benson, Oscar Wilde, and the Burning of Bridget Cleary." In McCormack, *Wilde the Irishman,* 36–46.

Bowlby, Rachel. *Virginia Woolf: Feminist Destinations.* New York: Blackwell, 1988.

Bradshaw, David. "Vicious Circles: Hegel, Bosanquet, and *The Voyage Out.*" In *Virginia Woolf and the Arts,* edited by Diane F. Gillespie and Leslie K. Hankins, 183–90. New York: Pace University Press, 1997.

Brivic, Sheldon. "Gender Dissonance, Hysteria, and History in James Joyce's *A Portrait of the Artist as a Young Man.*" *James Joyce Quarterly* 39.3 (2002): 457–76.

Brontë, Charlotte. *Jane Eyre.* 1847. Edited by Jane Jack and Margaret Smith. Rev. ed. Oxford: Oxford University Press, 1975.

Brown, Julia Prewitt. *Cosmopolitan Criticism: Oscar Wilde's Philosophy of Art.* Charlottesville: University Press of Virginia, 1997.

Brown, Wendy. *Politics Out of History.* Princeton: Princeton University Press, 2001.

Bruford, W. H. *Culture and Society in Classical Weimar, 1775–1806.* London: Cambridge University Press, 1962.

———. *The German Tradition of Self-Cultivation: "Bildung" from Humboldt to Thomas Mann.* London: Cambridge University Press, 1975.

Buckley, Jerome H. "Autobiography in the English Bildungsroman." In *The Interpretation of Narrative: Theory and Practice,* edited by Morton W. Bloomfield, 93–104. Cambridge, Mass.: Harvard University Press, 1970.

————. *Season of Youth: The Bildungsroman from Dickens to Golding*. Cambridge, Mass.: Harvard University Press, 1974.

Budgen, Frank. *James Joyce and the Making of "Ulysses."* 1934. Bloomington: Indiana University Press, 1960.

Bullock, Alan. *The Humanist Tradition in the West*. London: Thames and Hudson, 1985.

Butler, Judith. "Contingent Foundations: Feminism and the Question of 'Postmodernism.'" In *Feminists Theorize the Political*, edited by Judith Butler and Joan W. Scott, 3–21. New York: Routledge, 1992.

Carlyle, Thomas. *Past and Present*. 1843. Edited by Richard D. Altick. New York: New York University Press, 1977.

Cascardi, Anthony J. *Consequences of Enlightenment*. Cambridge: Cambridge University Press, 1999.

Castle, Gregory. "Ambivalence and Ascendancy in Bram Stoker's *Dracula*." In *Dracula*, by Bram Stoker, edited by John Paul Riquelme, 518–37. Case Studies in Contemporary Criticism. Boston: Bedford Books, 2002.

————. *Modernism and the Celtic Revival*. Cambridge: Cambridge University Press, 2001.

[Chambers, Jessie]. *D. H. Lawrence: A Personal Record*. By "E.T." 1935. Reprint, Cambridge: Cambridge University Press, 1980.

Chaudhuri, Amit. *D. H. Lawrence and "Difference."* Oxford: Clarendon Press, 2003.

Childs, Donald J. *Modernism and Eugenics: Woolf, Eliot, Yeats, and the Culture of Degeneration*. Cambridge: Cambridge University Press, 2001.

Church, Margaret. "The Adolescent Point of View toward Women in Joyce's *A Portrait of the Artist as a Young Man*." In *Irish Renaissance Annual*, edited by Zack Bowen, 2:158–65. Newark: University of Delaware Press, 1981.

Cohen, Ed. "Writing Gone Wilde: Homoerotic Desire in the Closet of Representation." In *Critical Essays on Oscar Wilde*, edited by Regenia Gagnier, 68–87. New York: G. K. Hall, 1991.

Cohen, Monica F. *Professional Domesticity in the Victorian Novel: Women, Work, and Home*. Cambridge: Cambridge University Press, 1998.

Cooley, Elizabeth. "'The Medicine She Trusted To': Women, Friendship, and Communication in *The Voyage Out* and *Night and Day*." In *Communication and Women's Friendships: Parallels and Intersections in Literature and Life*, edited by Janet Doubler Ward and JoAnna Stephens Mink, 65–76. Bowling Green, Ohio: Popular Press, 1993.

Corcoran, Timothy. *State Policy in Irish Education, A.D. 1536 to 1816, Exemplified in Documents Collected for Lectures to Post-graduate Classes*. Dublin: Fallon Brothers; London: Longmans, Green, 1916.

Cowan, James C. *D. H. Lawrence: Self and Sexuality*. Columbus: Ohio State University Press, 2002.

Cowan, Marianne. Introduction to *Humanist Without Portfolio: An Anthology of the Writings of Wilhelm von Humboldt*, 1–25. Detroit: Wayne State University Press, 1963.

Cross, Richard K. *Flaubert and Joyce: The Rite of Fiction*. Princeton: Princeton University Press, 1971.

Crotty, Raymond. *Ireland in Crisis: A Study in Capitalist Colonial Undevelopment*. Dingle, Ire.; Dover, N.H.: Brandon, 1986.

Crump, Ian. "Refining Himself out of Existence: The Evolution of Joyce's Aesthetic Theory and the Drafts of *A Portrait*." In *Joyce in Context*, edited by Vincent J. Cheng and Timothy Martin, 223–40. Cambridge: Cambridge University Press, 1992.

Cummins, Maria Susanna. *The Lamplighter*. 1854. Edited by Nina Baym. New Brunswick, N.J.: Rutgers University Press, 1988.

Daleski, H. M. *Thomas Hardy and Paradoxes of Love*. Columbia: University of Missouri Press, 1997.

Daly, Mary, and David Dickson, eds. *The Origins of Popular Literacy in Ireland: Language Change and Educational Development, 1700–1920*. Dublin: Modern Irish History, Trinity College, 1990.

Danson, Lawrence. *Wilde's Intentions: The Artist in His Criticism*. New York: Oxford University Press, 1997.

Danto, Arthur C. *Narration and Knowledge*. New York: Columbia University Press, 1985.

Davis, Alex. *A Broken Line: Denis Devlin and Irish Poetic Modernism*. Dublin: University College Dublin Press, 2000.

Davis, Richard. *The Young Ireland Movement*. Dublin: Gill and Macmillan, 1987.

Davis, William A. *Thomas Hardy and the Law: Legal Presences in Hardy's Life and Fiction*. Newark: University of Delaware Press, 2003.

Deane, Seamus. *Celtic Revivals: Essays in Modern Irish Literature, 1880–1980*. Winston-Salem, N.C.: Wake Forest University Press, 1987.

———. Introduction to *A Portrait of the Artist as a Young Man*, by James Joyce, vii–xliii. New York: Penguin, 1993.

———. *Strange Country: Modernity and Nationhood in Irish Writing since 1790*. New York: Oxford University Press, 1997.

DeKoven, Marianne. *Rich and Strange: Gender, History, Modernism*. Princeton: Princeton University Press, 1991.

DeLaura, David J. "Arnold and Goethe: The One on the Intellectual Throne." In *Victorian Literature and Society: Essays Presented to Richard D. Altick*, edited by James R. Kincaid and Albert J. Kuhn, 197–224. Columbus: Ohio State University Press, 1984.

———. *Hebrew and Hellene in Victorian England: Newman, Arnold, and Pater*. Austin: University of Texas Press, 1969.

———. "Heroic Egotism: Goethe and the Fortunes of *Bildung* in Victorian England." In *Johann Wolfgang von Goethe: One Hundred and Fifty Years of Continuing Vitality*, edited by Ulrich Goebel and Wolodymyr T. Zyla, 41–60. Lubbock: Texas Tech University Press, 1984.

———. "Matthew Arnold and Culture: The History and the Prehistory." In *Matthew Ar-*

nold in His Time and Ours: Centenary Essays, edited by Clinton Machann and Forrest D. Burt, 1–16. Charlottesville: University Press of Virginia, 1988.

Dentith, Simon. *Society and Cultural Forms in Nineteenth Century England*. New York: St. Martin's Press, 1998.

Derrida, Jacques. *Of Grammatology*. Translated by Gayatri Chakravorty Spivak. Baltimore: Johns Hopkins University Press, 1976.

DeSalvo, Louise A. *Virginia Woolf's First Voyage: A Novel in the Making*. Totowa, N.J.: Rowman and Littlefield, 1980.

Devlin, Kimberly. "The Romance Heroine Exposed: 'Nausicaa' and *The Lamplighter*." *James Joyce Quarterly* 22 (1985): 383–96.

Dilthey, Wilhelm. "Friedrich Hölderlin (1910)." Translated by Joseph Ross. In *Poetry and Experience*, vol. 5 of *Selected Works*, edited by Rudolf A. Makkreel and Frithjof Rodi, 303–83. Princeton: Princeton University Press, 1985.

Dollimore, Jonathan. *Sexual Dissidence: Augustine to Wilde, Freud to Foucault*. New York: Oxford University Press, 1991.

Donnell, Alison, and Pauline Polkey, eds. *Representing Lives: Women and Auto/Biography*. New York: St. Martin's Press, 2000.

Dougill, John. *Oxford in English Literature: The Making, and Undoing, of "The English Athens."* Ann Arbor: University of Michigan Press, 1998.

Dowling, Linda. *Hellenism and Homosexuality in Victorian Oxford*. Ithaca: Cornell University Press, 1994.

DuPlessis, Rachel Blau. *Writing beyond the Ending: Narrative Strategies of Twentieth-Century Women Writers*. Bloomington: Indiana University Press, 1985.

Eagleton, Terry. *Heathcliff and the Great Hunger: Studies in Irish Culture*. London: Verso, 1995.

————. *The Ideology of the Aesthetic*. Oxford: Blackwell, 1990.

————. "The Limits of Art." In Bloom, *Hardy's "Jude,"* 61–71.

Edwards, Owen Dudley. "Impressions of an Irish Sphinx." In McCormack, *Wilde the Irishman*, 47–70.

Eliot, George. *Middlemarch*. 1871–72. Edited by Gordon S. Haight. Boston: Houghton Mifflin, 1956.

Eliot, T. S. *Selected Essays, 1917–1932*. New York: Harcourt, Brace, 1932.

Ellis, David. *D. H. Lawrence: Dying Game, 1922–30*. Cambridge: Cambridge University Press, 1998.

Ellis, Lorna. *Appearing to Diminish: Female Development and the British Bildungsroman, 1750–1850*. Lewisburg, Pa.: Bucknell University Press, 1999.

Ellmann, Maud. "Disremembering Dedalus: 'A Portrait of an Artist as a Young Man.'" In *Untying the Text: A Post-Structuralist Reader*, edited by Robert Young, 189–206. Boston: Routledge and Kegan Paul, 1981.

Ellmann, Richard. *Oscar Wilde*. New York: Knopf, 1988.

Fachinelli, Elvio. "Lacan and the Thing." *Journal of European Psychoanalysis*, no. 3–4 (Spring 1996–Winter 1997). www.psychomedia.it/jep/number3-4/fachinelli. htm.

Fanon, Frantz. *Black Skin, White Masks*. Translated by Charles Lam Markmann. New York: Grove, 1967.

———. *The Wretched of the Earth*. Translated by Constance Farrington. New York: Grove, 1963.

Federico, Annette. *Masculine Identity in Hardy and Gissing*. Rutherford, N.J.: Fairleigh Dickinson University Press, 1991.

Fernihough, Anne. *D. H. Lawrence: Aesthetics and Ideology*. Oxford: Clarendon Press, 1993.

Ferrer, Daniel. *Virginia Woolf and the Madness of Language*. Translated by Geoffrey Bennington and Rachel Bowlby. London: Routledge, 1990.

Flaubert, Gustave. *Sentimental Education*. 1869. Translated by Robert Baldick. Harmondsworth, U.K.: Penguin, 1964.

Flexner, Abraham. *Universities: American, English, German*. 1930. New York: Columbia University, Teachers College Press, 1967.

Forster, E. M. *Howards End*. 1910. Edited by Paul B. Armstrong. New York: Norton, 1998.

Foucault, Michel. *The History of Sexuality*. Vol. 1, *An Introduction*. Translated by Robert Hurley. New York: Pantheon, 1978.

———. *The Order of Things: An Archaeology of the Human Sciences*. New York: Pantheon, 1971.

———. *Power/Knowledge: Selected Interviews and Other Writings, 1972–1977*. Edited by Colin Gordon. Translated by Colin Gordon, Leo Marshall, John Mepham, and Kate Soper. New York: Pantheon, 1980.

———. "The Subject and Power." Afterword to *Michel Foucault: Beyond Structuralism and Hermeneutics*, by Hubert L. Dreyfus and Paul Rabinow, 2nd ed., 208–26. Chicago: University of Chicago Press, 1983.

———. *Technologies of the Self: A Seminar with Michel Foucault*. Edited by Luther H. Martin, Huck Gutman, and Patrick H. Hutton. Amherst: University of Massachusetts Press, 1988.

———. "What Is Enlightenment?" In *The Foucault Reader*, edited by Paul Rabinow, 32–50. New York: Pantheon, 1984.

Fraiman, Susan. *Unbecoming Women: British Women Writers and the Novel of Development*. New York: Columbia University Press, 1993.

French, Marilyn. *The Book as World: James Joyce's "Ulysses."* Cambridge, Mass.: Harvard University Press, 1976.

Freud, Sigmund. *The Standard Edition of the Complete Psychological Works of Sigmund Freud*. Translated under the general editorship of James Strachey in collaboration with

Anna Freud, assisted by Alix Strachey and Alan Tyson. 24 vols. London: Hogarth, 1953–74.

Friedman, Susan Stanford. "(Self)Censorship and the Making of Joyce's Modernism." In *Joyce: The Return of the Repressed*, edited by Susan Stanford Friedman, 21–57. Ithaca: Cornell University Press, 1993.

———. "Spatialization, Narrative Theory, and Virginia Woolf's *The Voyage Out*." In *Ambiguous Discourse: Feminist Narratology and British Women Writers*, edited by Kathy Mezei, 109–36. Chapel Hill: University of North Carolina Press, 1996.

———. "Virginia Woolf's Pedagogical Scenes of Reading: *The Voyage Out, The Common Reader*, and her 'Common Readers.'" *Modern Fiction Studies* 38.1 (1992): 101–25.

Friel, Brian. *Translations*. London: Faber, 1981.

Froula, Christine. *Modernism's Body: Sex, Culture, and Joyce*. New York: Columbia University Press, 1996.

———. "Out of the Chrysalis: Female Initiation and Female Authority in Virginia Woolf's *The Voyage Out*." *Tulsa Studies in Women's Literature* 5.1 (1986): 63–90.

Fuss, Diana J. "'Essentially Speaking': Luce Irigaray's Language of Essence." *Hypatia* 3.3 (1988): 62–80.

Gagnier, Regenia. *Idylls of the Marketplace: Oscar Wilde and the Victorian Public*. Stanford: Stanford University Press, 1986.

Gellner, Ernest. *Nations and Nationalism*. Ithaca: Cornell University Press, 1983.

Gibson, Nigel. "Rethinking an Old Saw: Dialectical Negativity, Utopia, and *Negative Dialectic* in Adorno's Hegelian Marxism." In *Adorno: A Critical Reader*, edited by Nigel Gibson and Andrew Rubin, 257–91. Oxford: Blackwell, 2002.

Giddens, Anthony. *Modernity and Self-Identity: Self and Society in the Late Modern Age*. Stanford: Stanford University Press, 1991.

Gilbert, Sandra M., and Susan Gubar. *The Madwoman in the Attic: The Woman Writer and the Nineteenth-Century Literary Imagination*. 2nd ed. New Haven: Yale University Press, 2000.

Gillespie, Michael Patrick. *Oscar Wilde and the Poetics of Ambiguity*. Gainesville: University Press of Florida, 1996.

Giordano, Frank R., Jr. "Jude the Obscure and the Bildungsroman." *Studies in the Novel* 4 (1972): 580–91.

Gittings, Robert. *Young Thomas Hardy*. Boston: Little, Brown, 1975.

Goethe, Johann Wolfgang von. *Wilhelm Meister's Apprenticeship*. 1795–96. Edited and translated by Eric A. Blackall. Princeton: Princeton University Press, 1995.

Goldberg, S. L. *The Classical Temper: A Study of James Joyce's "Ulysses."* New York: Barnes and Noble, 1961.

Gomersall, Meg. *Working-Class Girls in Nineteenth-Century England: Life, Work, and Schooling*. New York: St. Martin's Press, 1997.

Goodlad, Lauren M. E. "Beyond the Panopticon: Victorian Britain and the Critical Imagination." *PMLA* 118 (May 2003): 539–56.

———. *Victorian Literature and the Victorian State: Character and Governance in a Liberal Society*. Baltimore: Johns Hopkins University Press, 2003.

Gosse, Edmund. Review of *Jude the Obscure*, by Thomas Hardy. *Cosmopolis*, January 1896. Reprinted in Page, *Jude*, 383–88.

Gregor, Ian. "An End and a Beginning: *Jude the Obscure.*" In Bloom, *Hardy's "Jude,"* 37–60.

Groden, Michael. *"Ulysses" in Progress*. Princeton: Princeton University Press, 1977.

Grote, Georg. *Torn Between Politics and Culture: The Gaelic League, 1893–1993*. Münster and New York: Waxmann, 1994.

Habermas, Jürgen. *Legitimation Crisis*. Translated by Thomas McCarthy. Boston: Beacon Press, 1975.

———. "Modernity versus Postmodernity." *New German Critique* 17 (Spring 1979): 3–22.

———. *The Philosophical Discourse of Modernity*. Translated by Frederick Lawrence. Cambridge, Mass.: MIT Press, 1987.

———. *Theory and Practice*. Translated by John Viertel. Boston: Beacon Press, 1973.

Hardin, James, ed. *Reflection and Action: Essays on the Bildungsroman*. Columbia: University of South Carolina Press, 1991.

Harding, James M. "The Signification of Arabella's Missile: Feminine Sexuality, Masculine Anxiety, and Revision in *Jude the Obscure.*" *Journal of Narrative Technique* 26.1 (1996): 85–111.

Hardy, Barbara. *Thomas Hardy: Imagining Imagination in Hardy's Poetry and Fiction*. London: Athlone, 2000.

Hardy, Thomas. *The Collected Letters of Thomas Hardy*. Edited by Richard Little Purdy and Michael Millgate. 7 vols. Oxford: Clarendon Press, 1978–88.

———. *Jude the Obscure*. 1895. Edited by C. H. Sisson. London: Penguin, 1978.

———. *The Life and Work of Thomas Hardy*. Edited by Michael Millgate. Athens: University of Georgia Press, 1985.

Heath, Stephen. "Ambiviolences: Notes for Reading Joyce." Translated by Isabelle Mahieu. In *Post-Structuralist Joyce: Essays from the French*, edited by Derek Attridge and Daniel Ferrer, 31–68. Cambridge: Cambridge University Press, 1984.

Hechter, Michael. *Internal Colonialism: The Celtic Fringe in British National Development, 1536–1966*. Berkeley and Los Angeles: University of California Press, 1975.

Hegel, G.W.F. *Introduction to "The Philosophy of History": With Selections from "The Philosophy of Right."* Translated by Leo Rauch. Indianapolis: Hackett, 1988.

Henke, Suzette A. "De/Colonizing the Subject in Virginia Woolf's *The Voyage Out*: Rachel Vinrace as La Mystérique." In *Virginia Woolf: Emerging Perspectives*, edited by Mark Hussey and Vara Neverow, 103–8. New York: Pace University Press, 1994.

———. *James Joyce and the Politics of Desire*. New York: Routledge, 1990.

Heyck, Thomas William. "Educational." In *A Companion to Victorian Literature and Culture*, edited by Herbert F. Tucker, 194–211. Oxford: Blackwell, 1999.

Higonnet, Margaret R., ed. *The Sense of Sex: Feminist Perspectives on Hardy*. Urbana: University of Illinois Press, 1993.

Hirsch, Marianne. "Spiritual *Bildung*: The Beautiful Soul as Paradigm." In Abel, Hirsch, and Langland, *The Voyage In*, 23–48.

Hobsbawm, E. J. *The Age of Empire, 1875–1914*. New York: Pantheon, 1987.

Holderness, Graham. *D. H. Lawrence, History, Ideology, and Fiction*. Dublin: Gill and Macmillan, 1982.

Hollis, Patricia, ed. *Class and Conflict in Nineteenth-Century England, 1815–1850*. London: Routledge and Kegan Paul, 1973.

Holmes, Colin. "A Study of D. H. Lawrence's Social Origins." In Pilditch, *Critical Response*, 41–52.

Horkheimer, Max, and Theodor W. Adorno. *Dialectic of Enlightenment*. Translated by John Cumming. New York: Continuum, 1973.

Howe, Suzanne. *Wilhelm Meister and His English Kinsmen: Apprentices to Life*. 1930. Reprint, New York: AMS Press, 1966.

Humboldt, Wilhelm von. *Humanist Without Portfolio: An Anthology of the Writings of Wilhelm von Humboldt*. Edited and translated by Marianne Cowan. Detroit: Wayne State University Press, 1963.

———. *The Limits of State Action*. Edited by J. W. Burrow. London: Cambridge University Press, 1969.

Hutcheon, Linda. *Narcissistic Narrative: The Metafictional Paradox*. Waterloo, Ont.: Wilfrid Laurier University Press, 1980.

———. *A Theory of Parody: The Teachings of Twentieth-Century Art Forms*. New York: Methuen, 1985.

Ingersoll, Earl G. *D. H. Lawrence, Desire, and Narrative*. Gainesville: University Press of Florida, 2001.

Ingham, Patricia. *The Language of Gender and Class: Transformation in the Victorian Novel*. London: Routledge, 1996.

Irigaray, Luce. *Speculum of the Other Woman*. Translated by Gillian C. Gill. Ithaca: Cornell University Press, 1985.

Jaffe, Audrey. *Scenes of Sympathy: Identity and Representation in Victorian Fiction*. Ithaca: Cornell University Press, 2000.

Jameson, Fredric. *The Political Unconscious: Narrative as a Socially Symbolic Act*. Ithaca: Cornell University Press, 1981.

———. *Postmodernism, or, The Cultural Logic of Late Capitalism*. Durham: Duke University Press, 1991.

———. *A Singular Modernity: Essay on the Ontology of the Present*. London: Verso, 2002.

JanMohamed, Abdul R. "The Economy of Manichean Allegory: The Function of Racial Difference in Colonialist Literature." *Critical Inquiry* 12 (1985): 59–87.

———. *Manichean Aesthetics: The Politics of Literature in Colonial Africa*. Amherst: University of Massachusetts Press, 1983.

Jeffers, Thomas. "Lawrence, *Sons and Lovers*, and the End of Sex." *Hudson Review* 52 (Summer 1999): 191–204.

———. "'We Children Were the In-Betweens': Character (De)Formation in *Sons and Lovers*." *Texas Studies in Literature and Language* 42.3 (2000): 290–313.

Joyce, James. *Finnegans Wake*. New York: Viking, 1939.

———. "Oscar Wilde: Poet of 'Salomé.'" In *The Critical Writings of James Joyce*, edited by Ellsworth Mason and Richard Ellmann, 201–5. 1959. Reprint, Ithaca: Cornell University Press, 1989.

———. *A Portrait of the Artist as a Young Man*. 1916. Edited by Chester G. Anderson. New York: Viking, 1964. Reprint, Harmondsworth, U.K.: Penguin, 1977.

———. *Stephen Hero*. Edited by John J. Slocum and Herbert Cahoon. Norfolk, Conn.: New Directions, 1959.

———. *Ulysses*. 1922. Corrected ed. New York: Modern Library, 1961. Reprint, New York: Vintage, 1990.

Keane, Robert N., ed. *Oscar Wilde: The Man, His Writings, and His World*. New York: AMS Press, 2003.

Kenner, Hugh. *Ulysses*. Rev. ed. Baltimore: Johns Hopkins University Press, 1987.

Kiberd, Declan. *Inventing Ireland*. Cambridge, Mass.: Harvard University Press, 1996.

Kilroy, James, ed. *The "Playboy" Riots*. Dublin: Dolmen Press, 1971.

Klein, Scott. "Speech Lent by Males: Gender, Identity, and the Example of Stephen's Shakespeare." *James Joyce Quarterly* 30.3 (1993): 439–49.

Kontje, Todd. "The German *Bildungsroman* as Metafiction." *Michigan Germanic Studies* 13.2 (1987): 140–155.

———. *Private Lives in the Public Sphere: The German Bildungsroman as Metafiction*. University Park: Pennsylvania State University Press, 1992.

Kristeva, Julia. *Desire in Language: A Semiotic Approach to Literature and Art*. Edited by Leon S. Roudiez. Translated by Thomas Gora, Alice Jardine, and Leon S. Roudiez. New York: Columbia University Press, 1980.

Kucich, John. "Moral Authority in the Late Novels: The Gendering of Art." In Higonnet, *Sense of Sex*, 221–41.

Larson, Jil. *Ethics and Narrative in the English Novel, 1880–1914*. Cambridge: Cambridge University Press, 2001.

Law, Jules David. "'Pity They Can't See Themselves': Assessing the 'Subject' of Pornography in 'Nausicaa.'" *James Joyce Quarterly* 27 (Winter 1990): 219–39.

Lawler, Donald. "The Gothic Wilde." In *Rediscovering Oscar Wilde*, edited by C. George Sandulescu, 249–68. Gerrards Cross: Colin Smythe, 1994.

Lawrence, D. H. *The Letters of D. H. Lawrence*. Edited by James T. Boulton. 8 vols. Cambridge: Cambridge University Press, 1979–2000.

————. *Sons and Lovers*. 1913. Edited by Helen Baron and Carl Baron. Cambridge: Cambridge University Press, 1992. Reprint, London: Penguin, 1994.

————. *Study of Thomas Hardy and Other Essays*. Edited by Bruce Steele. Cambridge: Cambridge University Press, 1985.

Lawrence, Karen. *The Odyssey of Style in "Ulysses."* Princeton: Princeton University Press, 1981.

Ledger, Sally. *The New Woman: Fiction and Feminism at the Fin de Siècle*. Manchester: Manchester University Press, 1997.

Leonard, Garry. "The Virgin Mary and the Urge in Gerty: The Packaging of Desire in the 'Nausicaa' Chapter of *Ulysses*." *University of Hartford Studies in Literature* 23:1 (1991): 3–23.

Levin, Harry. *James Joyce: A Critical Introduction*. Norfolk, Conn.: New Directions, 1941.

Levine, George. *Dying to Know: Scientific Epistemology and Narrative in Victorian England*. Chicago: University of Chicago Press, 2002.

Lewiecki-Wilson, Cynthia. *Writing Against the Family: Gender in Lawrence and Joyce*. Carbondale: Southern Illinois University Press, 1994.

Lima, Maria Helena. "Decolonizing Genre: Jamaica Kincaid and the *Bildungsroman*." *Genre* 26.4 (1993): 431–59.

Littleton, Michael, ed. *From Famine to Feast: Economic and Social Change in Ireland, 1847–1997*. Dublin: IPA, 1998.

Locke, John. *An Essay Concerning Human Understanding*. 1690. Edited by Peter H. Nidditch. Oxford: Clarendon Press, 1975.

Longenbach, James. *Modernist Poetics of History: Pound, Eliot, and the Sense of the Past*. Princeton: Princeton University Press, 1987.

Loptson, Peter. "Locke, Reid, and Personal Identity." *Philosophical Forum* 35.1 (2004): 51–63.

Low, Lisa. "'Listen and Save': Woolf's Allusion to Comus in Her Revolutionary First Novel." In *Virginia Woolf: Reading the Renaissance*, edited by Sally Greene, 117–35. Athens: Ohio University Press, 1999.

Lowe-Evans, Mary. "Sex and Confession in the Joyce Canon: Some Historical Parallels." *Journal of Modern Literature* 16 (Spring 1990): 563–76.

Lyotard, Jean-François. *The Postmodern Condition: A Report on Knowledge*. Translated by Geoff Bennington and Brian Massumi. Minneapolis: University of Minnesota Press, 1984.

Maddox, James H., Jr. *Joyce's "Ulysses" and the Assault upon Character*. New Brunswick, N.J.: Rutgers University Press, 1978.

Mahaffey, Vicki. *States of Desire: Wilde, Yeats, Joyce, and the Irish Experiment*. New York: Oxford University Press, 1998.

Manganiello, Dominic. "Reading the Book of Himself: The Confessional Imagination of St. Augustine and Joyce." In *Biography and Autobiography: Essays on Irish and Ca-*

nadian History and Literature, edited by James Noonan, 149–62. Ottawa: Carleton University Press, 1993.

Martini, Fritz. "Bildungsroman—Term and Theory." In Hardin, *Reflection and Action*, 1–25.

Marx, Karl, and Friedrich Engels. *The German Ideology*. Edited by C. J. Arthur. New York: International Publishers, 1970.

Mattar, Sinéad Garrigan. *Primitivism, Science, and the Irish Revival*. Oxford: Clarendon Press, 2004.

Mattisson, Jane. *Knowledge and Survival in the Novels of Thomas Hardy*. Lund, Sweden: Lund University, 2002.

McBride, Lawrence W., ed. *Reading Irish Histories: Texts, Contexts, and Memory in Modern Ireland*. Dublin: Four Courts Press, 2003.

McCombe, John P. "Besteglyster and Bradleyism: Stephen Dedalus's Postcolonial Response to English Criticism." *James Joyce Quarterly* 39.4 (2002): 717–34.

———. "*The Voyage Out*: No 'Tempest' in a Teapot: Woolf's Revision of Shakespeare and Critique of Female Education." *ARIEL* 31.1–2 (2000): 275–306.

McCormack, Jerusha, ed. *Wilde the Irishman*. New Haven: Yale University Press, 1998.

McElligott, T. J. *Secondary Education in Ireland, 1870–1921*. Dublin: Irish Academic Press, 1981.

McGee, Patrick. *Paperspace: Style as Ideology in Joyce's "Ulysses."* Lincoln: University of Nebraska Press, 1988.

Memmi, Albert. *The Colonizer and the Colonized*. Translated by Howard Greenfeld. Boston: Beacon Press, 1967.

Meredith, George. *The Egoist*. 1879. Edited by George Woodcock. Harmondsworth, U.K.: Penguin, 1968.

———. *The Ordeal of Richard Feverel*. 1859. Reprint, New York: Holt, Rinehart and Winston, 1964.

Miles, Andrew. *Social Mobility in Nineteenth- and Early Twentieth-Century England*. London: Macmillan, 1999.

Mill, John Stuart. *On Liberty*. 1859. In *Essays on Politics and Society*, vol. 18 of *The Collected Works of John Stuart Mill*, edited by John M. Robson, 213–310. Toronto: University of Toronto Press, 1971.

Miller, J. Hillis. *Fiction and Repetition: Seven English Novels*. Cambridge, Mass.: Harvard University Press, 1982.

———. "Virginia Woolf's All Souls' Day: The Omniscient Narrator in *Mrs. Dalloway*." In *The Shaken Realist: Essays in Modern Literature in Honor of Frederick J. Hoffman*, edited by Melvin J. Friedman and John B. Vickery, 100–27. Baton Rouge: Louisiana State University Press, 1970.

Miller, Kerby. "The Distortions of Post-Modern Ireland." *Irish Literary Supplement* 23.2 (2003): 12–13.

Miller, Nicholas Andrew. *Modernism, Ireland, and the Erotics of Memory*. Cambridge: Cambridge University Press, 2002.

Minden, Michael. *The German Bildungsroman: Incest and Inheritance*. Cambridge: Cambridge University Press, 1997.

Mitchell, Breon. "*A Portrait* and the *Bildungsroman* Tradition." In *Approaches to Joyce's "Portrait": Ten Essays*, edited by Thomas F. Staley and Bernard Benstock, 61–76. Pittsburgh: University of Pittsburgh Press, 1976.

Moers, Ellen. *The Dandy: Brummell to Beerbohm*. New York: Viking, 1960.

Mohanty, Chandra Talpade. "Under Western Eyes: Feminist Scholarship and Colonial Discourses." *Feminist Review* 30 (Autumn 1988): 65–88.

Moore, George. *Confessions of a Young Man*. 1888. Edited by Susan Dick. Montreal: McGill-Queen's University Press, 1972.

Moretti, Franco. *The Way of the World: The Bildungsroman in European Culture*. London: Verso, 1987.

Morgan, Ellen. "Humanbecoming: Form and Focus in the Neo-Feminist Novel." In *Images of Women in Fiction: Feminist Perspectives*, edited by Susan Koppelman Cornillon, rev. ed., 183–205. Bowling Green, Ohio: Bowling Green University Popular Press, 1973.

Muller, Jill. "John Henry Newman and the Education of Stephen Dedalus." *James Joyce Quarterly* 33 (Summer 1996): 593–603.

Mulrooney, Jonathan. "Stephen Dedalus and the Politics of Confession." *Studies in the Novel* 33 (Summer 2001): 160–79.

Musselwhite, David. *Social Transformations in Hardy's Tragic Novels: Megamachines and Phantasms*. Houndmills, Basingstoke: Palgrave Macmillan, 2003.

Myers, Elyse. "Virginia Woolf and *The Voyage Out* from Victorian Science." In *Virginia Woolf: Turning the Centuries*, edited by Ann Ardis and Bonnie Kime Scott, 298–304. New York: Pace University Press, 2000.

New Catholic Encyclopedia. 17 vols. New York: McGraw-Hill, 1967–79.

Newman, John Henry. *Fifteen Sermons Preached before the University of Oxford between 1826 and 1843*. London: Longmans, Green, 1898.

———. *The Idea of a University Defined and Illustrated*. 1873. Edited by Martin J. Svaglic. New York: Holt, Rinehart and Winston, 1960.

Nicholson, Peter. *The Political Philosophy of the British Idealists: Selected Studies*. Cambridge: Cambridge University Press, 1990.

Nietzsche, Friedrich. *The Gay Science*. 1882–87. Translated by Walter Kaufmann. New York: Random House, 1974.

Nolan, Emer. *James Joyce and Nationalism*. London: Routledge, 1995.

Norris, Margot. "Modernism, Myth, and Desire in 'Nausicaa.'" *James Joyce Quarterly* 26 (1988): 37–50.

North, Michael. *Reading 1922: A Return to the Scene of the Modern*. New York: Oxford University Press, 1999.

Nunokawa, Jeff. "Homosexual Desire and the Effacement of the Self in *The Picture of Dorian Gray*." *American Imago* 49.3 (1992): 311–21.

———. *Tame Passions of Wilde: The Styles of Manageable Desire*. Princeton: Princeton University Press, 2003.

O'Brien, Kate. *The Land of Spices*. 1941. Reprint, London: Virago Press, 1988.

Ochoa, Peggy. "Joyce's 'Nausicaa': The Paradox of Advertising Narcissism." *James Joyce Quarterly* 30.4/31.1 (1993): 783–93.

O'Connell, Maurice R., ed. *People Power: Proceedings of the Third Annual Daniel O'Connell Workshop*. Dublin: Institute of Public Administration, 1993.

O'Connor, James. *Accumulation Crisis*. New York: Blackwell, 1984.

O'Grady, Standish James. *All Ireland*. 1898. Washington, D.C.: Woodstock, 1999.

———. "Ireland and the Hour." In *Standish O'Grady: Selected Essays and Passages*, 199–266. Dublin: Talbot Press, 1918.

Oliphant, Margaret. "The Anti-Marriage League." *Blackwood's Magazine*, January 1896. Reprinted in Page, *Jude*, 379–83.

Page, Norman, ed. *Jude the Obscure*, by Thomas Hardy. 2nd ed. New York: Norton, 1999.

Parry, Benita. "Problems in Current Theories of Colonial Discourse." *Oxford Literary Review* 9.1–2 (1987): 27–58.

Pater, Walter. "A Novel by Mr. Oscar Wilde." In Wilde, *Dorian Gray*, 352–54.

———. *The Renaissance: Studies in Art and Poetry; the 1893 Text*. Edited by Donald L. Hill. Berkeley and Los Angeles: University of California Press, 1980.

Paul, Janis M. *The Victorian Heritage of Virginia Woolf: The External World in Her Novels*. Norman, Okla.: Pilgrim Books, 1987.

Peake, C. H. *James Joyce: The Citizen and the Artist*. Stanford, Stanford University Press, 1977.

Pearse, Patrick. *A Significant Irish Educationalist: The Educational Writings of P. H. Pearse*. Edited by Séamas Ó Buachalla. Dublin: Mercier Press, 1980.

Pecora, Vincent. "Arnoldean Ethnology." *Victorian Studies* 41.3 (1998): 355–79.

Perl, Jeffrey M. *The Tradition of Return: The Implicit History of Modern Literature*. Princeton: Princeton University Press, 1984.

Peters, Gerald. *The Mutilating God: Authorship and Authority in the Narrative of Conversion*. Amherst: University of Massachusetts Press, 1993.

Peterson, Linda. "Harriet Martineau's *Household Education*: Revising the Female Tradition." In *Culture and Education in Victorian England*, edited by Patrick Scott and Pauline Fletcher, 183–94. Lewisburg, Pa.: Bucknell University Press, 1990.

Pilditch, Jan, ed. *The Critical Response to D. H. Lawrence*. Westport, Conn.: Greenwood Press, 2001.

Pinion, F. B. *Hardy the Writer: Surveys and Assessments*. Houndmills, Basingstoke: Macmillan, 1990.

Pinkney, Tony. *D. H. Lawrence and Modernism*. Iowa City: University of Iowa Press, 1990.

Platt, Len. *Joyce and the Anglo-Irish: A Study of Joyce and the Literary Revival.* Amsterdam: Rodopi, 1998.

Pratt, Mary Louise. *Imperial Eyes: Travel Writing and Transculturation.* London: Routledge, 1992.

Punter, David, ed. *A Companion to the Gothic.* Oxford: Blackwell, 2000.

Radford, Andrew. *Thomas Hardy and the Survivals of Time.* Aldershot: Ashgate, 2003.

Redfield, Marc. *Phantom Formations: Aesthetic Ideology and the Bildungsroman.* Ithaca: Cornell University Press, 1996.

Richards, Thomas. *The Commodity Culture of Victorian England: Advertising and Spectacle, 1851–1914.* Stanford: Stanford University Press, 1990.

Richardson, Angelique, and Chris Willis, eds. *The New Woman in Fiction and Fact: Fin-de-Siècle Feminisms.* Houndmills, Basingstoke: Palgrave, 2001.

Riquelme, John Paul. "Oscar Wilde's Aesthetic Gothic: Walter Pater, Dark Enlightenment, and *The Picture of Dorian Gray.*" *Modern Fiction Studies* 46.3 (2000): 609–31.

———. *Teller and Tale in Joyce's Fiction: Oscillating Perspectives.* Baltimore: Johns Hopkins University Press, 1983.

Roach, John. *A History of Secondary Education in England, 1800–1870.* London: Longman, 1986.

———. *Secondary Education in England, 1870–1902: Public Activity and Private Enterprise.* New York: Routledge, 1991.

———. "Victorian Universities and the National Intelligentsia." *Victorian Studies* 3 (1959): 131–50.

Rose, Margaret A. *Parody: Ancient, Modern, and Post-Modern.* Cambridge: Cambridge University Press, 1993.

———. "Parody/Post-Modernism." *Poetics* 17.1 (1988): 49–56.

Rosenman, Ellen Bayuk. *The Invisible Presence: Virginia Woolf and the Mother-Daughter Relationship.* Baton Rouge: Louisiana State University Press, 1986.

Rowe, Karen. "'Fairy-born and human-bred': Jane Eyre's Education in Romance." In Abel, Hirsch, and Langland, *The Voyage In*, 69–89.

Rubin, Gayle. "Traffic in Women: Notes on the 'Political Economy' of Sex." In *Toward an Anthropology of Women*, edited by Rayna R. Reiter, 157–210. New York: Monthly Review Press, 1975.

Ruddick, Nicholas. "'The Peculiar Quality of My Genius': Degeneration, Decadence, and *Dorian Gray* in 1890–91." In Keane, *Oscar Wilde*, 125–37.

Ruotolo, Lucio P. *The Interrupted Moment: A View of Virginia Woolf's Novels.* Stanford: Stanford University Press, 1986.

Sagar, Keith. *The Life of D. H. Lawrence.* New York: Pantheon, 1980.

Said, Edward W. *Culture and Imperialism.* New York: Knopf, 1993.

———. *Orientalism.* New York: Pantheon, 1978.

Saldívar, Ramón. "*Jude the Obscure*: Reading and the Spirit of the Law." *ELH* 50.3 (1983): 607–25.

Sammells, Neil. *Wilde Style: The Plays and Prose of Oscar Wilde.* New York: Longman, 2000.

Sammons, Jeffrey L. "The Bildungsroman for Nonspecialists: An Attempt at a Clarification." In Hardin, *Reflection and Action*, 26–45.

———. "The Mystery of the Missing Bildungsroman: What Happened to Wilhelm Meister's Legacy?" *Genre* 14 (1981): 229–46.

Sanders, Scott R. *D. H. Lawrence: The World of the Major Novels.* London: Vision Press, 1973.

Scheckner, Peter. *Class, Politics, and the Individual: A Study of the Major Works of D. H. Lawrence.* Rutherford, N.J.: Fairleigh Dickinson University Press, 1985.

Schiller, Friedrich. *On the Aesthetic Education of Man, in a Series of Letters.* Translated and edited by Elizabeth M. Wilkinson and L. A. Willoughby. Oxford: Clarendon Press, 1967.

Scott, Bonnie Kime. "Emma Clery in *Stephen Hero*: A Young Woman Walking Proudly Through the Decayed City." In *Women in Joyce*, edited by Suzette Henke and Elaine Unkeless, 57–81. Urbana: University of Illinois Press, 1982.

Sedgwick, Eve Kosofsky. *Between Men: English Literature and Male Homosocial Desire.* New York: Columbia University Press, 1985.

Senn, Fritz. "Nausicaa." In *James Joyce's "Ulysses": Critical Essays*, edited by Clive Hart and David Hayman, 277–311. Berkeley and Los Angeles: University of California Press, 1974.

Sheehan, Paul. *Modernism, Narrative, and Humanism.* Cambridge: Cambridge University Press, 2002.

Sicker, Philip. "'Alone in the Hiding Twilight': Bloom's Cinematic Gaze in 'Nausicaa.'" *James Joyce Quarterly* 36.4 (1999): 825–50.

Small, Ian, and Josephine M. Guy. *Oscar Wilde's Profession: Writing and the Culture Industry in the Late Nineteenth Century.* Oxford: Oxford University Press, 2000.

Smith, Craig. "Twilight in Dublin: A Look at Joyce's 'Nausicaa.'" *James Joyce Quarterly* 28 (1991): 631–35.

Smith, John H. "Cultivating Gender: Sexual Difference, *Bildung*, and the *Bildungsroman*." *Michigan Germanic Studies* 13.2 (1987): 206–25.

Smith, Patricia Juliana. "'The Things People Don't Say': Lesbian Panic in *The Voyage Out*." In Barrett and Cramer, *Virginia Woolf: Lesbian Readings*, 128–45.

Smith, Philip E., II, and Michael S. Helfand. *Oscar Wilde's Oxford Notebooks: A Portrait of Mind in the Making.* New York: Oxford University Press, 1989.

Smith, Sidonie. *Subjectivity, Identity, and the Body: Women's Autobiographical Practices in the Twentieth Century.* Bloomington: Indiana University Press, 1993.

Smith, Sidonie, and Julia Watson, eds. *De/Colonizing the Subject: The Politics of Gender in Women's Autobiography.* Minneapolis: University of Minnesota Press, 1992.

Solow, Barbara L. *The Land Question and the Irish Economy, 1870–1903.* Cambridge, Mass.: Harvard University Press, 1971.

Spivak, Gayatri Chakravorty. "The Burden of English." In *Postcolonial Discourses: An Anthology*, edited by Gregory Castle, 53–72. Oxford: Blackwell, 2000.

——. "Can the Subaltern Speak?" In *Marxism and the Interpretation of Culture*, edited by Cary Nelson and Lawrence Grossberg, 271–313. Urbana: University of Illinois Press, 1988.

——. "Poststructuralism, Marginality, Postcoloniality, and Value." In *Literary Theory Today*, edited by Peter Collier and Helga Geyer-Ryan, 219–44. Ithaca: Cornell University Press, 1990.

Stendhal. *Scarlet and Black*. 1830. Translated by Margaret R. B. Shaw. Harmondsworth, U.K.: Penguin, 1953.

Suleri, Sara. "Woman Skin Deep: Feminism and the Postcolonial Condition." *Critical Inquiry* 18 (Summer 1992): 756–69.

Sultan, Stanley. "Lawrence the Anti-Autobiographer." *Journal of Modern Literature* 23.2 (1999): 225–48.

Sunder Rajan, Rajeswari. *Real and Imagined Women: Gender, Culture, and Postcolonialism*. London: Routledge, 1993.

Swales, Martin. *The German Bildungsroman from Wieland to Hesse*. Princeton: Princeton University Press, 1978.

——. "Irony and the Novel: Reflections on the German Bildungsroman." In Hardin, *Reflection and Action*, 46–68.

Sweet, Paul R. *Wilhelm von Humboldt: A Biography*. Vol. 1, *1767–1808*. Vol. 2, *1808–1835*. Columbus: Ohio State University Press, 1978–80.

Tennyson, G. B. "The *Bildungsroman* in Nineteenth-Century English Literature." In *Medieval Epic to the "Epic Theater" of Brecht: Essays in Comparative Literature*, edited by Rosario P. Armato and John M. Spalek, 135–46. Los Angeles: University of Southern California Press, 1968.

Thomas, David Wayne. *Cultivating Victorians: Liberal Culture and the Aesthetic*. Philadelphia: University of Pennsylvania Press, 2004.

Thompson, E. P. *The Making of the English Working Class*. New York: Pantheon, 1963.

Tyson, Nancy Jane. "Caliban in a Glass: Autoscopic Vision in *The Picture of Dorian Gray*." In *The Haunted Mind: The Supernatural in Victorian Literature*, edited by Elton E. Smith and Robert Haas, 101–21. Lanham, Md.: Scarecrow, 1999.

University Extension Congress, London 1894: Report of the Proceedings. London: P. S. King and Sons, 1894.

Upchurch, David A. *Wilde's Use of Irish Celtic Elements in "The Picture of Dorian Gray."* New York: Peter Lang, 1992.

Valente, Joseph. *Dracula's Crypt: Bram Stoker, Irishness, and the Question of Blood*. Urbana and Chicago, University of Illinois Press, 2002.

——, ed. *Quare Joyce*. Ann Arbor: University of Michigan Press, 1998.

——. "'Thrilled by His Touch': The Aestheticizing of Homosexual Panic in *A Portrait of the Artist as a Young Man*." In *Quare Joyce*, 47–75.

Van Ghent, Dorothy. *The English Novel: Form and Function*. New York: Harper and Row, 1953.

Verdon, Nicola. *Rural Women Workers in Nineteenth-Century England: Gender, Work, and Wages*. Woodbridge, U.K.: Boydell Press, 2002.

Waldrep, Shelton. "Economics and Performance: Wilde's Aesthetics of Self-Invention." In Keane, *Oscar Wilde*, 113–24.

Wallace, Robert. "'Laughing in Your Sleeve': James Joyce's Comic Portrait." *Essays in Literature* 3 (1976): 61–72.

Wardle, David. *English Popular Education, 1780–1975*. 2nd ed. Cambridge: Cambridge University Press, 1976.

Weinstein, Philip M. *The Semantics of Desire: Changing Models of Identity from Dickens to Joyce*. Princeton: Princeton University Press, 1984.

Whiteley, Patrick J. *Knowledge and Experimental Realism in Conrad, Lawrence, and Woolf*. Baton Rouge: Louisiana State University Press, 1987.

Widdowson, Peter. *On Thomas Hardy: Late Essays and Earlier*. New York: St. Martin's Press, 1998.

Wilde, Oscar. *The Artist as Critic: Critical Writings of Oscar Wilde*. Edited by Richard Ellmann. New York: Random House, 1969.

———. *De Profundis and Other Writings*. 1905. London: Penguin, 1973.

———. *Intentions: The Decay of Lying; Pen, Pencil and Poison; The Critic as Artist; The Truth of Masks*. 1891. New York: Brentano's, 1905.

———. *Miscellanies*. Vol. 14 of *The First Collected Edition of the Works of Oscar Wilde, 1908–1922*, edited by Robert Ross. New York: Barnes and Noble, 1969.

———. *The Picture of Dorian Gray*. 1890/91. Edited by Donald L. Lawler. New York: Norton, 1988.

———. "The Portrait of Mr. W. H." In *The Artist as Critic*, 152–220.

———. "The Rise of Historical Criticism." In *Essays and Lectures*, edited by Robert Ross, 4th ed. London: Methuen, 1913.

———. *Selected Letters of Oscar Wilde*. Edited by Rupert Hart-Davis. Oxford: Oxford University Press, 1979.

———. "Some Literary Notes." *Woman's World* 2 (1889): 389–92.

———. "The Soul of Man under Socialism." In *The Artist as Critic*, 255–89.

Williams, John R. *The Life of Goethe: A Critical Biography*. Oxford: Blackwell, 1998.

Williams, Louise Blakeney. *Modernism and the Ideology of History: Literature, Politics, and the Past*. Cambridge: Cambridge University Press, 2002.

Williams, Raymond. *Culture and Society: 1780–1950*. New York: Columbia University Press, 1958.

———. *The English Novel from Dickens to Lawrence*. London: Chatto and Windus, 1970.

———. *The Long Revolution*. New York: Columbia University Press, 1961.

Wood, Jane. *Passion and Pathology in Victorian Fiction*. Oxford: Oxford University Press, 2001.

Woolf, Virginia. *The Letters of Virginia Woolf.* Edited by Nigel Nicolson. Vol. 3, *A Change of Perspective, 1923–1928*. New York: Harcourt Brace Jovanovich, 1977.

———. "Modern Fiction." In *The Common Reader*, 184–95. London: Hogarth Press, 1925.

———. "Mr. Bennett and Mrs. Brown." In *Essays of Virginia Woolf*, edited by Andrew McNeillie, 3:384–89. London: Hogarth Press, 1988.

———. *Mrs. Dalloway.* 1925. Reprint, New York: Harcourt Brace Jovanovich, 1990.

———. *A Room of One's Own.* London: Hogarth Press, 1929.

———. *Three Guineas.* London: Hogarth Press, 1938.

———. *The Voyage Out.* 1915. Edited by Lorna Sage. Oxford: Oxford University Press, 1992.

———. *A Writer's Diary.* Edited by Leonard Woolf. New York: Harcourt, Brace, 1954.

Worthen, John. *D. H. Lawrence: A Literary Life.* New York: St. Martin's Press, 1989.

———. *D. H. Lawrence: The Early Years, 1885–1912*. Cambridge: Cambridge University Press, 1991.

Žižek, Slavoj. *Tarrying with the Negative: Kant, Hegel, and the Critique of Ideology.* Durham: Duke University Press, 1993.

Index

Gregory Castle is associate professor of modern British and Irish literature at Arizona State University. In addition to essays on James Joyce, John Millington Synge, Bram Stoker, and the Irish historian Standish O'Grady, he has published *Modernism and the Celtic Revival*, *Postcolonial Discourses: An Anthology*, and *Literary Theory*.